# Psychological Methods
## of
## Child Assessment

# Psychological Methods
# of
# Child Assessment

Jacquelin Goldman

Claudia L'Engle Stein

Shirley Guerry

BRUNNER/MAZEL, *Publishers* • New York

SECOND PRINTING

**Library of Congress Cataloging in Publication Data**

Goldman, Jacquelin.
  Psychological methods of child assessment.

  Includes bibliographical references and index.
  1. Psychological tests for children.  I. Stein, Claudia
L'Engle, 1940-    .  II. Guerry, Shirley, 1931-
III. Title.  [DNLM: 1. Child development.  2. Child
psychology.  3. Psychological tests—In infancy and child-
hood.  WS 105.5.E8 G619p]
BF722.G62  1984        155.4′028′7        83-20889
ISBN 0-87630-348-3

Copyright © 1983 by Jacquelin Goldman, Claudia L'Engle Stein
and Shirley Guerry

Published by

BRUNNER/MAZEL, INC.
19 Union Square
New York, New York 10003

MANUFACTURED IN THE UNITED STATES OF AMERICA

# Contents

## PART II. METHODS OF CHILD ASSESSMENT

PART III. APPLICATIONS OF PRINCIPLES
AND METHODS

# Acknowledgments

We would like to express our grateful appreciation to the many students who participated in clinical reviews of many of the instruments covered in this volume. These practicum students and interns provided stimulation and interest. We would also like to thank the graduate students in the clinical psychology program at the University of Florida who read various sections of drafts of the work. In particular, we would like to thank Mary Morris and Roberta Isleib for their thoughtful review of major portions of the manuscript. Finally, we are especially grateful to our colleague and good friend, Dr. Eileen B. Fennell, for her helpful comments and information which contributed greatly to the chapter on neuropsychological assessment.

# Introduction

The sensitive clinician must be familiar with the basic tools of the profession and must also have a fund of information which includes an understanding of developmental processes and abnormal deviations from normal development. In addition, the practicing clinician will need to know what types of services and facilities are available for various types of child care. Yet even this is not sufficient for the assessment of children, for a basic issue integral to all child assessment situations is that adults are seeking services for children whose understanding of what is involved in the evaluation may be quite different from that held by the responsible adults. It is the exception for a child to seek services directly. Therefore, it is easy for the clinician to overlook how the assessment process is experienced by the child, even though most of us would at least give lip service to the contrary.

We believe that the consistent sensitivity to the child's experience of the assessment experience is of primary importance. It may develop that the appraisal of referral questions as reported by responsible adults will change when the child's point of view about the referring problems and about the assessment experience are taken into account. The clinician bears the responsibility to enlarge the examination of the referral questions so that it does include information that can only come from the child's perceptions.

Since children are dependent upon adults for their information about the reasons for referral and about the assessment process, it is frequently the case that the child comes to an appointment either ignorant or misinformed. Because problems have precipitated the appointment, the child may feel a loss of self-esteem, suffer confusion, or wonder if there is a question about his* sanity when learning of the assessment session. In any case, the child may be less able than the adult to view the assessment as a personally helpful process. Very likely the child will not understand that the evaluation is a means of gathering information which will be used ultimately in his best interests.

The child may not have knowledge of the results of the assessment in many cases. Sometimes this is unavoidable, as when the child is brought to an appointment by a social worker or someone who does not have continuity of contact with the child. Moreover, the child may not understand who will learn the results of the evaluation or what effect the evaluation may have upon his life. The issue of confidentiality is colored by the fact that the child always knows that someone else, either his parents, teachers, social workers, or some other authority figure will know how he has performed, even if he himself does not receive this knowledge. Further, the child may be aware that decisions affecting his life will be made on the basis of his performance and these are decisions about which he will have very little, if any, input. Our view is that the child should be involved and informed as much as possible about the reasons for the referral and what will be done with the findings.

## THE PRACTICE OF CHILD ASSESSMENT

The past 15 years have been characterized by changes in our view of the child and by the development of a significant number of new child assessment procedures. In 1970 when Palmer published *Psychological Assessment of Children*, he traced a theoretical position (ego-developmental) and described procedures and techniques which he related directly to that position. Since that time, broad thrusts in our knowledge about children have focused attention on individual differences in biologically-based characteristics, in cognitive aspects of development, and on specific learning problems such as dyslexia. We have also seen the rise of both behavioral methods and cognitive behavioral approaches to the conceptualization of problematic behavior.

Hunt (1960) has reviewed philosophical ideas about children and has

---

*The use of the masculine form both here and throughout the text is only for the express purpose of brevity. It is assumed that when speaking of the child, both sexes are included in consideration, unless otherwise noted.

shown how these ideas both direct the nature of research and are challenged by new research findings and new conceptualizations. His excellent review follows the change through history from the idea that the child was a miniature adult, to the child as a passive recipient of adult shaping, to the notion that the child is an active, developing participant in the growth process. The period since the publication of *Intelligence and Experience* has been marked by technological changes in child assessment, as well as many new ideas.

Much of the refocused interest in children over the past 15–20 years has been devoted to biologically-based processes and how these processes affect psychological growth. We can think of biologically-based characteristics as a horizontal, more stable dimension, and cognitive growth as a vertical, developmental dimension of human functioning. In this light, ego development becomes clearly related to individual differences in activity level, attentional styles, and other features which delimit the nature of interpersonal and cognitive growth. For this reason our book will focus upon the complexity of outcomes which are possible given different patterns of personal organization, different personal response styles. Questions of assessment must take into account developmental issues as well as questions of psychopathology or situational problems which prompt adults to refer children to clinicians.

The knowledge base from which clinicians now operate has expanded to include significant information about both cognitive development and social development, together with the biological influences which affect their course and outcome. To cite only a few examples, we know specifically how genetic endowment limits intelligence (Down's Syndrome), how malnutrition affects intellectual potential, and how hyperactivity and attentional disorders may be mitigated by the use of drug therapies. Piaget's work has influenced conceptions of cognitive growth on both sides of the Atlantic, while American investigators have directed their attention to specific cognitive processes within briefer intervals of growth. Likewise, conceptions of social development have been reinterpreted in terms of self-esteem and the effect of the child upon his own social milieu, as well as in terms of the peer culture to social values. The child has also been construed not so much as an individual, but rather as part of a family system which should be considered as a whole (Satir, 1969; Minuchin, 1974). Rather than focus upon the extensive literature relevant to all aspects of child assessment, we will illustrate selective areas of development and deviation most relevant to assessment issues. The interested reader will find excellent texts on various aspects of child development and child psychopathology which will provide a more comprehensive background.

## CLINICAL SETTINGS

Psychologists now work in a broad range of settings. Recent texts on clinical psychology (Korchin, 1976; Phares, 1979; Sundberg, Tyler, & Taplin, 1973) have described many of these settings. In the main, these settings reflect employment opportunities which are affected by social forces including both funding patterns and legislation regulating and addressing social problems. Early in the history of American psychology when children's services became a major sphere of activity for psychologists, clinicians functioned within child guidance centers. Today the pattern of distribution of clinicians has moved toward the community mental health centers. These centers are settings which attempt to provide comprehensive mental health care for people of all age groups. Therefore, to some extent purely child-centered programs must compete with other programs within these centers. Differences among community mental health centers exist and the result is that some settings provide excellent care for children while others fall short.

Many of the practitioners who have entered private practice offer some assessment services for children, whether or not their basic training included child assessment as part of the curriculum. A third setting is the university-based clinic which serves both teaching and service functions. Here the quality of care is usually excellent as well-trained and experienced clinicians serve as faculty and supervise the work performed in the settings. Yet a fourth group of clinicians provides service within other institutional environments, e.g., schools and retardation facilities.

With all of the different groups of psychologists offering child assessment services, there is some overlap in function among them. To some extent the graduate training of these clinicians has overlap, as well. However, examination of the graduate training in 15 predoctoral programs which offer a specialty in child clinical psychology indicates that at least four different models are required to account for the curricula (Roberts, 1979). These models vary from developmental to school to clinical core curricula. With all too few programs and so little consistency among the few that exist, it is clear that clinicians may not share enough of a common knowledge basis from which problems of assessment should be approached.

Between the changing social situations and the diversity in training of child clinical psychologists, parents have difficulty in identifying providers of competent child assessment services. Information is frequently gained by word of mouth, or sought in desperation when some crisis occurs. Some practitioners are known because they donate time to meet with various community groups. Still, the anxious parent is generally unaware of credentialing issues. Credentialing is generally based on generic state laws which insure that the provider is trained as a psychologist, but does not offer much in the way of guidelines which would be helpful in selecting a practitioner for the child assessment services. Credentialing in specialty services is voluntary at the present time, as is the training in child clinical psychology (Goldman, 1982).

## PURPOSE OF THE BOOK

Given this state of affairs, many students and providers of child assessment services will find a basic reference which examines psychological methods of child assessment helpful. We did not plan to provide a definitive background in child development, psychopathology, or test and measurement theory. Nor did we intend to write an exhaustive, complete list of all psychological instruments and techniques available to the clinician. There are excellent texts on measurement and some superb compendia reviewing tests of intelligence, achievement, skills, personality, aptitudes, and personal and social characteristics of children.

Rather, the purpose of our book is to provide some common background and to assist the provider of child assessment services to determine appropriate procedures to answer referral questions and investigate specific problems. The instruments we chose for inclusion are mostly easy to obtain and adequately standardized (with the exception of some more clinical procedures which are included for other reasons), usually with information available as to their reliability and validity. These techniques have been found to be useful across a variety of settings and for a wide range of evaluation purposes. To our knowledge, there is no single source to which an examiner can go for considering the most commonly used assessment techniques for children.

In the information provided for each instrument reviewed in this book we describe the purpose of the instrument, its administration and scoring, and data on its standardization, reliability, and validity. The statistical information comes from test manuals, unless otherwise noted. Our critiques are based on personal experience and the use of standard reference materials such as the Mental Measurement Yearbooks, Anastasi (1976), and current journal literature. In each description of a test or clinical instrument, our purpose is to provide the reader with enough information so that it will be possible to decide whether examination of the test itself is likely to prove fruitful and might result in its use in an assessment situation. However, we will not attempt to reproduce exact instruction and detailed repetition of information given in manuals.

In the final part of the book, we provide illustrative material and case discussion. These examples are meant to demonstrate the thoughts that the examiner considers and the approach that is taken with regard to referral questions. The data are reproduced for the reader so that the clinical evaluation of the material can be followed. Reports relevant to each case are included in Chapter 12. This arrangement will permit the reader to reflect upon the material presented from the chapter, arrive at conclusions, and compare conclusions with the report prepared on the basis of the data.

We hope that this book will help providers of child assessment services in their efforts to render high quality work. If psychologists are able to evaluate better the advantages and disadvantages of psychological methods of child assessment for their clients, the authors will be richly rewarded for their part in writing this book.

## REFERENCES

Anastasi, A. *Psychological Testing,* 4th edition. New York: Macmillan, 1976.

Goldman, J. Clinical child psychology training and credentialing. *Journal of Clinical Child Psychology,* 1982, *11,* 8–11.

Hunt, J. McV. *Intelligence and Experience.* New York: Ronald Press, 1960.

Korchin, S. J. *Modern Clinical Psychology. Principles of intervention in Clinic and Community.* New York: Basic Books, 1976.

Minuchin, S. *Families and Family Therapy.* Cambridge: Harvard University Press, 1974.

Palmer, J. O. *Psychological Assessment of Children.* New York: John Wiley, 1970.

Phares, E. J. *Clinical Psychology: Concepts, Methods, and Profession.* Homewood, IL: The Dorsey Press, 1979.

Roberts, M. C. Clinical child psychology programs: Where and what are they? Presented at American Psychological Association Meeting: Clinical Child Psychology: Mapping a Future (Symposium, chaired by Allen Barclay). New York, Sept. 5, 1979.

Satir, V. *Conjoint Family Therapy.* Palo Alto, CA: Science and Behavior Books, 1969.

Sundberg, N. D., Tyler, L. E., & Taplin, J. R. *Clinical Psychology: Horizons.* New York: Appleton-Century-Crofts, 1973.

# PART I

# *Psychological Considerations in Child Assessment*

# CHAPTER 1

# *Principles of*
# *Child Assessment*

## ETHICAL ISSUES

When should a psychologist see a child? Under what conditions may the child be seen? Who should be privy to the information about the child? These are not idle questions.

Several months ago a man walked into the clinic room where I (JG) was working on a report. He announced his name and said he was the biological father of Shirley B., a child whom we had seen for evaluation several weeks before. He wanted to get a copy of the report. I was a little taken aback by the man's sudden appearance and authoritative manner, but at the same time something in the back of my mind was alerted to inquire more. "Biological father," I repeated, "Do you have custody of the child?"

To make a long story short, it developed that this father was divorced from the mother of the child who had custody of the child. He was interested in obtaining the information to aid him in a custody battle so that he could prove the mother to be unfit as a parent. There were many legal and ethical issues involved in this situation. The legal issues may vary from state to state as there are no uniform guidelines as to legal rights of divorced parents. The ethical issues are also very complex. The mother of the child had brought the child in for an evaluation voluntarily to get information to help her in providing for the child's interests.

3

The child, who was in her custody, was the family member not represented by legal counsel. Each parent retained the services of an attorney in their custody battle.

The psychologist who provides assessment services may easily encounter similar situations. The ethical guidelines for psychologists are not clear on all points. Most psychologists would try to take the child's needs into account. In some states both parents have rights to access to information about the child, even though one of them may retain custody. In other states only the parent with custody would be legally entitled to this information. Sometimes ethical questions are so predominant that even when legal rights are clear-cut, the psychologist may want to consider and discuss the possibility of conflict between ethical and legal issues with the child's legal custodian. Not all problems can be anticipated in advance, but many potential difficulties are predictable and can be discussed so as to minimize any negative effect on the child.

In bringing the ethical issue out early in this chapter, our purpose is to underscore the fact that in working with children, many ethical issues should be expected to arise. Because children are dependent upon others who are legally responsible for them, and because parents are often at legal odds with one another or with juvenile authorities, there are many times when the psychologist will be called upon to consider at what point the child is truly served. In some cases the most ethical part that a psychologist can play may be to refuse to provide services, if those services appear to ensnarl a child as a pawn in a fight between parents. Sometimes confronting the parents with this reality is of greater service to a child than would be the assessment which is requested. On the other hand, many times matters are more straightforward, parents are not divided in their efforts to do the best thing for the child, and everyone is cooperative. At the outset, the psychologist must determine enough of the familial situation to be able to act in the child's best interests.

## DEFINING THE QUESTIONS

Referral complaints are raised by adult caretakers who feel ineffective or who are confronted with others who are dissatisfied with their children's performance. The complaints may be roughly grouped into retardations, fixations, regressions, and deviations. Retardations involve lack of or slower than normal development. Fixations imply that a child developed normally until some period at which further growth failed to occur in the expected way. Regressions involve a return to a more primitive form of functioning than that which has been previously attained. Deviations occur when growth takes a distorted form. Different forms of psychopathology occur if the deviation relates to cognitive function, affective functions, or conduct.

The psychologist must consider the statements and questions posed by the referral sources and entertain the general nature and content implied by them. From this process the psychologist begins to define questions in the terms which will direct the nature and content of the assessment process. In a later chapter we will discuss in more detail the decisions which the psychologist makes. However, here we will simply note that the psychologist will decide whether the evaluation will entail an intellectual assessment, a personality assessment, a family assessment, other specialized techniques, and/or further consultations. It may be helpful, for example, to make either home or school visits in some cases. Since these procedures are costly, few practitioners outside of university settings employ them consistently. However, in some cases, the utility of extramural consultations is so clear that they should be considered and employed as appropriate.

## THE CHILD

Each child comes to the assessment situation with some sort of preparation. The preparation may range from nothing, to exasperated threats by a parent to take the child to someone who can "straighten him out," to empathic understanding that the child is suffering. Regardless of what parents or others mention on the telephone or by other contact, the psychologist should not assume that the child has experienced the preparation in the manner that the parents perceive it to be given. Both the child's cognitive understanding and the child's motivational set will influence the manner in which the assessment situation will be received.

Small children who do not really understand what a psychologist is may have no understanding of the purpose of their visit. In fact, they are likely to attribute the reason to something that they have done to displease their parents or to some shortcoming on their own part. Older children may have an appreciation of parental frustration or concern but may not see the problems in the same light. In extreme cases, in which adolescent suicidal attempts are involved, there may be very little overlap between parental and child views of problems (Jacobs, 1971). The cognitive level of development of the child will determine, in part, whether the child attributes behavior alone or intentionality also as part of the reason for the referral. Other significant cognitive developmental factors will include the child's understanding of causality in terms of time, space, and number, which in turn may affect how he interprets sequences of events that have taken place and caused concern among adults. In other words, the degree of egocentricity which limits the child's ability to consider other points of view will influence his understanding of problems.

Aside from these cognitive factors, a child's understanding of reasons for referral is affected by the social and emotional variables that characterize familial and peer relationships. The degree to which a child's needs to be accepted, valued, and competent are frustrated, together with the strength of psychological defenses which protect the child from feelings of rejection, worthlessness, and incompetence, will affect the particular interpretation that the child makes of the problems that lead to referral. Parents, teachers, and others may have some appreciation of the child's understanding and may be able to help the psychologist anticipate some of the child's response to evaluation. However, frequently these adults are frustrated because they do not understand the child or cannot accept the child's point of view. The psychologist will need to be open so that such differences can be observed where they exist.

## ESTABLISHING A WORKING RAPPORT

Some people feel very much at home working with children. Others do not or have to learn or relearn how to relate to children. Children who are docile or cooperative present few problems. One simply has to explain to these children what is expected and they will comply and produce whatever the examiner requires in the nature of performance. The shy or nonverbal child presents a different picture. The psychologist must take a stance which puts the child at ease so that discomfort on the child's part does not interfere with performance. Before this can be done the psychologist will have to do a little self-analysis to make sure that the child has not made the situation so stressful that the examiner has become defensive.

Very often shy children want to be able to enter a situation cautiously and test it out. The examiner can help the child by engaging him briefly in conversation in a casual manner about a topic which is not very personal: When did the child have to get up to come to the session, if it is in the early morning, or was the child in school, if the session occurs later in the day? The idea is simply to get the child to interact on a casual basis. The examiner can then ask what the child understands about the reason for the visit, clarify matters if there is some confusion, and explain the child's role in the evaluation.

Some children present more difficulty in establishing a working rapport. These are children who have been brought unwillingly to the assessment situation. They may be belligerent, defensive, angry, or simply determined not to cooperate. The examiner usually will do well to acknowledge that the child seems unhappy about being in the situation and to inquire about why. Often the child will perceive that the parents or others have brought him to someone who will act as their agent in getting him to accept their views of the problems and problem behavior. As such the psychologist is in the enemy camp and has to be resisted. To the extent that can be managed, the examiner will usually find it helpful to explain to the child that by his participation the child will be able to influence the outcome of problem situations that he confronts. When children are able to see that cooperation does not signify defeat, but rather a way to exert some control over situations, they usually will try to take advantage of the opportunity.

A few children are not trusting enough to permit themselves to take part in an examination. Others, if they go through the motions, give only the minimal performance to get the experience over and done. The psychologist has to decide whether it is better to terminate the attempt to perform an evaluation in such cases, or whether to continue to push for better performance. While there is no advice that can be written in stone, it usually works better to recognize the child's discomfort when it is so extreme and to offer to terminate the session, which will sometimes prompt a child to decide to continue. Other times the offer is accepted. In those cases the psychologist should recognize that there may be a future time when the child will want to return. If at all possible, this should be offered as a potential later choice. If it is not possible, the psychologist should simply say so and accept the decision. Likewise, if a session has to be terminated, the psychologist should explain why this was done to the parents and discuss the value of whether and when a new session should be scheduled.

In those cases in which a session has had to be terminated, the psychologist will want to review the events. Very few sessions have to come to this point and, if the frequency of terminated sessions is high, it probably means that the practitioner is mishandling the situation. However, it is probably vanity to expect to be able to evaluate all children, regardless of their attitudes and perceptions.

## KEEPING THE CHILD ON TASK

After a working rapport has been established, the examiner will need to set conditions so that the child will work on task. A good working rapport is neither so distant that the examiner appears uninterested in the child so that only the task is important, nor so personal that the task becomes unimportant and all that matters is the child. It is difficult to keep a child on task if the child is so preoccupied with how the examiner responds on a personal basis that the task is denigrated by comparison.

Clear instructions will help to keep a child on task. Only those instructions for the immediate task at hand should be given. If there is any hesitation or some sign of discomfort, the examiner should take time to determine whether the child understands the task. Shy children will often say they understand a task when they do not so that they do not have to be embarrassed by the admission. Sometimes inquiring about signs of discomfort will reveal that the child needs to visit the bathroom. It is best to get all these problems resolved so that the child can attend to the instructions and feel more at ease.

The physical environment of the assessment is a major determinant in how well a child can remain on task. If the child has problems with distractibility, the nature of the physical environment becomes even more important. The room should be well lit, but not so brightly lit that it is noticeable. Furniture should be comfortable, of a size that the child's feet can reach the floor. Work tables should permit the child to reach test materials without straining or having problems seeing the materials. The room should be pleasant in tone but without many decorations, which can be distracting to some children. If a viewing mirror is present, the child should be seated so that reflections do not create distractions.

The examiner should sit near the child so that they can both reach materials easily. However, it is wise to keep materials on the side of the examiner away from the child. In the case of children with attentional disorders these materials should be kept out of view as much as possible. The examiner wants to set up a situation in which the task at hand is a very clear figure against neutral background conditions. This will permit the child to give a good performance. Of course, in the case of children who are distractible the difference between performance under these ideal conditions and performance in the classroom may be a measure of the deficits incurred when distraction occurs. The examiner should not assume that good performance under ideal conditions implies a similar level of performance under other conditions.

## SELECTING ASSESSMENT TECHNIQUES

In a later chapter we will discuss the rationale for selection and order of assessment techniques. For the time being let us confine our discussion to the selection of age-appropriate tasks and some of the situational factors which may be important in ordering their administration. For children who need structure to help them calm down and stay on task, it is often best to give intellectual assessment procedures or achievement tests first. There is less likelihood that the child will stray from the task or resent being brought back to it by the examiner. With children who are very worried about being able to do well, just the reverse may be necessary. With these children it is often helpful to use unstructured play, projective techniques, or methods in which it is not clear whether a child has done well or poorly. Likewise the nature of the reason for the referral may help the examiner decide which instruments to administer first. Children who are anxious may want or need to participate in tasks which permit a lot of interaction with the examiner. Once having gained confidence they may be able to work more independently on other tasks which require less personal contact.

## THE EXAMINATION

The examiner should be familiar with the procedures. It is very important to review materials well in advance of the assessment situation. The examiner needs to know not only the administration procedures and be able to perform them well, but also to know the nature of standardization data relative to the test. Poor preparation can lead to invalid results. If the examiner has difficulty, for example, with enunciating sound blends required by a test, it is unfair to administer the instrument to the child. Likewise, if reliability data suggest that factors known to be operative in a case will result in poor estimates of performance, the examiner will be able to substitute a more suitable measure.

When the examiner is familiar with the procedures, a smooth performance is possible during which the examiner has more opportunities to observe the child's behavior. There is no problem of fumbling with a manual or poorly standardized administration. The examiner should take time to explain the instructions to the child. Usually some initial statement should indicate to the child that the examiner and the child will be engaging in a variety of activities and that the examiner will explain each of them as they begin.

The child should be permitted to work steadily so long as performance remains satisfactory. If the child requests a rest or break, this should be permitted so long as the request does not constitute an avoidance. If the examiner notes signs of fatigue or distraction it may be necessary to stop and either restructure the situation or to take a break. If the child attempts to avoid tasks by wanting to rest, or take frequent bathroom or water breaks, the examiner should consider making such time off tasks contingent upon the child's satisfactory performance while on task. By and large most children will respond to such conditions without any other special reinforcement. Some children, however, because of attentional problems, resistance, or dependency will not perform without more reinforcement. The first and most effective reinforcer for most children is social approval. Simply by noting approval of the child's performance, the examiner will usually be able to get the child back on task. In the case of retarded children and those with more pervasive problems, other reinforcers are sometimes needed. A typical reinforcer of this sort might be to let the child play with a desired toy for a brief time after satisfactory performance. Some other children will work well for food reinforcers – small bits of candy or salty food. Needless to say, before administering food reinforcers, the examiner should make sure that there are no medical contraindications.

The examiner should be in control of the session. To this end, the examiner should make sure that reinforcement schedules are set by the examiner rather than the child. If the child becomes cranky, sleepy, or uncooperative near lunch, the examiner should consider stopping while still in control, in order to give the child a happy feeling so that the afternoon session will be more attractive.

Some children may be taking medication. If a child has a seizure disorder or attentional problems, the medication may be administered several times per day. The examiner will want to note any changes in attentiveness, quality of performance, and activity level, as well as whether these changes appear related to the time since medication. If there are many procedures to administer and the child becomes fatigued, has to cope with medication effects, or for some other reason cannot profitably accomplish everything in one session, it is better to recognize the limitations. Most evaluations are scheduled for one session for the convenience of the adults who are involved. However, sometimes it may be important to spread the evaluation over several shorter sessions in order to accommodate the child's needs.

## SUPERVISION AND CONSULTATION

In addition to providing the professional with an opportunity to learn and improve performance, supervision and consultation serve as a means of insuring quality control. If the examiner is a new graduate or not experienced in working with children, it is especially important to schedule a time to discuss the case with the supervisor. Students should be supervised regularly and should also be observed in direct work with children so that the most efficient learning can occur. The more experienced professional will rarely need such close supervision but should be involved in some sort of peer review activities and should seek consultation whenever questions or issues make it desirable. Responsible professional activity includes communication and learning whenever good service to the patient would be improved.

## REPORTS

There are no ironclad rules to follow about reports, in terms of form or style. The outline suggested here arises from the fact that many children are seen, some of them return for reevaluation, and often, cases require legal depositions. For these reasons it is convenient to be able to read a report which may be several years old, know what data led directly to what conclusions, and be able to compare the child's current status with previous results.

What should go into a report? The report should include sufficient *referral information* so that the reader understands the questions which prompted referral and by whom the child was referred. In addition, it is helpful to have a *developmental history* which surveys major aspects of the child's medical, cognitive, family, and social history. Further discussion of the details of history-taking will be discussed in a later chapter. *Behavioral observations* should be included which describe the child's waiting room, leave-taking from adult, and within-session behavior. Results should include information from the *clinical interview* and separately for *each instrument* administered. The *summary and recommendations* should give a succinct picture of the child with regard to cognitive, affective, and social functioning in terms of productivity, organization, and level of function. Special problems and suggestions for remediation should be stated. In many settings a diagnostic classification label and number are required. Samples of several reports may be found in Chapter 12.

## DIVULGING INFORMATION

No report should be given, either verbally or in writing, to anyone who does not have a right to the information. The legal parent or guardian has the right to make that decision in most cases. However, in some cases insurance companies have the right to reports. In some states both parents have a right to information even if one parent retains custody. The psychologist should be careful to determine *in advance* those persons who have a right to information and should secure *written consent* from the parent or guardian for all copies of reports which are to be sent to people involved with the child's welfare.

Some cautions are in order with regard to giving information. A visit to a psychologist is a personal and private matter. The psychologist does not have the right to inform anyone, unless under court order, even of the fact of a visit unless the person or guardian of the person permits that disclosure. In cases involving court action or potential court action, telephone contacts are often received requesting information. These should be treated in the same manner as written reports. Without a signed release the psychologist does not have the right to release information.

Because of the sensitive nature of material contained in psychological reports they should be written with the idea that they may be read by many people who have conflicting views about the child in question. Statements should be straightforward and nonpartisan. Reports which are not directly based on observation or which are interpretations made by informants should be carefully evaluated before inclusion, and if they serve no useful purpose they should be excluded. It does not help much to include angry statements by a parent about the other parent. Moreover, when reports are read by others, statements at the level of rumor are often inflammatory and damaging. Information which is to be shared should be based on data and verifiable reports. Otherwise it is better to note that there is dissension between parents, for example, than to go into detail.

## REFERENCE

Jacobs, J. *Adolescent Suicide.* New York: Wiley-Interscience, 1971.

# CHAPTER 2

# *Testing Normal Children*

Why would a psychologist see a normal child? Of course, the answer to this question depends upon what is seen as normal. Normal children often experience problems based on situational circumstances. If the circumstances change, the problems are transient and may never require assessment or intervention. If the circumstances are chronic or debilitating, assessment may be appropriate.

Recently one of the authors received a referral for evaluation. The mother was concerned because her child was reading far below grade level. She was worried that the child might be dyslexic. The psychologist met with the child and mother and performed a psychological evaluation. The child proved to be of normal intelligence and able to achieve at grade level. There were no motivational problems. The only finding that indicated difficulty was a poor score on word attack skills on the Woodcock-Johnson Achievement Test. The psychologist was somewhat puzzled by the results. Fortunately, at the same time two independent referrals were received which presented similar problems. In the course of thinking about these children the psychologist discovered that all the children were in the same grade. They were all taught by the same teacher. It developed that this teacher was hired on a temporary basis due to an emergency leave by the regular teacher. The substitute taught word attack skills very poorly. These children had compensated somehow for the lack of word attack skills, probably by memorizing the vo-

14

cabulary items word by word, but they did not know how to approach new items. Given the achievement test the deficiency appeared, although comprehension was good when the child could recognize words previously learned.

A report written about this child might have begun: "This normal child with poor word attack skills is experiencing difficulty because she has been poorly instructed and thus is ignorant." In other words children can suffer problems based upon variables quite independent of psychopathology. A second point of interest is that such children often do compensate for situational stresses, at least initially. A child of more limited intelligence or one who was poorly motivated might have shown greater deficits on evaluation. In the case just described the psychologist saw a normal child who had a poor teacher.

Most normal children seen by psychologists for evaluation present placement problems. Does my child belong in a gifted program? Does my child need a special class for reading? Is this boy appropriate for foster home placement? These are the usual questions which might bring a normal child into assessment. The questions are raised because there are doubts about the child who proves upon evaluation to be normal.

A slightly different reason for adults to bring a normal child to a psychologist is because they want a description of the child by a disinterested party. While they are satisfied with the child and current adjustments, they want to get some help in thinking ahead. Examples of such reasons might be:

- If we travel abroad for a year, will it be likely to disrupt his educational progress?
- Should we think of him as very bright or does it only seem that way to us?
- My child has been through a very traumatic experience but isn't showing any signs of being disturbed. Is he covering up something or is he all right?

These are responsible reasons for parents to consult a psychologist. Sometimes the need is really for parental support or simply to get information that parents do not have.

In opening our discussion of testing the normal child, we urge a strong caution about the interpretation of psychopathology. As a rule, psychopathology should be seen as accounting for behavior when other explanations can be ruled out. The psychologist should start with the child, not with the explanation. When the data have been presented, explanations that are the most parsimonious should be examined first: How good is the teacher? Did the child have opportunities to talk about the traumatic event?

## A WORKING FRAMEWORK

We have already enunciated the first principle of our eclectic working framework, that is, psychopathology is the explanation of last resort. There is no normal child in the sense that there is no one way to be normal. Children are characterized by variability or individual differences along many continua which are important for their psychological functioning. Our working framework takes into account both cognitive, behavioral function and social, affective function. The literature which prompts this stand will only be sampled rather than reviewed exhaustively. Theories of development are restricted in terms of the amount of material they attempt to explain. Thus, Piaget focused upon cognitive development while taking note that there were rich domains of affective development which he did not try to explain. Theories of social development concentrate on early attachment and later interpersonal experience and usually relegate material on cognitive development to others. Consequently, the psychologist who works with children has to read and integrate material that covers cognitive, social, and emotional development. Neglect of any of these aspects of child development will result in a highly skewed notion of normality and deviance. Yet, because theories of cognitive development and theories of social development have grown out of different milieus, total theoretical congruence is only to be hoped for; certainly, it is not the status quo.

Psychologists often find themselves engaged in child assessment without basic background, because many programs in graduate psychology departments offer little basic coursework in child development. For those who have missed such coursework, Baldwin (1967) offers a survey of theories of child development. *Carmichael's Manual of Child Development* (Mussen, 1970) presents a survey of empirical research in child development. Journals such as *Child Development, Monographs of the Society for Research in Child Development,* and the *Journal of Clinical Child Psychology* are good sources for current research which is relevant to both normal and disturbed children. Among these references it is doubtless possible to extract a variety of expositions of normal development.

We have chosen to focus upon cognitive development first. We believe that the reader who becomes sensitive to cognitive growth will be able to be a more acute observer of interpersonal interaction and less likely to overinterpret behavior in terms of social meaning. For example, an infant who has not yet attained object constancy should not be seen as oppositional when he does not retrieve a hidden object. While this may seem a trivial example, it is not uncommon for abusive parents to attribute motivation to children who do not obey their commands because they are not yet able to understand or perform some desired tasks. The psychologist unfamiliar with cognitive landmarks is likely to misinterpret lack of compliance, hopefully in a more benign manner, but misinterpret all the same.

## COGNITIVE DEVELOPMENT

One approach to cognitive development was established when Alfred Binet began his testing program (Binet, 1908; Terman & Merrill, 1973). Binet began with a selection problem (he had to group children according to cognitive abilities) and devised a test which would help him with the problem. This approach establishes norms for different groups and permits one to describe differences among groups. It does not, however, necessarily provide any information about the course of cognitive development. Incidental information about the development of cognitive functions may be surmised if a series of tests spans enough years and if the items which contribute to differences over time are studied. While tests may function efficiently for selection purposes, the identification and study of basic cognitive functions are incidental and nonprogrammatic.

Guilford's model of intellectual function is based upon an analysis of types of thinking which characterize adulthood (Guilford, 1956). Of course, such a model can be used to generate studies of children and young adults, but it lacks epistemological sophistication. Research from this point of view results in knowledge about types of intellectual functions. Disproportionate amounts of emphasis may be given to some functions within the model, depending upon the interest of the investigator. The representativeness and developmental aspects of the model may vary considerably from typical child development.

A third approach to the study of cognitive functions is followed by Piaget (Flavell, 1963; Piaget, 1950, 1952). Using his own three children as subjects, Piaget began his observations of their cognitive functions soon after birth and followed the development of these functions longitudinally. He was able to establish a descriptive sequence of events which, later researchers found, were characteristic of other children as well. These studies are based on the natural development of cognitive functions within the cultural milieu which was present for European children. Since the time that Piaget made his observations, many cross-cultural studies have been done both in this country and on other continents. Piaget's account of cognitive development is epigenetic, i.e., one form or stage of development grows out of the preceding stage or form.

Piagetian theory spawned an enormous amount of research devoted to children's cognitive development. Numerous controversies arose about theoretical issues, among them what Piaget called "the American question," which is whether children's cognitive development can be accelerated by various types of experience. Other issues which arose were even more basic, such as whether children who are much younger than those described by Piaget were capable of systematic thinking. Some of these issues have implications for curriculum planning, e.g., the point at which mathematical reasoning in young children can be expected. Some writers, notably Gelman and Gallistel (1978), have produced evidence that children are better able to reason with regard to number functions than previously was thought, if the material does not exceed their memory capacities. Findings of this type also indicate how various cognitive functions (such as memory and reasoning) interact in limiting the behavior of children.

Young children (largely preschool) are characterized by what Piaget termed preoperational thinking, a nonsystematic and illogical approach to explaining matters. For children at the preoperational level of thought, words often do not mean the same thing as they mean to adults. Thus a child may understand that A is bigger than B, but may not understand that B is smaller than A. Adults who think transitively (and think nothing of it) may not realize that such performance is beyond that of young children. For the child, terms which imply relativity to the adult may have no such meaning. Many studies have been done which have shown that children's understanding of terms such as more, less, some, etc. is not uniform. In order to test reasoning capacities, investigators have had to make sure that children were trained to understand any relative language terms which were used in the instructions for specific tasks. Very young children, given a Stanford-Binet, may not understand such terms as *alike* and *different*.

Likewise, other terms which have standard meaning for adults will not necessarily mean the same thing to children. Very young children will not be aware of the difference between one hour and three hours, a week and a month. Since children do not have ratio scales of measurement underlying their notions of time, they have only crude methods of judging and anticipating duration. To the child who has not achieved a systematic appreciation of number concepts, a week may not mean seven days. It may mean that the sun has to rise and set many times before mommy and daddy get back from a trip. In working with preschool children in assessment, the examiner should be sensitive to the fact that children may appear to understand but may lack appreciation of relative terms and estimates based on number concepts. The child may use the word in speech but have limited understanding of exact denotation of what the word means to adults.

Another aspect of preoperational thought is that children are more limited than adults in the number of bits of information which can be remembered and manipulated (memory span). Thus, a child may be able to remember instructions with three bits of information but not with seven, or the child may be able to order objects as large or small, but may overlook ordinal relationships among the array of objects. Later in the preoperational period the child may be able to arrange ordinal arrays of objects but not transpose an order. These abilities to reverse the arrangement of an array and to maintain the ordinal relationship among its elements are important evidence that judgments of relativity can be made. Such operations may apply to understanding the relationships among ages of children in a family, cost of items in a store, etc. Thus, for very young children one cannot assume that because a child knows that both of his sibs are older than he, and that one sib is older than the other, he will be able to arrange himself and his sibs in correct order of age, or that he will be able to give the order from youngest to oldest, even if he can give the order from oldest to youngest.

As thought is becoming operational, i.e., systematic, other cognitive functions also mature. For example, memory strategies begin to become prominent and the nature of the strategies becomes more complex (Dempster, 1981). When children remember by categorizing objects rather than simply trying to remember items, they are also better able to organize their thinking. However, these cognitive developments are usually too subtle for adults who are not interested in memory to notice.

Intelligence tests for children at the stage which Piaget described as preoperational usually include tasks which depend upon nominal classification (Which one is different? Which one is ugly?) and upon memory of three or four items used in verbal commands, definitions of words, and similar cognitive operations. Such intelligence tests do not use items requiring use of transitivity. Examination of items on the Wechsler Preschool and Primary Scales of Intelligence, the Stanford-Binet, and some of the items on the Wechsler Intelligence Scale for Children (Revised) reflect this level of measure concepts, although these tests do come out of the psychometric tradition initiated by Binet's attempts to measure general intelligence.

The achievement of concrete operational thought marks the first period at which the child is capable of systematic thought in which reversibility of operations (and a number of other cognitive functions) is available to the child. Now the child can compensate for changes in appearance, which do not affect basic characteristics of substance, weight, and volume of a given quantity of matter. This ability has been called *conservation*, and requires an ability to coordinate at least two variables in such a manner as to understand that changes in one variable (e.g., area of the base) require compensatory changes in the other variable (e.g., height), if some basic characteristic (e.g., volume) is to remain constant. Ordinal relationships are mastered as are operations on classes, i.e., addition and multiplication.

The exact relationship between operations performed on classes and mathematical reasoning has been a controversial issue in cognitive developmental research. Piaget held that concrete operational thought depended upon empirical correspondence rather than upon hypothetico-deductive reasoning. Thus, the child should be able to perform operations on classes, and deal with ordinal relationships and correspondence, but only in terms of concrete situations. No intelligence test has been constructed with the notion of using these Piagetian concepts as the basis of item selection. Although some special procedures such as the Concept Assessment Kit – Conservation (Goldschmid & Bentler, 1968) are constructed on this basis, they do not provide intelligence quotients.

Interestingly, we have a tradition of test construction which was initiated by social pressure to identify groups of children by level of ability, and it is out of this model that most of our tests of cognitive function have been derived. We have a second thrust stemming from longitudinal work which has identified various cognitive processes available to children; but while this work has spawned many empirical studies of children's thinking, it has not resulted in standardized intelligence tests. Aside from Concept Assessment Kit – Conservation, the Uzgiris – Hunt scales, which were constructed to measure the development of object permanence, are the most durable measures which have been developed (Uzgiris & Hunt, 1975).

## SOCIAL DEVELOPMENT

Current views of children were developed only within this century. Neither the public notions of children nor those accepted in the academic world took account of how much change and growth had to be accomplished in the social development which children experience. American psychology had been preoccupied with content for most of its existence. By content, we mean to distinguish between what is known as opposed to how it is known. Content is generally defined as what is known. American psychology had its roots in the British tradition of associationism which had as a major idea the mind as tabula rasa, the passive recipient of impressions etched upon it by stimuli.

Predisposed in this manner, American psychology was most concerned with stimulus variables and how these variables *determined* responses. This predisposition gave rise to Hullian learning theory and to other S-R theories. Naturally, as these theories were applied to concepts of childhood and child development, the idea was also accepted that children were more passive and pliable than they are seen today. The rigidity of Watsonian dicta to mothers about scheduling feedings, together with many other rules about childrearing, was based on this view of children. Also, the type of research which was produced out of the S-R schools was preoccupied with stimuli, e.g., how similarity of stimuli would affect learning-paired associates or how number of trials to learn might be affected by other characteristics of the stimulus. The subject was relatively neglected by comparison with the interest in the effects of stimulus materials.

By contrast, psychology which developed in continental Europe was oriented not only to the problems of content but also to how content was acquired. Thus Piaget, who came out of this tradition, was interested in children's conceptions of time, substance, morality, and physical laws and equally interested in the processes by which the child explained the world to himself. As a result Piaget's work concentrated on cognitive processes such as conservation and operational thinking, while work that grew out of logical positivism was interested in how well the children could learn when situations were manipulated or stimuli were varied. The Piagetian notion of childhood implies an active, exploratory, and increasingly socialized and self-directed child. The implications for mothering and for education included focusing attention on the child and studying what the child was able to do at various points in development as a participant.

Piagetian theory posits an invariant order of development for cognitive functions. Other psychologists have accepted the idea of an invariant order of development based on biological functions. Some of these psychologists took direction from Galton's early work measuring various biologically-based reactions. In this group we have researchers such as Gesell and Ilg whose work has produced several volumes which chart children's performance from infancy through childhood on both motor and mental tasks (Gesell et al., 1940; Gesell & Ilg, 1943, 1946; Gesell et al., 1956). From these studies we have group norms of behavior. Other psychologists have been deeply interested in activity level, sensitivity to stimulation, patterns of responsivity, and temperamental style. Some researchers have described processes which underlie information-processing (such as orientation and habituation), while others have been interested in social behavior.

The data produced by psychological studies of child development early in this century have changed the face of theory about child development. For several decades the literature was full of debates between the proponents of psychoanalytic theory and those of S-R learning theories. The topics included scheduling versus permissiveness, practice versus unguided development. Parents were advised to keep to the schedule, then to be permissive, and now to enrich early experience.

By the middle of this century the importance of early experience had captured the imagination of most psychologists. One of the drawbacks of the acceptance of this new concept was that parents were seen as focal causes of later problems, often to the exclusion of other factors. With this focus on the parents, particularly on the mother as primary caretaker, came the implication that psychopathology was the fault of the family. Cognitive development was not exactly ignored, but emotional adjustment was a matter of primary concern. Advice about parenting was devoted to suggestions about how to help a child feel secure and loved.

An alternative to the extreme environmental position is found in the work of Chess and Thomas who integrated biological and social aspects of development in their investigations of "primary reaction patterns." This work on primary reaction patterns (and thence to temperamental or behavioral style) spans over 20 years' study of the interaction between behavioral style and environmental stimulation. According to Chess and Thomas, when the child's temperament and the demands of the environment are a good fit, optimal development occurs and moves in the right direction. When the match of temperament and circumstances is inappropriate, distortions and maladjustments may be expected to occur. Other writers (e.g., Escalona, 1968) have also studied this proposition, but at present the idea does not appear to have much impact on those primarily concerned with child assessment.

The recognition that the infant is an active participant in the social process has now been demonstrated and popularly accepted (Hunt, 1961; Maccoby, 1980). Much of the credit belongs to Piaget (Flavell, 1963) and his careful descriptions of his own children's developmental progress. This longitudinal and individual method of observation is a method which grew out of Piaget's background in biology and his interest in epistemology. Cross-sectional methods of investigation which characterized much of early American psychology prevented in-depth study of individual differences. Individual differences within groups are thought of as variability and often the object has been to minimize group variability so as to be able to better gauge the effect that some stimulus might have on performance. Yet studies which follow individuals through time are able to identify personal styles of responsivity which indicate that the way individuals react to stimulation may differ consistently from one another (Escalona, 1968).

Piaget concluded from his observations of cognitive and moral development that each of us "constructs" our own world. In our physical similarities and in the common forces of nature which act upon us (e.g., gravity), we have the basis for genuine shared experience. However, due to the idiosyncratic features of our experiences, we manifest many individual differences. Piaget began his observations during the first month of life, a time when the infant sleeps, eats, eliminates, orients to physical stimuli, and begins to develop some visual accommodation. At this time the infant's dependency upon parents, especially the mother, is great. At the same time, the infant's response to the mother and her ability to satisfy her baby set in motion one of the major social processes of human life – attachment, i.e., "a relatively enduring emotional tie to a specific other person" (Maccoby, 1980, p. 53).

Children who are attached to a person want to be near that person, are distressed at separation, are happy when they are reunited with the object of attachment, and are oriented toward watching for and listening for that person even when the person is not immediately present. Attachment occurs at the same time as the cognitive achievement of object constancy and may depend upon, in part, the same underlying cognitive functions. Following closely upon the development of attachment to a specific caretaker, an avoidance of strangers becomes prominent in children. While some children demonstrate this avoidance of strangers more extremely than others, it is a common occurrence during the second half of the first year of life. Having the mother or some other object of attachment present contributes to a calming effect in the presence of a stranger or of a strange situation.

With the development of language, children become less frightened of separation, probably because they are able to maintain distal contact with the mother (e.g., by calling out to her if she is in another room) until they become absorbed in some activity which captures their curiosity. Indeed, early attachment seems to be characterized by contact comfort, eye contact, and the ability to elicit response from the object of attachment, such as signaling distress by crying. As language and cognitive functions mature, children depend on a broader range of attachment objects who serve a broader range of social functions for them, probably contributing to the diminution of the intensity of attachment to the mother. In time, physical proximity, while pleasurable, can be interrupted for long periods of time without loss of emotional attachment.

Interpersonal contact with others leads to the necessity to coordinate individual activities and desires with those of one's companions. This need to reconcile differences leads, according to Piaget, to the growth of moral development, on the one hand, and empathy and social awareness, on the other hand. Maccoby (1980) has reviewed the literature on the attachment process. Three patterns bear particular attention: the secure, the avoidant, and the resistant. Maccoby concludes that children who are characterized by secure attachment during the first year are able to meet and deal with new experiences during the next few years, while resistant children suffer greater difficulty in coping with new tasks. There is no direct comparison in the literature between the temperamental styles studied by Chess and Thomas and attachment patterns reviewed by Maccoby, although it seems reasonable that some relationships might be expected, since the socialization process is influenced by contributions from both caretakers (usually the mother) and from the infant. It is expected that infants who are fussy, active, and difficult to comfort, who respond intensely to stimulation, and who have trouble achieving regularity demand much more concern and care from their mothers. Consequently, mothers who are insecure, insensitive, or resent the demands of the infant are likely to experience feelings of frustration and/or inadequacy. In other words, the temperamental style of the infant and the mother's style of caretaking are likely to interact in such a manner that the socialization process will reflect both of these influences and, in this case, be likely to result in either a resistant or avoidant attachment.

Some studies have been performed which examined early attachment and later differences in the interactions of infants and mothers. Both in this country and in cross-cultural studies (Ainsworth, 1967; Ainsworth, Bell, & Stayton, 1971), babies who can elicit a maternal response by signaling distress early in life show fewer signs of later distress.

Let us pursue this idea of how temperamental styles may be involved in the development of a particular type of attachment pattern. Using the work of Chess and Thomas, we will exemplify how children within a normal range of temperamental differences produce different social response styles. Some cohesive patterns of child behavior were identified and define three general classes of temperament. About 65% of the original New York Longitudinal Study (Thomas, Chess, & Birch, 1968) could be classified using these three temperament clusters. The definitions of temperament rested upon reliable categories of observed behavior including: activity level, regularity or rhythmicity, approach or withdrawal, adaptability, threshold of responsiveness, intensity of reaction, quality of mood, distractibility, and attention span and persistence. The clusters derived were temperamental styles labeled: the Easy Child, the Slow-To-Warm-Up Child, and the Difficult Child. (For a good review of this work, including information on correlates of temperamental styles, see Thomas and Chess, 1977.)

The Easy Child is the child everyone finds easy to like, to manage, and to enjoy having in the family. This child with this temperamental style has a positive expression of mood, adapts well to new experiences, and has regular habits. By contrast, the Slow-To-Warm-Up Child is hesitant about approaching new situations, but adapts well if not pressured too much or too quickly. The Difficult Child reacts strongly and negatively to change and to new situations. The child with the Difficult temperamental style is likely to be irregular in sleeping and eating patterns and to adapt slowly.

Now let us consider the consequences of interactions of particular temperamental and caretaking styles. For example, if a Difficult Child were born into the home of a mother with a relaxed attitude toward mothering, the mother would be able to tolerate quite a lot of disturbance and temper problems. By comparison, a tense or insecure mother might take fussing and temper to mean that she was at fault in some way. She might be less comfortable about herself as a mother, less confident, and less able to manage her child, to calm him down, and to provide pleasant experiences for him. The Difficult Child with the more relaxed and competent mother would be expected to have a better chance of developing a secure attachment during early life.

A Slow-To-Warm-Up temperament style appears to require an interested but calmly nurturant mother in order for the child to experience a low level of frustration. One might expect that a child with this temperament style and a somewhat cool and distant mother might not get enough nurturance for a secure attachment, whereas a pushy mother might easily provoke such a child to resist and withdraw from much contact.

Interviews with mothers of children who are brought to clinical situations frequently provide some clues as to the early adjustment of children and parents. When the interviewer inquires about what sort of baby the child was, it is not uncommon to hear parents say: "We knew he would be difficult from birth. He didn't like to be held and I could never satisfy him"; or "She was such an easy baby. She ate well, slept a lot, and she smiled early. I couldn't have asked for a better baby."

## SOCIAL DEVELOPMENT AND
## THE DEVELOPMENT OF PSYCHOPATHOLOGY

Just as there may be a relationship between temperamental style and the nature of the attachment pattern formed, there may be a relationship between temperamental style and the development of psychopathology. Recent work (Earls, 1981; Johnson et al., 1982; Webster-Stratton & Eyberg, 1982) supports this view. Whether parental behaviors mediate the developmental patterns is not clear, but a study by Cameron (1978) based on reanalysis of data from the New York Longitudinal Study is consistent with this interpretation.

Social development varies among normal children. The more active, difficult, and less securely attached children require more help in learning to control emotions, particularly those of a frustrating nature. Impulse control is more likely to be a problem for these children than would be the case for the more placid and securely attached children. These differences in impulse control are obvious in situations which require children to delay gratification, to take the point of view of another person, and to take responsibility for their own behavior. Thus children with different individual response styles are likely to exhibit behavior which will be reflected in the assessment process. We will discuss some of the implications for assessment later in the chapter.

As can be surmised, personal response styles, particularly those which are extreme, may be associated with risks for impaired cognitive and social behavior. Studies of deviant children indicate that those children who have active behavior problems constitute a major portion of the population which comes to the attention of mental health professionals (Robins, 1966). Moreover, these children have more problems when they grow up than these who suffer neurotic problems in childhood. In other words, the active, difficult child may be not only more of a problem for parental management, but also, at the extreme of that style of response, at greater risk for the development of psychopathology than other children. Quiet and withdrawn children are not as often identified as problems and, even when they do have problems in early childhood, they have a better chance of good adjustment later on. Whether a number of these deviant children who are withdrawn are extremes of the normal Slow-To-Warm-Up Child is not known. Regardless of whether there is a specific relationship between temperament styles and specific forms of psychopathology, it is clear that more deviant withdrawn children recover and show less psychopathology later than do acting-out children.

Efforts to classify child psychopathology (Achenbach & Edelbrock, 1978) usually identify some problems with undercontrol (such as aggressive behavior), some problems with overcontrol (such as obsessive and phobic problems), some somatic complaints, and a variety of smaller categories which appear to represent learning problems, and neurotic and psychotic psychopathology. The broadband factors, Internalizing (for problems characterized by overcontrol) and Externalizing (for problems characterized by undercontrol), may sort out differently by sex and age groups. When the narrow-band factors are examined, conduct and personality problems seem to constitute the bulk of child disorders which might be related to poor social development. Learning problems may have more biologically-based sources, at least for children who are distractible, have memory problems, or specific developmental disturbances of cognitive functions.

In the work reviewed both on temperament and on socialization styles, we have found descriptions of children who are relatively free and easy, children who are more cautious and withdrawn, and children who are more active, aggressive, and more easily frustrated. It is tempting to think of these children in terms of personality styles described by Horney (1937). She described a personal style of moving toward people, one of moving away from people, and a third style of moving against people. While the exact procession from temperament and socialization history to personality style has not been charted, it is clear that children at greater risk for social and cognitive disruption are more vulnerable to possible deviance than children who do not suffer these disruptions.

We have described social developmental factors: temperamental style and attachment patterns, and their interaction with parental behaviors to produce an *individual* or *personal response style*. From our discussion it is clear that within the normal range of development there are different personal response styles which will be developed as a function of individual differences among children and their parents. Moreover, when a child with a particular individual response style encounters situations with specific demands, there will be some degree of fit between the response style and the situational demands. In cases where the fit is good, there will be low stress, easy adaptability, and less vulnerability to all sorts of developmental deficits. In cases in which the fit is poor, there will be high stress, more difficulty in adapting to the situation, and higher vulnerability to the production of developmental deficits.

This model is similar in form to a model described by Zubin and Spring (1977). Zubin and Spring were interested in the appearance of overt psychopathology in schizophrenics and they proposed a vulnerability model to account for the appearance of schizophrenic symptoms. In their model, threshold for symptoms is a function of the relationship between vulnerability and challenging events. Vulnerability is defined in terms of genetic contributions and "acquired" vulnerability due to factors such as disease or life events. Challenging events constitute stressors, and Zubin and Spring make the point that some patterns of living may be identified as "stress-prone."

The significance of this model for the present discussion is that normal children may be more or less vulnerable to problem production, and that they may be embedded in more or less "stress-prone" patterns of living. The interaction between vulnerability represented in personal response style and situational demands will determine whether a normal child develops a problem.

## IMPLICATIONS FOR TESTING

We have examined some of the developmental processes involved in cognitive and social maturation. We have considered how parental behavior may mediate patterns which emerge among children. We have discussed how personal response styles and situational variables may interact to result in problems which lead adults to refer children for psychological assessment. We will now discuss some implications for testing normal children which are suggested by the material covered.

The psychologist cannot simply evaluate a child. The child must be evaluated relative to the situational stresses experienced by the child. Many problems are situationally determined and before one can assume that the child needs modification or treatment, it is important to make sure that either placement or environmental change is not indicated. We reiterate that the interpretation of psychopathology should occur only after other factors have been ruled out.

Children who are labeled a problem by adults have to contend with the labeling process. Children may identify and internalize a negative self-image which sets up expectations for future problems. The psychologist needs to be sensitive to this process for it is at work in all problem-related referrals.

Implications for testing normal children also proceed from differences among personal styles. As we mentioned in the first chapter, the inattentive child will be expected to require more structure to stay on task during an examination than the child who has no attentional problems. Likewise, the child who has a difficult temperamental style will experience frustration frequently and will need help in staying on task. These children require extra effort on the part of the examiner to function at their best. Moreover, when they are in a group of children, as in most classroom situations, performance may be well below what they are able to do with one-to-one support.

Similarly, the child who is slow to warm up will need encouragement and time to become familiar with both the examination room and the examiner before formal assessment procedures are likely to be accepted. The method of establishing rapport will differ with the needs of the child based upon the child's socialization history and the biologically-based aspects of his personality. The psychologist will have to be observant of these differences and will have to be flexible in order to maximize the child's freedom to respond well.

Aside from the establishment of rapport, other facets of the assessment procedure will be affected by the child's personal response style. For example, the determination of basal and ceiling levels employed in many tests depends upon the child's ability to stay on task and to control frustration. Children who are slow to warm up may give up easily without gentle encouragement. Difficult children, on the other hand, may require firm limits and some time away from the task in order to discharge their frustrations.

Finally, the child should never leave the test situation without some chance to discuss what has transpired. Many children have no basis for understanding their performance or what it means. The examiner should ask the child how he enjoyed the day, and then inquire as to his impressions ("What was it like for you today?"). A little general feedback is helpful ("I could see that you are a hard worker. You seemed to like some of the tasks better than others. Did you like _____ better?"). If a child had difficulty or was uncooperative, one should not make an issue of the fact, but neither should it be ignored. ("This wasn't a day when you wanted to be here, but you worked hard anyway," or "I know you didn't like being here, but when you did get involved you showed me that you were able to do well"). If the child would not perform or only complied minimally with the tasks, the examiner may acknowledge that fact ("You really didn't want to be here and so you wouldn't let me know what you could do. That's all I can say about it. Maybe sometime you will feel differently and we can schedule another appointment").

At the point of feedback, children will sometimes startle the examiner with questions such as, "Well, am I crazy?" The examiner can explain that the examination was not to answer that question (unless, of course, it was) but to find out what would help the child in school or to get along with parents. If the feedback part of the day is not included, children sometimes leave with misconceptions about what went on and the purpose of the examination. A few moments spent with the child in discussion of the day can prevent unnecessary discomfort on the part of the child.

## REFERENCES

Achenbach, T. M. & Edelbrock, C. S. The classification of child psychopathology: A review and analysis of empirical efforts. *Psychological Bulletin,* 1978, *85,* 1275-1301.

Ainsworth, M. D. S. *Infancy in Uganda: Infant Care and the Growth of Attachment.* Baltimore, MD: The Johns Hopkins Press, 1967.

Ainsworth, M. D. S., Bell, S. M., & Stayton, D. C. Individual differences in strange-situation behavior of one-year-olds. In: H. R. Schaffer (Ed.), *The Origins of Human Social Relations.* London: Academic Press, 1971.

Baldwin, A. L. *Theories of Child Development.* New York: John Wiley, 1967.

Binet, A. Nouvelles recherches sur la mesure de niveau intellectual chez les enfants d'ecole. *Ann. Psychol.,* 1908, *14,* 1-94.

Cameron, J. R. Parental treatment, children's temperament, and the risk of childhood behavior problems. *American Journal of Orthopsychiatry,* 1978, *48,* 140-147.

Dempster, F. N. Memory span: Sources of individual and developmental differences. *Psychological Bulletin,* 1981, *89*(1), 63-100.

Earls, F. Temperament characteristics and behavior problems in three-year-old children. *Journal of Nervous and Mental Disease,* 1981, *169,* 367-374.

Escalona, S. K. *The Roots of Individuality.* Chicago: Aldine, 1968.

Flavell, J. H. *The Developmental Psychology of Jean Piaget.* New York: Van Nostrand, 1963.

Gelman, R. & Gallistel, C. R. *The Child's Understanding of Number.* Cambridge, MA: Harvard University Press, 1978.

Gesell, A., Halverson, H. M., Thompson, H., Ilg, F. L., Castner, B. M., Ames, L. B., & Amatruda, C. S. *The First Five Years of Life.* New York: Harper & Row, 1940.

Gesell, A. & Ilg, F. M. *Infant and Child in the Culture of Today.* New York: Harper & Row, 1943.

Gesell, A. & Ilg, F. M. *The Child from Five to Ten.* New York: Harper & Row, 1946.

Gesell, A., Ilg, F. M., & Ames, L. B. *Youth: The Years from Ten to Sixteen.* New York: Harper & Row, 1956.

Goldschmid, M. L. & Bentler, P. M. *The Concept Assessment Kit—Conservation.* San Diego, CA: Educational and Industrial Testing Service, 1968.

Guilford, J. P. The structure of the intellect. *Psychological Bulletin,* 1956, *53,* 267-293.

Horney, K. *The Neurotic Personality of Our Time.* New York: Norton, 1937.

Hunt, J. McV. *Intelligence and Experience.* New York: Ronald Press, 1961.

Johnson, J. H., Basham, R., & Gordon, B. N. Temperament and indices of psychological adjustment in preschool age children. Paper presented at American Psychological Convention, Washington, D.C., 1982.

Maccoby, E. E. *Social Development: Psychological Growth and the Parent-Child Relationship.* New York: Harcourt, Brace, Jovanovich, 1980.

Mussen, P. H. *Carmichael's Manual of Child Psychology, Third Edition.* New York: John Wiley, 1970.

Piaget, J. *Psychology of Intelligence.* New York: Harcourt, Brace, 1950.

Piaget, J. *The Origins of Intelligence in Children.* New York: International Universities Press, 1952.

Piaget, J. *The Moral Development of the Child.* New York: Free Press, 1965.

Robins, L. N. *Deviant Children Grown Up.* Baltimore, Williams & Wilkins, 1966.

Terman, L. M. & Merrill, M. A. *Stanford-Binet Intelligence Scale (Third Edition, Form L-M, 1960, 1972 Norms).* Boston: Houghton-Mifflin, 1973.

Thomas, A. & Chess, S. *Temperament and Development.* New York: Brunner/Mazel, 1977.

Thomas, A., Chess, S., & Birch, H. *Temperament and Behavior Disorders in Children.* New York: New York University Press, 1968.

Uzgiris, I. & Hunt, J. McV. *Assessment in Infancy: Ordinal Scales of Psychological Development.* Urbana, IL: University of Illinois Press, 1975.

Webster-Stratton, C. & Eyberg, S. M. Child temperament: Relationship with child behavior problems and parent-child interactions. *Journal of Clinical Child Psychology,* 1982, *11,* 123-129.

Zubin, J. & Spring, B. Vulnerability—A new view of schizophrenia. *Journal of Abnormal Psychology,* 1977, *86,* 103-126.

# CHAPTER 3

# Clinical Populations

Whereas in the previous chapter we focused upon several patterns of normal development and some of the consequences of those patterns for individuals, in this chapter we will direct our attention to special populations of children. Our discussion will include intellectual deviation, academic deviation, and personality problems. For each of these clinical populations, we will consider issues related to definition, incidence, etiology, and assessment.

In discussing clinical populations, classification procedures are necessarily implied. In the case of mental retardation the most extensive classification work has been done by the American Association of Mental Retardation (AAMD) (Grossman, 1973). The classification of retardation employed by the Diagnostic and Statistical Manual, Third Edition (DSM-III, 1980) of the American Psychiatric Association overlaps but is not entirely consistent with the AAMD classification scheme. Because schools often tend to prefer the AAMD classification while hospitals and psychiatrists may use the DSM-III, we will discuss both systems and make comparisons in the section of this chapter dealing with mental retardation.

The DSM-III is more consistently used with other clinical populations which are served by psychologists. There are other classification systems used by hospitals, notably the International Classification of Diseases, Ninth Revision, Clinical Modifications (ICD-9-CM, 1978) but

DSM-III is more widely used across a variety of settings, and hence will be the system to which we refer in this chapter. Essentially, DSM-III provides a formal psychiatric diagnosis and information on the severity of the stressors as well as the highest level of adaptive functioning during the past year. However, DSM-III remains atheoretical with regard to etiology and makes no assumption that each mental disorder is a discrete entity. Also, DSM-III has been criticized on the basis that it almost totally neglects social psychological variables and interpersonal behavioral variables (McLemore & Benjamin, 1979). Consequently, the usefulness of DSM-III for predictive purposes, especially those which might bear on research in etiology, is far from clear.

## MENTAL RETARDATION

Edna, a nine-year-old who has repeated the second grade and who is large for her age and slightly overweight, is worrying her parents due to her poor academic performance. Edna's school problems include poor reading and arithmetic skills, as well as being a very slow worker. Edna is quiet, doesn't volunteer information, and is frequently observed avoiding eye contact. She does not seek out other children, tending to relate to younger girls if they approach her first. More often she is seen at the fringe of social activity.

As observers of children like Edna, we are faced with a number of questions in trying to understand what accounts for their academic and social performance. We might wonder if Edna were overly shy, slow to warm up, inept, or did not understand very well. We would have questions about her sensory modality receptiveness, including her sight and hearing. We would wonder if Edna's behavior at school was typical of other situations as well.

*Definition*

Lambert et al. (1975) have pointed out that adaptive behavior has been an essential focus in the definition of retardation and that the psychometric approach to defining retardation is a relatively new tradition stemming from Binet's work in 1905 in the Paris schools. The AAMD includes the measurement of intelligence as an essential component of the diagnosis and classification of retardation, but also includes the evaluation of adaptive behavior as central in the determination of an individual's retarded or nonretarded status. Prior to this psychometric evaluation of children, schools were not involved much in the process of assessment. With the advent of funding for special programs in American schools during the middle of this century, assessment of mental retardation acquired new importance for schools, and emphasis on IQ test scores for entry into these school programs also gained new importance. Grossman (1973), in the statement of the AAMD definition of mental retardation, includes both subnormal general intellectual functioning and concurrent deficits in adaptive behavior. This behavior-descriptive approach does not attempt to speak to questions of causality and prevention and is, therefore, distressing to some who are very concerned with the plight of retarded children.

Not all agencies and people responsible for the assessment of retarded children use the AAMD definition. Psychiatrists employ DSM-III, which uses the criteria for mental retardation of significantly subaverage general intellectual functioning (defined as an IQ of 70 or below on an individually administered intelligence test or, in the case of infants, a clinical judgment of retardation), and concurrent impairments or deficits in adaptive behavior, the person's age being taken into account. Also, the onset has to be before the age of 18. Psychiatrists have to rule out specific or pervasive developmental disorders and borderline intellectual functioning in order to assign the diagnosis of mental retardation. The numerical values for levels of retardation employed by DSM-III are compared with those required for the AAMD definition in Table 3.1.

*Incidence*

Due to problems of definition, diagnostic criteria, and methods of sampling, reliable incidence data are not available (Knopf, 1979). Using IQ scores below 70 results in estimates of about 3% of the population being defined as retarded. Males, blacks, and lower socioeconomic segments of the population have been found to be at greater risk for being diagnosed as retarded. Various experiential factors have been suggested as influential in the demographic distribution of retardation. The AAMD Manual on Terminology and Classification (Grossman, 1973) describes four levels of intellectual functioning used to classify mentally retarded people. These levels vary slightly in numerical value, depending upon whether the Wechsler Scales or the Stanford-Binet is used to obtain the intelligence test score. Some schools require the use of one or another of these instruments specifically in the classification of

# Table 3.1
## Level of Retardation With Respect to School, Psychological, and Psychiatric Conventions

| Retardation Level | Educational Level | AAMD Criteria Obtained Intelligence Quotient Stanford-Binet (s.d. = 16) | Wechsler (s.d. = 15) | DSM-III Criteria not specified as to which individually administered test |
|---|---|---|---|---|
| Mild | Educable Mentally Retarded (EMR) | 67–52 | 69–55 | 70–50 |
| Moderate | Trainable Mentally Retarded (TMR) | 51–36 | 54–40 | 49–35 |
| Severe | | 35–20 | 39–25* | 34–20 |
| Profound | | 19 and below | 24 and below* | Below 20 |

*Due to the fact that the Wechsler scores were not computed for values this low, scores in this range are extrapolations.

children as retarded. Table 3.1 indicates the levels of intellectual functioning as defined by the AAMD for these tests and relates these levels to the type of educational program to which they are usually assigned and to the levels which are employed by DSM-III in the classification of retardation.

The Educable Mentally Retarded (EMR) child does not perform as well as most children of the same chronological age and school placement. Usually these children are first identified in the early period of academic experience. Often these children are less emotionally stable, frequently in response to academic frustration, and they may have problems socially, in terms of being independent and responsible. Generally, there is no particular physical defect associated with retardation in this range. The school situation which is most helpful for these children includes small classes, considerable individual attention and tutoring, and tasks structured so that the children can work at their own pace. With proper support and guidance these children can often learn enough skills to be employed later in sheltered work situations with supervision. Without adequate education and continued support, many of these people cannot maintain employment or satisfactory living situations. Depending upon which criteria are employed, the IQ for the EMR child ranges from 50–70.

The Trainable Mentally Retarded (TMR) child is even more limited in rate and attainable level of learning. The IQ range includes scores from about 35–51 depending upon which criteria are employed. Reference to Table 3.1 indicates that this range covers all of the moderately retarded level and the upper part of the severely retarded level. The training typically successful with children at this level is related to self-help, such as toilet behaviors, dressing, eating, and some routine chores. Frequently children in this range do have physical deficits and coordination problems. If the resources of the home are not sufficient and if these children come to the attention of social agencies, they may be institutionalized. These children look and act differently from the normal child and are unable to learn the minimal vocational skills which are attained by the EMR children.

Severely and profoundly retarded children usually suffer physical and neurological deficits. They are limited in their ability to communicate and their social and motor development is undeveloped. Emotional disturbance is frequent and the most profoundly retarded are often bedridden, requiring constant attention with regard both to their everyday functioning and medical problems. Within these levels of retardation,

IQ scores are usually estimates because of the many attentional and response handicaps characteristic of these children, which make formal assessment difficult and sometimes impossible.

## Etiology

Mental retardation may result from a number of different etiological conditions, including various chromosomal aberrations with which retardation is associated, metabolic disturbances (usually associated with autosomal chromosomal defects) that lead to retardation, and complications of pregnancy and delivery associated with toxicity, trauma, nutritional problems, and prematurity. In addition to these biologically-based determinants, about one quarter of the cases of retardation appear to be affected by social and familial factors which are related to socioeconomic deprivations (often associated with poverty) and to unstimulating environmental conditions. Assessment of retardation should include careful historical investigation to determine whether the etiology can be discovered. Since some forms of retardation are reversible, this point is especially important.

Chromosomal abnormalities have usually been diagnosed prior to referral for psychological evaluation. The role of the psychologist usually is as a consultant rather than as the primary diagnostician. In the case of mongolism or Down's Syndrome the condition is irreversible. Usually the children are distinctive in appearance, more likely to be born to mothers over 35 years of age, and clumsy and slow. In the case of children who are born with Down's Syndrome, psychological assessment is helpful to parents who are trying to plan for the child and who may need to have a more realistic estimate of how much the child can understand, as well as what kind of support and supervision would be most helpful. Most children with Down's Syndrome function within the moderate to severe level of retardation. Boys are at greater risk than girls.

Boys are also subject to another chromosomal abnormality, Klinefelter's Syndrome, in which an extra X chromosome is present. This results in more feminine body build. In approximately 25% of the cases, mental retardation occurs. There is also a high incidence of psychosis and antisocial behavior.

Girls are subject to Turner's Syndrome, which results from an anomaly of the sex chromosome. The girls are usually of short stature with webbed necks, epicanthal folds, flat nasal bridge, and low-set ears. A phenotypically similar disorder also occurs and is associated with retardation. According to Menkes (1974), Turner's Syndrome itself is not associated with mental retardation, but because of the right-left disorientation which occurs and because of defects in perceptual organization, girls with Turner's Syndrome may have deficits on the performance portion of the Wechsler instruments.

Metabolic disorders which result in nervous system damage and which may be associated with mental retardation are sometimes reversible. Medical history in cases in which such disorders are suspected should be examined to determine whether screening tests for metabolic defects have been performed.

One of the better known metabolic disorders is phenylketonuria (PKU) which results in mental retardation, seizures, and imperfect hair pigmentation. About 1 in 14,000 children is born with PKU. While PKU babies look normal at birth, vomiting (including projectile vomiting) during the first two months of life develops, as does a musty odor. If uncorrected, seizures, restlessness, and hyperactivity will develop along with mental retardation (usually IQs are below 50 although there are cases in which normal IQs are obtained). Screening tests for PKU are routinely performed in most hospitals. If dietary regimes are not started early in life, both intellectual and neurological deficits are more likely to appear.

There are a number of other rare metabolic disorders, such as Maple Syrup Urine Disease and diseases of the urea cycle metabolism (Menkes, 1974), which will not be reviewed here. More familiar is a group of disorders due to defective lipid metabolism, of which Tay-Sachs Disease and Niemann-Pick's Disease are the best known. These diseases are more frequent among Jewish children of Eastern European backgrounds and are progressive and fatal. No treatment is known for either of these disorders. Related disorders include a variety of defects of lipid metabolism with varying onsets, some of which, while not fatal in childhood, do result in marked neurological symptoms and blindness. Most of these disorders will never come to the attention of psychologists either because of the early deaths of these children, or because the physical complaints bring them to the attention of pediatricians and the diagnosis is accomplished through review of neurological and biochemical evidence.

Due to the educational programs which have been available to prospective parents, many people are aware of the problems that toxicity, trauma, infection, nutritional problems, and prematurity pose with respect to mental retardation. Drug intake, particularly alcohol, has been implicated in birth problems related to mental retardation. Likewise, infections of various types, especially during the first three months of pregnancy, have been shown to be associated with retardation. However, mental retardation can be the result of infections such as those due to venereal disease after the first trimester. Radiation, trauma, toxic intake of various types, and nutritional deficiencies, particularly of A and E vitamins, have been shown to be related to retardation. Premature babies are at high risk for retardation due to the complications of labor and delivery as well as to the previously mentioned conditions. Similarly, anything which interferes with the growth and appropriate supply of nutrients and oxygen to the brain increases the likelihood of retardation. For the clinician it is important to be aware of these factors and to include a history which explores such possibilities. Since more of these factors are likely to be associated with a history of poverty (and hence little or no prenatal care), it is particularly important to take a thorough history to rule out various factors which might contribute to retardation or which suggest the need for medical referral.

In addition to physiologically-based reasons for mental retardation, it has been demonstrated that there are environmental contributors to functional mental retardation. Indeed, not too many years ago mental development was thought to be entirely predetermined (Hunt, 1961) and environmental influences were thought to be to no avail. This resulted in the scientific community discounting the work of Harold Skeels, who demonstrated with the children in an Iowa orphanage the dramatic effects of social stimulation on the intellectual performance of formerly low-functioning children. The follow-up study conducted by Skeels some 30 years later indicates the powerful effects of environmental stimulation and differences in later social, vocational, and economic adjustment (Skeels, 1966). The effects of poverty which are mediated through both physical and psychological channels exert an influential role in the incidence of mental retardation (Robinson & Robinson, 1970).

## Assessment of Retardation

For the psychologist who is involved in the assessment of children who may be mentally retarded, neither an intelligence test nor a history is sufficient data basis for decisions which result in a diagnosis. It is quite noticeable to anyone who has worked with retarded children for any length of time that several children of the same age may have the same measured IQ and histories which do not indicate any physiological basis for differences among them, and yet the children may be quite different in terms of their adaptability and social skills. For this reason, the recommendation of the AAMD that a diagnosis of mental retardation include both an individually administered intelligence test and assessment of adaptive behavior is especially important.

There are a number of psychological instruments which may be used in the determination of adaptive behavior. The AAMD Adaptive Behavior Scale was constructed especially for this use and includes domains which assess independent functioning in daily care, physical development, economic activity, language development, concepts of numbers and time, domestic activity, vocational activity, self-direction, responsibility, and socialization. There are also measures of maladaptive behavior which include violent and destructive behaviors, antisocial behavior, rebellious behavior, untrustworthy behavior, withdrawal, stereotyped behavior, inappropriate interpersonal manners, unacceptable vocal and egocentric habits, self-abusive behavior, hyperactive tendencies, sexually aberrant behavior, psychological disturbances, and use of medications. The AAMD Scale may be completed by parents and teachers which permits one to determine whether situational differences in the child's behavior are experienced by caretakers, which information may be employed in constructing management plans for the child. Many of the items on the AAMD Scale are designed more for older children and adults. Therefore, in the case of very young children other developmental scales which assess self-help behavior and developmentally appropriate domains of social and cognitive development may prove more helpful.

Motivation and social support may be of primary importance for the eventual adjustment of retarded children. Neither the IQ nor the mental age concepts take these personal characteristics and environmental influences into account, yet these may be the most important variables at work given children of approximately the same mental endowments. Assessment and planning for retarded children cannot afford to ignore or underestimate these factors since they may spell the difference between independent living or supervised living and working conditions for many individuals, and the difference between institutionalized versus shelter conditions for others.

Assessment of mentally retarded children should take into account both the adaptive and maladaptive behaviors which are observed by parents and teachers. Frequently children who are well socialized and have sufficient environmental support will show few maladaptive behaviors and will be motivated to achieve at the best level they can produce. Children who have been subjected to ridicule or who have suffered parental abuse will be found to achieve at lower than their possible levels of productivity and to indicate poorer levels of social and independent functioning. If the children have endured these circumstances long enough, there may be various forms of maladaptive behavior present as well. Infantalized children will tend to be more immature and inappropriate in their behaviors, while children whose experience includes ridicule and lack of support often suffer poor self-esteem leading to withdrawal and lack of motivation, and sometimes to self-abusive behavior. Recommendations for placement and treatment should rely not only on the intellectual level of the child, but also upon these adaptive patterns and the resources which are available for helping the child.

## UNDERACHIEVEMENT

Jimmy, an alert 10-year-old, is popular and active in sports. His teachers usually like him and consider him an attractive child. Although both Jimmy's family and school mates think of him as bright, Jimmy is having trouble in school. Because of his popularity Jimmy has a good fund of self-esteem but tends to disown any interest in school, particularly reading. Jimmy's parents are beginning to fear that Jimmy may have a problem which is causing his apparent underachievement. They want to know whether Jimmy can't do his school work or is just not trying.

### Definition

Regardless of specific definitions, the concept of underachievement denotes academic performance which is below expectation, based on intellectual capacity and experience (usually represented through chronological age). It follows that underachievement cannot be due to impairments of intellectual ability or to youth and inexperience. For example, a child who has been promoted to a higher grade based on intellectual endowment, but who is younger than other students, may not be able to function at that level due to social immaturity or lack of requisite academic skills at that level; however, he should not be considered an underachiever. Likewise most people would agree that the blind or deaf child of average intelligence may perform below grade level because of the obvious handicaps which prevent him from maintaining a level consistent with that of unimpaired children.

Referrals of children thought to be underachievers are presented in terms of whether the child is at an appropriate grade placement, or whether the child is as bright as previously thought, or whether some emotional or learning problem is interfering with academic performance. These referrals may be construed as falling into roughly two categories: those associated with external determinants of performance and those which are due to intrapersonal determinants. Both possibilities should be examined before one can be comfortable with a judgment of etiology and recommendations for intervention.

A significant issue which confronts the clinician focuses upon the less obvious emotional or learning handicaps characteristic of many children who would be defined as underachievers, based on the definition with which we opened this discussion. For example, the dyslexic child, the child who has specific arithmetic dysfunction, and the child whose social background actively discourages academic performance all have handicaps despite good intelligence. The problem, then, which confronts the clinician is whether the child presented for assessment should be considered as an underachiever or whether this is a child whose below-normal academic performance is due to subtle and previously undetected handicaps.

*Incidence*

Incidence figures for underachievement are incomplete. There are data for some groups of children who appear to have normal intelligence or even superior intelligence but who have impediments to performance. These include children whose underachievement is due to learning disabilities. The figures for dyslexia suggest that at least 15% of American school children are dyslexic (Gibson & Levin, 1975). As with so many other disorders of childhood, a sex ratio of 3:1 to 5:1 with males predominating is found among dyslexic children (Myklebust & Johnson, 1962). Definitional differences, as well as differences in the availability of neuropsychological examiners, contribute to the unreliability of the incidence data. Even so, it is clear that dyslexia and other special learning disabilities are widespread enough to account for the poor school performance of many children who would otherwise be expected to perform adequately.

*Etiology*

### Internal determinants of underachievement

Even though some children are bright, have parental support and peer relationships which facilitate academic achievement, and are in supportive school situations, they do not do well. Some of these children are self-motivated (at least early in their school years) but fail anyway due to reasons unknown to parents, teachers, or themselves. Among these children are those who suffer neuropsychological deficits, including many who are dyslexic.

There has always been a group of children who fail to master reading at a level normal for age. This failure, furthermore, is not due to mental retardation, documented central nervous system dysfunction, or emotional instability. A general guideline for determining if a child is exhibiting a significant reading problem has been suggested in the HEW report (1969). According to this report, if a child is reading one or more years below expected grade level, based on chronological age in the primary grades, and is one-and-a-half years behind expected placement in later school grades, this child exhibits a significant delay in reading skills.

This group of children has been classified in diverse ways. The terms "specific learning disability," "reading retardation," "word blindness," "developmental lag," and "primary reading disability" have been used interchangeably with dyslexia. All refer to a communality of symptoms in the otherwise normal child who has difficulty learning to read and who may be first identified as an underachiever, since expectations are that he will be able to perform adequately. On gross neurological examination, these children are intact; however, a careful family history often reveals reading difficulties, spelling problems, and poor academic achievement in close relatives, suggesting a genetic component to the etiology of the problem. Advocates of the genetic view find compelling evidence for this position from twin and family studies. For example, a twin study using 388 pairs of twins was carried out by Bakwin (1973) and indicated that identical twins were alike in reading disability in 84% of the cases, in contrast to only 29% of fraternal twins.

For most parents there are no indicators of dyslexia prior to the child's attempts to learn to read and write. When the beginning reader exhibits difficulty in developing phonetic skills, or fails to relate higher order relationships in orthography to those in his oral language, or has problems dealing with spatial relationships, dyslexia may be suspected. Some signs are more equivocal because many children manifest them developmentally but do not develop dyslexia. These equivocal signs include reversals of letters and numbers, left-right confusion, deficient intermodal integration, fine motor problems, and figure-ground difficulties. Clinicians should be cautioned not to interpret these equivocal signs as diagnostic of dyslexia in the developmental period prior to approximately eight years of age since so many children who never develop dyslexia also manifest these signs. For example, Shankweiler and Liberman (1972) found that single letter reversals accounted for only 10% of reading errors of very poor readers among third-grade children.

Debate exists whether dyslexia can be accounted for by a developmental lag which compromises the child's ability to learn reading during age-appropriate intervals. More specifically, Satz and his associates (Satz & Sparrow, 1970; Satz, Rardin, & Ross, 1971) have suggested that a lag in the maturation of the left hemisphere with a corresponding lag in functional specialization of language results in dyslexia.

Some children do appear to recover later when appropriate intervention (in the form of reading programs) has occurred, but others appear intransigent to attempts at intervention. Early identification of the problem appears to be a crucial variable in the successful prevention of chronic reading problems in children. Schiffman and Clemmens (1966) reported that 80% of children diagnosed and treated remedially by age eight were achieving at expected grade levels two years later. However, with the group of children diagnosed as reading failures at age 10, only 15% achieved expected reading levels after two years of remediation. Thus, early diagnosis and effective remediation programs at an early age would appear to alleviate the chronicity of reading failures for at least some of the children found to have severe reading problems.

Another group of underachievers are those who perform poorly because of emotional problems. They lack confidence, are distrustful, may be school phobic, highly anxious, or maladjusted in some other way. To observers, these children appear somewhat reticent but are not necessarily obvious as problem children. By comparison with children who are conduct disorders, these children exhibit appropriate classroom behaviors but fail to achieve academically. Because they are not conduct disorders and do not manifest obvious academic problems, they may be overlooked for a long time until the academic performance deteriorates alarmingly.

Finally, among the children whose underachievement cannot be accounted for due to external causes, there are some who suffer none of the problems discussed previously. They come from intact homes, loving parents, adequate socioeconomic levels, good schools, and have no neurological or learning problems. Despite the tendency for many mental health workers to assert that something must be wrong with children who do not achieve at the level of their potential, clinicians who assess children will find some who simply are not interested in school. They comply minimally with expectations and show no evidence of major psychological disorder.

*External determinants of underachievement*

Three sources of external pressure which result in underachievement are subcultural value systems, family attitudes, and peer pressures among socialized delinquent children. Subcultural value systems which are at variance with the belief that children should achieve up to their academic potential include religious, ethnic, and social groups which concentrate on the value of manual labor and on social organization, which characterized pre-industrial revolution social structure. For some of these groups, simple trade or craft skills are valued because they are consistent with a nonconsumer and nonacquisitive social organization. When academic achievement becomes symbolic of greed or evil or even of assimilation of the subculture into the mainstream of society, these groups actively discourage and condemn participation in the academic process. For many of these groups the school is seen as the corruptor of youth. Strong pressures are exerted to bind children to the in-group and to terminate or attenuate any influence that the majority might exercise through the educational process. Sometimes school officials or relatives who become concerned about the inadequate performance or social isolation of the children initiate referrals for assessment.

Among family influences which actively discourage school achievement are parental attitudes such as those of the parents who debunk the value of a higher education than they have achieved. Other parents insist that the child contribute to the financial support of the family. Work and family responsibilities interfere with the child's participation in school work. Still other parents are emotionally disabled and depend upon their child in such symbiotic or abusive ways that the child's presence in the home is demanded to the exclusion of school attendance.

There is another group of children for whom parental support or encouragement has simply been lacking. These children are often wards of the state, having been placed in foster homes or institutions where consistent interest in their academic achievement was not a priority.

Peer groups in which academic achievement results in loss of face may act as powerful deterrents to school performance. Socialized juvenile delinquents are among the children most characterized in this manner. Even though the peer groups may have high esteem for leadership and intelligence, they depend upon antisocial behavior which runs counter to goals set by social institutions, including the school. A child desiring membership in such a peer group is forced to choose between group membership and academic involvement.

Another group of externally determined causes of underachievement can be classed as those of transient situational nature. These would include traumatic episodes due to accident, illness, death, and divorce. Also among this group would be poor relationships with specific teachers, poor school environment such as that characterized by social disruption, poor curriculum, and disorganization.

*Assessment of Underachievers*

From the previous discussion we can see that data from life history materials, the child's style of relating, and various assessment techniques are all important in the diagnosis of underachievement and its distinction from other presenting problems. After the referral and history have been taken, and before the question of underachievement can be properly entertained, the child should be assessed intellectually to insure that expectations regarding potential are reasonable. The IQ, usually in the form of WISC-R scores, can be helpful in formulating hypotheses which account for the low academic performance.

The history may be informative with regard to complications of pregnancy, birth, and developmental history, including trauma, illness, and family attitudes. For foster or adoptive children these types of data may not be available. When the history does contain relevant information, the clinician may be able to detect a longstanding pattern of poor school performance.

Duration of poor school performance will be expected to have an effect on test findings. For a child with a long history of academic underachievement one should expect significantly lower performance on tasks which are highly dependent upon acquired knowledge. For example,

Bannatyne (1971, 1974) has described a triad of Wechsler subtests (Information, Arithmetic, and Vocabulary) which indicate that the child has not absorbed knowledge available from academic sources. Other subtests on the Wechsler may be unimpaired. In the absence of a good history, as in the case of many foster children, this triad may be suggestive of chronicity of the school problem.

Given the child's approach and level of performance on the Wechsler, the next step is to document further the nature and extent of the underachievement through the use of pertinent achievement tests. Let us suppose that we find consistent evidence of underachievement not only as reported by the school, but also on the testing materials. Projective testing may elucidate the nature of the child's unproductiveness in school settings. If the projectives indicate no evidence of psychological disturbance, the clinician may rule out emotional disturbance and usually neuropsychological disturbance, which often have associated emotional reactions, as probable sources of the underachievement. The projectives may indicate identification with subcultural or familial patterns which serve as deterrents to school achievement. On the other hand, disinterest in school achievement may be indicated in the absence of other factors mentioned above. Table 3.2 illustrates some of the expected patterns for groups of underachievers discussed in this section.

## HYPERACTIVITY AND ATTENTIONAL PROBLEMS

David, an eight-year-old who can't sit still, is a problem at home and at school. Complaints about David include restlessness, impulsivity, short attention span, distractibility, irritability, and disruptive behaviors. This red-headed, freckled-faced boy literally bounces into the room and is in constant motion, fidgeting with objects, while his eyes explore the room continuously. While David makes friends, he has frequent fallings-out with them so that his friendships are brief and usually end with unpleasantness.

*Definition*

The definition of hyperactivity found in DSM-III supports the recently reported research data that hyperactivity may, indeed, be a long-term problem having serious consequences in later life. The general term, "Attention Deficit Disorder," is broken down into "Attention Deficit with Hyperactivity," with inattention, impulsivity, and hyperactivity as the

# TABLE 3.2
## Underachievement

| Type of Data | Internally Determined | Externally Determined |
| --- | --- | --- |
| History | Family and situation may be supportive | Family or situation may be nonsupportive or obstructive |
| Observation | Child's behavior may be informative (anxious, reticient, lacks confidence) | Child's behavior may not be informative |
| Self-report | Child reports either wanting to perform or disinterest | Child reports trauma, group membership, or attitudes antithetical to school performance |
| Parent report | Usually sympathetic toward school achievement | Unsympathetic toward school achievement or report trauma or situational problems |
| IQ | Grossly unimpaired | Grossly unimpaired |
| Achievement | Specific problems related to either SLD or emotional problems or neither (more likely to show uneven pattern of performance) | School achievement low; test achievement low if long history of external problems |
| Projectives | Variable | Variable |

cardinal symptoms in young children. In addition, the diagnostic category "Attention Disorder without Hyperactivity" suggests that the individual so diagnosed need not manifest excessive motoric activity; however, he may exhibit the other symptoms. "Attention Deficit Disorder, Residual Type" clearly states that "signs of hyperactivity are no longer present; and the symptoms of inattention and impulsivity may result in some impairment in social or occupational functioning."

Unfortunately for the clinician involved with the assessment and treatment of children, there are no clear-cut normative data which define what overactive behaviors are or how much activity, inattention, or impulsivity are needed to make a diagnosis. There are no activity level norms for children of any age, although there have been many attempts to define operationally excessive activity. The value of gross activity level norms is questionable, as researchers have demonstrated that hyperactive children often do not exhibit higher levels of gross motor activity than do normal children in a variety of settings. Studies have shown that hyperactive children show significant intra-individual variability across situations (Schleifer et al., 1975) as well as intervariation within specific situations (Rapoport & Benoit, 1975).

Thus, the overactive behavior per se is not the major concern with hyperactive children but, rather, a high level of activity is significant only in its detrimental influence on other areas of the child's functioning. It is the qualitative aspects of hyperactivity which are important rather than the simple quantitative ones. Hyperactivity becomes significant in certain situations in which the child is unable to inhibit hyperactive behavior despite social pressures to do so and in which overly active behavior is clearly inappropriate (e.g., formal, structured academic settings). Regardless of the myriad descriptive terms applied to children considered to be hyperactive, four descriptors are commonly found: hyperactivity, distractibility, impulsivity, and emotional lability or excitability.

Several researchers have differentiated hyperactivity into a variety of groups. Regardless of the terminology employed by these researchers, several general classifications have been conceptualized in terms of etiological factors which in turn have led to particular treatment paradigms.

Fine (1976) suggests four general classifications of behavior which take into account the social learning position, the developmental lag hypothesis, the psychological basis, and the organic or biological position. Conditional hyperactivity is conceived of as a syndrome of behaviors resulting from external environmental factors that maintain and control hyperactive behaviors. Developmental hyperactivity is assumed to consist of a syndrome of activities that may be transmitted genetically and aberrant behaviors are the result of maturational delays in CNS functioning. Psychological hyperactivity is seen as a syndrome of behaviors which are the results of ineffective psychological systems, such as faulty ego development, with ensuing lack of impulse control. Organic hyperactivity results from a demonstrable abnormality in either the structure or function of the brain and/or the biochemical processes of the body.

*Incidence*

While there is little consensual agreement regarding the etiology, prognosis, treatment and educational management, there is considerable agreement that "hyperactive" children exist and that they exist in great numbers. The incidence rates range from 3-10% in normal populations of school children (Stewart & Olds, 1973) and increase to 10-30% among previously identified problem children (Wender, 1971). The approximate 3-4:1 male-female ratio is also characteristic of a number of other childhood disorders.

*Etiology*

Ross and Ross (1976) suggest that the lack of significant relationships between abnormal history, neurological findings, EEG, intelligence, and behavioral indices indicates that the exhibited symptoms are the result of multiple etiological factors. It is beyond the scope of this book to review the major theoretical positions with regard to etiology of hyperactivity. The interested reader is referred to many excellent reviews in this area (Cantwell, 1975; Fine, 1976; Fish, 1971; Safer & Allen, 1976).

Most professionals agree that hyperactivity has profound effects on the education and emotional and social development of young children. For some time, it was thought that hyperactivity was a problem confined to young children which disappeared during adolescence. Therefore, the problem could be expected to somehow resolve itself by adolescence and there would be no long-term detrimental sequelae in terms of adult functioning. Recently, the results of longitudinal research suggest that the notion that children "outgrow" hyperactivity may be overly simplistic. It appears more likely that the obviously disturbing, overactive, and restless behaviors decrease with age. It is becoming evident that the more subtle disabilities associated with hyperactivity continue to manifest serious educational, social, and psychological problems well into adulthood.

Several studies have shown that on measures of behaviors commonly associated with hyperactivity (e.g., restlessness, disorders of attention and concentration, distractibility, emotional immaturity, and inability to maintain goals), children previously so diagnosed continued to have problems as adults. In addition, reports indicate that hyperactive children showed residual effects of learning disabilities and poor social adjustment at least five years after the initial diagnosis was made. There is also evidence that adult men, previously diagnosed as hyperactive in childhood, had a high rate of psychiatric problems and that despite normal IQ scores these men had not achieved a socioeconomic status equal to that of their fathers or brothers (Borland & Heckman, 1976; Weiss, 1975).

In summary, it would appear that there is a multiplicity of etiological factors which produce hyperactivity. As the hyperactive children mature, some of the overt behaviors moderate, but other more covert behaviors persist and are associated with adult histories of underachievement, school failure, delinquency, and poor psychological adjustment.

## Assessment of Hyperactive Children

We turn our attention now to the assessment procedures used in the evaluation of hyperactive children. The problem of evaluating children who have been labeled as "hyperactive" by their parents, teachers, and pediatricians is complicated by the lack of operationally-defined criteria of characteristic symptoms. However, several excellent checklists and parent questionnaires are available which will aid the clinician in assessing the child's behavior across a variety of situations (see Chapter 10). Perhaps of major importance is the reported behavior of the child in the classroom. The teacher is often more aware of age-appropriate activity levels and has more realistic expectations of the child's ability to concentrate, attend, and maintain on-task behaviors than other adult caretakers. The teacher is also more likely to see the arousal effects of group stimulation than the parent, who may deal with the child more often on the one-to-one basis.

There is no clear-cut and definitive battery of tests nor distinctive intra-test pattern which has been shown to differentiate between hyperactive and normal children. There are, however, many types of data which help with the assessment process. The clinician depends heavily upon reports of the child's behavior (usually given by someone who is disturbed by the child), upon his or her own clinical observation and judgment of appropriate activity level, and upon the signs of distractibility and inability to concentrate during the evaluation. Often the hyperactive child has a hasty and impulsive response style, tending to answer quickly without regard to alternative possibilities, and his attention usually must be re-directed back to the task at hand. In addition, the child's behavior during the testing session gives the clinician valuable information in making an assessment. For example, the hyperactive child exhibits an inability to focus his attention on the specific task, becomes overly attentive to irrelevant stimuli in the test material, is unusually distracted by extraneous noises in his environment, and finds it exceedingly difficult to resume work on the task at hand. One begins to get clinical validation of reports of the child's behavior.

The test behavior of hyperactive children must be differentiated from that of the overly anxious child. In contrast to the hyperactive child who often shows little if any concern about his performance, the anxious child displays quite different behaviors, which result in poor performance on tests that require sustained attention and concentration (Kaufman, 1979). For example, anxiety is more often indicated by such behaviors as an excessive concern with the stop watch, fear of failure, tendency to give up easily as the tasks become more difficult, and the strong need for reassurance and encouragement.

Whenever either set of behaviors is found during the evaluation of a child and it is the clinician's opinion that these behaviors have had a depressing effect upon the child's performance, the test results must be interpreted with care. In particular, the obtained IQs may have limited meaning and may be an underestimation of his current levels of ability due to the behavioral interference with his performance. Extreme distractibility, short attention span, poor concentration or anxiety may have a depressing effect upon any test administered: intellectual, academic, or projective.

Frequently an analysis of the pattern of subtest scale scores on the Wechsler Intelligence Scale for Children (WISC-R) is used as the basis for a diagnosis of "cognitive hyperactivity." In particular, three subtests (Arithmetic, Digit Span, and Coding) are considered to be highly dependent upon concentration and attention. Therefore, significant decrements in performance on this cluster of subtests are assumed to be corroborating evidence for a diagnosis of hyperactivity (Kaufman, 1979).

A word of caution is in order if the clinician automatically interprets lower performance in these three subtests, labeled as "Freedom from Distractibility." First, a child's performance on any subtest may be significantly affected by anxiety or distractibility. Second, inferences about the meaning of the lowered performance must take into account the child's behavior during the examination. For example, poor performance on Arithmetic may be due to lack of computational skills, as well as a function of distractibility. An analysis of individual errors, together with consideration of the child's test behavior, must be made before the type of difficulty encountered can be interpreted.

Achievement testing with children who may be suffering the cognitive deficits associated with hyperactivity may be revealing. Tests such as the Metropolitan Achievement Test may indicate poor achievement whereas the PIAT (Peabody Individual Achievement Tests) or the Woodcock-Johnson may not show the same amount of deficiency. The difference may stem from the fact that on the latter tests the examiner interacts continuously with the child, which may serve to keep a more distractible child on task to a greater degree than would be the case with the Metropolitan.

Likewise, on various projective tests the pattern of minimal involvement and an impulsive response style will be obvious. Sometimes, but not always, hyperactive children will give content which reflects frustration or poor self-esteem.

In summary, it is the manifest behavior of children labeled hyperactive which remains the critical evidence in the diagnosis. It is also evident that various etiological factors can give rise to similar behaviors. The problems associated with making a diagnosis of hyperactivity are also compounded because there is lack of agreement among professionals about the definition, prognosis, or treatment. The presenting clinical complaints may vary greatly among children and at various times within the same child. In addition, there is no clear-cut test pattern which will differentiate reliably among hyperactive and normal children. The clinical diagnosis of hyperactivity, then, is confirmed by history, by reports of the child's behavior across a variety of situations, and by current behavior during evaluation, including response style, response characteristics, and response to behavior limits. With regard to the last item, the child's ability to attend and inhibit upon request is especially important. The clinician's subjective norms of age-appropriate levels of activity, distractibility, and ability to attend are also important. Some test results are consistent with the judgment of hyperactivity and these have been discussed with respect to intellectual, achievement, and projective testing, although no definitive operational criteria exist for the establishment of a diagnosis of hyperactivity in children.

## NEUROSIS

Bradley, an 11-year-old who was given her mother's family name, is overly concerned with cleanliness and being correct. She is known as a model child who is unhappy when she does not live up to her own perfectionistic standards. Even her parents, who are proud of their family tradition and have high expectations for Bradley's appearance and conduct, are impressed by their daughter's insistence on her own perfectionistic goals. Sometimes they worry when Bradley drives herself unmercifully, even on seemingly unimportant matters. While Bradley has a warm smile, she avoids physical contact. This perplexes her parents, who wonder if Bradley's behavior is a little too extreme. Because of her manner, the parents find it difficult to talk with her about their concern. When Bradley became very upset about taking showers after gym class, the parents recognized that something was wrong.

### Definition and Etiology

Historically, neurotic disorders were described by Freud who explained their origin and the meaning of their symptoms in terms of the psychoanalytic theory which he evolved in the course of studying his patients. For Freud and for subsequent psychoanalytic formulations, the key components to neurosis were the presence of anxiety and an internalized conflict. Symptoms arose as a function of the incomplete coping mechanisms which psychological defenses afford. Incomplete management of anxiety results in symptoms including anxiety, whereas if the defenses were more efficient conversion symptoms or displacement through phobic reactions might occur. If the anxiety were isolated from its original source, obsessive-compulsive disorders might result. Depression, according to psychoanalytic formulation, is based on a fixation in which the person's self-esteem is regulated by external supplies or in which a person has such guilt feelings that he regresses and constantly needs supplies of love and esteem from others. Depending upon the strength of the impulses, the ego, the superego, and the status of various introjects not yet assimilated into ego or superego, various expressions of psychopathology occur (Fenichel, 1945).

In the past 30 years we have seen the rise of behavior theory and behavioral interventions ranging from new attention to instrumental conditioning to the development of cognitive behavior therapy. The current status of the theory of neurosis is unsettled. Even greater disarray exists with regard to the current status of child psychopathology. Knopf (1979) devotes a short chapter to psychoneuroses and psychophysiological disorders. Quay and Werry (1979) mention anxiety-withdrawal as a pattern which includes separation anxiety and school phobia, depression-withdrawal and hysterical reactions, but in this empirically and behaviorally oriented text, neurosis is a term of historical interest rather than of theoretical significance. Schwartz and Johnson (1981) devote a chapter to "Neurotic" Behavior Disorders of Childhood, noting that DSM-III recommends the use of the term "neurotic disorder" only in a descriptive sense. The disorders discussed by Schwartz and Johnson include phobias, obsessions and compulsions, childhood hysteria, and childhood depression. Among the diagnostic categories devoted to childhood, DSM-III includes anxiety disorders, identity disorders, and sleep, eating and movement disorders, all of which might have been classified as neurotic disorders previously. In addition, phobias and affective disorders (including depression) can be applied to children by adapting different criteria than those applied to adults.

It is clear that we have moved away from the basis that Freud used in trying to classify disorders. While all workers start with observation of some complaints and behaviors, the amount of material that is organized with respect to any theoretical orientation varies considerably. At the present time, classification systems have moved toward an empirical approach which rests as much on the methodology of measurement as it does on notions of psychopathology. Quay and Werry call for operational definition of categories, reliability and validity, explanatory value, independence of categories, and parsimony while still offering completeness. One of the best examples of this approach is the work of Achenbach (Achenbach & Edelbrock, 1978), in which data from various sources have been grouped through multivariate techniques producing a taxonomy which takes account of age and sex in the identification of disorders. This approach may help to resolve some of the theoretical debates which are devoted to problems of child psychopathology. There is, for example, disagreement about the validity of the diagnosis of childhood depression, both from theoretical grounds and from incidence studies (which use varying forms of assessing depressive symptoms). Of course, these studies may be based on differing underlying theories about what constitutes childhood depression. One of the Achenbach and Edelbrock findings is that factors derived for boys and girls across different ages yielded a factor for all groups, except the 12–16-year-old boys' sample, which could be labeled depressed. Whether boys of this age may become depressed and, if so, mask the symptoms (as some writers would hold) are questions which data on related issues (e.g., incidence of suicide for boys of this age) may help to decide.

Regardless of the theoretical bent of the writer, there is a group of disorders characterized by an internalizing style and group of symptoms which is classified as distinct from the externalizing style of conduct disorders and which is not so severe as to represent major reality disturbance. The status of anxiety in these internalized disorders as either causal or merely associated with behavior disturbance appears to be a function of the theoretical orientation from which it is viewed. Likewise the status of family factors as contributors to the disturbance is not viewed with any kind of consensus. Some behavior that would be considered pathological at one time in childhood will be considered normal at other periods. Thus children of around one year of age may be afraid of strangers, a pattern which occurs in normally developing children. Fear of strangers at age 10 or 12 is not normal. For behavior to qualify as neurotic or psychopathological it is generally agreed that the behavior is not age- or stage-appropriate.

The characteristics which are usually associated with an internalizing style include anxious, fearful, tense, depressed, embarrassed, and worthless feelings. Even when considering the feared object, it is the internalized state that is preeminent – the anxiety is the focus for the child. The self is the focus, the other person or event is the occasion for the experience of the emotion. This is in sharp contrast to conduct disorders in which the focus is on the other person or event and the emotions are the signal for the child's criticality and dissatisfaction with the other person. Whereas the child who suffers from conduct disorder orients his behavior against other people, withdrawal is the common behavior characteristic of the internalizing child. The child who misbehaves may come to the attention of adults more readily than the withdrawn child who may be secretive about his discomfort. Therefore, it is likely that incidence data underestimate the number of children who suffer from neurotic or withdrawn and internalized conflicts.

*Incidence*

Two problems appear prominent with regard to estimating incidence of neurotic problems among children. First, one must consider the source of the reports of disturbance (child, parent, teacher, mental health worker) and, second, one must consider the nature of the sample. For some disorders which appear to be rare (such as obsessive-compulsive disorders) the rates are usually reported in terms of children who have been referred for child psychiatric services. Despite theoretical debate about its validity, childhood depression diagnosis is much more widely reported both with regard to the total population of children and to children referred for educational and emotional problems, than is obsessive-compulsivity. In our consideration of neurotic problems, we omit conduct disorders, psychoses, and specific problems of eating, sleeping, toilet behavior, and stereotyped movements. We also omit anxiety states which lack an internalized focus. Data cited by Knopf (1979) suggest that as many as 25%–50% of children referred to child guidance clinics were classified as psychoneurotic, while only 6%–11% was typical of other outpatient settings. The likelihood is that child guidance clinic data overestimate the proportion of neurotic children and other outpatient settings underestimate the proportion of neurotic children, due to the nature of the institutions and the samples which are likely to report to them.

*Assessment of Neurosis*

Assessment material pertinent to the different neurotic disorders must take account of the defining features of these behavioral patterns. Since no clinical approaches (interview, projective techniques, rating scales, self-reports, and observational assessment) possess the psychometric elegance of the instruments designed to assess intelligence, the psychologist must compensate for the possibility of greater error of judgment which might occur if only one clinical technique were used alone. For instance, a variety of assessment methods can be used and results compared across a number of instruments. Both confirming and disconfirming signs consistent with a diagnostic impression must be examined. The types of data available to the clinician include observation of behavior, interview material with the child, the parent, and sometimes the teacher or some other significant person in the child's life (not necessarily an adult), test material relevant to the child's level of intellectual and academic functioning, various projective and self-report devices, questionnaires, and check lists. For some disorders one class of data may be more revealing than for others. Let us examine and compare two cases in which such an approach might be utilized.

Consider the case of a child of elementary school age whose parents are concerned about withdrawal from activities and are aware of no reason for depression. The child's grades may have dropped but there are no signs of sleep disturbance or expressions of sadness. The child may not show signs of appetite disturbance or motor evidence of agitation or slowing. What is obvious is that the child's productivity has diminished and that there is loss of interest in previous sources of pleasure. Parental attempts to discover if anything is wrong have not turned up any incident or causal agent and they are perplexed, concerned, and perhaps irritated. A physical examination has been negative for any contributing physiological factor. The psychologist who examines the child also interviews the parents and decides to elicit material from them through the use of a problem checklist. In addition, the child is interviewed and fills out some self-report measures. Finally, intellectual, achievement, and projective data are obtained.

Observation reveals a child who is polite, cooperative, but passive. Responses are brief and somewhat stimulus-bound. The intelligence test reveals a child who is well above average in intelligence but shows loss of points on timed tests. Sometimes the child has to be prompted to provide fuller explanations of answers, and when this occurs, the explanations increase the point value of some answers. The achievement data indicate a much better grasp and understanding of academic material than is reflected in the child's school performance. In interview the child does not volunteer affective statements but tends to describe behavior and activity rather than feelings. No attributions of sadness, worthlessness, irritation, or apathy are produced. Projective data do reveal some themes of isolation, rejection, and preoccupation with affiliation. Both sentence completion and projective stories indicate that feelings of sadness at rejection and anger in response to it are prominent, although unverbalized through other methods of inquiry. History reveals that one of the child's friends has recently moved from town and that a teacher to whom the child is very attached has just had a baby. In passing, the parents mention that the father has just been promoted and that they are building a new and finer house in a better neighborhood.

In reviewing the data, the clinician is aware of the losses and potential losses that the child is facing. While vegetative symptoms are absent, there are signs of affective and productive disturbance which appear to be associated with the losses the child has incurred. The withdrawal, apathy, and feelings of rejection are indicative of depression, particularly in view of the fact that the child does not talk about the losses and is secretive with respect to negative self-attributions.

Consider now Bradley, the girl with whom we began this section. One might wonder whether Bradley was obsessive-compulsive, extremely distrustful to the point of paranoia, striving, and overachieving – in short, whether her behavior indicated an extreme amount of psychopathology and, if so, what kind.

The clinician who saw Bradley recognized that the family did have very high standards and that Bradley was extreme in her desire to seek parental approval and to meet her own high standards. In that regard she was an internalizer. However, no evidence was found that indicated a driven and unpleasant type of ideation nor was there any evidence of compulsive behavior. After becoming at ease in the clinical situation, Bradley confided that she was upset because the showers at school were dirty, some older girls were stealing the belongings of younger girls while they showered, and the teacher usually left to smoke while the younger girls showered. Bradley felt her parents would be very upset if she told them what was going on and they would want to take her out of the public school and place her in a private school. Because she was concerned about the money (which Bradley did not believe her parents could afford), she decided to keep her discomfort to herself. Projective techniques, self-report measures, problem checklists, and other material indicated that Bradley was overly concerned about approval but did not reveal any evidence that more serious psychopathology existed.

Bradley would benefit from intervention which can relax the rigid manner in which she drives herself and which can aid in her feeling of acceptance by herself and others. Her personal habits of cleanliness and avoidance of physical contact are not necessarily psychopathological, although they might be considered so if they interfere with her social relationships to any marked extent. No evidence from any sources indicated that Bradley had difficulty with her social relationships. Rather, it appeared that this somewhat perfectionistic child had reacted to a situation which was stressful beyond the normal limits of what should be expected in a school situation. Bradley's overconcern for her parents, and perhaps some residual anger at feeling that she had to please them so much, were maladaptive, but should only be considered neurotic if they persist and interfere with her ability to function appropriately. Had no situational stress of excessive proportions existed and if Bradley had shown signs of disturbed peer relationships, obsessive thinking or compulsive behavior, or such affective isolation that she did not relate well, there would have been reason for greater concern.

Table 3.3 summarizes some of the expected patterns of results from various sources of data for the phobic, depressed, obsessive-compulsive disorders and for the hysteric. The specific details of these data sources should be examined to ascertain whether they are consistent both within each instrument and across the various sources of data. In the absence of strong disconfirming data, a consistent pattern is support for diagnosis of a given disorder. With children, it is of course necessary to take into account the developmental status of the child for intellectual, affective, and personality variables. Ego development (Loevinger, 1976) for a child of 12 should be considered with regard to that developmental period and would be expected to be different from that of a child of three. The impulsiveness of the three-year-old, on the other hand, would be inappropriate for the 12-year-old. Given these differences in level of development, the patterns summarized in Table 3.3 are suggested as general guidelines for use in considering different sources of data helpful in the determination and severity of child neurotic personality problems.

## CONDUCT PROBLEMS

Bobbie, a 14-year-old well-developed ninth grader, has a reputation as sexually promiscuous. For a long time Bobbie has used marijuana moderately, although her parents have been unaware of either her drug use or her sexual behavior. A conference with school officials brought both of these matters to their attention when Bobbie was discovered with a boy in a parked car on the school grounds. Bobbie's response to the confrontation was that she had done what most other kids do and that she was old enough to know what she was doing. Bobbie has some sexual knowledge but her parents are worried about possible pregnancy, about the effects of her behavior on her reputation, and about controlling Bobbie's behavior.

### Definition

DSM-III makes the distinction between nonsocialized and socialized when examining conduct disorders. Not all writers use conduct disorder as a nosological term, although many of them make the distinction be-

TABLE 3.3

Neurotic Disorders of Childhood

| Type of Data | Phobia | Depression | Obsessive-Compulsive | Hysteria |
|---|---|---|---|---|
| Observation | Unimpaired except for phobia | Many possible impairments* | May be stereotyped ruminative, brooding | Ranges from unimpaired to indifferent to anxious |
| Self-report | Specific fear | May be indicative or masked | Content and style are both informative | Conversion has at least one physical symptom—otherwise may be immature, vague |
| Parent Report | Confirms | May not match self-report | Usually notes rigidity | May not match self-report |
| Intellectual | Unimpaired | May show some slowing and concentration problems | Indecisiveness | Unimpaired |
| Achievement | Unimpaired | | May be impaired | Unimpaired |
| Projectives | No major conflicts | Guilt, sadness, worthlessness, thoughts of death, anger, somatic focus | Ruminative thoughts, isolation, undoing, self-conscious-ness, perfectionistic | Body focus, evidence of psychological avoidance and/or anxiety |

*Sleep disturbance, eating disturbance, psychomotor agitation or retardation, apathy, dysphoric mood, which may not be the dominant feature. Sad face in children rather than verbal self-report of mood disturbance. Fatigue, possible indecision.

61

tween antisocial behavior and other forms of conduct disorder which rest on negative self-attributions and behavior characterized by anxiety or withdrawal. Others focus upon legal descriptions centering around delinquency. The age of the child, adolescent or younger, is also a variable of importance in some classifications. The thread which runs through these diverse attempts to classify conduct disorders is the focus on the violation of the rights of others. Quay (1979) observes that there is agreement on the diagnosis, with stable findings among a broad range of studies of children from different types of settings, different ages, and assessed by different techniques. Some of the variables used to describe these children are susceptibility to boredom, stimulus-seeking behavior, and poor attention. These children get into trouble and are less likely to improve than children with anxiety-withdrawal problems, immaturity, or socialized aggressive disorders. Quay believes that physiologically-based factors set in motion (through stimulus-seeking and resistance to punishment) a parent-child process which may contribute to parental frustration and ineffective control, leading to acceleration of the child's antisocial behavior.

*Incidence*

Boys are noted more often than girls to be characterized by behavior which is considered as evidence for conduct disorders (Graham, 1979), with younger children manifesting different behaviors than adolescents. The younger children are more often aggressive to peers, disobedient, and likely to steal from the home, while older children tend to engage in truancy and are more subject to property crimes.

Estimates of the incidence of conduct disorder vary with the items used to define the disorder and the locale of the studies, but appear to be in the range of 4%–8% (Knopf, 1979; Quay & Werry, 1979). Many children who have never been labeled conduct disorders admit to behavior which would qualify for the diagnosis if it had been brought to the attention of adult authorities. Conduct disorders are overly represented in the lower socioeconomic levels and also among children who have reading problems. Lax maternal and overly restrictive and rigid paternal disciplinary patterns are frequent among families of delinquents. Parental rejection, especially by fathers of their sons, and father absence due to family breakup are also frequent among conduct disorders. Children with conduct problems are likely to persist in being delinquent later in life relative to children who suffer other types of childhood problems.

Moreover, these children are likely to have poorer adult adjustment than children with other types of childhood disorders.

## Etiology

Many writers have been concerned with the nature of the parent-child relationship and some association of that relationship with forms of psychopathology. Jenkins (1973) has formulated three types of delinquency which he found to be associated with different family patterns. The gang delinquent, or socialized conduct disorder, is in many ways the most normal of the three types. These socialized delinquents are loyal to the gang, and their antisocial behavior may arise as a result of poor supervision and diffuse family relationships. The unsocialized conduct disorder is more likely to be hostile and impulsive and to have a background of parental rejection or abuse. The third type of delinquent is more conflicted and inhibited and the antisocial behavior is a function of the conflictual material. Rigid, cold family backgrounds were found to characterize the histories of these neurotic conduct disorders.

## Assessment of Conduct Problems

Assessment of conduct disorders involves a careful history which focuses on family and peer relationships, school history, and history related to antisocial acts. Because so many children and adolescents have school problems, particularly with reading, it is helpful to assess this area directly. Intellectual assessment and personality assessment are appropriate. Since family perceptions may vary, it is especially helpful to obtain both parents' perceptions, as well as those of the child. Sometimes the fact that hyperactive children exhibit conduct problems complicates the assessment. In those cases, one is in the position of trying to decide whether the behavioral problems are secondary to the physiologically-based components which first get the child into trouble, with the secondary social and emotional consequences accruing as a function of the labeling and self-attribution processes. In the following discussion we will assume that hyperactivity as a primary impetus to conduct disorder is not an issue and we will concentrate on the socialized, undersocialized, and neurotic varieties of conduct disorder.

It seems likely that the temperamental endowment of the child, the parental styles of discipline, the socioeconomic circumstances, and the child's ability to achieve in school (especially with regard to reading) are

all contributing factors to whether a child will or will not develop a conduct disorder and if so, what type of conduct disorder will be produced.
For example, it may be that difficult children who are initially very
similar in their behavior will turn out differently based upon the parental patterns of discipline and how available the parents are. Similarly,
it may be that a difficult child who is able to achieve well in reading will
enjoy enough success in school to compensate for some socioeconomic
deficiencies in family circumstances. A history which includes negative
indicators on several of these factors will be more likely to result in occurrence of a conduct disorder.

History will usually provide the cues for the socialized versus unsocialized status of the child. Before the age of adolescence, such information is helpful in aiding parents to facilitate the child into more normal
group situations which may provide opportunities for the development
of social relationships. Likewise, an unsatisfactory social development
may reflect either undersocialization or more neurotic problems due to
poor self-esteem. Planning and recommendations for these problems in
younger children are different and a good history helps to differentiate
the two patterns. It would be expected that the undersocialized child
will show less direct evidence of poor self-esteem and less frustration
in the absence of satisfactory social relationships. By contrast, the socialized child conduct disorder has friends and social support (usually
from a gang to which he is loyal). Gangs may compensate for diffuse
family relationships or even be congruent with family values which con-
done delinquent behavior. Whereas the neurotic delinquent acts most
often by himself, and the undersocialized delinquent acts impulsively,
the socialized delinquent commits antisocial behavior as part of the
group. The antisocial behavior has the advantage of permitting the
socialized adolescent delinquent to prove his mettle, substituting for
socially approved behaviors through which nondeviant adolescents
demonstrate mastery and independence.

Intelligence level varies for all these children, with the leader or undetected delinquent often being of high intelligence. Low intelligence
and high impulsivity both contribute to the risk of being caught. Self-
reports vary in the openness with which the adolescent will disclose to
the examiner. While school achievement may be impaired for the undersocialized and for the socialized delinquent, the neurotic delinquent may
not be doing poorly in school. The undersocialized delinquent is apt to
be impulsive, careless, and unmotivated when taking achievement tests.
Poor performance for the socialized delinquent is more likely to be due

to poor school attendance (hence, missing skills and information) rather than to distractibility or impulsivity. (See Table 3.4 for a summary of the assessment data for these groups.) It should be emphasized that these are general statements about groups. No one adolescent should be expected to conform to all the characteristics of any group as summarized.

For younger children who have conduct disorders, the socialization patterns mentioned may already be obvious. If school attendance and performance are not already disrupted and if there is no serious reading problem, prognosis is better. With either hyperactivity or reading difficulty, either of which interferes with successful and rewarding school participation, the younger child is at higher risk for continuation of conduct problems during adolescence.

The model proposed by Zubin and Spring (1977) for schizophrenia may also serve as a model for psychopathology in conduct disorders. This model, the vulnerability model, rests upon a genetic basis and attempts to deal with the influence of physiologically and psychologically traumatic experiences which might affect the development of psychopathology. In the case of conduct disorders, some evidence indicates that impulsivity and stimulus-seeking behavior may have a physiological basis, at least for the undersocialized adolescents (Quay & Werry, 1979). These stimulus seekers would have higher vulnerability according to the model. In the face of poor supervision, few intimate relationships, and low frustration tolerance, a conduct disorder would be likely to occur. The neurotic child would have less propensity for the development of the conduct disorder, and would probably require some additional interpersonal stressors or traumatic events to become antisocial. The socialized adolescent who lives in lower socioeconomic circumstances, has less supervision, and is part of a group or gang, may have sufficient social influence for the development of the antisocial behavior without high vulnerability based on physiological factors. In this sense the socialized adolescent has behaved adaptively considering his social environment. He is psychologically better off than either the undersocialized adolescent or the child who acts antisocially for neurotic reasons. Until he gets into trouble with authorities, he suffers little conflict and little interpersonal disturbance. In short, the addition of each factor increasing vulnerability (hyperactivity, stimulus-seeking, mesomorphic body build, poor reading) requires less social influence (poor supervision, opportunity for antisocial behavior, conflict or rejection by parents) to result in overtly antisocial conduct.

## TABLE 3.4
## Conduct Disorders of Childhood and Adolescence

| Type of Data | Socialized | Undersocialized | Neurotic |
|---|---|---|---|
| Observation | Relates easily, may be defiant | May be defiant or hostile, or distant | More reticent, troubled, distant |
| Self-report | Loyal to group, stimulus-seeking | Easily bored, impulsive, stimulus-seeking | May admit anxiety or conflict or may not disclose |
| Parent Report | No personality problems, trouble with authority, perhaps defiant | Impulsive, selfish, unrepentant; parent may reject or abuse | Not impulsive, may be overcontrolled, not usually a gang member |
| Intellectual | Level varies; leader often bright | Level varies | Level varies |
| Achievement | Deficit, if present, due to poor attendance | Deficits based on low motivation, impulsivity | Unimpaired or due to disturbed social relations, emotions which interfere with concentration and performance |
| Projectives | Unimpaired except for conflicts with authority and poor choice of models | Impulsive, self-centered, rebellious, manipulative | Conflicted, poor self-esteem, absence of impulsivity |

## PSYCHOSES

Sue, at age 16, has been a loner all her life. Born to older parents, she is an only child who until six months ago did well in school and seemed undisturbed. Sue was part of the social group but was never very close with any one person. She read a lot, liked music, and daydreamed. Her dating was entirely in groups or double dates until a boy began to call her frequently. With adults, Sue maintained a pleasant, correct manner, but was not self-disclosing. After a date one night, Sue returned home and her parents were awakened by her screams. They found her standing in the middle of the living room. She appeared confused and frightened, begging them to lock the door so that nothing would happen to them. Concerned that their daughter might have experienced some traumatic event, they tried to calm her to no avail. Sue's agitation continued until the next day when they took her to the emergency room at the local hospital. There Sue confided that she was afraid that someone wanted to kill her but refused to name the person because she was not sure that he didn't have friends who worked in the emergency room.

## Definition

Werry (1979), in his review of the history of efforts to diagnose the childhood psychoses, points out that several efforts have used developmental criteria, such as the age at onset. Controversy about other defining criteria of childhood psychoses represents attempts to include signs representing different theoretical points of view concerning the nature of autism, childhood schizophrenia, and the degenerative or symbiotic psychoses. As yet there is little agreement about definitions and criteria, and too little empirical research using operational definitions of symptoms.

Both Werry (1979) and Schwartz and Johnson (1981) have described the confusing problems of diagnosis which stem from the overlap of symptoms among the childhood psychoses and other conditions such as mental retardation. Prognosis varies for the childhood psychoses. Both biogenic and psychogenic theories have been proposed, although neither camp has provided convincing evidence. Prognosis for autistic children continues to be poor. The better prognosis for those autistic children with higher cognitive functioning may simply reflect less severe psychopathology than exists for those children with greater impairment of cognitive functioning. Neither psychotherapy, educational programs, nor pharmacological treatments have been encouraging in terms of recovery. These approaches have been somewhat more optimistic in terms of refining theories about the etiology of childhood psychoses.

*Incidence*

Incidence data on childhood psychoses are bimodal. A group of psychoses occurs prior to puberty and reflects developmental characteristics which are different from those which occur after puberty (Werry, 1979). Incidence figures for childhood psychoses are of questionable reliability due to definitional problems. Also, because of lack of diagnostic sophistication, it is probable that some psychoses go undiagnosed. It is known that more boys than girls are reported to suffer from childhood psychoses. The incidence rate in schoolchildren is about one per 1,000. Rates are higher for children who are referred for psychiatric services. These rates vary to some extent with concentrations of mental health professionals available to conduct evaluations.

Psychosis which occurs after puberty and before adulthood consists mainly of schizophrenic psychoses. Weiner (1970) estimates that between 5% and 7% of adolescents seen in psychiatric clinics are diagnosed schizophrenic, with girls slightly outnumbering boys. Among inpatient adolescents, slightly more than one quarter are diagnosed as psychotics, although the percentage of schizophrenias is not noted specifically. Some of the usual considerations of diagnosis prevail in the case of adolescent psychoses, e.g., differences in base rates among settings, reluctance to diagnose a major psychosis if a less severe diagnosis can be made. However, among adolescents the major psychosis diagnosed is schizophrenia, which is usually characterized by disorders of thought and affect, disorganization and deterioration of function, hallucinations and delusions. For adolescents the impairment of reality function may include looseness of association, confusion in thought, arbitrary reasoning, ideas of reference, inappropriate social relations, and poor judgment. Sometimes depression and conduct problems are con currently reported.

*Etiology*

It is known that childhood schizophrenia, as a rule, has a later onset than autism. For the child schizophrenic there is a period prior to onset in which children are seen as more normal than autistic children. Once the symptoms begin to occur, the schizophrenic children develop ritualistic and bizarre behavior. Prognosis is better than for autistic children, although estimates are that less than one third of these children develop satisfactorily. Stress has been suggested as a precipitating event (Brown, Birley, & Wing, 1972). These observations are compatible with the vulnerability hypothesis proposed by Zubin and Spring (1977) for adult schizophrenia.

Symbiotic psychosis and other degenerative psychoses are rare and probably stem from multiple causes. Practically all that is known is that children develop apparently normally for about three to five years and then decline in all their functions. In some cases neurological evidence has been found. Both psychogenic and neurological explanations have been advanced.

Children who have been schizophrenic from early childhood present a much more deteriorated condition than those whose onset is during adolescence. For the adolescent onset group, Weiner (1970) notes three guidelines for the clinician, namely, the persistence of symptomatology, the extent of normative adolescent concerns, and the prominence of formal manifestations of disturbance. These guidelines reflect similar views to those embodied in the process-reactive division proposed by Bellak (1948) in which reactive schizophrenics are characterized by more normal prepsychotic adjustment. In such cases, the psychotic episode usually begins in response to a severe stress or identified precipitating factor. The process schizophrenic, on the other hand, is more likely to have a poorer premorbid adjustment and a poorer prognosis for recovery.

The diagnostic criteria cited in DSM-III do not deal directly with the process-reactive distinction, although the criteria under sections on duration and prodromal or residual symptoms subsume some of the same concerns.

The status of motivational variables with regard to etiology is unclear. Research attempting to compare cognitive performance of psychotic and normal children is complicated by two possible motivational effects on performance: the ability to relate to people, thus affecting rapport during evaluation, which in turn may affect level and rate of performance; and second, arousal and physiological functions which may affect the ability to process information from various modalities. Just how these possible effects complicate the assessment procedure is unknown.

## Assessment of Childhood Psychosis

Assessment of childhood psychosis which occurs before puberty usually centers on the issue of whether the child is autistic or schizophrenic. The degenerative psychotic children are usually so anxious and withdrawn that formal assessment is not possible (see Table 3.5).

TABLE 3.5
Childhood Psychoses

| Type of Data | Autism | Childhood Schizophrenia | Degenerative (includes symbiotic) |
|---|---|---|---|
| Onset | At birth or before age three | Between two and 11 | Three to five |
| Behavior | Doesn't cuddle, make eye contact or attend; focus on inanimate objects | Blank look, can't get close, day-dreams; bizarre motor behavior | Can't separate from mother, with-drawn, anxious, low frustration tolerance |
| Language | Disturbed; echolalia; reverses pro-nouns; repeats commercials | Disturbed; echolalia | Deteriorates |
| Intelligence | Impaired, IQ predicts outcome | Impaired, often below 80 | Deteriorates |
| EEG | Less often impaired | Often impaired | Often untestable; severe impair-ment common |
| Special | Change in physical environment is disturbing; doesn't relate personally | Some pockets of competence (Idiot savants); may show lack of concern about body secretions; abnormal perceptual problems | Reality contact weakens, self-care deteriorates, may resemble autism when withdrawal and loss of reality contact occur |

Clinically, most autistic children show greater motor and spatial abilities than schizophrenic children. Often they are extremely fastidious, although in a bizarre and ritualistic manner. They appear to be sensitive to the inanimate environment, whereas schizophrenic children do not seem so concerned with it. Both autistic and schizophrenic children are difficult to test because of problems with attention and ability to relate or comprehend instructions. Therefore the history may be more informative than formal assessment through testing. When the children are testable, the level of cognitive functioning may be helpful in estimating outcome or in trying to structure care so that the child can understand better. Often the clinician is left with the question of whether interpersonal contact has been made and, if so, whether it is comforting or frightening to the child. Because so many autistic children are physically attractive, yet emotionally unreachable, they are intriguing and frustrating to the novice clinician, who may feel that there must be hope for children who are attractive, motorically clever, and able to mimic complex language which they do not produce spontaneously. By contrast, the child who is experiencing a degenerative psychosis may appear dull and hopeless. Yet the sad fact remains that neither of these groups of children have as much chance of recovery or improvement as the childhood schizophrenic, who also faces a guarded prognosis.

For adolescents, the diagnosis of schizophrenic psychosis is established through more formal assessment, as well as the history and the interpersonal contact derived in interview. The history should take note of the pattern of relationships and the level of social and academic competence attained by the teenager. Reactive schizophrenic adolescents may date a point at which things became different for them, or their parents may be able to identify a time at which they noticed the onset of symptoms. This endorsement of a definite time of onset is more likely to occur for the reactive schizophrenic than for the process schizophrenic. When such a point occurs with the process schizophrenic, it is more often tied to some irrelevant event which the parents use as a marker to locate things in time rather than because it relates to the teenager's problems. Higher premorbid social and academic performance are hopeful signs.

Observational material of primary importance can be described from the interpersonal contact attained during the assessment sessions. The adolescent's manner of relating is of primary importance. If the clinician feels there is good eye contact, interest in the assessment process, and relative openness to the process, there is less evidence for schizophrenia. By contrast, the schizophrenic adolescent is most often uninvolved, withdrawn, emotionally aloof or angry, with poor eye contact. By contrast with the conduct-disordered child, the schizophrenic's uninvolvement is usually less defiant and more withdrawn. The verbal content may be appropriate while the formal aspects of verbal processes are disturbed, namely, blocking, peculiar speech patterns and intonations, and inappropriate use of words. Either inappropriate or flattened affective responses are also frequent.

Formal assessment techniques often involve both cognitive and affective components. Most clinicians want to have an individually administered intelligence scale, projective techniques such as the Rorschach, a cognitive test which deals with concept formation, and usually personality inventory data such as the MMPI. The cognitive features which are usually present are concrete orientation, looseness of associations, and arbitrary reasoning. On the sorting and concept-formation tests, these patterns may be obvious, although schizophrenic adolescents may attempt to limit the scope of material to be organized in an attempt to organize the material at a higher level of abstraction. When these attempts fail, the level of concept attainment loses abstraction, falling to a functional or even a concrete level. The nature of the looseness which occurs is informative, i.e., whether a concept is overly general, overly symbolic, or personalized. Similar patterns can be observed on some of the Wechsler subtests (such as Comprehension and Similarities), although the range of content involved in each item offers less opportunity for indication of thought disorders.

Rorschach performances may indicate cognitive difficulties through the excessive use of abnormal locations, the use of confabulations, and other responses. The interested reader can find excellent discussions of these topics in Exner (1974), Klopfer, Ainsworth, Klopfer, and Holt (1954), and Weiner (1966). Reality contact is often reflected through the adequacy of the form level employed, a low F+% indicating that the patient is inaccurate and often poorly differentiated and poorly integrated. Frequently, these poor form responses have a personalized quality. Likewise, a failure to perceive popular responses may indicate atypical perception. The assumption is that failure to share recognition of consensually endorsed precepts may be associated with unusual thinking. Variables relating to perceptions of humans are less reliable because they occur with lower frequency in all records, but are especially likely to be of low frequency in the records of process or chronic schizophrenics. Likewise, Rorschach variables which involve color are sometimes suggestive but are less reliable indicators due to their low frequency.

Elevations in the use of pure color, however, may betoken some difficulty in integrating affective experience with cognitive aspects of perception

Scores on the MMPI which include elevations on the schizophrenia and F scales should be considered as consistent with the diagnosis of schizophrenia. However, because many of the items between the two scales overlap, it may be that the schizophrenia scale will be elevated as a function of a high F. Interpretation will depend upon the relative elevations and patterns in regard to other MMPI scales. It should be noted that adolescent profiles should only be interpreted with reference to adolescent norms. Discussion of the adolescent profiles may be found in Marks, Seeman, and Haller (1974). Of particular importance is the fact that profiles which do not employ adolescent norms for interpretation may be misclassified. Since higher raw scores are required for adolescents on the schizophrenia scale to obtain the same scale scores as would be the case for adults, misuse of norms will result in a high false positive rate of diagnosis of adolescents as schizophrenic. Because of the consequences of such misuse of test material, the importance of the use of proper norms must be underscored.

Most clinicians also elicit figure drawings during the course of assessment. The instructions generally request the patient to draw a complete person, not a stick figure. The patient is then requested to draw a person of the opposite sex. Sometimes kinetic family drawings are also requested. Inevitably, artistic ability will enter into the quality of the drawings, but artistic ability can be minimized as a variable through the use of instructions. Regardless of the artistic ability of the patient, some indications of reality contact and body distortion may appear. The most obvious of these signs which are more characteristic of schizophrenics than of other groups include the omission of body parts and confusion about the sexual differentiation (maybe a very impoverished drawing with little detail or ambiguous details). Body image may be distorted in terms of dimensions, posture, and other features. Likewise, overemphasis on sexual organs, particularly in the presence of other signs, is frequent among drawings of schizophrenics. Open or broken lines, and incomplete open figures are also more frequent. It should be remembered that drawings are not conclusive evidence for schizophrenic functioning, nor is the absence of such signs necessarily informative.

No single source of data should be considered sufficient to diagnose adolescent schizophrenic functioning. Rather, it is the consistency across several data sources — observational, historical, and test material — which provides the most reliable estimate of functioning.

## CHRONICALLY ILL AND HANDICAPPED CHILDREN

Billy is a handsome, slightly built 14-year-old boy having the physical appearance and behavior mannerisms of a boy several years younger. He was brought to the evaluation by his mother who related that Billy is failing in school, has few friends because he is a demanding bully, and is considered to be a discipline problem at home and at school. Billy fights constantly with his mother and sisters, a situation which has gradually become worse since his parents' divorce three years ago. Billy's medical history reveals that he was born with several serious congenital heart defects, e.g., ventricular septal defect, pulmonary stenosis, and a rudimentary, pulmonary valve. Prior to corrective cardiac surgery at age eight, Billy had recurring bouts of pneumonia with accompanying fevers of over 106°. Frequent hospitalizations and medical evaluations occurred during early childhood. His parents' reactions to their son's handicaps were different. As his physicians advised them that Billy should not be allowed to cry or become very upset, few attempts at discipline were made. Mrs. W. became almost totally concerned with her son's health, which caused her to neglect other members of the family. Mr. W. was more rejecting of his son, spending little time with him and complaining of his misbehavior. Within two weeks of Billy's return from open heart surgery, his father began divorce proceedings.

### Definition

The interaction between physical illness and psychological symptomatology is an area which is receiving increased attention from mental health professionals. As advances in neonatal care and other medical progresses are made, increasing numbers of children survive congenital defects, physical trauma, life-threatening diseases, and physical handicaps. It is becoming apparent that chronic and acute disease processes in a child may have long-term deleterious effects on both parents and children. The consequences of a congenital impairment or the effects of chronic illness that takes place in early childhood or adolescence are often highly traumatic. We are dealing with variables which may profoundly affect the developmental process. More specifically, children who are expected by their parents to die prematurely often react with serious disturbances in psychosocial development. That long-term physical illness in children puts them at high risk for future adjustment difficulties is well documented in a variety of studies of diverse illnesses and handicapping conditions. In addition it has been suggested that the social and psychological difficulties facing children with chronic physical disorders can be more debilitating than the direct effects of the disease or handicap per se (Mattson, 1972).

*Incidence*

Overall prevalence rates of persistent and socially handicapping mental health problems in epidemiological surveys of general populations suggest that between 6% and 9% of the total population of children included in the survey exhibited emotional problems (Goldberg et al., 1979; Rutter et al., 1976). In contrast, Rutter reported 13.2% of children with "physical handicaps" had significant mental health problems. Goldberg similarly reported that 12% of the children with chronic disorders had emotional problems.

With specific medical disorders, even higher rates of emotional problems among chronically ill children have been reported. Minde (1978) reported an incidence rate of 18% in a group of children with cerebral palsy; 79% of children with neurological defects in conjunction with congenital rubella exhibited three or more severe behaviorally abnormal symptoms (Chess, 1974); 59% of 114 survivors of childhood cancer indicated at least mild psychiatric symptomatology, with 12% rated as markedly or severely impaired (O'Malley et al., 1979).

*Etiology of Psychological Problems*
*Associated With Chronic Illness*

Several common psychological problems face children and adolescents who have serious illness, disabilities, or handicaps. These problems are accentuated in children and adolescents because the process of self-definition is in its formative stages and socialization undergoes many changes during these periods of development.

The child or adolescent may view his illness or handicap as a loss, either of part of his body or his ability or of some capacity that other people have. Losses of these kinds are commonly seen as grave misfortunes which evoke feelings of pity or sorrow on the part of others. The seriously ill or handicapped child is seen as being different from other children, as indeed he is, and as he perceives himself to be. Both of these factors have implications for the future development of the child's self-image and self-esteem.

With adolescents having serious health difficulties, a potentially serious problem can occur if the adolescent's body becomes a "battleground" between parents and child. The battle over who can, will, or should be responsible for the health and well-being of the adolescent is usually exacerbated during this period when the last serious battles of independence are being fought.

Additionally, the parents' response to a child's chronic illness becomes an important variable in the child's illness and self-perception. Repeated discussions of assumed parental guilt in response to discovery that their child is damaged are found throughout the psychiatric and psychological literature. Kanner (1963) emphasized that all parents experience some feelings of guilt about the handicaps in their children.

Anna Freud (1952) pointed out that there are few parents who do not change their attitudes toward an ill child. The majority of parents become preoccupied with an ill child, often to the exclusion of other family members. During periods of illness the child may find himself more loved than at any other time as the parents attempt to assuage their guilt feelings for having a child with a handicap or disability. The negative effects of this concerted parental attention upon the handicapped child are often seen among the siblings of the ill child. Minde (1978) reported that of 19 families of children with cerebral palsy, 14 families with other children claimed that the nonhandicapped children had experienced psychological problems as a result of being deprived of parental attention, especially in their early years.

Authorities in the field tend to agree that overprotection is the most frequently displayed parental attitude toward children who are seriously ill or impaired. Anna Freud (1952) indicated that anxiety for the child's health may cause the parent to suspend the usual considerations of discipline and expectations of appropriate behavior. These feelings often cause the parent to indulge the child's every wish to the detriment of his future emotional development. The overly protective parent may become excessively fearful of the recurrence of illness and tend to infantilize the child, thus interfering with the development of autonomous behavior.

Levy (1943) studied the effects of maternal attitudes on the child's development, conceptualizing maternal overprotection as often being dynamically related to unconscious rejection of the child. He considered that maternal overprotection might be manifested by four different groups of behaviors: 1) excessive contact (or "mother is always there"); 2) infantilization (or "she treats him like a baby ¡; 3) prevention of independent behavior (or "she won't let him grow up"); and 4) lack of maternal control (or "that child is a whining spoiled brat"). When all four types of behaviors are present, the effect is that of the "classic" overprotective mother who holds the child closely with one hand and pushes the world away with the other hand. The mother is often extraordinarily submissive to her child. The child's most outrageous demands for attention are met without question. As the child becomes more assertive, her attempts at discipline may become fewer, resulting in displays of childish temper tantrums if the child's wishes are not fulfilled.

Overprotective mothers may be either dominating or indulgent or a combination of both. The dominating, overprotective mother demands submission from her child and the child appears to yield readily. She dominates most areas of the child's life and he is passive, submissive, and often withdrawn. Mothers of dominating, disobedient children, on the other hand, are seen as excessively indulgent. These indulged children are characterized by disobedience, impudence, temper tantrums, crying spells, excessive demands, and usually exhibit varying degrees of tyrannical behaviors. Difficulties in establishing peer relationships are common for both groups of children. The dominating children tend to be bossy, selfish, and show-offs. The submissive children are more timid and withdrawn.

The expression of parental guilt for having produced a defective child may also take the reverse form from overprotection. These parents react with overt or covert rejection of the child in an effort to dissociate themselves from this living reminder of their own guilt feelings or imperfection. The child is reacted to with indifference, thinly disguised hostility, or outright rejection.

Both the overprotective parent and the rejecting parent may prevent the child from growing up normally. This is most clearly seen in terms of future goal-setting behaviors for the handicapped child. The setting of realistic goals for the child is complicated by a lack of knowledge concerning future limitations on ability or the possibility of recurring episodes of life-threatening illness. The parents are often faced with ambiguous information with regard to expectations and prognosis. The setting of goals and future possibilities for the child is influenced by the parental reaction to the child's handicaps. The overprotective parent frequently sets goals for the child that are too low; the rejecting or ambivalent parent, on the other hand, may be able to show the child affection only when he strives for unrealistically high goals.

The clinician is cautioned not to make the assumption that all parents of chronically ill or handicapped children feel guilty and become either overprotective or rejecting. Patterson (1975) cogently states that as one cannot generalize about handicapped children and their emotions, neither can one generalize about the emotion of the parents of handicapped children. What appears to be guilt feelings to professionals may merely be concern for the child's welfare, mingled with honest grief over his illness and suffering. Focusing on parental guilt feelings related to overprotection or rejection or upon parental depression following the birth of a handicapped child may be less worthwhile than consideration of other important interpersonal features of the parent-child relationship. Interpersonal factors may make a disability become a greater or lesser handicap depending on the way the child is treated.

Within the general areas of severe pediatric illness and its subsequent effects, Green and Solnit (1969) identified the "vulnerable child syndrome" in which children who are expected by their parents to die prematurely react with a disturbance in psychosocial development. Green and Solnit investigated the hypothesis that parental reactions to an acute, life-threatening illness in a child may have long-term psychologically deleterious effects on both parents and children. These chronically ill children were considered by their parents as being vulnerable to serious illness or accidents and destined to die during childhood. The authors considered some major patterns of symptomatology in the parent-child relationship: 1) difficulty with separation; 2) infantilization, in which the parents are unable to set disciplinary limits, are overprotective, overindulgent, and oversolicitous, while the child is overly dependent, disobedient, irritable, and uncooperative; 3) bodily overconcerns, in which the expectation of a premature death is one cause of academic difficulties. School failure is often the major manifestation of the vulnerable child syndrome. The reactions of the parents to an ill or handicapped child are seen as lingering aftereffects of a persistent, disguised mourning reaction that was evoked by the earlier life-threatening illness.

Parental reactions are viewed as caused by resentment, guilt, and fear which have continued as residuals from the time the parents had to cope with the expectation that the child might die. The child senses the parents' expectation of his vulnerability and accepts his parents' distorted mental image of himself. The vulnerable child syndrome should alert the clinician to the necessity for appropriate psychological intervention following serious illness, in order to prevent the development of future emotional problems for both parents and child.

The major defense mechanism or coping strategy employed by these chronically afflicted children is denial of the illness. By denial of the illness, we mean that the child himself does not recognize the limits imposed by his condition. Denial is manifested in many ways, including refusal to take medications, eating forbidden foods, and engaging in restricted physical activities. As mentioned before, these areas often become the battleground between the child and his parents or physicians. Denial can become pathological in extreme incidences resulting in the child's putting himself at risk for an exacerbation of symptoms or even a life-threatening circumstance. Parental attitudes are critical for the development of the adaptive coping techniques which the child needs.

*Special Problems in Assessment*
*of Handicapped Children*

Even a slight acquaintance with handicapped or ill children indicates that alterations of standardized testing techniques are required with resulting problems in the interpretation of the data. For example, Briggs (1960) has cautioned that a perceptual motor task (WAIS Digit Symbol) cannot be given routinely to a person who has suffered a disability to his dominant hand, even though the patient assures the examiner that he can easily substitute his nondominant hand. Often the clinician is asked to evaluate children while they are in a hospitalized setting. To compare the performance of a child on standardized tests when he is anxious, hospitalized, in pain, separated from his family, and forced to cope with numerous bodily insults with the performance of a child brought to an outpatient setting by his parents is fraught with danger of misinterpretation of the data. The timing of the evaluation in relationship to medical procedures is also crucial. For example, if the child is tested shortly after admission or trauma, the prevailing shock may obscure performance. The mourning periods which result from the experience of yet another life-threatening episode may also depress performance.

While the emotional state of the child during the evaluation is always a major factor to be considered, nowhere does it become more important than when assessing a physically ill child. This is clearly illustrated in the interpretation of depression in chronically sick children: Is the depression found in the interpretation of projective tests a core personality feature or is it a reactive response to the immediate effects of the recurrence of the disease and the subsequent hospitalization? Another factor which must be considered in these cases is that of fatigue, which fluctuates in intensity and must be considered in scheduling the assessment.

Finally, because each handicap or chronic illness has special features, the clinician should read and consult with appropriate caretakers to learn about the problem that each child must face. Sometimes medication effects will change vision, reaction time, concentration, and other cognitive behavior. The better informed clinician will be able to evaluate data and make better recommendations.

### SPECIAL BEHAVIOR PROBLEMS

Aside from the groups of intellectual, academic, social and emotional problems which we have reviewed, there are other behavior problems which are highly specialized. Some of these problems are widespread and become viewed as disorders when they persist beyond the developmentally expected period of life. In this category would be enuresis and encopresis. Other disturbances are more rare and more threatening in terms of both physical and emotional consequences. These would include eating disorders of anorexia nervosa and bulimia. Other eating disorders, such as pica, may be less threatening but still cause parental concern. Various movement disorders, including tics, stuttering, and sleepwalking and sleep terror also come to the attention of psychologists.

Given that physical causes for some of the special behavior problems can be ruled out, some of them are readily approached by behavioral techniques, e.g., enuresis. Others among the specialized problems are more resistant to behavioral management and may require considerable work with the patient, the family, and other caretakers. The assessment of many of these specialized disorders is based on life history material, observation, and absence of other signs of psychological disturbance which would indicate either intellectual or neuropsychological problems. Sometimes, as a result of frustration experienced by the child and family, other secondary emotional problems will also be observed. The diagnostician will always be interested in whether the behavior which resulted in the referral occurred prior to or as a consequence of other behavior problems. Poor self-esteem and disturbed parent-child relations may complicate the picture. An important part of assessment may involve determining whether the presenting complaints are the appropriate focus of treatment or whether other problems are more pervasive and need attention before or instead of the original complaint.

## REFERENCES

Achenbach, T. M. & Edelbrock, C. S. The classification of child psychopathology: A review and analysis of empirical efforts. *Psychological Bulletin,* 1978, *85,* 1275–1301.

Bakwin, H. Reading disability in twins. *Developmental Medicine and Child Neurology,* 1973, *15,* 184–187.

Bannatyne, A. *Language, Reading, and Learning Disabilities.* Springfield, IL: Charles C Thomas, 1971.

Bannatyne, A. Diagnosis: A note on recategorization of the WISC scaled scores. *Journal of Learning Disabilities,* 1974, *7,* 272–274.

Bellak, L. *Dementia Praecox: The Past Decade's Work and Evaluation.* New York: Grune & Stratton, 1948.

Borland, B. L. & Heckman, H. K. Hyperactive boys and their brothers: A 25-year follow-up study. *Archives of General Psychiatry,* 1976, *33,* 669–675.

Briggs, P. F. The validity of WAIS performance subtests with one hand. *Journal of Clinical Psychology,* 1960, *16,* 318–320.

Brown, G. W., Birley, J. L. T., & Wing, J. K. Influences of family life on the course of schizophrenic disorders: A replication. *British Journal of Psychiatry,* 1972, *121,* 241–258.

Cantwell, D. P. *The Hyperactive Child.* New York: Spectrum, 1975.

Chess, S. Behavior and learning of school-age rubella children. Final report of project MC-R-860184-03-0. Washington, D.C.: U.S. Department of Health, Education, and Welfare, 1974.

*Diagnostic and Statistical Manual of Mental Disorders, Third Edition.* Washington, D.C.: American Psychiatric Association, 1980.

Exner, J. E., Jr. *The Rorschach: A Comprehensive System.* New York: Wiley-Interscience, 1974.

Fenichel, O. *The Psychoanalytic Theory of Neurosis.* New York: W. W. Norton, 1945.

Fine, M. J. *Principles and Techniques of Intervention with Hyperactive Children.* Springfield, IL: Charles C Thomas, 1976.

Fish, B. The one child, one drug myth of stimulants in hyperkinesis. *Archives of General Psychiatry,* 1971, *25,* 193–301.

Freud, A. *The Psychoanalytic Study of the Child.* New York: International Universities Press, 1952, pp. 69–81.

Gibson, E. J. & Levin, H. *The Psychology of Reading.* Cambridge, MA: The MIT Press, 1975.

Goldberg, I. D., Regier, D. A., McInerny, T. K., Pless, I. B., & Roghmann, K. J. The role of the pediatrician in the delivery of mental health services to children. *Pediatrics,* 1979, *63,* 898–909.

Graham, P. J. Epidemiological studies. In: H. S. Quay & J. S. Werry (Eds.), *Psychopathological Disorders of Childhood.* New York: John Wiley, 1979.

Green, M. & Solnit, A. J. Reactions to the threatened loss of a child: A vulnerable child syndrome. Pediatric management of the dying child, Part III. *Pediatrics,* 1964, *34,* 58–66.

Grossman, H. J. *Manual on Terminology and Classification in Mental Retardation.* Washington, D.C.: American Association of Mental Deficiency, 1973.

HEW Report. *Reading Disorders in the United States.* Arleigh B. Templeton, (chairman). Report of the secretary's (HEW) national advisory committee on dyslexia and related reading disorders. August, 1969.

Hunt, J. McV. *Intelligence and Experience.* New York: Ronald Press, 1961.

*International Classification of Diseases – Ninth Revision – Clinical Modifications.* Ann Arbor, MI: Commission on Professional and Hospital Activities, 1978.

Jenkins, R. L. *Behavior Disorders of Childhood and Adolescence.* Springfield, IL: Charles C Thomas, 1973.

Kanner, L. Parents' feelings about retarded children. *American Journal of Mental Deficiency,* 1963, *67,* 375–383.

Kaufman, A. S. *Intelligent Testing with the WISC-R.* New York: Wiley-Interscience, 1979.

Klopfer, B., Ainsworth, M. D., Klopfer, W. G., & Holt, R. R. *Developments in the Rorschach Technique.* New York: Harcourt, Brace & World, 1954.

Knopf, I. J. *Childhood Psychopathology.* Englewood Cliffs, N.J.: Prentice-Hall, 1979.

Lambert, N., Windmiller, M., Cole, L., & Figueroa, R. *AAMD Behavior Scale – Public School Version, 1974 Revision.* Washington, D.C.: AAMD, 1975.

Levy, D. M. *Maternal Overprotection.* New York: Columbia University Press, 1943.

Loevinger, J. *Ego Development.* San Francisco: Jossey-Bass, 1976.

Marks, P. A., Seeman, W., & Haller, D. L. *The Actuarial Use of the MMPI with Adolescents and Adults.* Baltimore: Williams & Wilkins, 1974.

Mattson, A. Long-term physical illness in childhood: A challenge to psychosocial adaptation. *Pediatrics,* 1972, *50,* 801–811.

McLemore, C. W. & Benjamin, L. S. Whatever happened to interpersonal diagnosis? A psychosocial alternative to DSM-III. *American Psychologist,* 1979, *34,* 17–34.

Menkes, J. H. *Textbook of Child Neurology.* Philadelphia: Lea & Febiger, 1974.

Minde, K. K. Coping styles of 34 adolescents with cerebral palsy. *American Journal of Psychiatry,* 1978, *135,* 1344–1349.

Myklebust, H. R. & Johnson, D. Dyslexia in children. *Exceptional Children,* 1962, *29,* 14–25.

O'Malley, J. E., Koocher, G., Foster, D., & Slavin, L. Psychiatric sequelae of surviving childhood cancer. *American Journal of Orthopsychiatry,* 1979, *49,* 608–616.

Patterson, L. Some pointers for professionals. *Children,* 1975, *3,* 13–17.

Quay, H. C. Classification. In: H. C. Quay & J. S. Werry (Eds.), *Psychopathological Disorders of Childhood.* New York: John Wiley, 1979.

Quay, H. C. & Werry, J. S. *Psychopathological Disorders of Childhood.* New York: John Wiley, 1979.

Rapoport, J. L. & Benoit, M. The relationship of direct home observations to the clinic evaluation of hyperactive school-age boys. *Journal of Child Psychology and Psychiatry,* 1975, *16,* 141–147.

Robinson, H. B. & Robinson, N. M. Mental retardation. In: P. H. Mussen (Ed.), *Carmichael's Manual of Child Psychology* (Vol. 2, 3rd edition). New York: John Wiley, 1970.

Ross, D. M. & Ross, S. A. *Hyperactivity: Research, Theory, and Action.* New York: John Wiley, 1976.

Rutter, M., Tizard, J., Yule, W., Graham, P., & Whitmore, K. Isle of Wight studies. *Psychological Medicine,* 1976, *6,* 313–332.

Safer, D. J. & Allen, R. P. *Hyperactive Children: Diagnosis and Management.* Baltimore: University Park Press, 1976.

Satz, P., Rardin, D., & Ross, J. An evaluation of a theory of specific developmental dyslexia. *Child Development,* 1971, *42,* 2009–2021.

Satz, P. & Sparrow, S. Specific developmental dyslexia: A theoretical formulation. In: D. J. Bakker & P. Satz (Eds.), *Specific Reading Disability.* Rotterdam: Rotterdam University Press, 1970.

Schiffman, G. & Clemmens, R. L. Observations on children with severe reading problems.

In: J. Hellmuth (Ed.), *Learning Disorders, Vol. 2.* Seattle: Special Child Publications, 1966.

Schleifer, M., Weiss, G., Cohen, N., Elman, M., & Cuejic, H. Hyperactivity in preschoolers and the effect of methylphenidate. *American Journal of Orthopsychiatry,* 1975, *45,* 38–50.

Schwartz, S. & Johnson, J. H. *Psychopathology of Childhood: A Clinical-Experimental Approach.* New York: Pergamon Press, 1981.

Shankweiler, D. & Liberman, I. Y. Misreading: A search for causes. In: J. K. Kavanagh & I. G. Mattingly (Eds.), *Language by Ear and by Eye.* Cambridge, MA: The MIT Press, 1972.

Skeels, H. M. Adult status of children with contrasting early life experiences: A follow-up study. *Monograph of the Society for Research in Child Development,* 1966, *31,* Whole No. 105.

Stewart, N. A. & Olds, S. W. *Raising a Hyperactive Child.* New York: Harper & Row, 1973.

Weiner, I. B. *Psychodiagnosis of Schizophrenia.* New York: John Wiley, 1966.

Weiner, I. B. *Psychological Disturbance in Adolescence.* New York: John Wiley, 1970.

Weiss, G. The natural history of hyperactivity in childhood and treatment with stimulant medication at different ages. *International Journal of Mental Health,* 1975, *4,* 213–226.

Wender, P. H. *Minimal Brain Dysfunction in Children.* New York: John Wiley, 1971.

Werry, J. S. The childhood psychoses. In H. C. Quay & J. S. Werry (Eds.), *Psychopathological Disorders of Childhood.* New York: John Wiley, 1979.

Zubin, J. & Spring, B. Vulnerability – A new view of schizophrenia. *Journal of Abnormal Psychology,* 1977, *86,* 103–126.

# CHAPTER 4

# *Interview*

In this chapter we will review some of the differences between conversations and interviews. We will describe some of the misconceptions that children have about the interview situation. We will explore the interview process with children and adolescents as well as cover the basic functions that interviews serve. We will relate how individual differences among children require different interview techniques. We will also discuss interviews with parents. Although examiner effects are not peculiar to interview situations, they operate during interviews. We will point out how the examiner can avoid biasing the material obtained in the interview, since this clinical impression should avoid bias whenever possible. Finally, there are ethical issues which should be observed during all clinical contacts. Because interview situations are frequently less structured, the clinician bears a heavy burden in maintaining a professional observance of ethical issues even when these appear in subtle or attenuated form, or when the interviewee does not manifest concern about the ethical issues in question.

## COMPARISON OF CONVERSATIONS AND INTERVIEWS

Whenever two people exchange verbal material (and usually nonverbal behavior), there is some sort of dialogue. However, interviews are more formal verbal exchanges than conversations. One person is considered the interviewer by both parties and is given freedom to make inquiries about the other, while the interviewee is construed as playing a more respondent or information-providing role. The purpose of the interview is to elicit and appraise information. Both conversations and interviews have rituals, but conversations are often not directed and may be diversional, playful, or simply to maintain contact. Therefore, banalities centering on the weather, local current events, or world news may be very acceptable in conversations, but serve little purpose in most interview situations. Conversations may be mutually disclosing and may vary in level of intimacy; however, the interview is a situation in which disclosure is acceptable and desirable without having a personal relationship of great intimacy. In order for disclosure to take place, certain conditions have to be met and maintained. If the interviewee is a child, especially a young child, the interviewer will need to exercise sensitivity and vigilance to make sure that the child is not burdened too much with keeping conditions comfortable so that disclosure can take place.

In an interview one person assumes responsibility for directing and maintaining the activity. The interviewer assumes the right to ask questions and to continue the exploration of a topic until he or she is satisfied that the child's point of view and information have been understood fully. Neither the child's point of view nor his information are required to be factual. Indeed, many times further exploration with the child, family, teachers, or others is necessary before impressions can be verified or identified as nonfactual. Furthermore, the determination of fact is often less important than the feelings or perceptions held by the child. In the interview process, the examiner assumes the right to ask questions which are intrusive, invasive, and highly personal. The manner in which the examiner asks the questions keeps the material from being disrespectful or unkind. Even though the interviewer assumes the right to probe personal material, it would be unseemly if the questioning did not serve the purpose of obtaining relevant impressions from the child.

Children have rights to privacy which should not be disturbed unless the questions serve an appropriate purpose. Sometimes, despite gentleness and consideration on the interviewer's part, children become upset in the interview. The clinician will then be faced with the decision about whether the material should be continued or whether the child's need to regain composure is more important.

With very young children, questioning about family matters may be upsetting if the questions are presented directly. The examiner may find that less resistance will be found if the interview material is dealt with in a play or projective format. Since young children may feel that it is disloyal to express any dissatisfaction about a parent openly in answer to a direct question, the examiner may find indirect methods are the only form in which the child may be engaged. If the interviewer feels that material relevant to the family is important, part of the responsibility for directing the interview also involves the form of questioning. An example will illustrate this point.

*Examiner:* How are things at home?
*Child* (aged six): Fine.
*Examiner:* Is there anything you would like to change at home?
*Child:* No.
*Examiner:* Not anything? If you were going to change one thing, what would it be?
*Child:* I would paint my room blue.
*Examiner:* How about if you were going to change one thing about your mother?
*Child:* I would paint her room blue, too.

As one can see here, the child responds very concretely and does not get into any personal content. The examiner's questions may imply a criticism of the parent to the child, and the child may feel uncomfortable about this possibility. An alternative approach which permits the examiner to get at the same material but which is more playfully presented may feel more comfortable to the child.

*Examiner:* Have you ever played Three Wishes?
*Child:* No.
*Examiner:* Well, in this game you get to make any wish you want to. So for your first wish, if you could make any wish you want to make, what would it be?
*Child:* I would wish for a video game.
*Examiner:* OK. And what would your second wish be?
*Child:* I would wish for another video game.
*Examiner:* OK. Now make your third wish, but this time it can't be for a thing. It has to be for something you want to change at home.
*Child:* I would like to stay up until nine o'clock.
*Examiner:* OK. Now make a wish for something you would like to change about your mother.

*Child:* I wish she wouldn't get so mad at me.
*Examiner:* OK. Now one more wish about something you'd like to change
about your father.
*Child:* I wish he wouldn't yell at me and spank me.

The flow of this segment is smoother. The examiner avoids the concreteness by asking the child to make a wish, but carefully phrases the
question so that the child is not asked *what would he wish for*, which
is usually answered concretely by young children. He is asked instead,
what would his wish be, keeping the focus on the wish, not the content.
Although the focus is only slightly different on the first wish, the difference permits the examiner to shape the questions subtly into more
abstract content so that by the fifth question, the content is personal
and more abstract. Moreover, this line of questioning is still presented
in a less threatening manner than was the case before. If the examiner
accepts the content produced by the child and proceeds in a matter-of-
fact manner, the child will be put at ease.

*The child is an expert* on his own life and the interview is, in reality,
an exploration between two experts in their own fields. If this is kept
in mind, it may minimize the tendency of many adults to talk down to
children or to discount the importance of the child's perceptions. Only
the child can produce the perceptions and the examiner has to set up
an atmosphere in which the child feels comfortable enough to share the
perceptions. If the interviewer maintains an open, curious, and nonjudg-
mental stance, the child will feel invited to supply his impressions, feelings, and opinions. If the interviewer prejudges or is too quick to anticipate the child's experience or view, the process will become distorted
and misunderstanding may occur or unnecessary resistances may be
created. When the interview process becomes collaborative in tone, however, both the child and the interviewer sense that they are moving
toward a common goal, with the child making the interviewer aware of
how things seem from the child's point of view. Other methods of assessment, including formal testing, flow naturally from the establishment
of this relationship with the child.

Compare two excerpts from child interviews dealing with the same
material.

*Examiner:* Who lives at your house?
*Child:* Me and my mom.
*Examiner:* Where is your dad?

*Child:* He left because they didn't get along.
*Examiner:* What's that like for you?
*Child:* Well, I wish they were still together.

* * *

*Examiner:* Just you and your mom live together, right?
*Child:* Yes.
*Examiner:* Why doesn't your dad live with you?
*Child:* Because he had to move to another town.
*Examiner:* Why, didn't they get along together?
*Child:* I don't know.
*Examiner:* Do you feel badly about it?
*Child:* Yes.

In the first segment the examiner shows interest in the living arrangements but doesn't act as if the child's feelings were obvious. The child is given the chance to produce as much or as little as feels comfortable when asked about the experience. In the second segment the interviewer asks leading questions which presume a knowledge of the child's circumstances and feelings and "pull" for specific answers. If the child had a poor relationship with the father and was relieved to have him out of the house, he would have a very difficult time getting to the point of verbalizing those feelings in the second segment. If the child feels that the interviewer is getting too personal, he will have to resist either by refusing to answer, changing the subject, or making nonverbal protests of some type, all of which can be very stressful. The examiner is actually creating stress in the interview and the child's reluctance to answer may be incorrectly interpreted to signify that the tension observed is related to the home situation rather than to the interview situation. This is the type of negative examiner effect that should be avoided since it will result in an incorrect clinical assessment of family stress.

Interviews provoke reflection and explanation on the part of the child. As the interviewer evokes the child's explanations and perceptions, there is a second process which is at work. This is the interviewer's covert acceptance of the child and the covert communication that the child's understanding is valued. The examiner supports reflective thought on the child's part. Whether the child is being evaluated for continuation in therapy or for some other purpose, the experience will be constructive in that the child's self-esteem is enhanced as he comes to value his participation in the reflective process.

## MISPERCEPTIONS THAT CHILDREN HAVE
## ABOUT INTERVIEW SITUATIONS

Little children naturally identify being taken to a clinic or to a doctor with medical services, including such unpleasant procedures as hypodermic injections, getting undressed in front of strangers, and having their bodies poked or probed. Even when adults explain that a psychologist is a different kind of doctor, children may still respond with fear and want to avoid the situation.

Adolescents, on the other hand, have a history in which talking about conflicts and problems has been frustrating and unproductive. Coming to see a "shrink" may connote yet another unpleasant experience in which adults are only out to prove a point. Since the adolescent expects further dictates, fault-finding, or control of his behavior, initial resistance is high. This resistance must be resolved sufficiently for the evaluation to be a constructive process.

Both young children and adolescents may expect conflict resolution to result in fault-finding and blame. Since children referred to clinicians feel that adults think something is wrong with them, they fear the blame will be attributed to them as well.

Another misperception stems from parental manipulation of children. Many times parents do not inform or misinform the child of the purpose of the visit to the psychologist, either because they do not know how to explain this to the child or because they are afraid that the child will resist coming. Children who appear for the evaluation under these circumstances will feel betrayed and distrustful.

Prior to initiating the interview, it is important that the interviewer understands the child's perception of the reason for the visit. If the child doesn't understand or has some misconception which would interfere with the business to be conducted, the first order of business should be to discuss the visit with the child and explain its purpose. The interviewer should not expect such an explanation to result in the child's acceptance of the situation, although this may occur. The goal is to be aboveboard with the child and respectful of his feelings, whatever these may be.

### WHEN TO TALK WITH THE CHILD

The decision to talk only with the child is not a simple one and often cannot be made on an a priori basis. Usually the clinician has some referral information before meeting the child and the family members or others who accompany him to the evaluation. The amount of material may be very brief or may be extensive, but in any case referral information is almost always based on the report of some adult who is concerned about the child. If the interviewer formed an impression purely on the basis of the referral information, the child's behavior might appear more seriously disturbed or negative than when the child expresses his perceptions of the situation. Even when adults try to take into account how a child feels or the stresses which may be impinging on him, there are reasons which may keep them from fully appreciating the situation from the child's viewpoint.

Before actually meeting the child and family, it is a good idea to think about the possible way things may look to the child. Having read the referral material, including any questionnaires or history that you request prior to the first meeting, the interviewer should think about possible problems and different points of view that may be held by parents and children. The next step, prior to seeing the family, is to file this material away from one's thoughts and *to suspend all belief.* By this we mean to take nothing as fact, but only as a starting point for discussion and exploration. The second major step is to decide whom to interview and when and how to do it. Generally the child and adults are greeted in the waiting room. Unless there is a strong reason for speaking only with some one or more members of the group, it is usually better for the clinician to invite everyone to the interview room.

## WAITING ROOM BEHAVIOR

Experienced clinicians will tell you that the waiting room behavior of the child and family (or others) is informative and may be diagnostic in nature. For example, there is a real difference in the emotional atmosphere in the family when the clinician meets a child who is sitting calmly between his parents rather than meeting two adults seated at opposite ends of a couch with a child sulking across the room in a chair situated as far as possible from the parents. The way the patient and family (or other adults) handle the introduction and the walk to the interview room is similarly revealing. Usually, by the time the group reaches the interview room the interviewer has an impression of whether the family is a cohesive group and whether the child is at ease, angry, or frightened. Entry to the interview room gives the examiner an opportunity to observe the family dynamics, e.g., who sits next to whom, who directs the family traffic into the room, and who assumes responsibility for engaging the interviewer.

## FAMILY SESSION

After everyone is seated the clinician usually begins with some open-ended question, such as "What brings you here today?" Even though the interviewer may have received written material beforehand, it is a good idea to open in this way. Many times the way in which the family handles the purpose of the meeting is very different from the way it was handled on the telephone or in written communications. Sometimes parents are cautious in stating their reasons for coming, either because they are sensitive to the way the child may feel about the parents' statements or because they have difficulty in being direct. Other parents may give opening shots and structure the situation so that it is clear that they are in charge and expect the clinician to line up with them against the child. During the meeting in the waiting room, the walk to the interview room, the getting settled, and the answer to the opening question, the clinician is forming an impression of the family relationships and the level of comfort in the family. If no extreme level of tension characterizes the group, the interview may proceed with all members of the family present. The interview will then continue until the interviewer has solicited observations and explanations from each family member and also has determined how aware each family member has been of the viewpoints of the others prior to the interview. At this point, it is often time to talk separately with members of the family about matters which have been introduced either directly or covertly.

It is usually a good idea to ask the child whether he or she prefers to talk separately first or to wait. Many children would rather wait so that they can get the last word in with the clinician, but sometimes children feel that parents will have already ensnared the interviewer if they do not have an opportunity to speak first. The order of meeting frequently has importance to the child even when a façade of indifference has been adopted and the child rejects making a choice. The clinician who is not sensitive to these undercurrents may set up unnecessary distrust and resistance before ever talking privately with the child. For these reasons, giving the child an opportunity to choose when to talk is a good idea. The covert communication by the clinician that the child's point of view is valued will be received whether or not the child makes a choice.

If family tension is high during the initial part of the interview, the interviewer may follow an alternative procedure. It may become apparent that so much conflict and anger pervades the group that collaborative discussion is not possible. If family members interrupt one another, silence each other, disagree vehemently, and stalemate progress in discussion, the group should be confronted with this fact and/or separated if confrontation does not appear indicated or helpful. All family members will be experiencing higher tension as a result of their failure to work as a group. Regardless of the turmoil that just preceded, the child should almost always be offered the choice of whether to speak alone with the clinician first or later. The exception to this rule would be if the clinician believed that offering the child the opportunity to have the choice would somehow work against his best interests, perhaps by reinforcing his resistance.

### THE INTAKE INTERVIEW WITH THE CHILD

Once having decided to begin by interviewing the child, the clinician should take into account special requirements for that specific child. For example, two types of intake interviews are common for child assessment. One type occurs as part of the therapy process and is, in many cases, conducted by the therapist-to-be. In some settings the intake for therapy is conducted by someone else. When the initial interviewer is likely to continue as a therapist, there are some differences in approach which are possible. These consist of setting up expectations for future contact and expectations pertinent to the specific dyadic relationship which is being developed. If the intake is conducted by another person, the child will know that yet another person will be involved and may feel differently about some disclosures.

The other type of intake interview which is commonly performed is that which occurs as part of a child assessment after the child has been referred from therapists, agencies, or families. Typically, the expectation is that the child will be seen during the evaluation, but the expectation may be that no further contact will occur once the assessment is complete.

The tenor of the intake interview should reflect these differences in purpose. Intake interviews which do not promise later contact should have tighter limits in some crucial respects. While both types of intake process encourage self-disclosure and exploration of feelings and circumstances, the interview conducted for assessment only should respect the child's emotional needs for support differently than that conducted by the therapist-to-be. Specifically, the clinician should not encourage greater attachment and emotional dependence than is appropriate or the child will feel deserted and resentful when the contact terminates. Sensitivity to the establishment of an appropriate emotional distance for the occasion is important in keeping future resistance low. Among the examiner effects which are possible and undesirable, insensitive encouragement for feeling close to the interviewer is one which can easily be avoided. At the end of the interview the child should feel respected and encouraged, but not as though a loss will be sustained if contact with the examiner is terminated with the interview. The focus should be on helping the child feel better about his ability to communicate effectively rather than on how good contact with the interviewer feels.

Sometimes interviewers feel that getting information is sufficient justification for pulling a child closer, either emotionally or physically, than can be tolerated comfortably, but this is a psychological disservice. Rapport and openness can be encouraged through respect for the child's point of view. Any encouragement of closer attachment carries with it an implicit promise to continue the relationship. This implicit promise is unfair if the contact is to be brief and limited to the evaluation.

## Young Children

Intake interviews with young children require different techniques depending upon the child's personal response style, the level of tension with which the child enters the interview situation, and the type of problem which originated the appointment. When the meeting with the whole family has been collaborative it is usually possible to be direct with the child, even if severe problems have been acknowledged or the child is shy or somewhat withdrawn. Thus, one begins with a question such as, "What did your parents tell you about coming to see me?" or "Your parents said that you had a school problem when we were all together a few minutes ago. You sort of went along with that, but I'd like to know more about that now." In this manner we discover how the child sees the purpose of the visit. We follow with inquiries as to how the child views the situation (which may be different from his view of his parents' reasons for coming). Once the child begins to describe his perceptions, one follows up with questions which cause him to elaborate the material so that he gives a detailed description of the problems, what he thinks about the situation, and how it originated. Moreover, we learn what changes he would like to make and how he experiences his relationships with each person important to the situation being discussed.

After the information-gathering portion of the interview, it is constructive to thank the child for being helpful. It is important to summarize the child's point of view and make sure that he agrees that you have understood it. Even if there is disagreement about "facts," this expression of his point of view, including his feelings, is important. After the summary, the child should be asked if there is anything he has mentioned that he doesn't want discussed directly with his parents. If so, he should be assured that, while he will not be quoted directly, the information may be used in trying to work out a helpful solution to the problems. In some cases either the child or the interviewer will have raised the question prior to discussion of problems. Even when assurance has been given earlier, the interviewer should reiterate the limits of confidentiality near the end of the interview. If the child feels comfortable about the interviewer discussing material with the parents that, too, should be explicitly recognized.

The final work of the interview is the transition to the more formal testing situation. Usually, after thanking the child and recognizing his help in the interview, it is easy to continue by explaining that his help is needed with some other tasks. The examiner should explain that his performance on the tasks will help the examiner understand the situation better and will make it easier to work with him and the family. The child should be told that each task will be explained as it arises and that he will have a chance to ask questions. The child should be told in a general way what kinds of tasks will be used, e.g., "I'd like to see how you solve new problems, how you're doing in school, and let you tell me some stories and draw some pictures for me."

When the earlier family session has been tense, the examiner has to be sensitive to the child's personal style of responding even more than usual. One of the effects of tension in the family is to make everyone more defensive and this defensiveness will be expressed both in interpersonal styles and in cognitive functions. At this point it may be helpful to review some of the different ways in which personal response styles to tension may affect interview behavior.

A calm, easy child who comes out of a tense family session will generally respond quickly to comments such as "That was pretty rough, wasn't it?" and "Do things like that happen at home a lot?" Just the recognition of the situation with such a child is usually enough to establish rapport so that one can explore the reasons for the assessment and the child's view of the problems. A cautious, shy, withdrawn, or slow-to-warm-up child responds to tense situations by withdrawal and by becoming even more cautious than before. While the child may be intensely involved at an emotional level, the expression of these feelings interpersonally will require the child feeling in control of the time and rate at which the expression occurs. Following a tense interview session with the family, the first task of the interviewer should be to relax the atmosphere, lessen the demands on the child, and only after this has been accomplished should the interview proper begin. Even at this point the interviewer should approach the content more obliquely. This may be accomplished by offering a short break to go to the water fountain, bathroom, or for a snack. The idea is to change the situation, and have a little casual contact and conversation before going back to any further discussion of the reason for the visit and the child's report of his own experience. Coming back to the interview situation with the child, it is important to acknowledge what happened in the previous family session, e.g., "Your parents seem to be pretty upset today." Rather than focusing on the child's feelings at this point, it is better to continue with some structure and to let him know that one of the reasons for meeting is that people in the family are upset. The following excerpt illustrates this technique:

*Interviewer:* Your parents seem to be worried about how you're doing in school. *(Instead of demanding a response at this point it is better to ask an open-ended question which can be answered positively.)* Which subject do you like the best?

If the problems are centered more in the family and the family session has been tense, this might be reflected in a similar approach.

*Interviewer:* Your mom said that you and your sisters fight a lot. Which sister do you get along with the best?

The purpose of this maneuver is to put the child at ease and to give an experience of being in control and of expertness about the situation before probing into areas which might make the child anxious and defensive. If the child responds with a rejecting comment such as "I don't like anything at school" or "I don't get along with any of them," sometimes humor may break the ice. The interviewer may say solemnly, "What about lunch?" or "Not even when they're sleeping?"

Difficult or strongly resistant children present challenges even to very experienced clinicians. At the extreme, some of these young children become very frustrated, angry, and have temper tantrums, crying episodes, or sullen silences. Direct approach usually fails. Many of these children find it difficult to stop the protesting behavior without feeling a loss of face or control. On the other hand, if adults intervene directly and focus on the protesting behavior, they feel honor bound to resist. However, if the examiner is not frightened by the behavior or has to deal with it directly, the situation may improve quickly. One technique is to escort the child to the interview room and to attend to some paper work for a few minutes. Often the child will calm down and either approach the interviewer directly or respond to approach when the examiner looks up and makes eye contact with the child. The important thing here is to avoid power struggles with the child and to reduce the high level of negative feelings as rapidly as possible.

With difficult or oppositional children who are not at a high level of resistance, a variety of other procedures may work well. However, the procedures take into account that the interviewer is not engaging in power plays and is in control of the situation so that the choice open to the child is very structured and very limited, e.g., "I want a coke now. Would you like one, too?" Sometimes the child will not respond to indirect opportunities to ease into the interview situation. In such cases the following excerpt indicates a typical interaction which may be successful with an oppositional or difficult child:

*Interviewer:* It's time to get started now.
*Child:* I don't want to do this.
*Interviewer:* I know you don't, and I don't either, but we have to, so let's get started so we can both get out of here by lunch.

Once the child has entered into the interview process, there will be resistance to exploration and to spontaneous expression of feeling, other than the desire to leave the interview. A technique which works well with these children is to mobilize their oppositional stances and to structure situations so that their responses can only indicate the lesser of two evils. This is a form of presenting a double-bind situation to the child in which both sides are negative, e.g., "Who gives you more trouble, your brother or your sister?" or "You don't like school and you don't like your chores at home. Which is worse for you?" For children who have difficulty expressing positive feeling or who are more comfortable in a complaining stance, this form of question is more agreeable because the interviewer has not covertly asked them to act out of character. Many times children approached in this way become talkative, enjoy the interview (although they would deny it to the death), and cooperate fully. Even though these children might not be able to express verbally why they become compliant, it is clear that the examiner's respect for them has been important in their being able to feel a choice about how to respond. If permitted to continue to complain, the child feels understood in a basic way and no longer has to defend this right by silence or protest. Again, examiner effects can be produced here, either negatively, by attempting to force the child to respond in a manner which demands surrender, or positively, by structuring the situation so that the child does not have to lose self-respect in order to comply with the interviewer.

## Adolescents

Adolescents are able to think more abstractly than younger children. This permits them to have more ideas about what causes are responsible for the problems they confront and to formulate more complex explanations than young children have at their command. Despite the fact that adolescents possess this more analytic capability, the motivation for sharing and expressing viewpoints about their problems depends heavily upon the adolescent's perception that the interviewer is receptive and open-minded. Since most teenagers who are referred for evaluation have been criticized by significant adults in their lives, they are likely to enter the interview situation warily. In fact, the ability to think more abstractly and to argue hypothetico-deductively can be used as a powerful resistance if the adolescent feels distrustful and defensive. Even when realities are obvious, if the adolescent feels argumentative, there is great pleasure possible in frustrating adults by marshaling logical but irrelevant polemics.

For the interview to be successful, the interviewer must convey the attitude that the teenager's opinion counts for something and that it will affect some outcome important to him. This should be done without promising that the adolescent will agree with the outcome. It is important for the teenager to understand that he may have an effect without completely getting his own way. The major point is that the adolescent needs to know that it is in his best interests to state his position because decisions are about to be made which will affect him, and that this is his opportunity to have a major input into the decision process. Referrals of teenagers come from a variety of sources: families, schools, jails, probation officers, and social agencies. The motivational level of adolescents varies with the degree of coercion that they have experienced and with the perception of whether any choice about what happens is in their own hands. Many of these young people are both struggling for independence and clinging to dependent emotional strategies. An interviewer should not assume that the overt behavior and expressions of an adolescent are telling the whole story.

Even with adolescents who manifest bravado and disdain for the circumstances in which they find themselves, there are usually other more frightened, angry, and confused emotions present. The double-bind situation described with difficult younger children is one technique which may also work well with adolescents, but this should not be used if a more direct and open discussion is possible. Many times interviewers who are uncomfortable with adolescents, particularly if they are too close in age to the adolescent, will have a tendency to engage in more banter than necessary. This approach really treats the interviewer's anxiety rather than serves the teenager. Therefore, judicious consideration is a necessary forerunner to any use of flippancy, double-binding, or other indirect approaches. Otherwise, an unfortunate examiner effect may be to foreclose meaningful discussion. The examiner may be asking for the adolescent's approval rather than dealing with the problems which are presented.

So far we have discussed interpersonal considerations which influence interviews with children. However, all that these factors influence is the atmosphere established within which the interview takes place.

## WHAT THE INTAKE INTERVIEW ACCOMPLISHES

The intake interview fulfills a number of functions. It is the occasion for the establishment of a working relationship with the child. It is also the vehicle for enhancing the child's motivation to become involved in and productive within the assessment process. A third function is the determination of the child's perceptions and feelings about the situation which prompted the referral. This information should include the cast of characters, their interrelationships, and a statement of the problem, as well as the child's evaluation of the problem. Further, the interview should reveal how hopeful the child feels about change and what he thinks would bring about change. Finally, the intake interview provides the interviewer with observations of the child's style of approach, methods of relating, cognitive level and style, defensive maneuvers and response to both stimulation and limit-setting.

## INTERVIEWING THE PARENTS

While the child's point of view and understanding of the events which resulted in the decision to come for assessment are a necessary part of the picture which the clinician develops, they are only a part of that picture. The interview with the parents establishes an impression of whether the parents are reliable informants. Sometimes this is difficult to determine and additional measures need to be taken to establish the reliability of parental report. (For example, some paper and pencil measures have scales which permit one to assess parental defensiveness, e.g., Personality Inventory for Children.) In addition, the clinician forms some impression of whether parents see problems in a manner which is congruent with that of the child or of others (such as teachers), and how they explain the onset and development of the problem.

In addition to the clinician's impressions of the parents, the interview should also establish some factual information which will contribute to the formulation resulting from the assessment process. The vehicle through which most of the information can be gathered is the developmental history. Such a history should include several distinct types of information and can be organized so that the clinician will be able to integrate data relative to various possible explanations which might account for the presenting problems. We will review the content that comprises a good developmental history. Some aspects of the developmental history may prove to be much more helpful than others. In many cases some aspects of the developmental history are most useful in eliminating or ruling out potential interpretations of material which could account for the behavior in question. An intake interview which is too sharply focused on a behavioral description of the current problem may cause the examiner to overlook possibilities which should be explored during the assessment, thus resulting in too narrow a formulation and leading to inappropriate treatment considerations.

*Prenatal influences* include information indicating whether the child was a planned baby (which may reflect parental attitudes toward the birth), the course of pregnancy, including the type of prenatal care that the mother received, and the particulars of the delivery. Of potential significance are signs of familial conditions which might indicate genetic factors, illness, accidents, or nutritional features occurring during pregnancy. The term of the pregnancy, the nature of the delivery, its length, drugs used, and the condition of the baby at birth are all important. These historical details may have bearing on later development and may have effects which influence the child's functioning long after birth (Braine et al., 1966; Taub et al., 1977).

Even though possible genetic anomalies have been considered by the referring party, they may not have been thoroughly investigated. A child who was referred to one of the authors for psychological evaluation was suspected of being mongoloid by her teacher who had noticed some of her facial characteristics. The child was failing in school. Upon interview it was discovered that the child had one grandparent who was Eskimo (thus accounting for the eyelid features) and an IQ within the normal range, demonstrating another example of the Rosenthal effect! No one had taken a thorough history and, although the child was experiencing school problems, examination ruled out intellectual factors as the source of the difficulties. While not commonplace, there are enough similar incidents which occur in child assessment cases to make the carefully done history an integral part of the process.

More subtle prenatal problems may not be identified when abbreviated history procedures are employed. In our own practice we have the parents complete a questionnaire (see Chapter 10) which supplies historical material prior to the appointment for assessment. The data provided by the parents serve as the basis for exploration of significant areas during the parent interview.

*A health history* provides information concerning illnesses, accidents, surgery, and treatments. Factors which might influence central nervous system function are particularly important, including prolonged high fever, serious infections, blows to the head and other trauma, or problems affecting oxygen supply, e.g., choking, near drowning, and apnea. The use of life charts is a convenient method of displaying this information (Goldman, 1976). Consider Figure 4.1.

From this chart we learn that Joe's parents had Rh factor incompatibility, a circumstance that has been associated with heightened risk for the occurrence of mental retardation for children late in the birth order. The parents report that they kept hoping for a boy and were very happy when Joe was born. Joe has a problematic health history with several features suggesting risk factors which might have jeopardized Joe's neurological and psychological integrity. At birth Joe obtained an Apgar score of seven. The Apgar (named after its originator, Virginia Apgar) is used to rate the conditions of babies at birth based upon the status of their respiration, reflexes, sensory modality integrity, and other indications of physiological functioning. Scores of eight to ten are considered within normal limits. Joe's score of seven indicates a border-line condition and should be investigated if possible.

The interviewer should determine whether Joe needed help breathing at birth, whether he was in an incubator and, if so, for how long. All of the facts may help determine whether Joe suffered oxygen deprivation which might have resulted in some central nervous system damage early in life. Joe's history also includes several episodes of high fevers. Since fevers can compromise brain function, it is important to inquire as to the level of temperature attained, the duration, and the type of treat-ment Joe received. Likewise, the examiner will want to probe for infor-mation concerning the frequent ear infections listed. Joe's early years have been subject to frequent illness and to some extent his life has been shaped by these early experiences. How the family managed the illness-es is important, and how Joe learned to think about himself is also sig-nificant.

*Social histories* are important sources of biographical material. Among the features of a good social history are data relating to people and events which may have affected the child's life significantly. Such items include the composition of the household, births, deaths, divorces, changes in residence, schools, and jobs. The social history should describe the way the child relates to various family members. It should also provide information as to the child's peers, the nature of these re-lationships (e.g., does the child have close friends or only more distant acquaintances?), types of social activities, and the manner in which the child relates to others. Of interest will be such material as whether the child plays with children his own age or only with those much older or younger. Likewise, it will be helpful to know whether the child gets along better with either children or adults. Figure 4.2 indicates significant social history data for Joe. We write the material for the social history above the age line to separate it from the health history for easy inspec-tion.

From the social history we learn that Joe has already suffered vari-ous disruptions to the social stability experienced in his short life. His mother returned to work when he was three months old and, shortly after, Joe was very ill and had to spend a week in the hospital. When

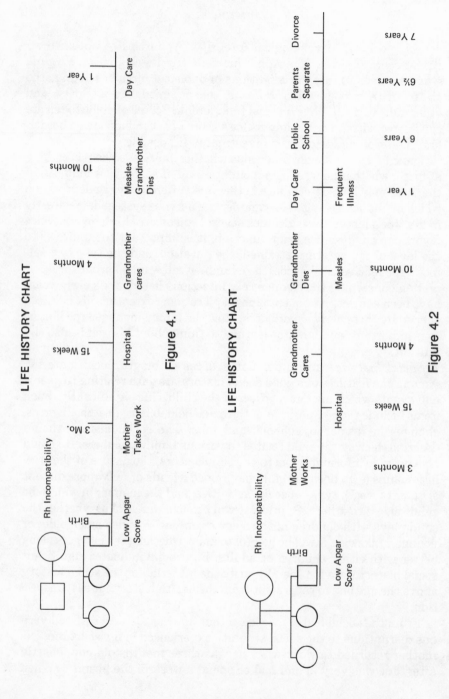

LIFE HISTORY CHART

Rh Incompatibility

Birth
Low Apgar
Score

3 Mo.
Mother
Takes Work

15 Weeks
Hospital

4 Months
Grandmother
cares

10 Months
Measles
Grandmother
Dies

1 Year
Day Care

Figure 4.1

LIFE HISTORY CHART

Rh Incompatibility

Birth
Low Apgar
Score

3 Months
Mother
Works

15 Weeks
Hospital

4 Months
Grandmother
Cares

10 Months
Grandmother
Dies
Measles

1 Year
Day Care
Frequent
Illness

6 Years
Public
School

6½ Years
Parents
Separate

7 Years
Divorce

Figure 4.2

the family moved, Joe's care was provided primarily by his grandmother, to whom he became deeply attached. The grandmother died while Joe was sick with the measles and the boy had difficulty understanding why his grandmother was not there to take care of him when he recovered. He missed her greatly and did not respond to explanations about her absence. Joe's parents placed him in a day care shortly thereafter, but Joe was ill and was absent frequently. When Joe entered public school he had barely gotten adjusted to the new situation before his parents, who had been having marital difficulties for the past two years, decided to separate and then obtained a divorce.

The overlap between the events noted in the health history and the social history raises issues for clarification, e.g., the relationship between the complaints regarding Joe's poor school work and the onset of enuresis and the recent divorce should be explored. Careful history-taking will establish sequences which may be significant and can easily have passed unnoticed by the parents.

Few histories devote much time to developmental milestones beyond the early ones: age at sitting up, walking, first words, and onset of puberty. However, particularly with regard to referral questions which imply possible intellectual deficits or learning problems, it is useful to get a *cognitive history*. The cognitive history will include such items as when the child learned to count, could repeat the alphabet, learned to say nursery rhymes, and learned to read and write. The history should indicate how interested the child was in these matters, whether the parents encouraged them, whether the child was read to by parents, and something about the level of cognitive stimulation in the home. The latter may be assessed by what books, magazines, television, and music the family and child have available. The cognitive history should also indicate whether the child experienced problems which might suggest neuropsychological difficulties, e.g., confusion of left and right, letter and number reversals, motor difficulties (either gross or fine coordination problems), memory problems, or difficulty understanding instructions. School problems are of special interest. They should be examined carefully to determine their nature, approaches to remediation that have been attempted, and the child's attitude and response to these interventions.

The *structure* of the interview usually begins with the parents' description of current problems. The examiner is wise to listen to the parental observations and to ask for their beliefs regarding the problem and its onset. Sometimes it happens that parents and teachers have very different views of children who are referred for assessment. The examiner should attend with an open mind to all sources of data. It may well happen that a child who is well-behaved and able to attend in one situation is a behavior problem and unable to concentrate in other circumstances, in which case parents and school officials find themselves at odds and become impatient with each other. During this period it often happens that incompatible approaches are desired by parents and teachers. The clinician who identifies too closely with any adult caretaker is in a position to ignore useful data and therefore may not be able to make the most appropriate formulation. When the psychologist feels pressured to take sides, it is a good sign that time should be taken to examine the situation and to try to understand how the child may be responding to these disparate influences or may be eliciting such different responses from adults. It may be that a child who becomes distracted in the presence of a whole classroom full of children is a well-behaved angel at home and is able to function academically with the lower level of stimulation in the home.

Once the reason for the visit has been discussed, the interviewer can explain that some developmental history would be helpful and can turn to obtaining health, social, and cognitive historical data. The parents should be asked to describe the conditions under which the child functions optimally. They will have already tried to alleviate the problems which resulted in the assessment appointment. Their attempts to change the child's behavior or situations in which the child encounters problems should be described in detail, partly to get an understanding of the parents' explanations and behavior, and partly to determine the child's responses to these interventions. From the parents' report it will be possible to learn how discouraged they feel, how consistent they have been in their attempts to elicit change, and whether they cooperate or act out problems between themselves as they attempt to bring about changes in their child's behavior.

Parents who bring their children for evaluation have positive motivations for doing so. While it is true that ambivalence and frustration are also usually present, it is important to remember that parents mean well. They also feel threatened and anxious when they are not able to understand and manage the problems which they and their children experience. Even when parents have gotten into power struggles with their children or with each other, even when they are angry and feel rejecting, they also want to be good parents and their child to be happy. These motivations should be recognized for the invaluable assets which they are and should be used in obtaining the parents' perceptions of the child and his problems.

Many times parents have had no formal training in child development. Other parents have themselves had poor parental models or very disrupted childhoods. They may not understand simple principles of reinforcement (Patterson, 1976). In their attempts to change the behavior of a child, parents may go through a long period of trial and error attempts with different methods, none of which is tried for very long. In some cases they inadvertently set up reinforcement schedules which maintain the problematic behavior. In the course of the trial and error approaches they have used, they may have even applied some good methods, but did not understand the importance of consistency on their own part. As a result they may have reinforced the negative behavior on a random and infrequent basis, making it difficult for them to understand why the behavior persists. In such cases it is usual for the parents to be upset because the child will not obey and they cannot control the behavior of the child, who often sees the parents as overly demanding and rigid. Both parents and children attribute unpleasant motivations to each other and the family is tense with the expectation that the child will misbehave at every opportunity and the child expects parental disapproval no matter what the behavior. In addition, out of insecurity the parents feel that they must demand obedient behavior rather than using modeling and socialization as means of obtaining appropriate child values and behavior (Hoffman, 1970).

After appropriate history has been gathered in the interview, it is important to learn *how the family operates as a group.* One way to find this out is to inquire about how the family makes decisions (Satir, 1967). In authoritarian-oriented families, the parents usually report that they make decisions. In very loosely organized families it may be that, although the parents claim that the family works democratically, nobody actually takes responsibility for decisions and many of them are made by default. Sometimes the child's problems (especially if conduct problems are the major source of concern) are expressions of inadequate time or inadequate involvement with the parents. (With adolescents, of course, many times the locus of problems is in the peer group.) The form of expression of the problem may reflect the nature of the family structure—whether the family rejects the idea of having problems and uses the children to keep the family intact or whether the developing children threaten the marital relationship, which, unable to tolerate the children, has to push them out. Stierlin (1974) has described how family structure may be involved in the form of symptom production in adolescents. Both the type of organization (authoritarian, egalitarian, irresponsible) and the level of parental psychopathology are factors in the type of response the child must make to survive in the family. The interview which explores decision-making will permit the psychologist to determine how the parents set conditions to which the child has to respond.

A final phase of the parental interview should include an explanation of the assessment which will be done. Frequently parents need some idea of how long the session will last and what will be done.

*Interviewer:* Johnny will be taking some tests which will help us get a better idea of what's going on with him. We will give him an intellectual evaluation, partly because we want to know at what level he can understand things, and partly to screen some of his cognitive functions so that we will know if some of his school problems might be related to them. We will give him some achievement tests to see if he has learned material perhaps even better than he is using it in the classroom. We will also give him some personality tests to get a better idea about how he feels about himself, his attitudes, and some of the problems he may be having. These may be things he hasn't talked about or doesn't know how to talk about. For example, you have wondered if he was depressed. Even if he is, he may not know how to talk about it. . . . When we have finished with all the tests we will look over the results and arrange a time to discuss the results with you. At that time we will also discuss recommendations with you and answer any questions that come up as a result of the findings.

FEEDBACK

We have now discussed the material that should be covered in intake interviews with parents and children. Whereas intake interviews are primarily designed to obtain information, feedback interviews are designed primarily to give information and answer questions. Feedback interviews should be conducted with the parents, sometimes with children present. The child should be present if old enough to understand the material and recommendations and if the family structure is such that this can be constructively accomplished. If the child cannot be present or the psychologist feels that it would be better to talk with the parents alone, the child should nonetheless be given some sort of feedback, whether this is in a separate session or at the end of the evaluation.

## Feedback to the Child

The examiner has an opportunity to give good feedback to the child immediately after the session. Consider this example:

*Interviewer:* Well, what was the session (day) like for you?
*Child:* It took a long time.
*Interviewer:* Yes it did. While you were talking (or taking some of the tests) did you notice anything about how you were doing?
*Child:* Like what?
*Interviewer:* Like what was easier for you to talk about (or do) and what was harder.
*Child:* Oh, yes. It was a lot easier when I had to answer the questions about words, but the numbers were hard.
*Interviewer:* Well, even though it felt that way, you did very well on both of them. I got the impression that you are better at working with numbers than you know you are. Could that be true?
*Child:* I guess so.
*Interviewer:* Another thing I noticed is that you feel more comfortable when somebody asks you a question that has a definite answer. You seem more unsure when it is a matter of your own opinion.
*Child:* Yes, because how do I know if that's the right answer?
*Interviewer:* Well, sometimes adults want a right answer. That's true, but sometimes your own ideas are very important. Maybe one thing you need to do is think about your ideas before you worry about how right they are.

## Feedback to the Parents

This same type of content would be communicated differently to the parents. The psychologist would state the results and recommendations in a form like this:

*Interviewer:* One thing I noticed about Johnny was that although he did well on the entire intelligence (or achievement) test, he was much more confident on the verbal part. On arithmetic he performed well, but he was pretty tense. Also, when he had to answer open-ended questions he was very tense. I got the impression that he was so motivated to get my approval that he was more worried about that than he was interested in the questions I was asking him. Does that fit with your own observations?

*Parent:* Well, yes. He's always been worried about math because he knew I was bad at it. And it's true he really wants us to think well of him.

*Interviewer:* I think one of Johnny's problems is that he needs to know that your approval will be there when he does his own thinking. Right now, he acts as though he has to agree with your ideas. Maybe we need to talk about how you can get this across to him so that he can relax more and get more involved with the material. Then he will not have to try to give answers he thinks you want to hear.

The major point is that a recitation of test results alone is not helpful to either parents or children. The results need to be imparted with a discussion of how the results bear on the interpretations of the presenting problems. The recommendations need to be focused upon the presenting problems and additional matters that may be of concern, which may far outweigh the problems which first caught the parents' attention.

*Interviewer:* I know you were worried about Johnny's math ability and his school performance. The results of our assessment point to something that seems more emotional than academic in nature. He's so concerned about approval that he's having a rough time concentrating on his work. Let's go back to when this began. You said he started doing poorly after his younger sister had to go to the hospital. . . .

In the above example, it may be that Johnny developed problems because he needed reassurance that he had not been displaced by the younger sister. It may be that his way of getting attention and concern was to produce his own kind of problem, particularly if a valued parent has also been reported to have a similar problem with which Johnny can identify. On the other hand, Johnny may have become tense when the family experienced the stress of a sick child. Unable to express this tension directly, he found it difficult to concentrate and developed a school problem. The examiner will need to explore the history and findings from the assessment in formulating the material. In the feedback session the parents should be reassured whenever a possible source of trouble has been ruled out. They should be given advice on how to reassure and support the child where this seems appropriate. If the support and advice are simple and straightforward and the parents understand and accept the advice, no further work may be necessary.

If parents need more than advice and simple suggestions, it may be appropriate to recommend treatment or management. The treatment may be family-oriented, either family sessions or separate sessions for the child and for his parents. Similarly, management sessions may include the entire family or subsets of it. In such cases the interviewer may respond:

*Interviewer:* Because Johnny's having some problems feeling that you approve of him and is having some school problems as well, I think he needs some help. I would recommend that he have someone to talk with about these things. I would also recommend that we set up a few sessions to help you work out some ways of helping him at home.

The final work of the feedback session should concern the communication of the results, via reports or consultations with others who should be involved in the child's care. The parents should be asked to sign informed consent statements which direct the psychologist to communicate with those who should receive information. If both parents and child are present at the feedback session, the interviewer should reiterate the agreement about any further treatment or the findings which are of particular relevance. Both parents and child should be thanked for their cooperation before leaving.

*Records*

The patient's file should contain not only the signed informed consent forms, but also the final report, the raw materials from testing, and any notes of patient contact. Impressions from the interview material at feedback should also be entered with any changes in recommendations that might have been decided upon after further discussion.

110     *Psychological Methods of Child Assessment*

## REFERENCES

Braine, M. D. S., Heimer, C. B., Wortis, A., & Freedman, A. M. Factors associated with impairment of the early development of prematures. *Monograph of the Society for Research in Child Development,* 1966, *31,* Whole No. 4.
Goldman, J. *Becoming a Psychotherapist.* Springfield, IL: Charles C Thomas, 1976.
Hoffman, M. L. Moral development. In: P. Mussen (Ed.), *Carmichael's Manual of Child Psychology.* New York: John Wiley, 1970, pp. 261-359.
Patterson, G. R. *Living with Children* (revised). Champaign, IL: Research Press, 1976.
Satir, V. *Conjoint Family Therapy.* Palo Alto, CA: Science & Behavior Books, 1967.
Stierlin, H. *Separating Parents and Adolescents.* New York: Quadrangle, 1974.
Taub, H. B., Goldstein, K. M., & Caputo, D. V. Indices of neonatal prematurity as discriminators of development in middle childhood. *Child Development,* 1977, *48,* 797-805.

# CHAPTER 5

# Measurement and
# Clinical Judgment

In the previous chapters we focused upon some patterns of normal development and some clinical populations of children who deviate from those patterns. Before we can examine in detail the methods of assessment which employ psychometric techniques, it will be helpful to review some measurement issues which are central to the assessment process so that the psychometric criteria for evaluation of these techniques will be clearly in mind. Our review will include standardization procedures for the development of assessment instruments, as well as the matters related to reliability and validity. Our discussion of clinical judgment will deal with evaluation of referral questions, hypotheses, selections of methods of assessment, and interpretation of clinical material.

Assessment procedures include both clinical methods and psychometric evaluation. These processes share some characteristics but are different in important respects. Some clinical procedures are structured and attempt to insure, as do psychometric tests, that each person receives a standardized presentation of material to which responses will be made. On the other hand, the structured clinical interview and questionnaire generally permit a variety of responses and are more open-ended, thus stimulating personal associations and life history material which cannot be anticipated in many multiple choice test formats. Also, the clinical procedures permit personal observation and interpersonal interaction, thus providing other sources of information to the clinician.

111

However, in both cases – structured interviews and questionnaires and psychometric tests – an attempt is made to elicit material and to observe both content- and task-relevant behaviors which may be informative. The guiding principle as to which type of format is chosen for eliciting information is usually that of efficiency. In those cases in which interpersonal contact is important, rapport needs to be established, and some specific testing of interpersonal approaches will be helpful, the clinical method is usually elected as the approach. In other cases in which more factual information needs to be reviewed, checklists, self-administered procedures and other forms of psychometric instruments may be more efficient. Some instruments, of course, combine clinical and psychometric methods, e.g., intelligence tests.

## STANDARDIZATION

What measurement principles do we need to keep in mind in the assessment process? The reason that we assess is to permit us to describe a person and to compare that person either with himself on some previous or future occasion, or to compare him with some group of people. Therefore, we need to know that any measurement technique which will be used in the assessment has been studied with regard to an appropriate sample so that the data we obtain for that individual can be compared to the standardization sample. This principle refers to the representativeness of the sample.

Sometimes the same instrument has been studied with regard to a number of different samples, as in the case with the MMPI (Minnesota Multiphasic Personality Inventory). The literature will contain a number of different manuals describing the samples and findings relevant to them. In those cases the practitioner must observe comparison with the correct sample in order to interpret findings appropriately. While this sounds simple-minded, errors do occur when readers hurriedly skip over descriptions of samples and search for rules of interpretation. For example, one MMPI handbook is based on patients in VA hospitals (Gilberstadt & Duker, 1965), while another deals with adolescents and adults from a much broader part of the population (Marks, Seeman, & Haller, 1974). Since most VA patients are men, it would be a mistake to use a VA sample as the basis of describing a female patient or an adolescent.

It is often the case, particularly with instruments devised for use with children, that the standardization sample really includes several sub-samples. The Wechsler instruments which will be reviewed in the chapter on intellectual assessment are good examples of how representativeness is achieved for such cases. In order to insure a representative sample the first step is to decide what major dimensions characterize the sample.

In child assessment procedures *age* is an important variable. Age itself is seldom important, but because of developmental changes which occur through time, any instrument which spans an age range must include subjects across that age range in its standardization sample. Likewise, because sample data exist which indicate that subjects from homes of different *socioeconomic levels* may perform differently, a range of socioeconomic levels must be included in the standardization sample. *Ethnic background* and *geographical location* have also been found to be variables which are related to subjects' performance on some instruments. In order to insure adequate standardization for comparison purposes, an adequate sampling of both ethnic backgrounds and of urban-rural locations is necessary. Since school systems vary, it is important to include a sampling of variables relative to school systems (e.g., size of school) in standardization of instruments related to school performance (e.g., achievement tests). *Sex* differences have been found for some kinds of performance. Regardless of whether these differences appear because of genetic or cultural reasons, it is important to include both male and female subjects in the standardization samples. Other variables may be pertinent for special tests, e.g., a range of children from very retarded to very bright or a sampling of children who have particular disabilities (deaf children or children with visual handicaps). In all cases the *number* of subjects used in the standardization sample must be large enough to obtain data which satisfy psychometric criteria for the establishment of adequate estimates of reliability and validity.

Several different methods have been used to sample groups for the purpose of standardization. One method applies random sampling with post hoc analyses which describe the parameters of the sample. A frequent method, as in the case of the Wechsler instruments, is that of the stratified random sampling. This insures that a given number of subjects can be selected representing each of the dimensions of interest, which is important for establishing norms. While not quite as desirable for psychometric reasons, the stratified random sampling method does insure that no dimension will be neglected and that the cost of standardization can be held within given limits.

Since the purpose of the standardization process is the acquisition of normative data for the purpose of comparing either groups or individuals to the standardization sample, some methods of comparison have been developed. Convenient practices insure that comparison can be made, which permits interpretation of the scores obtained by individuals on the instruments employed. In practice this has resulted in the use of transformations of the subject's raw scores to some kind of standard scores which may facilitate the comparisons to be made. Since standard scores may set the numerical value of the mean and standard deviation to represent the characteristics of the standardization sample (and since these values may vary with size and other parameters of the standardization sample), one cannot always assume comparability across different tests. Such comparability is legitimate only when the distributions of the standardization samples are comparable. As a result of the need to establish better means of comparison, a common practice has been to use standard scores expressed in terms of a transformed distribution which fits the normal curve. This is the case with the Wechsler Intelligence Scales. The deviation IQ concepts represent scores in terms of a distribution which has a mean of 100 and a standard deviation of 15. Various other types of scores are employed for a variety of tests and comparison purposes. For a fuller discussion of these types of scores, the reader is referred to Anastasi (1976).

An important point for the reader of reports in which several different tests have been used and which indicate different IQ scores is that the comparison of these scores will depend upon the equivalence of the scale units used in each test. If the tests have different standard deviations, even though the scores are presented relative to a mean of 100, it will be necessary for the reader to compare test scores relative to the different standard deviations before assuming that true change in performance has been indicated.

## RELIABILITY

Aside from chance variations which stem from irrelevant factors, it is desirable for scores obtained on a psychometric test to be stable, given certain circumstances related to the test itself or reflecting certain consistencies with regard to the person taking the test. The object is to reduce chance variation (error variance) to a minimum and to construct an instrument which measures accurately and consistently. Various approaches are used to derive estimates of reliability (expressed in terms of correlations). *Test-retest reliability* is the coefficient used to estimate the stability of scores likely to be received by the same person taking the same instrument on two different occasions. While the interest interval in adulthood may be lengthy, shorter intervals are desirable for instruments which are used for the assessment of children. Because the child is growing and developing, it is expected that the child's score on developmental instruments will rise between one occasion and the next. In considering test-retest reliabilities for children's tests, we need to have estimates based on a time interval that reduces, as much as possible, the likelihood of obtaining practice effects, while also reducing the likelihood that any change in scores is really due to the child's acquisition of knowledge and skills.

Another form of reliability which is relevant for tests measuring a specific trait or ability or including a broad range of material is *split-half reliability*. This comprises one index of content consistency and one measure of internal consistency. Test users will need to decide how important it is to have content consistency and/or internal consistency and select instruments on the basis of estimates of these features. (See Anastasi, 1976, and Wiggins, 1973, for fuller discussion.)

Parallel forms are developed for many tests so that an individual may be retested using similar but not identical content material. The *alternate-form* reliability estimate is based upon scores obtained on the two forms of the test. Of course, the intertest interval should not be too long or development may result in a lower estimate due to the child's increased knowledge or skill. While the use of parallel forms may reduce the practice effects which are prominent in some test-retest situations, interpretation of results should not ignore the fact that similar content is used and that generalization of problem-solving approaches will probably attenuate rather than eliminate practice effects. The use of parallel forms is especially helpful in situations in which pre- and post-testing with some intervening treatment occurs. Such situations may involve the use of a reading program with reading testing, or intellectual evaluation pre- and post-surgically.

All of these reliability estimates are based upon the performance of groups of subjects tested as part of the standardization procedures or in studies conducted especially for the purpose of obtaining normative data. Aside from knowing that the content is consistent, the alternate forms comparable, and that test-retest estimates are equivalent, it is important to know how much variability is to be expected in the performance of individual scores on a test when describing various estimates of its reliability. The estimate appropriate for the determination of individual variation in a score is the *standard error of measurement* or the standard error of a score.

The reader and user of tests will need to consider what types of reliability are most necessary for the purposes for which the test will be used. However, reliability may be quite high and still an instrument may be unsatisfactory because it fails to measure validly.


## VALIDITY

To the untrained person the most obvious type of validity is *face validity*. This is a term indicating that the material in a test appears to be a reasonable kind of content with regard to the purpose for which it was intended. However, face validity is subjectively determined and the appearance of suitability of material may be deceptive in that it may not result in high objective levels of validity. An example of face validity would be the use of a sorting test for a job which requires sorting as an activity. We now turn to other forms of validity which are objectively determined. (See *Standards for Educational and Psychological Tests*, 1974, and Anastasi, 1976, for more detail.)

Three principal types of validity which should be considered when using or selecting an instrument are content validity, criterion-related validity, and construct validity. Knowledge of what purposes these various estimates of validity serve will be necessary to understand manuals and to interpret findings appropriately.

*Content validity* insures that the instrument samples the material which is of interest, such as a skill or basic knowledge in an area. Many credentialing procedures depend upon content validity (e.g., knowledge of anatomy) with respect to a given area of knowledge. However, actual job performance may not be reflected as a function of the basic knowledge, even though that knowledge may be a prerequisite for the job (e.g., surgery). For this reason some critics of credentialing processes object to the use of content validity as a basis for examination procedures. Even more inappropriate would be the use of tests using content that is irrelevant to the function that will be important in later performance.

*Criterion-related validity* refers to an estimate based on an independent measure against which a desired performance may be compared, e.g., vocabulary scores may be highly related to achievement scores in science. In this type of validity procedure the content may not always be obviously related to the performance. Appropriately, we note that the criterion for concurrent validity, a form of criterion-related validity, is always available at the time of testing. This form of criterion-related validity is useful when it permits one to select a cost-efficient substitute for a longer procedure which has been used to provide the basic data of interest, e.g., a briefer reading measure has been shown to have high concurrent validity with respect to a longer instrument. Predictive validity, another form of criterion-related validity, refers to the ability of one measure to anticipate future performance on some other important measure, e.g., whether a test of intellectual function will actually predict performance in a program for gifted children. Most manuals and test reports will provide some description of the measures selected to establish validity, but the reader will need to reflect upon the propriety of the variables. Consultation with Mental Measurement Yearbooks (Buros, 1965, 1972, 1978) and other reviews of the materials will be invaluable if the prospective user of an instrument is unfamiliar with some of the clinical and psychometric problems which should be considered.

*Construct validity* is the term which indicates that a test is actually measuring some abstract descriptor, which may be theoretical in nature, such as anxiety or intelligence. Often test manuals report correlations between a particular instrument and other instruments which are purported to measure the same domain as that test. These correlations are reported as evidence of construct validity. Still other methods commonly used include cluster analyses, factor analyses, and other statistical approaches which identify relationships among items that are thought to support evidence of the construct in question. For example, clusters based on measures of reading and related performances may support neurologically-based estimates of dyslexic symptoms, such as trouble with spatial relationships, and problems with phonetic skills.

Developmental differences are used as evidence of construct validity, particularly for assessment instruments which are devised to evaluate the performance of children. Thus differences in the ability to manipulate certain types of content at different ages become criteria for establishing construct validity for some instruments. The appearance of certain types of verbal performance, as on the Stanford-Binet, would be evidence of developmental changes which are indicative of cognitive growth.

Given the level of precision which is possible in the construction of tests, it is somewhat ironic that we have not really needed many tests to become aware of clinical populations. That is because the social and academic consequences of the problems defining these populations are the bases upon which they have been identified initially. However, once we have become aware of the existence of such groups, clinical methods of evaluation and tests have played very important roles in our ability to detect less extreme forms of deviance and in our ability to detect whether interventions have been effective. We turn now to a discussion of how assessment procedures may contribute to the identification of psychological deviance discussed in the previous chapters.

## SELECTION OF ASSESSMENT METHODS

Selection of assessment methods is a process which begins as soon as the psychologist receives the first information from a referral source. Let us recall the cases discussed in the introduction. Each of these cases initiates questions and hypotheses about potential alternatives which may need to be explored diagnostically. A parent who asks for help with a child who is hyperactive will confront the psychologist with a different set of questions than a state agency seeking consultation to arbitrate a custody case. Even so, very few referral questions are entirely clear at the onset, and sometimes they evolve into more complex possibilities before the assessment has been completed. The clinician is wise to begin by taking referral questions at face value, but to consider other possibilities as the material develops. No purely mechanical use of assessment procedures will substitute for the active clinical judgment of the psychologist.

An essential part of the selection process is the clarification of the referral question. Thus, developmentally it makes sense to think about the integrity of function available to the child. If there are questions about the input from sensory modalities or processing of input by the brain in terms of associative processes or expressive responses, the neuropsychological soundness of the child is in question. Without an intact and functional nervous system, neither measures of intellectual function nor school achievement will be expected to survive without deficit. In such cases the assessment process will lean toward evaluation of these areas before any other questions can be clarified. In other cases no clear-cut neuropsychological questions enter into the picture. yet the possibility still exists that they may bear upon the child's behavior and problems, e.g., conduct problems associated with hyperactivity. In such cases the questions may center around whether the child has the capacity to inhibit behaviors, attend properly, and direct behavior appropriately. Given that all of these questions can be answered affirmatively enough, there will be questions relating to the personality and attitudes of the child which may be the primary focus of the assessment.

In some cases children suffer school problems which may be determined either by poor intellectual functioning or by motivational problems. Because these aspects of the child's functioning are so intertwined, especially once the child is identified as an academic problem, neither aspect of behavior should be ignored in the assessment process. Even when special class placement or schooling is recommended, children may take several weeks of adjustment to the new atmosphere, because they have previously developed such negative attitudes toward themselves that they are initially discouraged and unable to take advantage of more suitable learning conditions. Given good intelligence, children who are underachievers because of learning problems face different obstacles from those who have motivational problems. Poor performance on achievement tests may fail to differentiate these groups of children, while other cognitive and personality tests may be helpful to the clinician who is trying to decide whether special attention needs to be paid to the structure of the learning situation or to the social supports which reinforce motivational aspects of performance.

At the other end of the spectrum are children who are seen as having suffered major forms of psychopathology. One of the authors was asked to assess an adolescent inpatient with reference to whether she was schizophrenic. The staff suspected that she was schizophrenic because she was very concrete in her thinking and seemed to have poor judgment. Upon examination she was found to have a Wechsler score below 75, to be impulsive, and to be in a home situation in which she was inadequately supervised. There were no signs of psychosis or thought disorder. This young woman was functioning as well as she could given her intellectual endowment, her slightly impulsive temperament, and her inadequately supervised social life. Her thinking was somewhat concrete, but this was a function of her intellectual ability and not of psychopathology. Likewise her poor judgment was related to her poor ability to abstract and generalize and to her needs for more immediate gratification than could be properly obtained in many social situations. Personality testing revealed that this young woman was eager to please, unimaginative, and striving for an independence that she was unable to negotiate because of her limited cognitive abilities.

In general, if one can rule out neuropsychological problems, one should next examine the question of cognitive problems, including intellectual functioning. Given that the cognitive processes are intact and that no special learning problems exist, a variety of behavior problems remain to be investigated. As we saw in Chapter 2, these behavior problems can be investigated through life history, observation, and formal assessment procedures that include tests, questionnaires, and behavior rating measures.

Sometimes a question may arise as to the child's ability to work independently. Some indication may be given that the child is impulsive or lacks motivation and requires an examiner to keep on task or involved in performing. For example, in the case of achievement testing, instruments which involve direct examiner interaction with the child will likely provide different levels of performance than those which require the child to work only with the material. In some cases one is interested in the maximum level the child can attain for purposes of assessing the highest level of function or achievement. However, at other times one is more interested in how the child is likely to perform under conditions which do not exact his optimum performance. In those cases the choice of instruments would exclude those which provide a higher level of examiner interaction than usual.

At other times, the choice of instruments may depend upon the reliability of informants. If it is believed that parents and teachers are good observers and recorders, it may be helpful to obtain parent questionnaires and checklists. However, these instruments are virtually worthless if the informant is either a poor observer, biased, or unmotivated. In such cases a few minutes of interview will usually provide one with an indication of whether gathering the paper and pencil material is worth the effort. If not, and if the clinician cannot obtain information which is helpful from the informant, there is no choice but to spend enough time in observation and contact with others to collect whatever data are necessary for some reasonable interpretation of the assessment material. Occasionally, one will be unable to obtain information on current functioning.

## HYPOTHESES

The process of hypothesis formation begins with the referral questions and continues throughout the course of the evaluation. The entire diagnostic process is concerned with hypothesis formation, hypothesis-testing, and the integration of information which leads to further hypothesis formation, some of which may be concerned with the prediction of criterion behavior. After the referral information has generated questions, the clinician formulates some most probable hypotheses. Usually, intake interview will establish some of these hypotheses as more tenable than others. Some of the original hypotheses may be discarded entirely due to information about life history or to observations made by the clinician during the course of the interview. Finally, after all the sources of data have been considered, the formulation of the results and the integration of all the material should lead to an interpretation which best fits all the material which has been obtained about the person. This interpretation requires not only the input from various data sources but also the clinician's judgment and weighting of the material so as to derive the most probable account relative to the patient's behavior and attitudes.

The importance of the hypothesis formation process is recognized as the distinguishing feature of clinical prediction (Wiggins, 1973). In the sense that many formulations represent clinical judgments about individuals which imply predictability of their behavior and adjustment to particular treatment methods, the hypothesis formation process can be seen as an integral part of clinical prediction applied to assessment. Whereas the hypothesis used in statistical prediction applies to groups of people and is concerned with nomothetic laws, hypothesis formation applied to clinical prediction is often concerned with idiopathic relationships. Comparison of material generated both within and across data sources provides the clinician with something approaching consistency estimates for a given individual. Whereas the nomothetic laws and actuarial data gathered for *groups* permit standard scores and prediction equations, the consistency of the *individual's* performance across and within data sources provides some expectation that that individual is predictable within certain limits, in terms of personal characteristics.

Comparison of the individual with group data will permit some descriptions to be made (e.g., with regard to general level of intelligence and grade level achievement) where appropriate norm groups exist for comparative purposes. Discovery of consistent styles or conflicts, or perceptions provide information which must generally be judged clinically. To the extent that data are available on groups which also apply to the individual, some comparisons can be made. Even when statistical data on norm groups are available, the complexity of clinical material may require integration of more material than can be accomplished appropriately on a statistical basis. In such cases, the clinician's experience and judgment serve as the best approach to the task. Suppose, for example, we have a professor of Sanskrit who has been referred for assessment. While ethnic background and occupation are often important descriptors of norm groups, we find that we have none for comparative purposes for this person. Consequently, if no more suitable group norms exist, the clinician will rely more heavily upon clinical experience and judgment for interpretation of performance on assessment instruments.

## GUIDE KEY TO SELECTION OF INSTRUMENTS

The assessment process almost always begins with referral information and the clinician usually arranges an interview prior to deciding on further steps to be taken. Our guide key consists of several illustrated decision trees which reflect the points at which the clinician elects various general assessment methods. We will present these decision trees and discuss the decision points and issues involved in selection of specific assessment procedures.

*Mental Retardation*

Take, for example, the decision tree which applies to mental retardation. At each level the clinician must decide whether further information at the next level will be helpful on the basis of data obtained at the previous level. This decision tree may be represented as shown below:

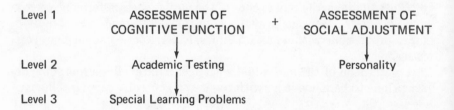

| Level 1 | ASSESSMENT OF COGNITIVE FUNCTION | + | ASSESSMENT OF SOCIAL ADJUSTMENT |
| --- | --- | --- | --- |
| Level 2 | Academic Testing | | Personality |
| Level 3 | Special Learning Problems | | |

At Level 1 we note that, following the referral and interview, the clinician administers an individual intelligence test and a measure of social adjustment. Observations and data from these tests may reveal areas of weakness and possible sensory, motor, or cognitive problems which require further investigation. The examiner chooses to assess the academic achievement or readiness of the child and finds some specific areas of weakness leading to questions of deficit which are best studied through the use of other clinical instruments. The clinician wonders whether the child has some visual-motor problems. Some of the tests which are employed separate out visual perception and visual-motor performance and indicate that the child is able to perceive accurately but is not able to reproduce what he sees accurately. The information will be useful in constructing a learning situation and curriculum which takes advantage of this child's good visual perception and his handicap at expression through visual-motor channels. He may need, for example, to learn to compensate for some problems by using oral rather than written or spatially represented modes of expression.

At Level 1 of our decision tree we assess social adjustment. This is accomplished by the administration of some measure, e.g., AAMD Adaptive Behavior Scale, which will provide us with information about the child's general level of development, special problems, self-care, social development, and other functions such as language and motor development. Based on the measure of social adjustment we have some indication of whether more psychopathological problems need to be considered. We are free to continue with other methods of assessment should those be indicated, e.g., projective play. You will notice that in using this decision tree model we are not specifying that some standard battery of tests be used given situation A, while another standard battery of tests be used in situation B. That is because the decision points will always be negotiated on the basis of specific characteristics of a given child and in some cases one specific assessment instrument may be indicated whereas in other cases one of several different instruments may be equally appropriate. Our decision tree model illustrates the types of questions that are being entertained by the clinician. At Level 1, the clinician asks "How bright is this child?" and "How well adjusted is this child?" If there are indicators of maladjustment (on the right side of the decision tree), the clinician may next ask, at Level 2, "How does the child feel about himself or other people who are important to him?" If intelligence is impaired, the clinician may ask at Level 2, "How much has this child learned?" or "What might this child's educational achievement level indicate about school placement or type of classroom?" If cognitive and academic impairments suggest specific modality impairment or learning problems, the clinician will ask, at Level 3, "What specific impairments may be affecting the learning and achievement process?"

The clinician may refer to later chapters which include reviews and critiques of some of the most commonly employed assessment procedures to help in the selection of specific instruments to be used with a given child. Of course, in some cases specialized instruments for quite specific purposes may be needed which are not commonly employed. In those cases, the same type of decision process will continue but the clinician will need to use judgment and consultation in selecting these more esoteric methods.

## Underachievement

A frequent reason for assessment of children is that parents have cause to believe that a child is bright but not working up to his or her level in terms of academic achievement. This underachievement may be either chronic or acute in terms of duration. Let us follow a decision tree which illustrates assessment for scholastic underachievement. Remember that you have received a referral and already held an interview. Let us suppose that neither the interview nor the referral information was very enlightening. Each source of information affirms the belief that this child is probably bright but not achieving up to potential.

In this decision tree we find that the clinician first asks, "How bright is this child?" (Level 1). Assessment of intellectual function must confirm the impression that the child is intellectually competent and at a level which fulfills the expectations of the concerned adults. Sometimes a well-socialized child from a relatively high socioeconomic background will impress those around him as being brighter than he actually is. In such cases the child may be achieving at the best possible level, but

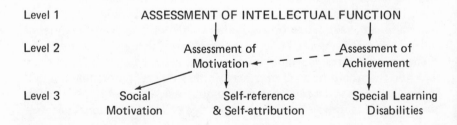

parents or teachers may have the impression that the child is an under-achiever. While this is not usually the case, it happens often enough so that the possibility should be ruled out, especially when the child is the youngest of several children who are bright and achieving.

Once the intellectual level has been verified, the clinician must decide whether to evaluate the possibility that the underachievement is a function of 1) inability to achieve due to specific learning problems, 2) motivational problems which have curbed interest, or 3) some combination of the first two alternatives. It may be that the child will perform well on achievement tests (Level 2), although performing poorly in school. In that case the clinician can rule out special learning problems and would not test for those types of disabilities. On the other hand, if the child does not perform well in school and on achievement tests, the clinician may wish to gather more information about the visual, auditory, and verbal processes which are necessary for learning retention and application of information to proceed normally. Let us assume that intellectual assessment indicates that the child is bright and at the level expected by the adults who are concerned about him. We are now in the position of investigating the left side of the decision tree. If achievement test data show no impairment, the motivational issues gain even greater prominence. If the achievement test data show impairments, the motivational issues still need to be investigated, although it remains to be seen whether they are primary or a secondary function of achievement problems. History and referral information may raise the question of motivation. Given an intact IQ, the issue of motivation is raised by the clinician in questions such as, "Is the child responding to situational or peer problems?" or "Is this child responding to feelings and attitudes he has developed about himself?" These questions are raised at Level 2, partly as a function of previous interview data and partly as a result of performance on the assessment of intellectual functioning (attitudes of inadequacy, defiance, etc.). At Level 3 we can use behavior problem checklists and parent questionnaires, teacher reports, and social history to evaluate the child's social development and relationships. If the child is socially adjusted and without major problems, we still need to examine self-reference material (projective tests) to determine whether conflict, poor self-esteem, or other motivational determinants of poor school performance are operating.

In the absence of confirming evidence from either achievement or motivational data, hypotheses are directed toward the school situation for some explanation. For example, overcrowded conditions or personality conflicts with teachers may be part of the problem. If consultation with teachers and parents is at variance with regard to the way the child is perceived, we may be able to find an answer in this difference. Most often, however, the assessment will be informative and helpful as to whether a learning problem is primary or a motivational problem is the main contributor to the child's underachievement.

## Neuropsychological Problems

Neuropsychological impairment may underlie the presenting complaints that often cause parents to refer their children for clinical assessment. In particular, many children who are referred for problems with learning, for hyperactivity and distractibility, for underachievement, or for retardation may be suffering from some underlying neuropsychological deficit.

Neuropsychological evaluation is complex and often not performed in many mental health clinics which do not have enough cases to make it worthwhile to devote staff resources for that purpose. However, for many mental health professionals who work in clinical settings and for private practitioners, enough sensitivity to the identification of cases which may require further specialized testing is a necessary clinical skill. Most clinicians who have not had specialized training in neuropsychology but who work with children will encounter assessment cases with histories of trauma, compromised development due to complications of birth or pregnancy, or special learning problems which may reflect neuropsychological problems. Without specialized training these clinicians need to obtain basic information about the anatomy and function of the brain. Walsh (1978) or some other general neuropsychology survey will supply survey information.

With both mental retardation and underachievement we enter the decision tree with an intellectual assessment. However, in neuropsychological cases there is also likely to be some disturbance of cognitive functions. Therefore, because the intelligence test is such a good screening device for cognitive functions, the practice is usually to begin assessment with an intellectual evaluation. The decision of where to begin at Level 2 of the decision tree will depend on the nature and pattern of results in intellectual evaluation. Also, the clinician is in the position of trying to determine whether the child has acquired basic functions on schedule, insofar as maturation and normal development would lead one to expect, or whether any noted discrepancies are due to deviant or disturbed processes which interfere with normal behavior.

Let us suppose that a child referred for evaluation has a known reading problem. His IQ test indicates normal-to-above-normal intelligence and no evidence of distractibility. Some difficulties are noticed on the block design and object assembly, which rate lower than other subtests, and on coding, which is poor because of very slow performance.

At Level 2 the clinician administers a reading test because reading has been identified as a problem. The examiner learns that the child is able to comprehend when read to by another person but he makes errors when he has to read either silently or aloud. The oral reading performance indicates that the child is reversing some letters and short words, possibly indicating some perceptual-motor problems, but an equivocal sign as far as dyslexia is concerned. At Level 3, based on both the IQ test and the reading test the clinician decides to administer drawings and copy of designs to test the hypothesis that the poor reading is based on visual-motor problems. Upon confirmation of the presence of such problems, the clinician elects next to determine whether these are primarily visual or motor problems. Motor tests prove normal and the child's performance indicates visual perception problems with figure-ground relationships and spatial relationships. These signs indicate enough deficit of function for the reading problem to be viewed as likely associated with neuropsychological dysfunction and not due primarily to motivation or curriculum problems.

The complexity of organization and the neural pathways involved leave the possibility that the same function (e.g., reading) can be compromised for many different reasons and in different manners. To know that a child has a reading problem does not inform the clinician whether the basis for the problem is neuropsychological, or if so, what functions may be involved. The child who has problems with organization and fluency suffers a different problem from the child who has poor visual-motor coordination, although they may both be poor readers. While our knowledge of how to help these children remains far below our ability

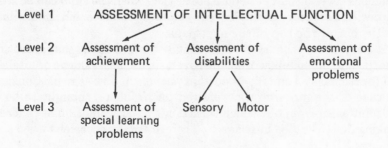

to identify them, it would be unfortunate if we did not approach the child in terms of specific strengths and problems characteristic of his performance. Disabilities may be so obvious that special achievement testing is unnecessary, but specialized tests which yield more direct neurological data may be appropriate, e.g., sensory and motor testing.

The specific tests which are used in neuropsychological assessment depend upon the known relationship of the task to the various kinds of brain function required for performance on the task. Most brain functions cannot be inferred from single tests, even when they require highly specialized function. Even if only visual tests are involved, for example, differences occur depending on whether the task requires construction, memory, or perception, and whether the stimulus requires the subject to use spatial relationships or separation from a background, permits the use of verbal labels, or is abstract. The hypotheses which direct the clinician to use one or another of these instruments will depend upon both the presenting complaint and the different structures of the brain which might be required to process the functions related to the reported deficit.

*Personality and Behavior Problems*

Aside from school problems, the reason why most parents seek assessment services for their children is that they are concerned about the child's behavior or the development of personality problems. Some parents are simply worried that their children are unhappy or do not have friends, but more often the complaints result from problems first noticed in the parent-child or sibling relationships. Other children are referred because of conduct problems which interfere with school performance or which have gotten them into trouble with the law or with other social institutions. In these cases, the clinician will find interviews with both the family and the child of immense importance. Often the parents and other adult caretakers can be asked to fill out checklists, questionnaires, and other material prior to the interview so that the clinician has several sources of data at the time when the child can be seen. The decision tree for personality and conduct problems will usually look like the one at the top of the next page.

At Level 2 the primary concern usually centers about the separation of social and personality problems; even so, the assessment of intellectual functions is an equally important part of the assessment. Consider the case of the girl who was referred for problems thought to be of schizophrenic origin but which turned out to be a function of concrete thinking due to limited intelligence. There are many occasions when chil-

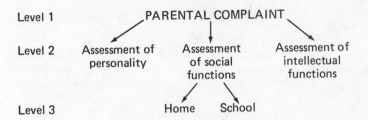

Level 1                       PARENTAL COMPLAINT

Level 2      Assessment of      Assessment      Assessment of
              personality        of social       intellectual
                                 functions        functions

Level 3                        Home    School

dren are easily led into antisocial behavior because they are not able to think independently and are eager to please. At the other extreme, children who are very bright and bored in school settings may get into trouble as they attempt to amuse themselves.

At Level 3, the clinician may find that one or both of the paths should be explored based on data from previous levels. If social behavior requires assessment, a variety of parent questionnaire and checklist material may be used, as well as teachers' reports or other data which will be helpful. If personality factors seem relevant, projective testing or special aptitudes and interests may be helpful.

Guide keys for four major classes of assessment problems have now been presented. In the case of mental retardation we saw that cognitive and social assessment was the primary concern. With underachievement, cognitive and motivational issues each could account for the problems or they could jointly produce the referral complaints. While neuropsychological problems may require the most complex set of decisions because of the cognitive and emotional patterns produced by brain dysfunction, in practice the questions may be resolved more simply, as data at Level 1 often rule out the need for further testing of a specific type. Personality and conduct problems often center on psychosocial instruments but should not ignore the basic intellectual endowment of the child as a factor in the child's adjustment.

## APPLICATION OF DECISION TREE MODEL
## TO A CLINICAL CASE

The special characteristics of each child and the special characteristics of the assessment instruments will help the clinician elect the most suitable specific test or technique. We will now illustrate how the decision tree model may be applied to a clinical case. Let us recall the decision tree for underachievement.

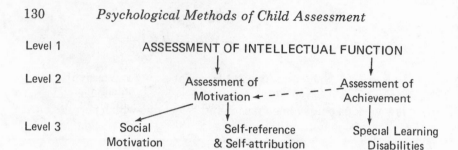

We will assume that a WISC-R has been administered at Level 1, and that the child has a Full Scale IQ of 94, Verbal IQ of 100, and Performance IQ of 90, with the following subtest scale scores:

| | | | |
|---|---|---|---|
| Information | 10 | Picture Completion | 12 |
| Similarities | 12 | Picture Arrangement | 9 |
| Arithmetic | 7 | Block Design | 9 |
| Comprehension | 11 | Object Assembly | 8 |
| Vocabulary | 10 | Coding | 6 |
| Digits | 6 | | |

What are the decision points for the application of the model? First we note that the child's IQ is well within the normal range and that there is no sizeable discrepancy between verbal and performance scores, which would ordinarily suggest integrity for both types of function. However, in this case the value of the Distractibility Factor (Kaufman, 1979) raises the question of the child's ability to function proficiently arithmetically. Had there been a significant verbal-performance discrepancy, we would have to entertain various hypotheses associated with specific learning problems which might have a neuropsychological basis.

Consider the right side of the decision tree. We want to investigate more fully the arithmetic question. Before deciding which specific instruments should be employed, we should analyze the errors made by the child on the Distractibility subtests (Arithmetic, Digits, and Coding) to determine if computational problems, concepts, speed, sequencing, or anxiety appear to have affected performance adversely. In this case, let us assume that the child worked steadily, attended, and showed no signs of anxiety or distractibility. However, he was slow and achieved all items up to the point where he was at his ceiling on subtests. This rules out distractibility as the determinant of his performance and suggests that we should examine his arithmetic performance in detail, since he may lack either computational skills, concepts or both.

Not all achievement tests are constructed so as to provide data on both concepts and computational skills. Therefore the clinician will need to review various achievement tests and select one which permits data to be obtained for both of these domains. The clinician should not be misled that because an achievement test has a mathematics subtest, it will provide the relevant data (see Chapter 7).

Now observe the left side of the decision tree. We can outline possible motivational questions which should be approached. From other testing we may wonder whether the child works well when interacting socially but not when working independently. This question can be resolved by administering two achievement tests which are so structured that the comparison can be made. A second motivational question may concern the child's feelings of inadequacy and failure; a variety of projective tests may be suitable for this type of evaluation (see Chapter 9). Perhaps the child does not get along well with his teacher or peers and does not function well in specific class settings because of these social factors, in which case questionnaires, checklists, and observations can be used to investigate this possibility (see Chapter 10).

Now, as an overview with the possible assessment instruments chosen, return to the decision tree. At each level the clinician has made a decision concerning whether to collect data. If he has chosen to collect data, a number of possible assessment techniques should have been compared, and the instrument most suitable for this child in terms of type of material, age range, normative data, and type of interaction required should have been chosen.

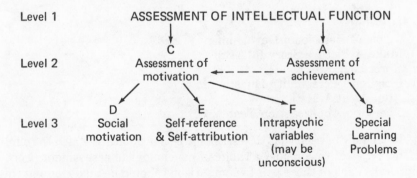

We find that at Level 2, Point A, considering only the most commonly used tests reviewed in Chapter 7, we have the following possible choices:

Metropolitan Readiness Tests
Metropolitan Achievement Tests
Peabody Individual Achievement Test
Diagnostic Reading Scales
Stanford Achievement Test
Woodcock-Johnson Psycho-Educational Battery.

If one is interested in a wide-range achievement test, there are several possibilities. If one wants an individually administered test, there are only two possibilities from the list. If one wants separate scores for mathematics computation and mathematics concepts, there is only one choice. On the other hand, if one wants to focus on reading tests, all of these instruments have some measure of reading. Other questions would be required to narrow the choice among them. The results of tests at this level will suggest further tests on specific learning problems at Level 3, Point B.

At Level 2, Point C, clinical judgment based on interview material, referral questions and information, together with the child's performance on the instrument used at Point A, leads the clinician to elect one, two, or all of the succeeding paths of inquiry. At Level 3, Point E, the possible choices reviewed in this book include seven or eight checklists and several parent questionnaires. At Point F, the possible choices include a variety of projective tests assessing intrapsychic variables (some of which may be at an unconscious level), including:

Incomplete Sentences
Drawings
Tasks of Emotional Development (TED)
Make A Picture Story (MAPS)
Rorschach
Children's Personality Questionnaire
Adolescent MMPI
Thematic Apperception Test.

It can now be seen that the decision tree has points at which the clinician may elect to consider a range of psychological assessment procedures. At each of these points comparisons should be made among the various instruments to decide which are most appropriate for the particular child being seen and with regard to the specific questions which need to be answered. Diagnostic problems for referral questions of underachievement served as the illustration, but other types of referral questions could be illustrated in similar detail.

## REFERENCES

Anastasi, A. *Psychological Testing, 4th Edition*. New York: Macmillan, 1976.
Buros, O. K. *The Sixth Mental Measurement Yearbook*. Highland Park, N.J.: Gryphon Press, 1965.
Buros, O. K. *The Seventh Mental Measurement Yearbook*. Highland Park, N.J.: Gryphon Press, 1972.
Buros, O. K. *The Eighth Mental Measurement Yearbook*. Highland Park, N.J.: Gryphon Press, 1978.
Gilberstadt, H. & Duker, J. *A Handbook for Clinical and Actuarial MMPI Interpretation*. Philadelphia: W. B. Saunders, 1965.
Kaufman, A. S. *Intelligent Testing with the WISC-R*. New York: Wiley-Interscience, 1979.
Marks, P. A., Seeman, W., & Haller, D. L. *The Actuarial Use of the MMPI with Adolescents and Adults*. Baltimore: Williams & Wilkins, 1974.
*Standards for Educational and Psychological Tests*. Washington, D.C.: American Psychological Association, 1974.
Walsh, K. W. *Neuropsychology: A Clinical Approach*. Edinburgh: Churchill Livingstone, 1978.
Wiggins, J. S. *Personality and prediction: Principles of Personality Assessment*. Reading, MA: Addison-Wesley, 1973.

# PART II

# Methods of
# Child Assessment

# CHAPTER 6

# *Intelligence Tests*

It would be very comforting if there were some universal guidelines for the selection and best use of intelligence tests, which are major components of psychological evaluations of children. Since no such guidelines exist, we will review the current tools of the trade and discuss some of the major considerations relevant to their use in clinical situations. One of the primary concerns of the clinician is to get the child's cooperation so as to arrive at the best estimate of his level of function, which includes the manner in which the child approaches the work presented through the test procedure.

One often has to use one's own judgment as to the most suitable clinical method of child assessment, including which intelligence test to employ. In a teaching clinic one has a little more time and freedom to compare techniques, to learn what is more likely to work, given certain conditions, and to take into account more thoroughly the handicaps that some children suffer. But for the busy practitioner, for the clinician who is only beginning to see children, and for the examiner about to try an instrument for the first time, this luxury is usually not in the realm of possibility.

In this chapter we will present a synopsis of the source, general purpose, format and content, administration, scoring, standardization data, and critique for each instrument covered. These synopses are arranged for a quick review of the instrument so that a clinician can determine the characteristics of a particular test and if it will fit the diagnostic purpose in mind.

Due to the state of the art and the materials available, it will sometimes happen that more than one assessment procedure is available. Here the clinician who is relatively unfamiliar with child assessment procedures may feel in a quandary. We have, therefore, made some comparisons, highlighting issues leading to possible choices among the instruments and we have illustrated some frequently encountered clinical situations in which choices have to be made.

We have chosen for review only individually administered tests, because of their generally desirable psychometric qualities and because the clinical method utilizes observation of the child as a basic source of information. Even with very well constructed tests, observation of the child's behavior provides important, sometimes crucial, information. The clinician will want to know, at the very least, whether the child is systematic, impulsive, competitive, oppositional, or approval-seeking. These are only a few of the factors which may affect performance on tests of intellectual functioning. It should be reemphasized that tests are standardized situations which permit observation of both on-task behavior and style. To the clinician both of these types of data are significant.

Because clinical observation relating to motivational and cognitive style are not available for group tests, and because many group tests have lower reliabilities, results from group tests are generally accorded less weight in the assessment process than data derived from individually administered procedures. However, clinicians will often receive reports from schools which include results of group-administered tests. Basic references such as Anastasi (1976), Buros (1978), and Cronbach (1960) may be helpful for specific critiques of group instruments and for measurement issues.

Our choice of instruments includes an infant assessment procedure (the Bayley Scale), which is often helpful in assessment of children when an early baseline of development is needed, as is the case in many pre-adoption studies. Likewise, many researchers use the Bayley to determine whether a child is developing normally. In cases of medical disabilities, the scale may be used to compare the infant's performance to determine whether improvement or loss of function is significant. We follow the Bayley with reviews of the Wechsler Scales (Preschool and Primary Scale of Intelligence, and the Wechsler Intelligence Scale for Children – Revised) and with the Stanford-Binet (1960 Revision, 1972 norms). We also review the Peabody Picture Vocabulary Test, which is widely (although sometimes inappropriately) used as a measure of intelligence, the Leiter International Performance Scale, the Hiskey-Nebraska, the Test of Nonverbal Intelligence, all of which are frequently used with children who have speech, language, and/or hearing impairments. We include the Culture Fair Intelligence Test. All of these tests are given primarily as supplementary procedures. There are often reasons why children's abilities to perform intellectually may be uncompromised, despite marked deprivation and physical handicaps. Many of these children will not have at their disposal information common to the culture and represented within the content of most intelligence tests. The clinician may want to evaluate the child so that the cultural component is minimized. The comparison of results from some of these supplementary procedures with the results from the Wechsler or the Binet may prove helpful. We will discuss these situations later in this chapter and also in Chapter 12.

In the information provided for each instrument reviewed, we will describe the purpose of the instrument and information on its administration and scoring and data on its standardization. The statistical information comes from test manuals, unless otherwise noted. Our critiques are based on personal experience and use of standard reference materials such as *Mental Measurement Yearbooks,* Anastasi (1976), and other relevant sources. In each description of a test, our purpose is to provide the reader with a brief review to determine whether the test itself might be helpful in the assessment. We do not intend to duplicate all of the information which can be found in manuals, nor to provide an exhaustive description of the information available on the tests.

## BAYLEY SCALES OF INFANT DEVELOPMENT

*Manual*

*Bayley Scales of Infant Development.* Bayley, N. New York: The Psychological Corporation, 1969. 757 Third Avenue, New York, N.Y. 10017.

*Purpose*

This scale is designed to ascertain the infant's developmental status and to determine the extent of any deviation from normal development. The test is designed for children from two months to 30 months of age.

*Format*

The test is made up of three parts: the Mental Scale (163 items), the Motor Scale (81 items), and the Infant Behavior Record (30 behaviors). The Mental Scale is designed to measure a variety of areas, some of which are sensory-perceptual acuities and discriminations, the acquisition of object constancy, and the beginning of verbal communication. For ease of administration and scoring, the areas in the manual concerning this scale are printed on yellow pages.

The Motor Scale is designed to measure the degree of control of the body, coordination of the large muscles, and fine manipulatory skills of hands and fingers. Instructions for this scale can also be easily found in the manual because they are printed on blue pages.

The Infant Behavior Record (IBR) is completed after the Mental and Motor Scales have been given. The IBR assesses the nature of the infant's social and objective orientations to his environment. Since the IBR differs from the other two scales in administration, it will be reviewed following their discussion.

*Administration*

Under optimal conditions administration takes approximately 45 minutes. For both the Mental and Motor Scales, the examiner establishes the child's basal and ceiling levels. The record form facilitates this process by having the test items arranged in order of difficulty. Beside each test item number is the age placement score in which 50% of the children tested will pass the item. Below this score are the age range values which provide estimates of the ages at which each item was passed by 5% and 95%, respectively, of the children in the standardization sample.

*Scoring*

The manual provides detailed criteria for scoring. Once the raw score (total number of items passed) is calculated, then a standard score can be obtained from tables printed in the manual. Both the standard score from the Mental Scale (Mental Development Index) and the Motor Scale (Psychomotor Developmental Index) have a mean of 100 and a standard deviation of 16. The standard score range of 50 to 150 covers more than three standard deviations on either side of the average Mental Development Index or Psychomotor Development Index.

*Standardization*

A stratified sample design based on the 1960 U.S. Census was used for the standardization of age norms. The sample was controlled for sex and race within each group, with further restrictions related to residence and education of the head of the household. In all, 1,262 children distributed in equal numbers across 14 age groups were used.

*Validity*

Both the Stanford-Binet and the Bayley were administered to 120 children aged 24, 27, and 30 months. The coefficient of correlation between the IQ obtained from the Stanford-Binet and the Mental Development Index was .57 for the children on whom the comparison was made for the six-month age overlap of the two tests.

*Reliability*

Split-half reliability was calculated by dividing both the Mental and Motor Scales into two equal parts. Raw scores for these half-tests were obtained for each of the 14 age groups of the standardization sample. The Mental Scale coefficients ranged from .81 to .93 with a median value of .88, and the Motor Scale coefficients ranged from .68 to .92 with a median value of .84. The standard error of measurement was obtained for both the Mental and Motor Scales. The $SE_m$ for the Mental Scale ranged from 4.2 to 6.9 standard score points; for the Motor Scale it ranged from 4.6 to 9.0.

The test-observer reliability in scoring was calculated on 90 eight-month-old infants by having a second examiner observe through a one-way mirror. An 89.4% agreement was found on the Mental Scale and a 93.4% agreement was found on the Motor Scale.

Test-retest reliability of one-week duration was done on 28 infants with a 76.4% agreement found on the Mental Scale and a 75.3% agreement found on the Motor Scale.

*Infant Behavior Record*

The IBR consists of a number of descriptive rating scales for behaviors characteristic of children up to 30 months of age. The behaviors include affective domains, motivational variables, and specific sensory experiences. The IBR record form is filled out after the Mental and

Motor Scales have been administered and usually just after the child has left. Inside the manual is a table of the distribution of ratings for each of the 14 age groups in the standardization sample. Also included in the manual is a descriptive paragraph of the characteristic behaviors of each age group.

*Critique*

The Bayley deserves the excellent reviews in Buros (1978) and Anastasi (1976). Damarin (1978) states: "The Bayley is a truly excellent instrument . . . the standardization of the Mental and Motor scales is as good or better than any other individual tests, whether for infants, children, or adults" (p. 292). Bayley cautions that the Infant Development Scale should be used descriptively and not predictively.

The examiner must be well trained in the mechanics of the instrument. An examiner should not expect to pick up the manual and give the test after a cursory reading. The same stimulus objects are used for several tasks at different age levels, although there is no easy way to know this from the arrangement of the scoring materials. Experience with the instrument will result in administration of all or most of these tasks while the examiner has a given object in hand. The novice will lose time since he or she will have to keep coming back to the same object at different age levels of testing. For the relatively untrained examiner, the Bayley is often administered with the help of an assistant who locates appropriate test materials and records performance, while the examiner works directly with the infant. Sometimes with difficult or fearful children help from the mother may be required so that the child can settle down and attend to the task.

The Bayley is one of the few tests in which scoring for the items is actually scaled along a developmental continuum. Other tests generally employ a total score or subtest scores which are then converted statistically into some type of developmental score or estimation.

## WECHSLER PRESCHOOL AND PRIMARY SCALE
## OF INTELLIGENCE (WPPSI)

*Manual*

*Wechsler Preschool and Primary Scale of Intelligence Manual.* Wechsler, D. New York: The Psychological Corporation, 1976. 757 Third Avenue, New York, N.Y. 10017.

*Purpose*

The Wechsler Preschool and Primary Scale of Intelligence, which was first published in 1967, is an individually administered test of intelligence for children ages four to six and a half. The reason the WPPSI was developed for children in this age range is because that period is a transitional stage in cognitive developmental maturity. It is also the time span during which the child commonly enters his first formal schooling, a time in which such an instrument is often helpful.

*Format*

The scale includes 11 subtests, only 10 of which are used in finding the IQ. Eight of the subtests are downward extensions and adaptations of the WISC subtests (Information, Vocabulary, Arithmetic, Similarities, and Comprehension; Picture Completion, Mazes, and Block Design). The three novel tests are Sentences, Animal House, and Geometric Design. The Sentences subtest, a supplementary task, involves repeating sentences read aloud by the examiner. This test was designed to replace the Digit Span test on the WISC. Animal House is similar to the WISC coding and involves matching colored discs with appropriate animals. Finally, Geometric Design was included because reproductions of geometric figures correlate highly with other measures of a child's intelligence.

*Administration and Scoring*

The subtests are grouped into a Verbal and a Performance Scale from which Verbal, Performance, and Full Scale IQs are derived. The administration of verbal and performance subtests is alternated to reduce boredom and to help maintain the interest of the younger child. Specific instructions are provided for each subtest, as are scoring instructions. Total testing time usually varies between 50 and 75 minutes. Raw scores for each subtest are transformed into normalized standard scores within each age group. Tables for scaled scores are provided by age range from 4.0 to 6.6 in three-month intervals. These scaled scores for subtests are added and converted into Verbal, Performance, and Full Scale IQs for which tables are provided in the manual.

*Standardization*

The WPPSI was standardized on a sample of 1,200 children who included 100 boys and 100 girls in half-year intervals from ages four to six and a half. The sample was stratified according to geographic region, urban-rural composition, racial origin, and occupational level. The norms for scaled scores are reported in quarter-year levels; sample size is not noted for the extreme ends of the age range.

*Reliability*

Split-half reliability was computed for each subtest except Animal House, which is a speeded task. Animal House reliability was assessed by administering a retest at the end of the testing session. The subtest reliabilities (Spearman-Brown formula) varied from a low of .62 to a high of .91 with the majority of the reliabilities falling in the .80s. Information concerning the standard error of measurement is also provided in the manual. According to these data a difference between the Verbal and Performance IQs of 11 points or more is significant at the .05 level. The manual advises that discrepancies of 15 points or greater are important and warrant further investigation.

*Validity*

Anastasi (1976) reviews several factor analytic studies which supported the validity of the use of Verbal, Performance, and Full Scale IQs. The validity data presented in the manual are meager. The only measure of criterion validity is a comparison of the WPPSI IQs of 98 children with three other intelligence tests. The correlation between the Stanford-Binet and the WPPSI was .75, with the Verbal Scale correlating more highly with the Stanford-Binet than the Performance Scale.

*Critique*

The WPPSI is a very carefully constructed and well-standardized test. It has the advantage of providing not only a performance score but also a verbal score. Its major limitations consist of a paucity of validity data and the fact that it was designed for use with children from a narrow age range. Eichorn (1972) and Oldridge and Allison (1972) criticize the WPPSI because of its long administration time, the limited sensitivity at the lowest age range, and because failure is obvious to the child.

A problem which can be encountered with the WPPSI is the determination of IQ scoring below 50. Since a four-year-old making no correct response would obtain an IQ above 50, the WPPSI may not be suitable for use in selection of children for some retardation programs and services.

On the positive side, Wechsler employed the deviation IQ in this test and in his other intelligence tests. The problem with the older use of the mental age, which has been employed in other tests, including the early versions of the Binet, arose from the fact that children of different chronological ages who had the same mental age weren't actually functioning in cognitively equivalent manners. Moreover, the necessary gain in mental age to maintain a given IQ increases nonlinearly with chronological age, making comparisons across different ages difficult to interpret meaningfully. For these reasons Wechsler employed the deviation IQ. This results in the case that the child's IQ will not vary unless his performance relative to his peers varies. (The IQ is based on age-related norms adjusted so that the mean total score for each age will equal an IQ of 100 and the standard deviation is made equal to 15 points.) Thus, the WPPSI is well standardized and offers advantages of comparison among children for those ranges at which it is sensitive.

## WECHSLER INTELLIGENCE SCALE FOR CHILDREN—REVISED (WISC-R)

*Manual*

*Manual for the Wechsler Intelligence Scale for Children – Revised.* Wechsler, D. New York: The Psychological Corporation, 1974. 757 Third Avenue, New York, N.Y. 10017.

*Purpose*

The Wechsler Intelligence Scale for Children was first published in 1949 and was designed to be a test of general or global intelligence, utilizing a variety of subtests administered and scored in a standard manner. The Wechsler Intelligence Scale for Children – Revised (WISC-R) was published in 1974, retaining as much of the WISC content and format as possible, while strengthening the reliability of individual subtests by the addition of test items and modification of those parts of the tests deemed ambiguous, obsolete, or unfair to particular groups of children. For example, the WISC-R includes more pictures of female and black children in the Picture Completion subtest. The age range for the WISC-R is from six through 16 years of age. At the younger ages (6.0 to 6.7) it overlaps with the Wechsler Preschool and Primary Scale of Intelligence (WPPSI), and at the older ages (16.0 to 16.11) it overlaps with the Wechsler Adult Intelligence Scale (WAIS).

The WISC-R is composed of 12 subtests, six designated as Verbal tests which yield a Verbal Intelligence Quotient (VIQ) and six designated as performance tests which yield a Performance Intelligence Quotient (PIQ). The combined tests yield a Full Scale Intelligence Quotient (FSIQ). The subtests are as follows: Verbal Scale – Information, Similarities, Arithmetic, Vocabulary, Comprehension, Digit Span; Performance Scale – Picture Completion, Picture Arrangement, Block Design, Object Assembly, Coding, Mazes. Digit Span and Mazes are supplementary tests and are not included in the computation of the IQ scores. The standard administration alternates verbal and performance subtests, although this order can be changed at the discretion of the examiner.

*Administration and Scoring*

The manual contains directions for the administration and scoring of each subtest. Verbatim directions are printed in red, with supplemental instructions and explanatory material printed in black. Some of the subtests are timed and require the use of a stopwatch. Administration can usually be completed in one to one and a half hours. To obtain the best estimate of the child's abilities, the battery should be administered in its entirety and only abbreviated in cases of handicapped or disabled children.

Raw scores on each subtest are computed and then changed into Scaled Scores. Tables for Scaled Scores are provided for each four-month interval from six years no months no days through 16 years 11 months 30 days. The Scaled Scores for the Verbal Scale (excluding Digit Span) are summed and transformed to yield the VIQ; Scaled Scores for the Performance Scale (excluding mazes) are summed and transformed to yield the PIQ. The sum of the Scaled Scores for all the subtests (excluding the Digit Span and Mazes) are transformed to yield the FSIQ.

*Standardization*

The WISC-R was standardized on 2,200 children, 100 boys and 100 girls at each year of age from six and a half to 16½. The sample was stratified with respect to geographic region, urban-rural composition, social origin, and the occupation of the head of the household. Anastasi (1976) states that the WISC-R standardization sample is possibly the most representative ever employed in developing norms for an individual test.

## Reliability

Average split-half reliabilities for Verbal, Performance, and Full Scale IQs were computed to be .94, .90, and .96 respectively. On tests administered at a one-month interval, the test-retest reliabilities were .93, .90, and .95 respectively. One outstanding feature of the WISC-R is that the standard error of measurement of the Full Scale IQ is only three points. Consequently, there is a 95% chance that the true WISC-R IQ differs from the obtained IQ by no more than plus or minus six points.

## Validity

Validity data consist of mean correlations across age groups between the FSIQ and the Stanford-Binet (r=.73). The Verbal Scale correlated more highly than the Performance Scale, .71 and .60 respectively. Other validity data are reported in the manual relative to the older WISC and other measures, as well as factor analytic studies of both WISC and WISC-R, which yielded three factors corresponding to a verbal comprehension factor, a perceptual organization factor, and a freedom from distractibility factor. Other data are included in the manual with regard to intercorrelations among subtests and with the various Full Scale, Verbal, and Performance Scales.

## Critique

The WISC-R is an extremely reliable and well-standardized instrument. It has the advantage of providing both a verbal and performance measure. The WISC-R has been compared with the WPPSI on a sample of 50 children aged six years exactly. The WISC-R IQs were about two points lower than the WPPSI.

One problem which may be encountered with the WISC-R also applies to the WPPSI. The IQ scores cannot be computed below about 45 points for the Verbal or Performance Scales or 40 points for the Full Scale IQ, even when minimal performances are obtained. Since some retardation programs depend upon lower ranges of IQ for placement, the WISC-R may not be the instrument of choice for these cases.

STANFORD-BINET INTELLIGENCE SCALE

*Manual*

*Stanford-Binet Intelligence Scale (Third Edition, Form L-M, 1960, 1972 Norms).* Terman, L. M. and Merrill, M. A. Boston: Houghton Mifflin Company, 1973. 110 Tremont Street, Boston, MA 02107.

*Purpose*

The purpose of the Stanford-Binet Intelligence Scale is to provide a measure of a person's general intelligence. This measure of general or global intelligence is obtained by presenting to the individual a variety of tasks of known increasing difficulty.

*Format*

The Third Revision of the Stanford-Binet Intelligence Scale (1960) combines into one form (L-M) items from each of the equivalent forms (L and M) of the 1937 Scale. In 1972, a re-standardization was published with updated norms but with no changes in test items. The age range for the Stanford-Binet is from two years through adulthood. At each of the age levels there are six items and one alternate item. From ages two through five, test levels are at half-year intervals with one month credit given for each item passed. From ages six through 14, test levels are at yearly intervals with two months' credit given for each item passed. There are also test levels for Average Adult, Superior Adult I, Superior Adult II, and Superior Adult III. The Stanford-Binet presents test items by age level rather than by subtests based on separate aspects of intelligence or on specific abilities (as is the case with the Wechsler instruments). For example, at year two content includes a form board, delayed response, identifying parts of the body, building block towers, word combinations, and an alternate — identifying object by name. At year six the content is vocabulary, differences, mutilated pictures, number concepts, opposite analogies, mazes, and an alternate — response to pictures. At year 12 the content is vocabulary, verbal absurdities, picture absurdities, repeating five digits reversed, abstract words, minkus completion, and an alternate — memory for designs.

## Administration and Scoring

In the administration of the Stanford-Binet the examiner must first establish the basal level. This is the highest age at which all the items are passed. All items below the basal level for a given child are considered passed. The examiner then continues sequentially to administer test items until an age level is reached at which all items are failed by the child; all items above this ceiling level are considered failed. Usually the examiner utilizes the child's score on either the Picture Vocabulary items (for children five years of age or younger) or the Vocabulary items (for children over six years), as a starting point to ascertain the basal age. The mental age is computed by adding the basal age and all additional months' credit received. The present version of the Stanford-Binet contains tables which permit the examiner to obtain a deviation IQ by entering the appropriate table with chronological age and mental age. Thus the child can be compared with his peers.

The manual contains verbatim instructions for administration as well as criteria for scoring. Each item is scored on a pass-fail basis as it is administered. Items for children under age six are presented in a game-like approach with a variety of toys. Most of the items are not timed.

## Standardization

The 1960 revision of the Stanford-Binet used 4,498 subjects of ages two and a half through 18 years. Children who had been individually referred for assessment of some special adjustment problem were not included in the sample. Also included were two stratified samples (100 six-year-olds and 100 15-year-olds) based on occupational grouping of the fathers. The 1972 standardization program, undertaken to update the norms for the 1960 Revision, used a sample of 2,351 subjects. Although earlier norms were limited to the white population of the United States, the 1972 norms include minority children from homes in which English was the primary language spoken.

## Reliability

In 1937, test-retest reliability, using Forms L and M, administered one week apart, yielded coefficients for different age groups ranging from .83 to .98. Greatest reliability was apparent at lower IQ levels and for older children. The two forms are combined in the 1960 revision with reliability coefficients in the .90s for subjects in most age groups. Thus most IQ scores will be within five points of the obtained scores over two-thirds of the time.

## Validity

Since the Stanford-Binet is basically an age scale, in which the content changes with age (e.g., more abstract tasks are demanded at upper levels), criterion validity of items and their distribution is established by evaluation of percentage passing items and tests at each age level, with regular increase from younger to older ages.

Factor analysis (McNemar, 1942) supports the conclusion that the Stanford-Binet performance is explainable by a single common factor. In the 1960 revision, most items with low first factor loadings were eliminated and all items highly saturated with the general factor were included.

## Critique

For older children whose functioning level is considerably below their chronological ages, the Stanford-Binet provides good information about the things the children *can* do rather than what they *cannot* do. Clinically such information is helpful in planning recommendations for the child. For younger children, the game-like format is an advantage and testing time can be shorter than with the WPPSI. The Binet norms are fairly recent and provide a wide range of IQ scores (useful when special placement of retarded children may be part of the referral question).

One drawback of the Stanford-Binet is that younger children are tested with items that use many small toys and objects, making it difficult for an inexperienced examiner to administer the test easily. The IQ which is obtained does not permit an easy breakdown into verbal and performance areas, or more specific areas of intellectual functioning. The standardization data have not assured racial balance, although minorities were included. Also, the 1972 norms did not include re-standardization of the new test as a whole. There is, however, high internal consistency of items.

## PEABODY PICTURE VOCABULARY TEST (PPVT)

*Manual*

*Expanded Manual for the Peabody Picture Vocabulary Test.* Dunn, L. M. Circle Pines, MN: American Guidance Service, 1965. Publisher's Building, Circle Pines, MN 55014.

*Purpose*

The Peabody Picture Vocabulary Test is designed primarily to measure a person's hearing or receptive vocabulary and to serve as a predictor of school success. It does not provide a comprehensive measure of general intelligence, even though results can be expressed in terms of an IQ score.

*Format*

The PPVT consists of a booklet containing 150 plates of four drawings each. Alternate equivalent word lists (Forms A and B) have been developed for use with the plates. The pictures and words are arranged in increasing order of difficulty for ages two years six months through 18 years.

At the lower levels of the test all four pictures on each plate are quite different; however, as the difficulty of the words presented increases, the picture choices are more similar, thus requiring finer discrimination to select the correct answer.

*Administration*

The subject is requested to identify the picture on each page which corresponds to the word spoken by the examiner. Generally, the subject will point to his answer choice, but when motor problems interfere with pointing, other arrangements can be worked out to indicate the subject's choice of picture.

In order to establish a basal (eight consecutive correct answers), the examiner begins testing at a level where the child can be expected to do well. The answer forms give suggested beginning items for different ages. After the basal level has been established, the examiner presents the items consecutively until a ceiling has been reached (six errors in eight consecutive items). The raw score is then computed. Tables are provided in the manual so that an IQ score, a mental age equivalent, and a percentile equivalent can be obtained.

*Standardization*

During the period of April through June 1958, 4,012 subjects ranging in age from two years six months to 18 years were administered both Forms A and B. All the subjects were from the Nashville, Tennessee, area and all were white. At the preschool levels (ages two years six months through six) examiners tested the children individually in their homes. At the lower elementary school level (six years six months through eight), the tests were individually administered. From upper elementary through high school levels (ages nine through 18) the PPVT was administered as a group test. The group testing was used only after a study was conducted which demonstrated no significant differences in results for individual and group administration.

*Reliability*

Using raw scores of the standardization subjects at each age level of Forms A and B, reliability coefficients were calculated. They ranged from a low of .67 at age six years zero months to a high of .84 at both ages 17.0 and 18.0. The standard errors of measurement were also obtained for the IQ scores at each age level and these ranged from 6.00 to 8.61.

*Validity*

To establish content validity, the words which could be depicted by a picture were selected from *Webster's New Collegiate Dictionary* (1953) to be included in the initial pool of 3,885 words. For item validity, only those words were retained which had a clearly increasing percentage of subjects passing from one age level to the next.

The extent to which PPVT scores compare with other intelligence tests has been calculated at .82 to .86 for mental age correlations with the Stanford-Binet, 1960 revision. Comparisons with the WISC IQ scores are as follows: WISC Verbal IQ correlations have a range of .41 to .74 and WISC Full Scale correlations have a range of .30 to .84.

*Critique*

The advantages offered by the PPVT include ease, simplicity, and quickness of administration and scoring. Also advantageous is the adaptability of the PPVT for use with handicapped persons, either with language and speech difficulties or with motor impairments.

The major disadvantage of the PPVT is the narrowness of the measure. It is basically a receptive vocabulary test and is not intended to be a measure of general intelligence equivalent to that offered by the WISC-R or the Stanford-Binet. The PPVT is best used as a supplemental procedure when complex questions of assessment are posed by the handicaps which prevent children from straightforward examination by one of the broader measures of intelligence.

## CATTELL CULTURE FAIR INTELLIGENCE TESTS

*Manuals*

Cattell, R. B. & Cattell, A. K. S. *The Culture Fair Series.* Scale 1, 1950; Scale 2, 1973; Scale 3, 1973. Champaign, IL: Institute for Personality and Ability Testing. 1602 Coronado Drive, Champaign, IL 61820.

*Purpose*

This series attempts to minimize cultural, verbal, and educational influences on intellectually directed performance. The tests rely on perception of relationships among figures and shapes. Scale 1 is designed for children ages four to eight and retardates. Administration takes about one hour if the full form is used. Several short forms are discussed in the manual. Scale 2 is designed for ages eight to 11 and adults. Scale 3 is directed toward senior high school and college students, as well as bright adults. Scales 2 and 3 are each estimated to take about 15 minutes and may be group-administered, as well as individually administered. All of these tests are asserted to measure *general mental capacity*.

*Format—Scale 1*

Scale 1 has eight subtests of 12 items each: *substitution, classification, mazes,* selecting named objects, following directions, wrong pictures, riddles, and *similarities*. The italicized subtests are purported to be more culture fair.

## Administration and Scoring

Instruction is given in the manual for each subtest for both administration and scoring. Raw scores may be converted to mental age, ratio IQ, or percentile rank.

## Standardization

The standardization is based on "more than 400 cases combining American and British samples" primarily of middle-class children. Standard deviations of the culture fair scale are set at 20. By use of the percentile standing, children can be compared with their peers. (However, the ratio IQ is not comparable to the deviation IQ scores now used on the Wechsler instruments and the 1960 revision of the Stanford-Binet.) The manual cites a Spearman-Brown coefficient of .91 and a Kuder-Richardson of .94. Scanty data with small samples are provided with regard to validity.

## Critique

Scale 1 has four subtests which are not culture fair as Cattell describes them in the manual. However, classification and mazes which are included in the four purely culture fair subtests are both timed subtests. Since different cultures and subcultures vary in their attitudes and practices toward speed performance, the degree of culture fairness of this scale is questionable. Given these facts, the value of Scale 1 as a culture fair test over the Stanford-Binet and the Wechsler (WPPSI) is also questionable. The full form of the Culture Fair Scale 1 takes longer for administration than either the WPPSI or the Stanford-Binet. The examiner is advised in the manual "to invoke a competitive spirit by referring fairly often to the way other children have done this test" (p. 6), a suggestion that could interfere with the performance of many children. A small number of children of skewed socioeconomic level comprise the standardization samples, raising questions about the validity of this scale.

## Format — Scales 2 and 3

Both Scales 2 and 3 contain four subtests: series, classification, matrices, and conditions or typology, all of which are timed tests.

*Administration and Scoring*

For both Scale 2 and 3 there are instructions for the administration and scoring of each subtest. Scores are converted into mental age, classical IQ (i.e., MA/CA), and percentile ranks. A and B forms are provided for each scale.

*Standardization*

Scale 2 has a Spearman-Brown coefficient of .79 for Form A and .71 for Form B, with Kuder-Richardson coefficients of .81 and .76, respectively, based on a sample of *102 female job-corps applicants.* Various cross-cultural studies comparing Scale 2 with performance on the Raven Progressive Matrices yield correlations between .51 and .64. Various other published sources report correlations within or lower than this range.

Scale 3 has Spearman-Brown coefficients of .68 and .64 and Kuder-Richardson coefficients of .51 and .53 for Forms A and B, respectively, on a sample of 200 male and female high school students. Validity data are low to moderate correlations with small samples reported.

*Critique*

Scales 2 and 3 have the disadvantage of being timed tests of questionable predictive and construct validity, with standardization data based on small samples of highly selected populations. The tests may be given on a non-timed basis, but interpretation of the findings is unclear given the current state of the standardization data.

## HISKEY-NEBRASKA TEST OF LEARNING APTITUDE (H-NTLA)

*Manual*

*The Hiskey-Nebraska Test of Learning Aptitude Manual* (Revised). Hiskey, M. S. 5640 Baldwin, Lincoln, Nebraska, 1966.

*Purpose*

The Hiskey-Nebraska Test of Learning Aptitude is designed for use with deaf and hearing-impaired children from the ages of three to 16 years. This is the only test of ability which is standardized on a hearing-impaired population. As the test is administered via verbal or pantomimed instructions, it is appropriate for use with speech-impaired, mentally retarded or other subject populations that may be penalized by verbal intelligence tests.

*Format*

The H-NTLA is an individually administered test which yields a Learning Age and Learning Quotient. There are 124 items arranged in order of increasing difficulty grouped into 12 subtests: Bead Patterns, Memory for Color, Picture Identification, Pictorial Associations, Paper Folding, Visual Attention Span, Block Patterns, Completion of Drawings, Memory for Digits, Puzzle Blocks, Picture Analogies, and Spatial Reasoning. None of the items requires verbal skills, and directions are given by pantomime. The Learning Age score is calculated by determining the median age level of the child's performance on the subtests administered.

*Standardization*

The normative sample included 1,107 deaf children, and 1,101 hearing children ranging in age from two-and-a-half to 17½ years. A definite bias exists in the selection of the normative sample as the deaf children were enrolled in state schools for the deaf, in contrast to the sample of hearing children who were selected on the basis of their parents' occupational level. Two sets of norms are available for converting raw scores into learning ages. Appropriate norms to be used are based upon the type of direction utilized in administering the test, e.g., verbal or pantomime. Norms for deaf children are appropriate when pantomime directions are employed, while the use of verbal directions requires utilization of norm conversions based on hearing subjects.

*Reliability*

Internal consistency for the scale was computed by the split-half method. Reliability estimates for deaf and hearing children of .90 have been reported for two age groups (3–10 and 11–17).

*Validity*

An early study (Hiskey, 1966) provided correlations of .82 between the H-NTLA and WISC for 52 hearing children. A later study (Wilson et al., 1975) conducted with 35 hearing-impaired children between the ages of seven and 10, who were given the Performance Scale of the WISC and the H-NTLA, yielded a correlation of .55. Hirshorn et al. (1977) conducted a study of 59 children between the ages of eight and 13 years who attended a school for the deaf. The children were given both the Performance Scale of the WISC-R and the H-NTLA. A t-test was conducted in order to determine whether a statistically significant difference existed between the WISC-R Performance IQ and the H-NTLA Learning Quotient. The obtained *t* of .62 was not significant. A Pearson product-moment correlation of .89 between the two tests suggests that both tests measure highly similar abilities. Predictive validity, in terms of school achievement, has been evaluated in a study of 59 black and white deaf children (Hurley et al., 1978). The WISC-R and the H-NTLA had significant correlations ranging from .34 to .64 with the Stanford Achievement Test for the 23 black children but not for the 36 white children. The authors suggest that the H-NTLA has little predictive validity for white deaf children and should not be used for placement or instructional decisions for children.

*Critique*

Although the standardization sample was biased, as all children attended state schools for deaf children, this is the only standardized test which is normed on deaf children. Correlations between the H-NTLA and the Performance Scale of the WISC-R suggest that the two tests are measuring the same abilities; however, some examiners have found that the H-NTLA is more difficult to administer and requires more time than the WISC-R. The H-NTLA has not been found to be predictive of school achievement. Additional reliability and validity data should be provided in order to determine whether the H-NTLA is a more appropriate test than the Performance Scale of the WISC-R for use with deaf children.

## LEITER INTERNATIONAL PERFORMANCE SCALE (LIPS)

*Manual*

Leiter, R. G. *Examiner's Manual for the International Performance Scale.* Chicago: Stoelting Co., 1969.

*Purpose*

The purpose of the Leiter International Performance Scale is to obtain a measure of general intelligence using tasks that require no verbal instructions or answers. In the manual of general instructions, Leiter defines general intelligence as "an individual's ability to analyze and synthesize materials with which he has no previous experience" (p. 4).

*Format*

There are four tests at each age level from age two through 10 and then four tests at each of the ages 12, 14, 16, and 18. The tasks are *assumed* to be of increasing difficulty and a basal consists of passing all tests for a specific age. Credit is given for all tests below that level on the assumption that since they are less difficult they would be passed if actually administered. Included in the test items are several levels of difficulty of matching colors and shades, reconstructing block designs, and arranging in logical order series of various items. Since there are no verbal instructions and very few demonstration or pantomime clues are provided, determining the nature of the task itself, as well as its solution, is considered a part of the testing process.

The presentation format for all the test items is essentially the same. A cardboard strip containing a series of pictures about one inch square is attached to a wooden frame. Below each picture space the frame forms a stall about one inch square into which a wooden picture block can be inserted. A ceiling level is established when all tests at two consecutive age levels have been failed. The mental age is then computed by adding the months of credit received (three months for each test passed for ages two through 10, and six months for each test passed at the upper age levels) to the basal age. The IQ is computed by dividing the mental age by the chronological age (a ratio IQ) and adding a constant of five points. Since the 1969 standardization of the Leiter International Performance Scale has an IQ norm of 95 for children in the continental United States, the five points are added, according to Leiter, to make the IQs directly comparable to other intelligence tests with a mean IQ score of 100.

*Administration and Scoring*

To compensate for the absence of verbal instructions, the author suggests starting the testing at an age level two years below the estimated mental age of the child; thus, with a six-year-old child of assumed normal intelligence, testing would start at the four-year level. When a basal is established, testing continues until a ceiling is reached, *including re-administering items which the child failed in the attempt to establish the basal.* The examiner presents each item by attaching the cardboard picture strip to the frame and then giving the picture blocks for that task to the child. The child must insert each block in its correct stall in order to receive credit.

The administration manual contains instructions and pictures of the presentation of each task as well as scoring criteria. Most of the test items are untimed and are scored on a pass-fail basis. No partial credit is given for varying degrees of correctness.

*Standardization*

The 1938 Hawaiian Standardization of the first Leiter Internation-al Performance Scale, using a population of children of Chinese and Japanese family origin, provided scores that Leiter reported were 18 months below the level scored by a later sample of children from the continental United States. Leiter's effort to offset this difference in per-formance and to construct a scale more applicable for the children from the continental United States resulted in the 1969 revision. This revision showed children from the continental U.S. now scored six months below the age level of the new revision, which resulted in a mean IQ of 95 with a standard deviation of 16. In communicating individual results, Leiter suggested that IQs to which a constant of five points had been added should be used and that an *adjusted* mental age (obtained from a table provided in the manual) be reported. Thus neither the IQ nor mental age reported are those actually obtained.

*Reliability and Validity*

No reliability and validity data are reported in the General Instruc-tions Manual for the 1969 revision. Anastasi (1976) reports some relia-bility and validity studies based on heterogeneous groups.

*Critique*

The Leiter International Performance Scale can be used to obtain a ratio IQ score for children with hearing impairments, for children who may not be able to understand verbal instructions, and for motor-im-paired children who may be unable to manipulate the more complex materials of other performance measures. Also, other performance measures usually have speed as a major component of the scoring system, whereas the Leiter has only a few timed items.

Disadvantages of using this measure are many. They include the cumbersomeness of the test materials, the question of determining whether the child cannot solve a particular task or cannot conceptualize the task itself from the materials presented, the issue of whether the order of the tasks really reflects increasing difficulty, and the lack of true comparability of IQs across age. Since the Leiter uses the ratio IQ rather than the deviation IQ, it is also not possible to make direct comparisons of general intelligence with such measures as the Wechsler scales and the Stanford-Binet.

Finally, since no data are reported on socioeconomic level and other important aspects of the standardization sample, it is unclear what kinds of bias may be present in the test.


### TEST OF NONVERBAL INTELLIGENCE (TONI)


*Manual*

*Test of Nonverbal Intelligence, A Language-Free Measure of Cognitive Ability.* Brown, L., Sherbenow, R. J., & Dollar, S. J. Austin, TX: Pro-Ed, 1982. 5341 Industrial Oaks Blvd., Austin, TX 78735.

*Purpose*

The purpose of the Test of Nonverbal Intelligence is to provide a nationally standardized measure of intellectual functioning which can be administered in a nonverbal format requiring no listening, speaking, reading, or writing by the individual being examined. It is designed for use with language- and/or hearing-impaired individuals.

*Format and Administration*

The test materials consist of two series (Form A and Form B) of 50 pictures each requiring that the subject choose from several pictured solutions the correct answer for each item. The pictures use only abstract content in order to reduce the effects of language and culture.

The basis chosen for the entire test is problem-solving with one or more of the following rules operating in the solution of each item:

1) Simple Matching
2) Analogies
   (a) Matching
   (b) Addition
   (c) Subtraction
   (d) Alteration
   (e) Progressions
3) Classification
4) Intersections
5) Progressions

Prior to administering the test items, a set of training items illustrating these rules is administered using gestures and pantomime, but no verbal instructions, to familiarize the subject with the problem-solving format, the test materials, and the method of response (i.e., pointing to the correct answer).

The TONI uses a basal and ceiling method of administration so that it is not necessary to administer all items to an individual. Five consecutive correct items are required to establish a basal level and three incorrect items out of five is used to find a ceiling level. The answer forms indicate appropriate beginning items by subject's age and the correct responses are indicated for each item. When the raw score has been computed, a TONI Quotient (Q) and percentile rank can be determined using the subject's chronological age and the normative tables provided for ages five years through 85 years 11 months. The TONI Quotient is a deviation standard score with a mean of 100 and a standard deviation of 15, with quotients from one standard deviation below the mean to one standard deviation above the mean (85-115) considered to be within the normal range of intellectual functioning.

*Standardization*

The final 100 test items selected for the TONI (50 items for Form A and 50 items for Form B) were derived from an initial pool of 307 items which the authors devised after reviewing nonverbal and performance measures of intelligence as well as literature in the area of problem-solving. These 307 abstract pictorial items were then submitted to professionals in the fields of education and psychology and those found to have ambiguous symbolic or linguistic content were removed from the pool, leaving 183 items. These were then administered to 322 subjects and the results analyzed to determine how well each item discriminated between high and low scores (item discriminating power) and the proportion of people who answered the item correctly (item difficulty). Items were kept if: 1) they fell within the .30 to .85 range of correlation with the total test score, which the authors assumed to be an indication that the item contributed significantly to the total score while not duplicating other items; and 2) they were answered correctly by 15% to 85% of the subjects. The two final forms (A and B) were then derived by using 50 items, each of equivalent item discriminating power and item difficulty.

Normative data were acquired by administering the TONI to 1,929 subjects from 28 states. Subjects were from five years through 85 years 11 months of age and were not intellectually impaired. The demographic characteristics of this sample were considered representative as they were similar to those of the 1980 census of the United States and took into consideration age, sex, race/ethnicity, domicile, geographic location, grade in school, and parental educational/occupational attainment (for child subjects) and current educational/occupational attainment (for adult subjects).

*Reliability*

The test authors have identified the TONI as an individually administered test with the primary function of diagnosis and screening rather than determination of individual placement, and have accepted reliability coefficients of .80 or greater as evidence that the TONI yields consistent results. The Kuder-Richardson Formula 21 was used to establish internal consistency for each age interval in the normative sample. These coefficients range from .6 and .7 for the five- and six-year-olds to .8 and .9 for all other age groups. Coefficients of equivalency were calculated for the alternate forms and ranged from .81 to .95, except for the age range 8 years 6 months to 10 years 11 months which has a coefficient of .78. In order to establish reliability of the TONI with groups having intellectual or sensory deficits, the TONI was administered to one group (N=10) of educable mentally retarded students, one group (N=30) of deaf students, and two groups (N=11, N=16) of learning-disabled students. All coefficients obtained for these groups were at least .80 or higher.

## Validity

To establish concurrent validity, studies were conducted to determine correlations with other standardized measures of intelligence and achievement: Raven's Progressive Matrices (Raven, 1938), the Leiter International Performance Scale, the WISC-R, the Otis-Lennon Mental Ability Test, the Iowa Tests of Basic Skills, the SRA Achievement Series, and the Stanford Achievement Test. All correlations were above the .35 criterion established by the test authors as necessary to indicate concurrent validity. The strongest correlations were found to be with intelligence rather than achievement measures and with language-free rather than verbal measures of intelligence.

Test results that successfully discriminated between a group of mentally retarded students and a group of normal subjects matched on the basis of age and sex from the standardization group are cited as evidence of construct validity and the TONI's usefulness as a diagnostic instrument.

## Critique

The TONI is easy to administer and score but the examiner must be very alert to the possibility of recording incorrectly the subject's answer choices, since the various choices are not numbered or otherwise identified on the test items. The test manual is clear and well written with the exception of the section on group administration, which is confusing.

Anyone using the TONI should read thoroughly the chapter on interpreting the results, particularly the section with regard to overgeneralizing from the results for a given individual. *The TONI should not be used alone as a definitive measure of intellectual functioning.* Rather, it is best used as a screening or supplemental measure in conjunction with other sources of data about an individual.

Despite the use of item difficulty data used in the construction of the test, it does appear that the sequencing of items may not represent uniformity or increasing order of difficulty. Also at the upper levels, the two forms may not be equivalent in terms of difficulty. Because material relevant to both functions and difficulty must be considered in the construction of the test, some unevenness may have occurred despite the attention to item difficulty for the test as a whole. Further study would be helpful on this question.

## COMPARISON OF TESTS OF INTELLECTUAL FUNCTIONING

For most purposes, when children across a broad range of intelligence are assessed, the Wechsler scales are desirable for a number of reasons. These have to do with the continuity of material across the various Wechsler tests so that comparisons can be made for the same child for most of the subtests. Likewise, comparisons of the same child across a span of years and on the same type of material aid in establishing whether the child's level of function has changed.

In addition, the comparisons among the component subtests of the Wechsler instruments permit convenient organization and examination of data which may be of special interest when the assessment questions focus on learning or neuropsychological problems. However, despite the strong psychometric advantages of the Wechsler instruments, there are some conditions under which other tests may be more helpful. The following discussion will illustrate some of these circumstances.

*Age of the Child*

Aside from the fact that there are instruments designed for both pre-school and school-age children, there are some more complicated problems which face the examiner with regard to the child's chronological age and the procedure of choice. These questions relate to the nature of the material tested through the particular instrument and the nature of the standardization data available to help the examiner with interpretation of the instruments.

The following example will illustrate one type of problem that an examiner may face in attempting to select the most appropriate instrument for the evaluation of intellectual function in a child. Let us suppose there is a referral of a boy six years four months old with some question of ability to attend appropriately and concentrate, and some concern over school placement. Should he be in a regular school classroom or in some special type of classroom? Here are some of the issues that need to be considered in selecting an instrument for intellectual assessment in this case:

*1) General intellectual level*

Do we think that this boy will be very dull or very bright? He is at the upper end of the age range for the Wechsler Preschool and Primary Test of Intelligence and at the lower end of the age range for the Wechsler Intelligence Scale for Children – Revised. If he is very dull and we give a WISC-R, we may not really learn a great deal about how he approaches problems because he will fail so quickly that we will not get a large sample of behavior (low ceiling). We will not have a basis for identification of the types of errors he makes. We will get an IQ score but a lot of the qualitative observation will be missing. If, on the other hand, he is very bright and we give him a WPPSI, we will get a score but there will be other considerations. Because of the differences in the subtests, there will be less continuity of material with those used later in retesting the child than if we use the WISC-R. Also, the testing may take an unnecessarily long time since the child can be expected to complete almost all the items on almost all the subtests (high base effect). In such cases where a child's age hits at the point of overlap between these two Wechsler tests and he is either very bright or suspected of being somewhat retarded, the Wechsler scales may not be the best choice.

The Stanford-Binet has the advantage of spanning this age gap without changes in content. Use of the Binet in such cases may avoid the awkwardness that a misjudgment of general level of functioning might result in with use of the Wechsler scales. However, the Stanford-Binet will not facilitate the inspection of perceptual and verbal components which may be of interest if learning problems are the major focus.

### 2) Attention span

In what ways will various tests be helpful if the child has a short attention span? Subtests on the Wechsler instruments usually focus on the same kinds of material for a longer time than the items on the Stanford-Binet, which is arranged so that the material is varied frequently. With children who have attentional difficulties this feature of the Binet may cause it to be less frustrating. This will be particularly true with children who have trouble sitting still. If the primary concern is whether the child can perform, then we may get a better performance with the Binet.

### 3) Poor self-concept

What about the child with a sense of failure, the child who dreads tests as yet another case that his/her incompetence is being documented? No test can avoid some indication that the child has not done well, but the Stanford-Binet is less likely to cause the child to focus upon his failure, because of the rapid changes in content which are characteristic of this test. These changes in content occur frequently whether or not the child has been successful, so that errors are less obvious to the child who may already be sensitive to failure. For children who are attuned to failure, the timed tests on the WISC-R and the WPPSI may also heighten anxiety and adversely affect performance.

As can be seen from the above discussion, clinical sensitivity plays a large role in the selection of the most appropriate test. It should be emphasized, however, that all of the tests reviewed above are well constructed. All of the Wechsler instruments are beautifully standardized and have excellent reliabilities. The standardization samples are well distributed across sex, age, socioeconomic level, urban-rural geography, and racial origin. The WPPSI has less validity information available than other Wechsler tests. The Stanford-Binet, although well standardized, does not report detailed information about minorities and sex distribution. Given these differences among the tests, it seems advantageous to rely on the Wechsler scales *unless* some of the problems of awkward transitional age, motivation, or self-reference regarding failure appear to be prominent considerations.

Not too surprisingly, another point of awkwardness for the examiner occurs in the selection of an appropriate intelligence test at the point of overlap between the WISC-R and the Wechsler Adult Intelligence Scale. The same type of problems with basal and ceiling effects may occur as we discussed for the situation in which the WPPSI and the WISC-R overlap. The dull 16-year-old will perform poorly and give less clinically relevant data on the WAIS. The bright 16- or 16½-year-old will take a long time to complete the WISC-R and may be more suitably tested as an adult. At this transitional period in adolescence, the Stanford-Binet is less desirable as a substitute for the WISC-R, since at the upper levels the Stanford-Binet is a highly verbal test in content. Therefore, the WAIS will more often be the instrument of choice.

*Children With Speech Problems*

Some children who are bright are mistaken for children of below average intelligence because of expressive language problems. In addition, children with developmental and learning problems are often referred to psychologists for assessment. Many of these children have multiple handicaps, including speech problems of either expressive or receptive language, or both.

Due to the nature of their content, both the Wechsler scales and the Stanford-Binet require the child to use verbal language, either in giving or explaining the answers. The highly expressive verbal performance of these tests may cause serious underestimates of children's comprehension in certain cases.

A second important language problem is encountered with children who cannot understand instructions on the basis of receptive language difficulties. The value of a test of receptive language in such cases is that the diagnostician is able to determine whether poor verbal performance is a function of expressive language alone, or whether it must be attributed to receptive language problems as well. This is often the situation faced by the examiner when the child has a history of hearing problems in addition to expressive language deficits.

For the child with speech problems, the Wechsler may provide a higher performance score than verbal score. Yet the child's speech production problems may not reflect some of the significant verbally mediated intellectual function at a higher level than the verbal scores indicate. Use of the Peabody Picture Vocabulary Test can serve to clarify whether the status of receptive language function is intact in these cases. If the clinician can establish that receptive language function is operative at a higher level than expressive language, the problem is more specifically related to speech production rather than general cognitive deficit.

Likewise children who function at a below-normal level of intelligence are often aware that they are performing poorly on intelligence tests. The Peabody with its pictorial content and less threatening format can be used to put such a child at ease. Analysis of PPVT items passed can also be used to determine whether the child understands only words with concrete direct referents (nouns) or whether more abstract words relating to action and feeling are also understood. Due to its narrow focus and lack of predictive power, the PPVT is best thought of as a descriptive aid in assessing the child's current level of receptive language comprehension. The child's ability to use information understood is *not* assessed by this instrument.

## Children With Hearing Problems

A second group of handicapped children often referred for psychological evaluation is that of hearing-impaired subjects. If the impairment is not too severe, many of the procedures used with otherwise normal children are appropriate with this group. A screening test for hearing sounds within the range of the human voice is often helpful prior to the psychological evaluation. The approach to evaluation and the instruments selected will depend upon the level of hearing impairment.

When hearing loss is severe, not only does speech suffer, but other problems may preclude the use of tests commonly employed with normal children. One major difficulty arises in making sure that the child understands the task. It is very understandable that speed tests may penalize the hearing-impaired child. Few children have proficiency with sign language so that use of the adaptation of the Wechsler Intelligence Scale for Children – Revised Performance Scales for deaf children is seldom a viable possibility. In such cases three other instruments are available: the Hiskey-Nebraska, the Leiter International Performance Scale, and the Test of Nonverbal Intelligence. Of these tests the Hiskey-Nebraska has the best standardization and has sizeable samples of both normal and hearing-impaired children. However, the Hiskey-Nebraska requires visual-motor performance of the complexity required by other individually administered intelligence tests (such as the Stanford-Binet or the WISC-R), which may be difficult for multi-handicapped children. Neither the Leiter nor the TONI require much coordination, but each of these tests surveys a more restricted range of cognitive activity and may suffer from being unfair to children who have problems with spatialization.

Tests devised for hearing-impaired children require great caution in their interpretation because of the restricted range of cognitive functions surveyed. The Leiter is also difficult to interpret because standard deviations of IQ across ages vary and item difficulty is uneven. Item difficulty also appears somewhat uneven across the TONI. However, the clinician will have an opportunity to observe the child's approach to the tests. Despite these shortcomings, tests for the hearing-impaired do permit systematic methods of observing children on these various performance tests.

This concludes our review of intelligence tests. In closing we must emphasize that tests of intellectual function are only a limited part of any psychological evaluation. Even when questions are directed primarily to the establishment of children's intellectual level (as in questions of retardation), both clinical interviews and observation and the use of other clinical instruments such as developmental scales and behaviorally based measures are important components of the evaluation. When more complex questions regarding achievement or emotional adjustment are involved, the contribution of the intelligence test, while important, is even more limited.

The picture of the child which develops from psychological evaluation is not a collection of disparate facts about that child. Rather, it should be a picture of the *child* and how he or she experiences the world. The intellectual evaluation gives us some notion of the cognitive assets with which the child tries to understand the world. From intellectual evaluation we learn how the child meets the world, actively or passively, curiously, systematically or impulsively, and how she or he processes the information which is available.

A great deal more work must be done in the evaluation before the data can be used to make recommendations for the child. The psychologist will need to learn about current and past situations relevant to the child, the personality and health of the child, the family, and so on. Some examples of the clinical process using all these types of material will be given in Chapter 12.

## REFERENCES

Anastasi, A. *Psychological Testing, 4th Edition.* New York: Macmillan, 1976.

Bayley, N. *Bayley Scales of Infant Development.* New York: The Psychological Corporation, 1969.

Brown, L., Sherbenow, R. J., & Dollar, S. J. *Test of Nonverbal Intelligence, a Language-free Measure of Cognitive Ability.* Austin, TX: Pro-Ed, 1982.

Buros, O. K. (Ed.) *The Eighth Mental Measurement Yearbook.* Highland Park, N.J.: Gryphon Press, 1978.

Cattell, R. B. & Cattell, A. K. S. *The Culture Fair Series.* Scale 1, 1950; Scale 2, 1973; Scale 3, 1973. Champaign, IL: Institute for Personality and Ability Testing.

Cronbach, L. J. *Essentials of Psychological Testing.* New York: Harper & Row, 1960.

Damarin, F. Review of the Bayley Scales. In O. K. Buros (Ed.), *The Eighth Mental Measurement Yearbook.* Highland Park, N.J: Gryphon Press, 1978.

Dunn, L. M. *Expanded manual for the Peabody Picture Vocabulary Test.* Circle Pines, MN: American Guidance Service, 1965.

Eichorn, D. H. Review of the WPPSI. In: O. K. Buros (Ed.), *The Seventh Mental Measurement Yearbook.* Highland Park, N. J.: Gryphon Press, 1972.

Hirshorn, A., Hurley, D. L., & Hunt, J. T. The WISC-R and the Hiskey-Nebraska test with deaf children. *American Annals of the Deaf,* 1977, *122*(4), 392–394.

Hiskey, M. S. *The Hiskey-Nebraska Test of Learning Aptitude Manual* (Revised). Marshall S. Hiskey, 5640 Baldwin, Lincoln, NE 68508, 1966.

Hurley, O. L., Hirshorn, A., Kavale, K., & Hunt, J. T. Intercorrelations among tests of general mental ability and achievement for black and white deaf children. *Perceptual and Motor Skills,* 1978, *46,* 1107–1113.

Leiter, R. G. *Examiner's Manual for the Leiter International Performance Scale.* Chicago: Stoelting Co., 1969.

Lindquist, E. F. & Hieronymus, A. N. *Iowa Tests of Basic Skills.* Boston: Houghton Mifflin, 1956.

McNemar, Q. *The Revision of the Stanford-Binet Scales.* Boston: Houghton Mifflin, 1942.

Oldridge, O. A. & Allison, E. E. Review of the WPPSI. In: O. K. Buros (Ed.), *The Seventh Mental Measurement Yearbook.* Highland Park, N.J.: Gryphon Press, 1972.

Otis, A. S., & Lennon, R. T. *The Otis-Lennon Mental Ability Test.* New York: Harcourt Brace Jovanovich, 1970.

Raven, J. C. *Standard Progressive Matrices.* London: Lewis, 1938.

Terman, L. M., & Merrill, M. A. *Stanford-Binet Intelligence Scale (Third Edition, Form L-M, 1960, 1972 Norms).* Boston: Houghton-Mifflin, 1973.

Wechsler, D. *Manual for the Wechsler Intelligence Scale for Children—Revised.* New York: The Psychological Corporation, 1974.

Wechsler, D. *Wechsler Preschool and Primary Scale of Intelligence Manual.* New York: The Psychological Corporation, 1976.

Wilson, J. J., Rapin, I., Wilson, B. C., Van Denberg, F. V. Neuropsychologic function of children with hearing impairment. *Journal of Speech and Hearing Research,* 1975, *18*(1), 634–652.

## SUPPLEMENTARY REFERENCES

Allen, R. M. C. & Collins, M. G. Suggestions for the adaptive administration of intelligence tests for those with cerebral palsy. *Cerebral Palsy Review,* 1955, *16.* 11–14.

Palmer, J. O. *The Psychological Assessment of Children.* New York: John Wiley, 1970.

Sattler, J. M. *Assessment of Children's Intelligence.* Philadelphia: W. B. Saunders, 1974.

Standardization of the WISC-R Performance Scales for Deaf Children. Series T Number L. Washington, D.C.: Office of Demographic Studies. Annual Survey of Hearing Impaired Children and Youth. 77-86305. Gallaudet College, 1977.

# CHAPTER 7

# Achievement Tests

Psychometrically, some intelligence tests are paragons of clinical assessment procedures. The conscientious efforts to gather nationally representative standardization samples with regard to race, socioeconomic scale, geography, age, and other relevant variables characterize the better instruments. However, even a cursory examination of the Mental Measurement Yearbooks will indicate that this is hardly the case with many of the instruments used to assess achievement in scholastic material. There are, of course, some notable exceptions, such as the Stanford Achievement Test.

The clinician or school psychologist who is attempting to determine how well a child compares with peers with regard to scholastic achievement must consider how to choose the most suitable instrument for the task. There is a variety of achievement tests marketed which vary with regard to the amount and fineness of detail which are assessed. While the needs of the classroom teacher may be for specific analysis of circumscribed skills appropriate to the subject matter of interest, this is rarely the case with a referral to the school or clinical psychologist. More often the question is whether the child has acquired material and whether the child is achieving at a level which could be expected on the basis of his capabilities. Thus, for the psychologist the type of achievement testing which is most useful is the screening type of test, whether this is for work in a single subject or for a broader range of achievements.

In this chapter we will review some of the most commonly used tests which are used to screen achievement. Not all of these tests are equally well standardized and their inclusion in this volume is not meant as an endorsement of their use. On the other hand, all of the tests we will cover are frequently used by psychologists and school programs (sometimes inappropriately). Consequently students and practitioners will encounter reports which include data based on these instruments and will find some discussion of these procedures helpful in the interpretation of the findings given in reports on children.

When the psychologist plans to use an assessment procedure to give some indication of a child's achievement, the clinician must decide how much time can be devoted to the measure. Usually achievement testing is included in an evaluation which will comprise interviews, intellectual assessment, and often some other specialized type of testing with regard to either personality or neuropsychological functions. As a rule the achievement tests that are most useful in these situations are of the screening variety, not the extensive batteries which take several hours and are used by teachers to specify remedial approaches to learning. Thus, the clinician will usually prefer a test which takes 30 minutes to an hour, depending on the range of questions to be answered. Regardless of the opportunities for clinical observation which should be a part of all assessment procedures, the better the test is psychometrically, the better the interpretation possible from the data.

Many achievement tests have poor normative and standardization data. Worse still, some of them have been printed in forms which appear to observe the psychometric amenities but in fact provide little information to the unsophisticated reader or the anxious student scanning quickly for reassurance that validity and reliability information has been provided. In the case of achievement tests, caveat emptor!

Using the same format we adopted with intelligence tests, we will review each test, describing its format and content, administration and scoring, and standardization data, followed by a critique. Finally, we will compare and discuss the instruments covered in the chapter.

### METROPOLITAN READINESS TESTS (MRT)

*Manual*

Metropolitan Readiness Tests, Fourth Edition. New York: Harcourt Brace Jovanovich, 1976. 757 Third Avenue, New York, N.Y. 10017.

*Purpose*

The Metropolitan Readiness Tests are designed to measure pre-reading skills of children enrolled in kindergarten or beginning first grade.

*Format and Content*

There are two levels of Metropolitan Readiness Tests with alternate Forms P & Q available for each level. Level I, used in the first half of the kindergarten year, contains the following tests: Auditory Memory, Rhyming, Letter Recognition, Visual Matching, School Language and Listening, Quantitative Language, and an optional test, Copying. Level II, used at the end of kindergarten or the beginning of the first grade, includes the following tests: Beginning Consonants, Sound-Letter Correspondence, Visual Matching, Finding Patterns, School Language, Listening, Quantitative Concepts, Quantitative Operations, and an optional test, Copying.

The tests are designed to be used as group tests administered by the classroom teacher. However, they can also be administered individually. For each level there is a manual with verbatim directions for administration and a separate manual presenting norms, interpretative information, and technical information on the development of the Metropolitan Readiness Tests.

*Administration and Scoring*

All test items are presented orally by the examiner and the child marks his answer choice directly in the test booklet. With the exception of the copying test all the answer choices are multiple choice pictures. No reading is required of the child, nor are there any timed sections on these tests. Time requirements for classroom administration are approximately 80–90 minutes.

Raw scores are computed and, using the norms in the second section of the teacher's manual, are converted to percentile rank and stanine scores. For Level I, composite scores are computed for Visual and Language areas, and a Pre-Reading Score is computed from the total raw score on all tests. For Level II there are composite scores for Auditory, Visual, and Language areas. The total raw scores for all areas yield a Pre-reading Composite Score. On Level II there is also a Composite Quantitative Score.

*Standardization*

Standardization for the MRT (Level I) samples was accomplished through November testing, with a second sample tested in April for both Forms P and Q. A total of 68,997 pupils participated in the samples, which contained subgroups for studies relating to equating of forms, levels and validation, and other purposes. The data were based on students chosen to represent a stratified random sample of the United States school systems with five levels of socioeconomic status, size of school system, geographic region, and ethnic background.

Standardization for the MRT (Level II) followed the same procedures with September testing for the first grade students and April testing for the kindergarten children. A total of 66,254 pupils participated in the samples, which were also a stratified random sample of U.S. school systems representative in terms of socioeconomic status, geographic region, ethnic background, and sex.

*Reliability*

Split-half reliabilities for Level I are variable but generally high for all subtests on Form Q. The only split-half reliability below .70 on Form P is School Language and Listening. Internal consistency estimates (KR-20, Kuder-Richardson Formula 20) are likewise supportive of acceptable reliability. The composite reliabilities for Pre-reading Skills are excellent on both forms and for both types of reliability, being in the .90s. For the Pre-reading Skills the Alternate Form Reliability is .85.

For Level II, split-half reliabilities and KR-20 estimates are all high for both Forms P and Q. The Pre-reading Composite reliabilities for both forms and both types of estimates are all above .90. The Alternate Form Reliability for the Pre-reading Composite is .87.

*Validity*

Content validity, based on an analysis of beginning reading skills, indicated that items on the MRT did indeed sample those skills. Predictive validity, assessed by comparing fall MRT Level I, Form P scores of kindergarten pupils with achievement scores in the spring (MAT), was generally high (N=719). Correlations were moderately high with the Pre-Reading Composite of the MRT (.68 with the MAT Primer Level; .72 with Mathematics; and .69 for Listening for Sounds). 
Content validity for Level II was assessed in the same manner as for

Level I. Predictive validity study indicated that a random sample of classes from the norm sample which took Level II, Form P in the fall had acceptable correlations with the MAT taken in the spring of the following year or performed as expected on the Stanford Achievement Test (correlations were generally in the .70s).

*Critique*

The MRT is simple to administer and to score. It has an easy-to-read manual, tables for conversion of raw scores into stanines, percentile ranks, and a clear discussion of test interpretation. The standardization work is well done and clear. The testing format is similar to that experienced by children in their everyday school experience. While the individual subtest scores cannot be interpreted accurately (the composite scores for pre-reading are more interpretable), they do offer some cues which may be tested out if specific strengths and weaknesses need to be assessed. The test does correlate well with other reading tests (Murphy-Durrell, r=.80).

Lower socioeconomic status (SES) is associated with lower reliabilities, making more caution appropriate in the interpretation of children's scores at the lower SES level. There is not a true measure of auditory skill at Level I and scoring for Level I copying is subjective. The MRT has the advantage of permitting one to observe a child functioning under classroom-like conditions with classroom-like materials. The MRT is frequently used to aid in decisions regarding whether a child possesses the necessary skills to enter the first grade.

### METROPOLITAN ACHIEVEMENT TESTS (MAT)

*Manual*

The Metropolitan Achievement Tests, Fifth Edition. New York: The Psychological Corporation, 1978. 757 Third Avenue, New York, N.Y. 10017.

*Purpose*

The purpose of the Metropolitan Achievement Tests is to provide a national measure of a student's acquisition of materials taught in classrooms from kindergarten through grade 12.

*Format and Content*

The 1978 revision of the MAT consists of a Survey Battery for each test level and separate Instructional Batteries in Languages, Mathematics, and Reading for each level. The Instructional Batteries are useful for detailed evaluation of specific skill areas, while the Survey Battery gives information regarding overall achievement and allows comparison of the relative strengths and weaknesses of a student in different subject areas. The Survey Battery can be used as a basic battery by administering only the Reading, Mathematics, and Language tests or as a complete battery by adding the tests in Science and Social Studies.

The MAT is designed for group administration by the classroom teacher and the teacher's manual includes verbatim instructions for each test, as well as general instructions for setting up the testing procedures. There is a separate teacher's manual for each level since the test batteries have slightly different formats due to the content areas measured and also the manner in which the material is presented to the student. For example, the teacher reads many of the test items aloud in the early grades.

*Administration and Scoring*

Most of the test items are presented as multiple choice items, with the answer choices including both a "Not Given" and a "Don't Know" selection. In the early grades the students mark their answer choices directly in the test booklet, while children in later grades use a separate answer sheet. Hand-scoring keys are available for each level. Raw scores are computed for each test as well as for the complete batteries and are converted to scaled scores. Scaled scores are then converted to grade equivalent, percentile rank, and stanine scores. The manual defines each type of score and explains its most appropriate use. The manual suggests stanine scores (in a nine-point scale based on percentile ranks) as the most preferable method of reporting test results to parents and pupils. Stanines 7, 8 and 9 are considered above average; stanines 4, 5, and 6 are designated average; and stanines 1, 2, and 3 are below average and indicate the need for a specialized or remedial curriculum. The manual cautions against using the Grade Equivalent as a means of reporting results of individual pupils on the MAT. For example, if a third grade pupil received a grade equivalent of 8.0 on the Mathematics tests, it does *not* mean that the third grader knows the eighth grade mathematics curriculum; it simply means that the average or typical beginning eighth grade student would score as well as the third grade student on the mathematics test for the *third* grade level.

*Standardization*

The 1978 edition is the fifth revision of the MAT, which was first designed to measure school achievement in the New York City area during 1930–32. The 1978 edition has norms for both fall and spring administration, and offers for the first time both a survey battery and an instructional battery for each test level. The development of this edition involved approximately 800,000 students in all 50 states. Teachers, administrators, and an independent panel of minority educators reviewed the approximately 14,000 test items which were administered to 93,000 students in order to select the 7,500 test items needed for the final two forms of the test. Over 550,000 pupils participated in the national standardization program of the final two forms. The sample was controlled for school system size, geographic region, socioeconomic status, and ethnic breakdown. Both forms were normed in October 1977 and April 1978 to provide fall and spring norms for each level.

*Reliability*

Reliability data are presented in the Teacher's Manual for the fall standardization. For the kindergarten level, Kuder-Richardson Formula 20 reliability estimates are: Language, .72; Mathematics, .77; Reading, .94; and Basic Battery, .95.

*Validity*

Content validity is designated as the most significant form of validity for an achievement test and the point is made that each school system must inspect both the content of the MAT and its own curriculum to estimate the MAT's content validity.

*Critique*

The MAT are designed as group tests and this must be kept in mind when evaluating their usefulness in a clinical situation. One advantage of the MAT is that the format allows the child to work with typical classroom test material, while it allows the examiner an opportunity to observe child behaviors such as the ability to follow directions, to use the materials correctly, to stay on task, and to persist for a fairly long period of time (tests range from 25-40 minutes each).

Some school systems require the administration of an individual rather than a group achievement test for the purpose of school placement. Clearly the MAT will not serve that purpose. However, valuable information about a child's ability to work with material under classroom conditions versus close one-to-one conditions can be elicited by comparing the results of the MAT with those of an individually administered achievement test such as the Peabody Individual Achievement Test.

## PEABODY INDIVIDUAL ACHIEVEMENT TEST (PIAT)

*Manual*

The Peabody Individual Achievement Test. Circle Pines, MN: American Guidance Service, 1970.

*Purpose*

The Peabody Individual Achievement Test is designed to measure academic achievement across a grade range of kindergarten through high school. The age ranges included are five years three months to 18 years three months.

*Format and Content*

The Peabody Individual Achievement Test is composed of five subtests: Mathematics, Reading Recognition, Reading Comprehension, Spelling, and General Information. Both grade level and age level norms are provided for each subtest as well as for the total test.

The test materials are contained in two volumes which form easels and may be conveniently placed on a desk or table in front of the subject. These volumes present either pictorial or written material to the subject. The Mathematics subtest presents four answer choices for each question and the examiner reads the questions aloud. The Reading Recognition subtest requires the subject initially to identify letters of the alphabet and subsequently to read aloud an increasingly difficult list of words. The Reading Comprehension subtest utilizes two pages for each question. The subject reads a sentence silently on the first page and then is required to choose from the four pictures on the next page the one that best represents the content of the sentence. Both the sentences and picture choices become more complex and precise as the subtest proceeds. The Spelling subtest is a recognition test, not a written spelling test. The examiner pronounces a word, gives an example of its use in a sentence, and then the subject identifies the correct spelling from one of four choices. The Information subtest consists of a series of questions read aloud to the subject with each answer recorded verbatim and scored immediately according to criteria given for each question.

## Administration and Scoring

Since the PIAT is a wide-range test, a basal and ceiling level approach is used in order to administer only the relevant portions of the test to an individual subject. The basal level for a subtest is established when five consecutive correct responses are obtained. The ceiling is established when the subject fails five out of seven consecutive items. Raw scores are obtained for each subtest and for the total test. These can then be converted into grade equivalent scores and percentile ranks by current grade placement and/or into age-equivalent scores and percentile ranks by chronological age. Normalized standard scores with a mean of 100 and a standard deviation of 15 can also be obtained from percentile ranks (a percentile rank of 50 equals a standard score of 100). Test administration usually requires 30 to 45 minutes. All subtests are untimed.

## Standardization

The data from which norms were derived are based upon a standardization of 2,889 students in "mainstream" public education classes across the continental United States (kindergarten through grade 12). The country was divided into nine districts and samples were obtained from an urban, suburban, and rural school in each district (total communities=27). Sampling procedures for the standardization population sought to maximize the congruence between the characteristics of the sample population and those of an equivalent population defined by the 1967 U.S. census data. Variables included the geographical distribution noted above, as well as the occupational level of the major parental wage earner, age, race, and sex.

*Reliability*

Test-retest reliability of the PIAT was assessed by readministering the test one month later to samples of 50 to 75 subjects at each of six grade levels (kindergarten, grades 1, 3, 5, 8, and 12). The sample of this reliability study was skewed towards the lower grade levels because the authors believed that the PIAT would probably be most often used and would be more sensitive at lower grade levels. Reliability coefficients ranged from a low of .42 for kindergarten subjects on Spelling to a high of .94 for third grade subjects on Reading Recognition (overall median, all tests=.78). The standard error of measurement is larger in higher grades, often being greater than six raw score points above the fifth grade level. Therefore, minimally discrepant subtest scores in these grade levels should not be construed as indicative of differences in ability levels.

Split-half reliability coefficients were not calculated since the authors felt spuriously high estimates would be obtained because the items had been selected and ordered by difficulty for use with a basal and ceiling technique of presentation.

*Validity*

Content validity was not chosen to provide a sample of critical skills but rather to select items which correlated most highly with total test score (internal consistency). Items were retained which showed curves of 50% of a grade level's subjects passing. Concurrent validity data consisted of giving subjects used in the test-retest reliability study Form A of the Peabody Picture Vocabulary Test at the time of the second administration of the PIAT. Variation in the correlations between PPVT and PIAT was found with regard to both subtest and grade level. Highest correlations, collapsed across grades, were obtained between the PPVT IQ and the PIAT General Information subtest (median $r$=.68), the Reading Comprehension subtest (.66), and the total test scores (.675). The lowest correlation was between PPVT IQ and the PIAT Spelling subtest (.40).

*Critique*

The advantage of the PIAT is that it is a wide-range power test which is quickly and easily administered and scored. It has good standardization and it can be adopted for use with handicapped populations.

The disadvantage of the PIAT is that it has scant validity data and no real content reliability data. There are no data at all on predictive validity. Since clinicians are frequently asked to estimate future performance, the PIAT is quite limited to a current description of the student's relative placement on a screening device. The PIAT does not make any direct assessment of computational skills on the Mathematics subtest, and the Spelling subtest is only a recognition test. Therefore, low scores on these subtests do not inform the examiner as to the nature of the math or spelling problem. The length of the subtests does mean that sometimes subjects who begin to fail will be kept at a failing task for a long time (in order to get the ceiling) and this may result in poor rapport if instructions are followed completely. Moreover, the establishment of a ceiling may result in spuriously high scores (due to the method followed). Another problem with the PIAT is that for many children one cannot really assume the same beginning level for each subtest, an assumption made by the test. Particularly for children with learning problems this assumption is unlikely to be true. Nonetheless, given all these cautions, the PIAT has better item selection than many tests of its type. Finally, the fact that the standard error of measurement is larger at higher grade levels means that small discrepancies at higher grade levels cannot be interpreted with the same confidence as the same discrepancies at lower grade levels.

## DIAGNOSTIC READING SCALES

*Manual*

Diagnostic Reading Scales – Revised Edition. Spache, G. D. Monterey, CA: CTB/McGraw-Hill, 1972. Del Monte Research Park, Monterey, CA 93940.

*Purpose*

The Diagnostic Reading Scales are designed to measure reading skills, both oral and silent, and auditory comprehension. These scales are for use with elementary school readers and for retarded readers at the junior and senior high school levels.

*Format and Content*

The Diagnostic Reading Scales are individually administered. Three word lists of 40 to 50 words are provided. These word recognition lists are used to estimate reading grade level. The subject reads aloud from a list chosen by the examiner (to represent approximate grade level).

The examiner obtains a raw score on the basis of words read correctly and calculates a grade level from a table which accompanies the word list. Errors made by the child also permit the examiner to detect patterns of word analysis and sight recognition.

After establishing the grade level, the examiner has the subject read aloud from the reading passage at that grade level. The examiner notes reading errors and, when the subject finishes reading the passage, asks the comprehension questions listed in the examiner's manual. Scoring criteria are listed with each passage for both maximum allowable errors and minimum correct (60%) comprehension questions. The subject continues reading oral selections in increasing order of grade level until failing either on reading or comprehension scores for a particular passage. The oral reading level, designated the Instructional Level, is the highest level at which the student passes both aspects of the scoring.

In order to establish the Independent Level, the student is asked to read silently the next higher level passage above that established as the Instructional Level. The reading time is recorded and comprehension questions are asked. This procedure continues with successive reading passages until the student fails to answer correctly the minimum number of comprehension questions. The Independent Level is the highest level at which the comprehension questions are passed. Speed of reading is computed as slow, average, or fast, based on a table provided in the manual (not in the examiner's booklet).

To establish the child's Potential Level of reading, the examiner reads aloud a passage to the child, and his comprehension indicates his understanding of the passage. If a student fails the first selection read, the potential level is considered to be equal to the independent level.

Alternate equivalent reading passages are provided for the first and second half of grades 1 through 3 and for grades 4 through 8. The alternate selections are intended for retesting within a six-month period, but may be utilized in the initial testing if the child has exhausted the first selections by reading passages beyond the appropriate grade level during the establishment of the instructional level.

Supplementary phonics tests are also included in the Diagnostic Reading Scales but no data are included as to their standardization or construction. Therefore these tests will not be reviewed here.

*Standardization*

Students from both urban and rural schools in Florida, Georgia, New York, and Rhode Island were used to establish norms. For Oral Comprehension or Instructional Level, 2,081 students were tested, while 1,269 of these students were used in the silent reading comprehension norms (Independent Level). Data were based on a minimum of 100 cases scoring at each reading level regardless of age or grade level. Testing was done either by reading clinicians or by teachers being trained as remedial reading teachers. Norms are given in the Examiner's Manual. Separate groups of students were used for the establishment of the alternate forms.

## Reliability

The examiner's manual provides data on internal consistency for word recognition lists which range from .87 for list 2 to .96 for list 1. Alternate form reliabilities were as follows: Instructional, .99; Independent, .98; and Potential, .99, on samples of 75 children each. Test-retest reliabilities on samples of 52 for the Instructional Level and 50 for the Independent Level were .84 and .88 respectively, but these samples are not described with regard to age and grade of students. Since the standard errors of measurement are .56 and .48 respectively for these levels but no data are provided for level by grade, it is not possible to determine whether the grade norms represent real differences in performance level.

## Validity

Reading materials selected for use in the Diagnostic Reading Scales were selected by either the Spache formula for primary grades or the Dale-Chall formula for higher grades. These formulae are based on sentence length and vocabulary analyses of classroom reading materials. Content validity was established by this method.

Construct validity was studied by having students who took selections from the Diagnostic Reading Scales also read parallel selections from similar tests. These comparisons were continued until each selection from the Diagnostic Reading Scales was considered valid against the criterion measure or had been replaced by a selection which appeared more valid against this criterion. However, the criterion tests are not described.

Concurrent validity was studied by comparing results on the Diagnostic Reading Scales with classes of students in Grades 1 through 6 on the California Reading Test. Other samples were compared on the Durrell Listening-Reading Series, the Gates-McKillop Reading Diagnostic Test teacher judgments, and the Primary Reading Level of the Metropolitan Achievement Tests. A technical bulletin (Spache, 1982) reports data on a 1973 sample of 361 pupils from 24 schools which compares performance on the Diagnostic Reading Scales and the 1970 edition of the California Achievement Tests (CAT). All correlations with reading levels are above .70 except for word recognition level which is .69. The highest correlation is between Instructional Level and total CAT-70 score (.77). Test-retest reliability was also reported in the 1975 technical manual as ranging from .68 for Potential Level to .97 for word recognition list.

*Critique*

The Diagnostic Reading Scales are easy to administer and require no special equipment. While the instrument is a good screening test and therefore attractive for general determination as to level, it is not good for specification of remedial approaches. The comprehension passing rate (60%) may result in an overestimate of levels due to the fact that it is low. Also, the comprehension section taps recall of specific material rather than understanding based on higher cognitive operations and functions. The nature of the validity and reliability information is not well specified, and while there appears a conscientious attempt to study the scales, insufficient data are available to know exactly how confidently to interpret results for a specific grade and level of performance with regard to peers.

## STANFORD ACHIEVEMENT TEST (SAT)

*Manual*

Stanford Achievement Test, Sixth Edition. Madden, R., Gardner, E. F., Rudman, H. C., Karlsen, B., & Merwin, J. C. New York: The Psychological Corporation, 1973. 757 Third Avenue, New York, N.Y. 10017.

*Purpose*

The Stanford Achievement Test, Sixth Edition provides a comprehensive set of testing for various types of achievement related to school curriculum in the primary, intermediate, and advanced secondary school levels.

*Format and Content*

The Primary Level I (grades 1.5 through 2.4) includes subtests for Vocabulary, Reading Comprehension, Word Study Skills, Mathematics Concepts, Mathematics Computation, Spelling, and Listening Comprehension. The Battery consists of 304 items and takes about 190 minutes to administer.

Primary Level II (grades 2.5 through 3.4) includes subtests for Vocabulary, Word Study Skills, Mathematics Concepts, Mathematics Computation, Mathematics Applications, Spelling, Social Science, Science, and Listening Comprehension. The Primary Level II Battery consists of 442 items and takes 260 minutes to administer.

Primary Level III (grades 3.5 through 4.4), Intermediate Level I (grades 4.5 through 5.4) and Intermediate Level II (grades 5.5 through 6.9) all include subtests for the same areas as does Primary Level II, but also includes an additional subtest for Language. The respective numbers of items and times for the Total Complete Battery are 504 items, 295 minutes; 588 items, 320 minutes; and 595 items, 320 minutes.

The Advanced Level (grades 7 through 9.5) consists of the same subtests as for the Primary III and Intermediate Levels except that the subtests for Word Study Skills and Listening Comprehension are omitted. The number of items for the Complete Battery is 503 and 260 minutes are required for administration.

The Basic Battery which consists of Reading and Mathematics subtests are available for Levels Primary II through Advanced. The Basic Battery takes from 185 minutes to 225 minutes to administer, depending upon the level given.

Alternate forms are available at every level. These forms are equated for content, format, and level of difficulty.

The manual gives instructions for administration and interpretation. The instructions are clear. Test booklets include examples and practice items.

*Administration and Scoring*

The SAT is usually group-administered by may be given individually. Scoring may be done by hand or by machine. Subtest scores, scores for Total Reading, Total Mathematics, and Total Battery, and where appropriate Total Auditory Score, National Percentile Rank, National

Grade Equivalent, and National Stanine scores are available, as are standard scores for each subtest.

## Standardization

The standardization sample consisted of 275,000 students in 109 school systems across 43 states. The standardization sample was chosen to fit closely the characteristics of the national population (1970 Census data) as to: community size, geographic region, family income, school class size, and ethnic background.

Items were chosen to represent material generally included in school curricula. However, the test is not a diagnostic test in the sense that specific skills are identified as present or missing.

## Reliability and Validity

Both the split-half and Kuder-Richardson Formula 20 reliability coefficients are generally high (only 30 below .80, all in Primary I or II). Validity concerns entered into the construction of the test, including review of the items by a panel of minority group representatives. Not all areas tested present material, so that general validity of the testing in that subtest cannot be assumed. For example, all the spelling items are based on multiple choice identification. Spelling recognition may not reflect the same skills as spelling from recall.

Some concern over the content of the science and social science material may be in order. This concern stems from lack of clarity of the items and some unevenness of objectives in these sections.

## Critique

The SAT is a well constructed test. Lehmann (in Buros, 1978, pp. 105–106) gives high marks to the SAT but does suggest that the listening comprehension test may rely too much on memory material. The tests were normed both in fall and spring. Separate norms are not available for boys and girls. The material in the Basic Battery seems open to less criticism regarding content than either the science or social studies sections. The SAT is much too long for use in its entirety in clinical settings. However, subsets of the SAT might be useful in situations in which brief instruments are undesirable, such as when one wishes to eliminate one-to-one interaction with the examiner (prominent in the administration of the PIAT and Woodcock-Johnson Psycho-Educational Battery).

## WIDE RANGE ACHIEVEMENT TEST (WRAT)

*Manual*

Wide Range Achievement Test, Fourth Edition. Jastak, J. F. & Jastak, S. Wilmington, DE: Jastak Associates, 1978. 1526 Gilpin Avenue, Wilmington, DE 19806.

*Purpose*

The Wide Range Achievement Test was intended to measure "reading word recognition and pronunciation, written spelling, and arithmetic computation" (p. 1).

*Format and Content*

Each of the three subtests of the WRAT (Reading, Spelling, and Arithmetic) is divided into two levels. Level I is administered to children from age five years zero months through 11 years 11 months. Level II is administered to persons 12 years of age and older. The test blank contains all necessary printed material for both levels.

The Spelling subtest is composed of three tasks: copying a series of marks that are printed on the form, printing or writing the person's name, and writing a list of dictated words. The first two tasks are always given to children from five years zero months through seven years 11 months, but only to older persons with a minimal score on the dictation portion of the test.

The Arithmetic subtest contains printed computational problems which the subject solves and answers on the test form itself. This portion of the test has a 10-minute time limit. If the subject cannot solve any of the problems, a short oral arithmetic test is administered.

The Reading subtest consists of pronouncing a list of printed words from the test form. If the subject cannot meet the minimum passing criterion for word reading, a pre-reading portion is administered which includes such tasks as reading letters aloud from the form and identifying letters in the person's own name.

*Administration and Scoring*

The three subtests can be administered in about 20 to 30 minutes and may be presented in any order the examiner chooses. The test form has the subtests in the following order: Spelling, Arithmetic, Reading. The directions in the manual are in the order of Spelling, Reading, Arithmetic – a discrepancy which seems likely to cause initial confusion for the inexperienced examiner.

The manual contains verbatim instructions printed in red and also has pronunciation guides for the spelling and word recognition lists. The 1978 test form has charts at the end of each subtest for the purpose of converting raw scores to grade ratings. The test items are *unchanged* from earlier editions and old test forms may still be used for administration; however, the examiner is cautioned to use the suplementary grade ratings provided with the manual. Grade ratings are converted to standard scores and percentile ranks from tables provided in the manual. Scores are given for individual subtests only; no total general achievement level is computed.

*Standardization*

The manual states that 15,200 children and adults participated in the standardization of the 1978 edition of the WRAT. These subjects were *not selected to provide a representative national sample along socioeconomic, racial, or intellectual dimensions*. At each of the 27 age levels listed, the sample consisted of 50% male and 50% female and all of them had scores on some kind of ability test, mainly the Wechsler Intelligence Scale for Children, the Wechsler Adult Intelligence Scale, and the Jastak Wide Range Intelligence and Personality Test.

*Reliability and Validity*

Statements about the standardization sample are written in such a manner that the manual is unspecific as to the nature of the distribution of ethnic, economic, intellectual, and age groups used in various analyses. This makes it unclear whether a standard score for one age is comparable to a standard score for another age as the samples upon which they are based may be quite different.

Likewise the manual provides no breakdown by year and subtest for reliability figures, the result being that it is impossible to know how reliable any subtest score at any given age should be considered. Split-half reliability coefficients were computed using odd-even scores, a procedure which should and does yield reliabilities in the .90s. However, the more important information concerning internal consistency and test-retest reliabilities is missing. Also, it is unclear that any further reliability work has been done since the 1965 edition. None of the references cited appear to indicate work on the reliability and validity data beyond the date of the 1965 edition.

While several pages in the manual are devoted to descriptions of various relationships between the WRAT and other instruments ranging from achievement tests to intelligence tests, the descriptions are vague, based on small samples, and otherwise unsatisfactory for the purpose of being able to interpret the data presented. Some of the data are based on the 1946 edition and some on the 1965 edition. Since the materials in the 1978 edition are identical to the 1965 edition, they might have some relevance if interpretable.

There is no description of why the items used should be considered appropriate as to content validity. The use of the term *achievement test* for this set of materials is questionable. Moreover, there is no evidence that the WRAT actually functions as intended.

*Critique*

As can be seen above, the claims of the authors of the WRAT appear unsubstantiated by the information they provide with the test. The WRAT has been criticized consistently in various editions of the Buros Mental Measurements Yearbook. A careful review of the WRAT manual leads the reader to believe that these criticisms have been written with restraint. A quotation from Thorndike (1978) clarifies the nature of the concern:

> However it is in the domain of validity that the most serious questions about this test would seem to arise. Here the authors appear to have some bizarre conceptions and to engage in somewhat exotic procedures (p. 68).

Later in his review, Thorndike observes with regard to Jastak's description of *a clinical factor analysis* that "the exact nature of the procedure is apparently known only to the authors and God and He may have some uncertainty" (p. 68). The use of the WRAT is highly questionable;

its data and claims are uncertain. In the face of other, better constructed and better standardized instruments it would appear that the WRAT has little to recommend it. Because of the format of the manual and the vague statements, a naive and inexperienced examiner could assume greater confidence than is merited by the instrument and could be in the position of overinterpreting or misinterpreting the child's performance. Since such misinterpretation could have grave consequences for a child, the examiner should be aware of this danger and consider carefully before choosing an instrument to be used for the screening of a child's achievement performance.

## WOODCOCK-JOHNSON PSYCHO-EDUCATIONAL BATTERY

*Manual*

Woodcock-Johnson Psycho-Educational Battery, Part Two: Tests of Achievement. Woodcock, R. W. & Johnson, M. B. Hingham, MA: Teaching Resources Corporation, 1977. 50 Pond Park Road, Hingham, MA 02043.

*Purpose*

Part Two of the Woodcock-Johnson is a wide-range achievement test designed to provide measures of subjects' performances in reading, mathematics, and written language and their knowledge of science, social science, and humanities. Subjects may range in age from preschool to old age.

*Format and Content*

The test materials are contained in a volume which may be folded to form an easel and this may be conveniently placed on a desk or table in front of the subject. In addition, a copy of the response booklet and two sharpened pencils with erasers should be provided. The test manual is included in the volume. Each of the 10 subtests is numbered and headed by a tabulated sheet for easy access. On the title page for each subtest are specific instructions indicating the examiner's task, rules for determining basal and ceiling performances, guidelines for starting points, scoring instructions, and the like. Verbatim instructions are printed in blue at appropriate points in the instructions. The examiner's page also includes appropriate answers for the specific subtests. Letter-Word Identification contains 54 items; Word Attack has 26 items but is not administered unless a subject scores above 10 on Letter-Word Identification. Passage Comprehension contains 26 items; Calculation has 42 items. Applied problems (mathematics) has 49 items. Dictation consists of 40 items. The Proofing subtest, which is not administered unless the subject received a score of at least 10 on Letter-Word Identification, includes 29 items. Science contains 39 items, Social Studies, 37 items, and Humanities, 36 items. With the exception of Word Attack and Proofing, all subtests have both ceiling and basal rules. Items are scored either one or zero. About 30 minutes' administration time is estimated, although the manual advises that some subjects may take 45 minutes.

## Administration and Scoring

The test requires some training on the examiner's part. At least two practice tests are recommended to become familiar with the materials should precede an observed administration by an experienced examiner. Proper pronunciation is essential to administration of some parts of the test and a tape is provided (it is actually contained in Part One of the Woodcock-Johnson) for correct pronunciation of the material which is essential to administration of some parts of the test. Seating instructions are suggested for both right- and left-handed examiners.

A preschool form of the battery consists of six subtests: Letter-Word Identification, Applied Problems, Dictation, Science, Social Studies, and Humanities. No particular order of administration is required.

Raw scores are computed, which consist of all items below the basal level and all correct items between the basal and ceiling levels. Age and grade are recorded and used in further computations. Cluster scores are computed: Reading (Letter-Word Identification, Word Attack, and Passage Comprehension); Mathematics (Calculation and Applied Problems); Written Language (Dictation and Proofing); Knowledge (Science, Social Studies, and Humanities). Grade equivalent scores compare the subject's performance to those of the norm group appropriate for that subject. Age equivalent scores compare the subject's performance to that in the norm group and state the performance in terms of the age of that portion of the norm group. Percentile rank scores compare the subject's performance to those in an appropriate part of the norm group and reflect the subject's relative standing with regard to the norm sample. A Relative Performance Index (RPI) is a predictive score indicating the expected performance of the subject with regard to a stated reference group (average, for example). The RPI is based on 90% mastery. Cluster difference scores are computed by subtracting the average cluster value (given in table) from the subject's cluster scores. These cluster difference scores are used to obtain the subject's percentile rank scores from another table (for age or for grade). Likewise the cluster difference scores are used to obtain the subject's RPI and functioning level.

Several profiles may be constructed based upon the scoring. These include a Subtest Profile (based on raw scores), which indicates both subtest scores and cluster scores. A Percentile Rank Profile is also computed and an Instructional Implications Profile, the latter giving information about the subject's instructional range.

*Standardization*

Data were collected from 49 communities and 4,732 subjects distributed across the United States in 1976 and 1977. Each subject's contribution was weighted to provide equivalence with characteristics of the U.S. population. The pilot battery was administered to 1,000 subjects and then refined by dropping useless items. After 2,000 subjects were tested, the process was repeated and further items were dropped. When all data were obtained, all statistical analyses were completed, including multivariate analyses. Using a Rasch model, the authors calibrated the items for difficulty for each subtest.

The age range included subjects from three years to over 65 years. The sample was constructed using the 1970 Census data with regard to sex, race, occupational status, geographic region and urban-nonurban status. Some grade levels were over-represented to permit factor analyses and regression analyses.

*Reliability*

Prior to data collection clusters were identified by determining which subtests should be included and the weight of each subtest for the cluster. Median reliabilities across several studies were reported (Woodcock, 1978). The Reading Cluster included those subtests which represented the most significant aspects of reading ability. The median reliability across several studies was .96 for the Reading Cluster. The

Written Language Cluster can be rescored to obtain measures of punctuation, capitalization, spelling, and usage. Its median reliability was .94. The Knowledge Cluster had a median reliability of .93, while the Skills Cluster produced a median reliability of .90. This cluster included Letter-Word Identification, Applied Problems, and Dictation. No data are provided as to other aspects of reliability.

Since no subject is administered complete subtests (for most subtests) reliability coefficients had to be computed to include the easiest items likely to be presented at an age or grade level, and all items likely to be presented to a subject who falls at a point one standard deviation above the mean. Median reliabilities were computed for subtests (as well as for the clusters noted above) and ranged from .83 to .95. Specific values for age and grade for either subtest or cluster are not included in the reported data (Woodcock, 1978).

*Validity*

Content validity was established by the use of textbooks with broad sampling of content in an area, by experts, and by the use of the Rasch model to select items. Construct validity was dealt with by using clusters (predetermined data were collected) analyzed for relationships among subtests within clusters and between other clusters. Predictive validity was studied only with regard to the Cognitive Abilities Tests (Part I) but not with regard to Part II (Achievement Tests). Concurrent validity coefficients based on samples of 83, 86, and 75 for the third, fifth, and twelfth grades, respectively, yield values in the high .80s to low .90s with the Woodcock Reading Mastery Test, and similar correlations with the PIAT Reading. The Mathematics Cluster correlates with Key Math in the low .80s and somewhat lower with other mathematics tests. Written language has similar correlations with the Iowa Language Test. Data for clinical groups are based on smaller samples and produce lower coefficients where available.

*Critique*

The Woodcock-Johnson Psycho-Educational Battery (Part II – Tests of Achievement) appears to be an excellent instrument in terms of its coverage and psychometric properties. The subtests are superior to those of other tests which require a comparable amount of time for administration in that they sample broadly across a range of material that is more representative of the school curriculum than is the case for many other instruments. The test is attractively packaged and relatively easy to administer. Instructions are well stated. Because of its recent development, there are no data which use outside validation criteria, large-scale clinical samples, or longitudinal samples. However, given the thoroughness with which the test has been constructed, it is to be expected that such information will be available shortly. The material provided in Woodcock (1978) indicates that some sex differences were obtained in that girls achieved higher scores on the written language cluster than boys with the same aptitude scores on Part I and that these differences increased with age. The major question to be answered with regard to the Woodcock-Johnson Battery is whether the model underlying it is appropriate for clinical as well as normal populations. While the sample-free characteristics of the test are attractive and seem reasonable for normal samples, it is not clear whether the hoped-for predictive and prescriptive statements based on the model will be equally applicable to clinical samples. In any case, the test is superior to most instruments currently available.


## COMPARISON OF ACHIEVEMENT TESTS

Despite the widespread use of achievement tests by schools, reviews of some of the most frequently used instruments lead us to urge caution in the manner of their use. We are led to a number of conclusions. First, with regard to *content validity*, the Metropolitan Readiness Test, the Metropolitan Achievement Test, the Stanford Achievement Test, the Woodcock-Johnson, and the Diagnostic Reading Scales all use some systematic examination of curriculum-based analyses to guide the selection of items. The PIAT includes items passed by 50% of the students taking the test at a given grade level (in the standardization sample, but how closely this sample of items approximates a representative sample of curriculum for a grade level is not clear). Of the tests we have reviewed, only the WRAT offers no justification for the item selection in terms of content validity. Psychometrically the construction of the Woodcock-Johnson Achievement Battery appears to be excellent and its content seems more comprehensive than any of the other tests which take comparable amounts of time for administration. The Woodcock-Johnson is also a broader range test than the PIAT and includes both concept and skill assessment across a number of content areas.

Since school curricula vary with regard to region and school system, the use of standardized tests may be helpful in comparing a child's performance with peers in terms of a national sample, but may not be helpful in terms of grade placement if the local curriculum differs greatly from that tested in the standardized instrument. Referrals which include questions about appropriate grade placement must take into account local curriculum characteristics as well as standing on achievement tests, which are constructed on the basis of national representative samples. Likewise, the skills tests must be broad enough to permit the examiner to address questions raised by the referral source.

Remedial programs and tutoring should be evaluated with regard to the specific curriculum requirements. Scores given in terms of grade level on screening instruments are not very helpful with regard to the construction of a remedial program. Tests such as the Stanford Achievement, Metropolitan Readiness, and Metropolitan Achievement offer greater specificity than screening tests; however, they are not diagnostic tests as such. Detailed analysis of specific areas of underachievement may, in some cases, require even more detailed analysis of difficulties through the use of a diagnostic skills test. None of the tests reviewed has demonstrated predictive validity. Consequently, *it would be improper to suggest, on the basis of these tests, how a child will perform in the future.*

The clinician interested in child assessment will find achievement tests very helpful in several respects. First, achievement tests can be used to rule out specific areas of current underachievement. Given a child whose school performance is below expectation, good performance on an adequately constructed achievement test appropriate with regard to the school curriculum tells us that the child has been able to absorb, retain, and use information. This knowledge often permits the clinician to differentiate between motivational and learning problems.

Second, high scores on intelligence tests and low scores on achievement tests often reveal patterns which indicate problems with processing information on specific modalities. Likewise, attentional problems can be detected. In the case of low achievement scores on instruments such as the SAT, MRT, or MAT, it is sometimes helpful to administer the Woodcock-Johnson or the PIAT. If social interaction, support, and reinforcement result in markedly higher Woodcock-Johnson or PIAT scores, there is reason to believe that one-to-one teaching techniques may result in improved school performance. Such information is valuable in consultation with teachers and parents. For example, many hyperactive children or children with learning disabilities are unable to function under usual classroom conditions but are able to do so in a tutorial situation.

Even children who are disruptive and over-dependent may be able to function under regular classroom conditions. It may be that their behavior stems from social reinforcement rather than from learning problems. The knowledge that distractibility and inattention are not sources of poor achievement may help in the formulation of the child's problems. It may be that parent counseling or child treatment (psychotherapy) are more appropriate in these circumstances. Thus, achievement tests, even with their psychometric limitations, provide valuable data which may aid in formulating and planning for children who are experiencing school problems.

One of the most frequent and serious school problems encountered is reading difficulty. We have reviewed a number of instruments which permit some analysis of reading performance. The choice of instrument depends partly on the type of questions and partly on the amount of time available for the assessment. The Diagnostic Reading Scales offer a screening test which requires relatively little time for administration. The comprehension questions focus on the recall of specific information (whereas some tests such as the SAT, particularly in the advanced battery, stress interpretation of the information which is presented to the child).

The examiner must attend to the content of the various instruments in order to make sense out of the results. For example, one cannot make interpretations with regard to the child's mathematical computation skills based on the PIAT, since that test does not include items which would be helpful in that regard. The important point here is that the examiner must understand the content and limitations of the achievement tests used, if the results are to be helpful in understanding and planning for a child. Since school systems often want achievement testing and often base academic decisions upon their results, it is part of the ethical and responsible practice to use only instruments appropriate for the purposes that they serve. Likewise, a common error commited by inexperienced examiners is to interpret a grade level equivalent score as meaning that the child has all the necessary skills to perform at that grade level. Such an equivalence score is limited to the material covered by the test.

The tests we have reviewed here take from about 20 or 30 minutes up to several hours for administration. Any examiner who is confronted with a child with school problems faces a myriad of complex issues. Seldom is a referral source interested only in whether a child can spell or perform arithmetic computations. The achievement test will be one source of information about the child's performance. There will be other sources of information from the history, interview, intelligence tests, teacher reports, parent reports, and so on. Depending upon the nature of the referral and the time for the total evaluation, several good options for assessment of school-related achievement have been reviewed. We will consider further, in a later chapter, how batteries of tests are selected. However, a good guideline for the selection of achievement tests is that they should serve the purpose of determining whether a child can perform the type of academic skills tested and has the appropriate knowledge without taking a longer or more comprehensive sample of performance than is necessary. The test should be selected to answer questions about how the child works, in addition to how well and how quickly he works.

## REFERENCES

Buros, O. K. *The Eighth Mental Measurement Yearbook.* Highland Park, N.J.: Gryphon Press, 1978.

Dunn, L. M. & Markwardt, F. C., Jr. *The Peabody Individual Achievement Test.* Circle Pines, MN: American Guidance Service, 1970.

Jastak, J. F. & Jastak, S. *Wide Range Achievement Test, Fourth Edition.* Wilmington, DE: Jastak Associates, 1978.

Madden, R., Gardner, E. F., Rudman, H. C., Karlsen, B., & Merwin, J. C. *The Stanford Achievement Test, Sixth Edition.* New York: The Psychological Corporation, 1973.

Nurss, J. R. & McGauvran, M. E. *Metropolitan Readiness Tests, Fourth Edition.* New York: Harcourt, Brace, Jovanovich, 1976.

Prescott, G. A., Balow, I. H., Hogan, T. P., & Farr, R. C. *The Metropolitan Achievement Tests, Fifth Edition.* New York: The Psychological Corporation, 1978.

Spache, G. D. *Diagnostic Reading Scales, revised edition.* Monterey, CA: CTB/McGraw-Hill, 1972.

Spache, G. D. *Diagnostic Reading Scales, revised edition.* Monterey, CA: CTB/McGraw-Hill, 1982.

Thorndike, R. L. Review of the WRAT. In O. K. Buros (Ed.), *The Eighth Mental Measurement Yearbook.* Highland Park, N.J.: Gryphon Press, 1978.

Woodcock, R. W. *Development and Standardization of the Woodcock-Johnson Psycho-Educational Battery.* Hingham, MA: Teaching Resources Corp., 1978.

Woodcock, R. W. & Johnson, M. B. *Woodcock-Johnson Psycho-Educational Battery, Part II: Tests of Achievement.* Hingham, MA: Teaching Resources Corporation, 1977.

# CHAPTER 8

# Developmental Instruments

Developmental instruments are generally broad spectrum devices used to assess a variety of both biologically-based and socially-developed skills. In this regard developmental assessment procedures differ from intelligence tests with which they share some overlapping purposes. Although intelligence test performance may rest upon such features as fine motor ability or language skills, IQ tests are not constructed specifically to assess these functions, which may be involved to a greater or less extent in the assessment of cognitive skills.

In the case of infant assessment procedures, the distinction between intelligence tests and developmental instruments no longer holds, since because of the predominance of motor items, the content of developmental and cognitive tasks overlaps to a significant degree. For this reason, we have included the Bayley Scales of Infant Development both in the section on intellectual assessment and in the section on developmental procedures. As we will see in the specific reviews of procedures and the discussion which compares them, the construction of the Bayley Scales differs markedly from other developmental procedures.

Developmental assessment procedures were devised to serve functions important to those who are responsible for the care and welfare of children. These functions include help in discriminating children who are handicapped, retarded, or deviant in some other way from children who are progressing normally. Parents, adoption agencies, pediatricians,

198

educators, and mental health professionals often need to know how normally children are developing and in what ways they are deviant in order to plan for them. Errors in judgment may have serious consequences for children, including inappropriate placement and ineffective or harmful treatment.

Most developmental assessment procedures take into account various biologically-based milestones. For the examiner who does not have much experience with children, there are helpful summaries of expectations regarding developmental milestones. These can be found in a series of books by Gesell and his associates (Gesell et al., 1940; Gesell & Ilg, 1946; Gesell, Ilg, & Ames, 1956). If the reader is unfamiliar with developmental assessment procedures, it would be helpful to review some of the developmental milestones for the first five or six years of life. Most pediatricians observe the motor and language behavior of children, as well as their social behavior, ask several questions relative to the history of attainment of developmental milestones, and arrive at a reasonably good estimate of a child's developmental level. This approach should be familiar to those who use child assessment procedures as it will offer a quick estimate for children who do not deviate markedly from normal development. However, many children who come to the attention of psychologists are not progressing normally, and while they may have attained many milestones on schedule, there may be significant deviance from normal development. For these children, more detailed screening devices or very detailed broad spectrum developmental assessment devices may be appropriate.

Some developmental assessment procedures depend upon direct examination of the child or infant, while others are based on parent reports. Each type of assessment procedure has its advantages and its drawbacks. If the parents are good observers and reliable historians, parent report may be more thorough and cover observations over a broader range of situations than can be obtained in the examiner's time and place of observation. However, many times early history is not available or parents are unreliable informants. In such cases, direct examination is the only approach available. Even so, care must be taken to determine whether the child appears secure and able to participate in such a way as to derive a representative sample of behavior. The report of developmental level should include some statement about the examiner's level of confidence in the results obtained.

The examination of infants and young children can be affected by the child's rapport and by various physical handicaps. If a child appears unresponsive or minimally responsive to auditory stimuli, the examiner should question the parents or caretakers about their observations, about ear infections and other possible sources of hearing defects. Even if parent report and health history are negative, when the child does appear to have difficulty in hearing or understanding directions, a hearing examination should be scheduled before proceeding with further psychological evaluation. Many young children do have hearing impairments which are not detected prior to psychological examination. Similar problems may occur with vision, but these are usually noticed by parents or caretakers who observe children holding toys or books close to their faces or sitting close to television screens. A third type of interference with performance often noted in examination of infants and young children is distractibility, which may result from attractive toys or other stimuli which the child sees and wants, from noise, or even from strangers in the testing situation (such as students or observers). In such cases, the examiner needs to simplify the environment, seating the child or infant in such a manner that attention is directed to the examiner and testing materials and away from mirrors, lights, and irrelevant objects. In the case of infants and young children who are uncomfortable in the testing situation, the presence of the mother, father, or caretaker may calm the child and make it possible to get a better idea of how well the child may perform. In the case of extremely difficult children it may be necessary to involve the parent in the presentation of material, although the examiner will need to be careful to provide the parent with specific instructions so that no inappropriate cueing or feedback is given.

We turn now to a description of various developmental assessment procedures, after which we will compare and discuss their various merits.

## BAYLEY SCALES OF INFANT DEVELOPMENT

*Manual*

*Bayley Scales of Infant Development.* Bayley, N. New York: The Psychological Corporation, 1969. 757 Third Avenue, New York, N.Y. 10017.

*Purpose*

This measure is designed to ascertain the infant's developmental status and to determine the extent of any deviation from normal development. The test is designed for children from two months to 30 months of age.

*Format*

The test is made up of three parts: the Mental Scale (163 items), the Motor Scale (81 items), and the Infant Behavior Record (30 behaviors). The Mental Scale is designed to measure a variety of areas, some of which are sensory-perceptual acuities and discriminations, the acquisition of object constancy, and the beginning of verbal communication. For ease of administration and scoring, the areas in the manual concerning this scale are printed on yellow pages.

The Motor Scale is designed to measure the degree of control of the body, coordination of the large muscles, and fine manipulatory skills of hands and fingers. Instructions for this scale can also be easily found in the manual because they are printed on blue pages.

The Infant Behavior Record (IBR) is completed after the Mental and Motor Scales have been given. The IBR assesses the nature of the infant's social and objective orientations to this environment. Since the IBR differs from the other two scales in administration, it will be reviewed following their discussion.

*Administration*

Under optimal conditions administration takes approximately 45 minutes. For both the Mental and Motor Scales, the examiner establishes the child's basal and ceiling levels. The record form facilitates this process by having the test items arranged in order of difficulty. Beside each test item number is the age placement score in which 50% of the children tested will pass the item. Below this score are the age range values which provide estimates of the ages at which each item was passed by 5% and 95%, respectively, of the children in the standardization sample.

*Scoring*

The manual provides detailed criteria for scoring. Once the raw score (total number of items passed) is calculated, then a standard score can be obtained from tables printed in the manual. Both the standard score from the Mental Scale (Mental Development Index) and the Motor Scale (Psychomotor Developmental Index) have a mean of 100 and a standard deviation of 16. The standard score range of 50 to 150 covers more than three standard deviations on either side of the average Mental Development Index or Psychomotor Development Index.

## Standardization

A stratified sample design based on the 1960 U.S. Census was used for the standardization of age norms. The sample was controlled for sex and race within each group, with further restrictions related to residence and to the education of the head of the household. In all, 1,262 children distributed in equal numbers across 14 age groups were used.

## Reliability

Split-half reliability was calculated by dividing both the Mental and Motor Scales into two equal parts. Raw scores for these half-tests were obtained for each of the 14 age groups of the standardization sample. The Mental Score coefficients ranged from .81 to .93 with a median value of .88, and the Motor Scale coefficients ranged from .68 to .92 with a median value of .84. The standard error of measurement was obtained for both the Mental and Motor Scales. The $SE_m$ for the Mental Scale ranged from 4.2 to 6.9 standard score points; for the Motor Scale it ranged from 4.6 to 9.0.

The test-observer reliability in scoring was calculated on 90 eight-month-old infants by having a second examiner observe through a one-way mirror. An 89.4% agreement was found on the Mental Scale and a 93.4% agreement was found on the Motor Scale.

Test-retest reliablity of one-week duration was done on 28 infants with a 76.4% agreement found on the Mental Scale and 75.3% agreement found on the Motor Scale.

## Validity

Both the Stanford-Binet and the Bayley were administered to 120 children aged 24, 27, and 30 months. The coefficient of correlation between the IQ obtained from the Stanford-Binet and the Mental Development Index was .57 for the children on whom the comparison was made for the six-month age overlap of the two tests.

*Infant Behavior Record*

The IBR consists of a number of descriptive rating scales for behaviors characteristic of children up to 30 months of age. The behaviors include affective domains, motivational variables, and specific sensory experiences. The IBR record form is filled out after the Mental and Motor Scales have been administered and usually just after the child has left. Inside the manual is a table of the distribution of ratings for each of the 14 age groups in the standardization sample. Also included in the manual is a descriptive paragraph of the characteristic behaviors of each age group.

*Critique*

The Bayley deserves the excellent reviews in Buros (1978) and Anastasi (1976). Damarin (1976) states: "The Bayley is a truly excellent instrument . . . the standardization of the Mental and Motor scales is as good or better than any other individual tests, whether for infants, children, or adults" (p. 292). Bayley cautions that the Infant Development Scale should be used descriptively and not predictively.

The examiner must be well trained in the mechanics of the instrument. An examiner should not expect to pick up the manual and give the test after a cursory reading. The same stimulus objects are used for several tasks at different age levels, although there is no easy way to know this from the arrangement of the scoring materials. Experience with the instrument will result in administration of all or most of these tasks while the examiner has a given object in hand. The novice will lose time since he or she will have to keep coming back to the same object at different age levels of testing. For the relatively untrained examiner the Bayley is often administered with the help of an assistant who locates test materials and records performance, while the examiner works directly with the infant. Sometimes with difficult or fearful children help from the mother may be required so that the child can settle down and attend to the task.

The Bayley is one of the few tests in which scoring for the items is actually scaled along a developmental continuum. Other tests generally employ a total score or subtest scores which are then converted statistically into some type of development score or estimation.

## McCARTHY SCALES OF CHILDREN'S ABILITIES (MSCA)

*Manual*

McCarthy Scales of Children's Abilities. McCarthy, D. New York: The Psychological Corporation, 1970, 1972. 757 Third Avenue, New York, N.Y. 10017.

*Purpose*

The McCarthy Scales of Children's Abilities are designed to serve as a single instrument to measure the overall development of young children from two and a half to eight and a half years old.

*Format and Content*

The MSCA consists of 18 subtests administered in a specified order which has been carefully sequenced to encourage rapport, provide a variety of tasks, and allow for gross motor tasks to serve as an activity break during a fairly lengthy testing session (one to one-and-a-half hours). Fifteen of the 18 subtests are summed to determine the General Cognitive Index (GCI). Included in the GCI are three separate and non-overlapping scales: Verbal, Perceptual-Performance, and Quantitative.

Five subtests (Pictorial Memory, Word Knowledge, Verbal Memory, Verbal Fluency, and Opposite Analogies) comprise the Verbal Scale. Seven subtests (Block Building, Puzzle Solving, Tapping Sequence, Right-Left Orientation, Draw-A-Design, Draw-A-Child, and Conceptual Grouping) comprise the Perceptual-Performance Scale and three subtests (Number Questions, Numerical Memory, and Counting and Sorting) comprise the Quantitative Scale. The remaining subtests (Leg Coordination, Arm Coordination, and Imitative Action) are not included in the General Cognitive Index, but are combined with the Draw-A-Design and Draw-A-Child subtests to yield a separate Motor Scale. Scores from four of the subtests included in the GCI (Pictorial Memory, Tapping Sequence, Verbal Memory, and Numerical Memory) are combined to form a separate Memory Scale.

*Administration*

The MSCA manual is organized so that directions for administering each item include verbatim instructions printed in red and the scoring criteria printed immediately following the instructions for each item rather than in a separate section or appendix. Most of the items are not timed; only four subtests (Puzzle Solving, Pictorial Memory, Leg Coordination, and Verbal Fluency) require a stopwatch. Most of the test items are quite similar to those included in measures of intellectual development used with young children, i.e., the Stanford-Binet Intelligence Scale and the Wechsler Preschool and Primary Scale of Intelligence.

*Scoring*

Each item is scored as soon as it is administered and generally a qualitative or judgment component is included in scoring each item. Certain raw scores are changed to weighted scores as indicated on the record form, then summed to give Composite Raw Scores for each of the scales. The chronological age of the child is computed and the manual contains tables which show Scale Index Scores for Composite Raw Scores on each scale at quarter-year intervals from ages two years four months and 16 days through eight years seven months and 15 days. The front of the record form provides a profile on which to chart the Scale Index Scores obtained. The General Cognitive Index which includes the Verbal, Perceptual-Performance and Quantitative Scales has a mean of 100 with a standard deviation of 16, while the scales have a mean of 50 and a standard deviation of 10. While the GCI is purposely not termed an IQ score, the table listing General Cognitive Ability levels in the manual is very similar to a table of IQ levels.

*Standardization*

A sample of 1,032 children was tested in the standardization of the MSCA. Ten age groups were designated (2½, 3, 3½, 4, 4½, 5, 5½, 6½, 7½, 8½) with 100 to 106 children in each group with equal numbers of boys and girls in each group. Other major variables of the sample included white-nonwhite, geographic region (Northeast, North Central, South, and West), father's occupation, and urban-rural residence. The sample was stratified on the basis of the 1970 Census and was designed to be representative of children in the United States from age two and a half through eight and a half. However, no known mentally retarded or physically handicapped children were included in the sample and bilingual children were included only if they could speak and understand English.

*Reliability*

Test-retest reliability data with a time interval of three to five weeks are presented for the MSCA on a sample of 125 children at three age levels (3 to 3½, N=40; 5 to 5½, N=40; and 7½ to 8½, N=45). Reliability coefficients of .89 to .91 were obtained for the General Cognitive Index, while the Motor Scale had the lowest reliability coefficients, ranging from .69 at ages seven and a half to eight and a half to .78 at ages three to three and a half. The standard error of measurement was computed for each scale of the MSCA at each age level. The standard error of measurement for the GCI ranges from 3.4 at age three and a half to 5.0 at age six, with an average for all age groups of 4.1.

*Validity*

A study was conducted with a small group of six-year-old first grade children (N=35), testing each of the children with the Stanford-Binet Intelligence Test, Form L-M (1960), the Wechsler Preschool and Primary Scale of Intelligence, and the MSCA. The GCI correlated .81 with the Stanford-Binet IQ and .63 with the WPPSI Verbal IQ, .62 with the WPPSI Performance IQ, and .71 with the WPPSI Full Scale IQ. The Metropolitan Achievement Tests, 1970 Edition, Primary I, Form F was used with 31 of the children four months after the initial testing to secure an indication of predictive validity. Coefficients for the GCI were significant at the .01 level for the Mathematics and Total Raw Scores; and at the .05 level for the Reading and Total Reading Scores.

*Critique*

The MSCA is well constructed and organized. Administration and scoring instructions are well presented and a variety of useful information is gained from the MSCA about a given child. Because the content is varied with game-like tasks, the material is likely to hold the child's attention. Sattler (1978) notes that the MSCA has greater potential for providing information, especially with exceptional children, than the Binet or Wechsler Scales. The major disadvantage is that in most evaluations the MSCA would not suffice as a substitute for either the Binet or the WPPSI with which it has sizable correlations. Moreover, the time required for administration would generally rule out its use as a supplementary measure. There is no information about minority children. Because the GCI appears to be a measure of intelligence, the use of the entire MSCA as a measure of anything other than intelligence is questionable. Some of the subtests of motor, memory, or neuropsychological interest (Tapping, Left-Right Orientation) may be useful as supplementary information when questions of neurological problems occur.

## DENVER DEVELOPMENTAL SCREENING TEST (DDST)

### Manual

Denver Developmental Screening Test. Frankenburg, W. K., Dodd, J. B., & Fandal, A. W. Denver, CO: Ladora Project and Publishing Foundation, 1973.

### Purpose

The Denver Developmental Screening Test is intended to aid in the early identification of developmental problems and delays in preschool children. It is designed to be easy to administer, score, and interpret by examiners with no specific training in psychological testing and for use in such settings as neighborhood health clinics, physicians' offices, and Headstart programs.

### Format and Content

The DDST contains 105 test items divided into four categories: Personal-Social, which samples interpersonal and self-help behaviors; Fine-Motor Adaptive, which checks the child's ability to see and samples eye-hand coordination; Language, which checks the ability to hear and samples both receptive and expressive language; and Gross Motor, which samples such behaviors as sitting, walking, and jumping. Since a basal and ceiling are established in each category, it is necessary to administer only a portion of the items to any individual child. Test materials needed are red wool, a box of raisins, a rattle, eight one-inch cubes, a small bottle, a small bell, a tennis ball, and a pencil. Some items can be scored based on the report of the parent, but most require the child to demonstrate certain skills and abilities.

*Administration and Scoring*

The manual is also a training workbook for the prospective examiner and contains detailed and specific instructions and quizzes on all phases of administration, scoring, and interpretation. A training film is also available. Prior to beginning the actual testing, the child's chronological age is calculated and entered on the test form. Test items are arranged on the test form itself to indicate the chronological age at which 25%, 50%, 75%, and 90% of the children in the standardization sample were able to pass each item. A basal level is established by the child's successfully responding to at least three easy items in a category. A ceiling is established in that category in which the child fails three items. Failure of an item which the test form indicates was passed by 90% of younger children is designated a delay. Based on the number of delays and refusals of test items by the child, results are interpreted as Abnormal, Questionable, Untestable, or Normal. A child who does not score in the Normal range on the first testing should be given the DDST again within two-to-three weeks. If the results are still categorized as Abnormal, Questionable, or Untestable, the authors of the DDST recommend that the child be referred for a more extensive diagnostic evaluation by a qualified specialist in child development.

*Standardization*

In the development of the DDST at the University of Colorado Medical Center, 240 test items were selected from various infant developmental tests and preschool intelligence tests and were administered by four medical students to 200 infants and preschool children. From these 240 items, 105 were selected for administration to the standardization sample of 1,036 (543 boys and 493 girls) normal children from the Denver area. The children's ages ranged from two weeks to 6.4 years and demographic characteristics of the group, such as occupation of father and ethnic background, reflected those of Denver according to the 1960 Census. The standardization sample includes more children in the younger age ranges because the time spans for the age groups are shorter in order to reflect the faster rate at which developmental changes occur at these younger ages. There is no indication in the manual as to whether each age group was divided equally among boys and girls but there are separate norm tables for boys and girls, as well as for different occupational groups with respect to fathers.

*Reliability*

To determine test-retest reliability, the DDST was administered to 20 children from ages two months to five-and-a-half years and one week later the same examiner re-administered the measure to these children. Written results of the first administration were not available to the examiner for the retest. Basal and ceiling levels were established for all four sections on each administration and, for the total group, 95.8% of items were performed the same way after a one-week interval.

During the standardization phase of the DDST, an attempt was made to determine reliability among the four medical students who were serving as examiners. Each examiner tested 12 children, four of whom were also tested by each of the other three examiners. Agreement by the examiners as to items passed or failed was 90%.

*Validity*

Only one validity study was reported in the 1973 edition of the test manual. A group of 236 children was administered the DDST and either the Stanford-Binet or the Bayley Scales of Infant Development. The data presented indicate that of the 36 children who scored in the abnormal range on the DDST (which would indicate either a Stanford-Binet intelligence quotient or a Bayley developmental quotient below 70), 17 or 47% scored 70 or above on the Stanford-Binet or Bayley. Of the 152 children who were rated as normal on the DDST, 16 or 10.5% scored 79 or below on the Stanford-Binet or Bayley. Of the 48 children rated Questionable on the DDST, only five or 10% scored below 70 on the Stanford-Binet or Bayley, while 11 or 23% scored 70-79, and 32 or 67% scored 80 or higher. Especially at the three-year level, the DDST over-selected children as abnormal.

*Critique*

The standardization, reliability, and validity of the DDST are questionable. Sample sizes were too small and too limited in demographic distribution of socioeconomic, ethnic, and geographical factors to be widely applicable. Item selection and sectioning appear to be arbitrary. The Denver would appear to improve only slightly over a casual observation of current functioning and recording of developmental milestones which are routinely accomplished in pediatric examinations. In the very situations in which the screening of children would be most helpful, e.g., Headstart programs and day care situations, the population of children for which such an instrument would be most useful is not included in the standardization sample.

## DETROIT TESTS OF LEARNING APTITUDE (DTLA)

*Manual*

Examiner's Handbook for the Detroit Tests of Learning Aptitude, Revised. Baker, H. J. & Leland, B. Indianapolis, IN: Bobbs-Merrill Co., 1967. 4300 W. 62nd Street, Indianapolis, IN 46206.

*Purpose*

The Detroit Tests of Learning Aptitude are designed to provide a graphic representation of an individual child's psychological strengths and weaknesses and to relate these to learning problems.

*Format and Content*

There are 19 different subtests, of which a minimum of nine and maximum of 13 are selected by the examiner for administration to the child being evaluated. To aid in the selection of appropriate subtests, a chart indicates eight mental faculties (reasoning and comprehension, practical judgment, verbal ability, time and space relationships, number ability, auditory attentive ability, visual attentive ability, and motor ability) and the subtests to which they seem to relate. The manual recommends that all eight mental classifications be included in the selection of subtests administered. The instrument is designed for subjects aged three to adulthood.

*Administration and Scoring*

The manual includes verbatim instructions for the administration of each subtest, suggested beginning and stopping points for the subtest, and a scoring key to determine the correctness of the child's answers. Each subtest is arranged to begin with the easier items and continue to more difficult ones. Normative tables of mental ages for scores on each subtest are presented and are entered on the record form. These mental age scores are then arranged in rank order from highest to lowest and the median mental age ascertained. In order to find the IQ the median mental age is divided by the chronological age and the result is entered on the record form. A profile is also constructed on the record form using the mental ages for each subtest with the lowest scores interpreted as disabilities and the highest ones as special talents or abilities.

*Standardization*

The initial standardization sample was selected from the Detroit Public Schools and included 50 children at each age level. Those students selected were categorized as being in the expected grade placement for their chronological age and having an IQ between 90 and 110 based on group intelligence measures. Later the number for each age level was increased to 150 students.

*Reliability and Validity*

The manual reports minimally regarding data on reliability and validity. A comparison of the distribution of IQ scores obtained with the DTLA on over 4,000 cases was made with a similar number of cases using another unspecified individually administered intellectual measure and showed that the distributions agreed within one point of IQ at the first quartile, the median, and the third quartile. Test-retest reliability was reported as .959 for 48 cases, with a five-month interval between testings, and as .675 for 792 cases with a two-to-three-year interval between testings.

*Critique*

There are many criticisms of the DTLA based on its method of administration and its standardization. The practice of using different combinations of subtests as selected by the examiner makes it impossible to compare scores on the DTLA between children who may have had different combinations of subtests or even for multiple testings for the same child, if different combinations were used.

The use of the median subtest score to determine an individual's IQ ignores the full range of scores on the measure. Likewise the IQ computed is not a deviation IQ and suffers from the inadequacy of its statistical basis. The standardization, reliability, and validity data presented in the manual are significantly lacking in the detailed information needed to clarify the details essential for evaluation of the instrument and its usefulness.

These disadvantages and the limited geographical and other demographic characteristics of the standardization sample lend credence to the consistent criticisms of this instrument since it was first published in 1935.

## MINNESOTA CHILD DEVELOPMENT INVENTORY (MCDI)

*Manual*

Manual for the Minnesota Child Development Inventory. Ireton, H. & Thwing, E. Minneapolis: Behavior Science Systems, 1974. Box 1108, Minneapolis, MN 55440.

*Purpose*

The Minnesota Child Development Inventory is designed to be completed by the child's mother and to yield information about the developmental level of the child from one to six years of age. The MCDI is meant to be considered a supplementary measure and is not intended to serve as a substitute for a parental interview.

*Format*

The MCDI contains 320 items about observable child behaviors. The statements are grouped into eight scales: General Development, Gross Motor, Fine Motor, Expressive Language, Comprehension-Conceptual, Situation Comprehension, Self-Help, and Personal-Social. The scales were not selected by a factor analytic method but by the authors as those which would be most meaningful to clinicians, teachers, and parents, and which would generally be included in the child developmental literature.

*Administration and Scoring*

The MCDI booklet and an answer sheet are given to the child's mother to be completed. Instructions are printed on the booklet, but the examiner should be aware that the MCDI requires an eighth grade reading comprehension level. Raw scores are calculated for each scale by the use of scoring templates and are recorded on a profile form and transformed into developmental age levels for each scale. Scores below the mean score for children 30% younger than the child being evaluated are considered to provide an indication of developmental retardation. Scores below the mean score of children 20%-30% younger are considered to be in the borderline range of development.

## Standardization

The 320 items of the MDCI were derived from an original item pool of about 2,000 statements collected from child development literature and psychological tests for preschool age children. The items were selected as representative of developmental skills, observable in everyday situations, readily described and possessing age-discriminating power. The age level of an item is that age at which at least 67% of mothers first answered yes to the statement and is thus considered characteristic of that age.

An item validation study was conducted to determine the age discrimination power of 673 items from the original item pool. From this study the final 320 statements of the questionnaire were established. The normative study was then conducted in Bloomington, Minnesota, a suburb of Minneapolis. The sample consisted of 796 white children (395 males and 401 females) from six months to six and a half years of age. Most of the parents had 12 or more years of schooling (94% of fathers and 95% of mothers), most of the mothers were full-time housewives (86%), and most of the fathers' occupations (92%) were above the level of unskilled labor with 43% being classified as professional-managerial. The families in the sample were small and intact. The authors state that other normative studies of urban, urban poor, and minority children will be conducted, and caution against using the current norms for children from lower socioeconomic levels or from other races.

## Reliability and Validity

Internal consistency for each scale was computed using the split-half method. The data are presented in the discussion section for each scale. The General Developmental Scale, which consists of 131 of the most age-discriminating items from the other scales, has the most uniformly high reliability coefficients (.83 to .93) for ages nine months to five years eleven months. Scale validity is demonstrated in the manual with graphs for each scale showing a systematic increase in the number of items passed with increasing age. Several of the scales have a limited age range, reflecting the pattern of development for certain skills. For example, gross motor skills beyond age three generally consist of refinement of established skills rather than the acquisition of new ones; therefore, this scale tops out at age three. The profile form indicates the age range for which each scale can be interpreted with confidence.

*Critique*

The MCDI samples a wide range of behaviors over the ages included. It is quick and convenient to administer and score and has a very good manual with adequate explanations, charts, and appendices. Its limitations include the requirement that the informant have an eighth grade reading level and its highly selective normative sample. While the inventory is not a substitute for an interview with parents of white, middle-class, suburban children, it is useful in that specific observable behaviors are reported by the informant and these behaviors can be used in the context of a comprehensive assessment to supplement other data. The first entry in the *Eighth Mental Measurement Yearbook* (Buros, 1978) contains a review by Goodwin, who cites in detail shortcomings in the nature of the standardization sample and who points out that validity has not yet been convincingly established. Despite these obvious inadequacies in the psychometric foundation of the instrument, the items do appear to be well chosen and it can be hoped that future work will place the MCDI on a more substantial measurement basis.

## PURDUE PERCEPTUAL-MOTOR SURVEY (PPMS)

*Manual*

*The Purdue Perceptual-Motor Survey.* Roach, E. G. & Kephart, N. C. Columbus, OH: Charles E. Merrill, 1966. 1300 Alum Creek Drive, Columbus, OH 43216.

*Purpose*

The Purdue Perceptual-Motor Survey is designed to provide teachers with a measure to identify children in the first through fourth grades who may be lacking in certain perceptual-motor skills deemed to be prerequisite for normal acquistion of academic skills and to indicate major areas for training. The survey is based on the developmental theory presented in *The Slow Learner in the Classroom* (Kephart, 1960).

*Format*

There are 22 items in the survey covering three major areas: Laterality, Directionality, and Perceptual-Motor Matching. A number of the items sample all areas simultaneously. All of the items require motor performance rather than verbal responses and include tasks of balance and postural flexibility (Walking Board, Jumping, Identification of Body Parts, Imitation of Movement, Obstacle Courses, Kraus Weber exercises, and Angels-in-the-Snow); a series of tasks of perceptual motor match (Chalkboard, Rhythmic Writing); tasks of ocular control (Ocular Pursuits); and tasks of form perception (Visual Achievement Forms).

*Administration and Scoring*

The manual gives clear descriptions of each task and qualitative scoring criteria on a scale of 1-4 for each item. A relatively large open area is need to administer the items so that the child and the examiner can be afforded freedom of movement. Since the survey requires the active involvement of the examiner in a number of the tasks, the examiner will need to memorize the administration of those sections. The manual also presents a short chapter on the rationale and development of the survey, and indicates that those who use this measure should be knowledgeable of the perceptual-motor theory upon which it is based. The theory embodies the notion of a hierarchical sequence of increasingly complex learning stages. The manual provides little specific information regarding the interpretation of the total score, stating that the purpose is only to identify areas for remediation.

*Standardization*

The standardization sample consisted of 200 children, 50 each in the first through fourth grades. The children had no known motor defect, nor had any of them been referred for achievement-testing. All children were rated by their classroom teachers as being superior, high average, or low average students. No non-achieving students were included in the normative sample. The Wide Range Achievement Test was administered and all children selected for the normative sample scored at least within their assigned grade level on the WRAT (see review of the WRAT in Chapter 7). The school in Lafayette, Indiana, selected for the standardization study had students from both urban and rural homes and a wide range of socioeconomic groups; occupation, designated on the basis of head of household as professional, semi-professional, farming, service occupation, skilled labor, and unskilled labor, was listed for the sample. Also selected and matched for age and grade level was a group of 97 non-achievers; 25 each in the first, second, and third grades and 22 in the fourth grade. None of the children in this non-achieving sample was known to be retarded or to have specific physical handicaps. Each child in both groups was administered all 30 items of the original survey (Kephart, 1960), using Kephart's directions for administration and scoring (a score of three or four on an item was considered passing, while a score of 1 or 2 was considered failing). The results of the first group (achievers) were used in the normative phase. The results of the second group (non-achievers) were included in the validation phase to determine the feasibility of using a total score and designating a cut-off score for separating achievers and non-achievers. For the standardization survey of 29 items (Rhythmic Writing was omitted), the cut-off score of 65 included 85% of the non-achieving sample and only 17% of the achieving sample. However, the manual does not indicate a total score which can be used as a cut-off score with the final version of 22 items.

Thirty children in the achieving sample were selected for retesting by a different examiner one week after the first administration. A coefficient of stability of .946 was found and is considered to represent both the stability of the scoring criteria and the stability between examiners. Intercorrelations for each item were computed and the authors feel that many areas of perceptual-motor behavior are being sampled and that there is minimal overlap between items.

*Critique*

This instrument lacks clear information on its generalizability. A major disadvantage is lack of standardization across a representative sample with adequate demographic distributions. Likewise all the data were apparently collected by a very limited number of examiners. The test-retest data confound examiner and retest effects. The psychometric analysis of the data is limited. More importantly, the selection of subjects by the use of WRAT is of questionable value, and the interpretation of the scores appears clouded by the lack of information about the final 22-item survey. Other than to provide some sort of standard tasks for observation, the use of the Purdue appears to be of little benefit for an individual child since so many ambiguities about both the theory and the tasks would cloud interpretation. Jamison (1972) raises the question of the basis for the items which were included in the Purdue Perceptual-Motor Survey. She points out that the skills assessed have not been shown to be necessary for academic learning or characteristic of particular age groups. Factor analysis indicates lack of factor stability and inappropriate item grouping. The assumption that the items are related to achievement is unsubstantiated. Although Landis (1972) was more positive about the potential usefulness of the PPMS, there seems to be little solid basis for employing it when other tasks and methods are known to be more reliable and better tied to validity data.

## ILLINOIS TEST OF PSYCHOLINGUISTIC ABILITIES (ITPA)

*Manual*

Examiner's Manual for Illinois Test of Psycholinguistic Abilities, Revised. Kirk, S. A., McCarthy, J. J., & Kirk, W. D. Urbana, IL: University of Illinois Press, 1968. 54 E. Gregory Drive, Sta A, Champaign, IL 61820.

*Purpose*

The Illinois Test of Psycholinguistic Abilities was developed to provide a diagnostic aid in determining the specific abilities and disabilities which might be important with regard to children's learning. It was hoped that the ITPA would also serve as a basis for designing instructional programs based on the individual characteristics of children with learning disabilities. The ITPA is intended for use with children ages two to 10 years.

*Format and Content*

The ITPA is based on the communication model of Osgood (1957a, b). The ITPA assumes three dimensions of cognitive abilities: channels of communication (e.g., auditory, visual), psycholinguistic processes (receptive processes, expressive processes, and central mediating processes), and levels of organization (symbolic, representational versus a more perceptually based level of activity). This model logically generates a number of communication functions, not all of which are represented among the subtests of the ITPA. However, 12 tests are given. At the representational level are Auditory Reception and Visual Reception; Auditory-Vocal Association and Visual-Motor Association; Verbal Expression and Manual Expression. At the automatic level are Grammatic Closure (and two supplementary tests, Auditory Closure and Sound Blending), Visual Closure, Auditory Sequential Memory, and Visual Sequential Memory. Each subtest is designed to detect problems in the channels of communication, the levels of language organization, and the channels of input and output. For example, on Visual Closure the child is asked to identify an object from incomplete pictures of the object which portray varying degrees of the object.

*Administration and Scoring*

Training is required to administer the ITPA in the manner intended (the authors recommend 10 practice tests observed by an experienced examiner). Specific starting points have been indicated for each subtest which take the age of the child into account. For children who are thought to be gifted or retarded, an estimate of mental age is suggested as a guideline for starting point. Each subtest has specific instructions for the establishment of basal and ceiling levels where these are appropriate. Demonstrations are given for all subtests. The subtests are given in a specific order which was predetermined on the basis of maximizing rapport and minimizing fatigue effects. Instructions for scoring are given in the manual as well as criteria for establishing base and ceiling levels. A summary sheet is provided for recording the 12 subtests. For each subtest a raw score, age score, and scaled score are recorded. The summary sheet organizes the form of recording so that level (representational versus automatic) and channels of communication are displayed. A number of summary statistics are computed, including Psycholinguistic Age (a global measure) and Mean Scaled Scores for level. The Psycholinguistic Age (PLA) is compared to a ratio IQ measure because of the correlation between the Short Form of the Stanford-Binet and the ITPA. Guidelines for interpretation of differences between subtest scores and mean scaled scores are provided. Tables of Scaled Score Norms by age level at three-month intervals are provided for ages two years four months to 10 years three months. In a later publicaiton (Kirk & Kirk, 1971), guidelines for conversion of ITPA scores to deviation IQs are suggested, as well as some revised suggestions for interpretation of the patterns of scores among subtests.

*Standardization*

Standardization data are reported for the original version of the ITPA in McCarthy and Kirk (1963), but not in the manual for the Revised ITPA (Kirk et al., 1968), or in Kirk and Kirk (1971). Data relative to standardization, validity, and reliability are, therefore, difficult to obtain.

*Critique*

Carroll's (1972) review in the Seventh Mental Measurement Yearbook criticizes the ITPA for being called a test of psycholinguistic abilities and suggests that it really is a test of cognitive functioning which has serious shortcomings, both in the model upon which it is based, and in terms of the factor analytic studies which do not support the idea of an "automatic" level or of different "processes." Rather, Carroll notes, the factor studies suggest that vocabulary accounts for much of the test and introduces a socioeconomic bias. While the reliability of the test seems adequate, its usefulness as a diagnostic tool is called into question, since it may be another test of intellectual function rather than a psycholinguistic test as purported. The norm group of 962 children of average intelligence underrepresents minorities and is geographically narrow (all Midwestern). The children who constituted the sample were not learning-disabled children and so the usefulness of the instrument for describing and prescribing learning activities with learning disabled children is questionable. Because of the cultural bias involved in the vocabulary used in the test, it might be impossible to separate low performances on the basis of cultural differences from those obtained as a result of learning problems.

A second review by Chase (in Buros, 1972, pp. 442–445) indicates that the data supporting both validity and reliability are weak for some of the subtests of the ITPA.

It would be comforting if one could describe learning disabilities specifically and prescribe clear-cut remedial procedures, both of which were the intent of the authors of the ITPA. So far, there is not sufficient evidence to suggest that the instrument fulfills those hopes or that the model upon which it is based is congruent with the neurobiological system which mediates psycholinguistic behavior.

## COMPARISON OF MEASURES OF DEVELOPMENT

We have included measures which are based on direct observation of the child (Bayley Scales of Infant Development, McCarthy Scales of Children's Abilities, Denver Developmental Screening Test, Detroit Test of Learning Aptitudes, Purdue Perceptual-Motor Survey, and the Illinois Test of Psycholinguistic Abilities) and one parent report measure (Minnesota Child Development Inventory). Among the instruments which are based on direct observation of the child, the psychometric properties of the Bayley and the McCarthy are excellent. Both of these instruments require training in administration and both are helpful in estimating development in a manner which shares much of the information that would be gained from individual intelligence tests.

The Denver Developmental Screening Test does not require special training in psychological testing. The items which are grouped into four categories (Fine-Motor, Personal-Social, Language, and Gross Motor) overlap with much of the material included in the parent report measure (Minnesota Child Development Inventory). These two measures, used in conjunction, may be of aid in determining the reliability of parent report when this is in question. While the standardization data on the Denver is weak, an examiner who uses the instrument frequently will have a clinical impression based on a broad sample of the child's behavior. This sample of behavior may serve to focus questions for further investigation. The use of screening techniques such as the Denver is more likely to be economical in settings which provide screening services. For diagnostic work which includes full batteries assessing developmental and clinical functions, such an instrument is less efficient since there are more comprehensive and better standardized techniques available. What has been said about the Denver is even more true for the Purdue Perceptual-Motor Survey, an instrument designed for somewhat older children than the Denver. While there is a paucity of evidence supporting the Denver, our review suggests that there is evidence which calls the assumptions of the Purdue into serious question.

The Detroit Tests of Learning Aptitude hardly justify the use of the term *tests* as a descriptor. Poor standardization of the instrument and lack of any uniform administration of subtests makes interpretation tentative at best. Because many school systems employ the instrument, the psychologist should understand these limitations. Another test frequently used by schools is the Illinois Test of Psycholinguistic Abilities, Revised. Communication skills are intended to be of examination. However, as our review indicates, the ITPA has been criticized as less a test of psycholinguistic ability than a test of cognitive functioning.

The psychologist who wishes to assess developmental aspects of children's functioning enters a wasteland in which unreliability of instruments, or instruments which do not test what they purport to test, are the rule rather than the exception. Basic knowledge of normal child development and literature about the course of motor and cognitive functions may supply the clinician with better criteria for evaluating a child's performance than many of the instruments on the market. Exceptions have been noted, but these are often restricted in the age range (Bayley) or the socioeconomic level (MCDI) to which they apply. The cost efficiency of using a developmental assessment procedure will involve the time, psychometric properties of the test, the type of information actually produced, and the population for which they are useful. Many times the clinician will find little improvement over careful observation and a good history which focuses on motor, cognitive, and social developmental milestones.

## REFERENCES

Anastasi, A. *Psychological Testing, 4th Edition.* New York: Macmillan, 1976.

Baker, H. J. & Leland, B. *Examiner's Handbook for the Detroit Tests of Learning Aptitude,* Revised. Indianapolis, IN: Bobbs-Merrill Co., 1967.

Bayley, N. *Bayley Scales of Infant Development.* New York: The Psychological Corporation, 1969.

Buros, O. K. *The Seventh Mental Measurement Yearbook.* Highland Park, N.J.: Gryphon Press, 1972.

Buros, O. K. *The Eighth Mental Measurement Yearbook.* Highland Park, N.J.: Gryphon Press, 1978.

Carroll, J. B. Review of the Illinois Test of Psycholinguistic Abilities. In: O. K. Buros (Ed.), *The Seventh Mental Measurement Yearbook.* Highland Park, N.J.: Gryphon Press, 1972.

Chase, C. I. Review of the ITPA. In O. K. Buros (Ed.) *The Seventh Mental Measurement Yearbook.* Highland Park, N.J.: Gryphon Press, 1972.

Damarin, F. Review of the Bayley Scales of Infant Development. In: O. K. Buros (Ed.), *The Eighth Mental Measurement Yearbook.* Highland Park, N.J.: Gryphon Press, 1978.

Frankenburg, W. K., Dodd, J. B., & Fandal, A. W. *Denver Developmental Screening Test.* Denver, CO: Ladora Project & Publishing Foundation, 1973.

Gesell, A., Halverson, H. M., Thompson, H., Ilg, F. L., Castner, B. M., & Ames, L. B.

222       *Psychological Methods of Child Assessment*

*The First Five Years of Life: A Guide to the Study of the Preschool Child.* New York: Harper & Row, 1940.

Gesell, A. & Ilg, F. L. *The Child from Five to Ten.* New York: Harper & Row, 1946.

Gessell, A., Ilg, F. L., & Ames, L. B. *Youth: The Years from Ten to Sixteen.* New York: Harper & Row, 1956.

Ireton, H. & Thwing, E. *Manual for the Minnesota Child Development Inventory.* Minneapolis: Behavior Science Systems, 1974.

Jamison, C. B. Review of the Purdue Perceptual Motor Survey. In: O. K. Buros (Ed.), *The Seventh Mental Measurement Yearbook.* Highland Park, N.J.: Gryphon Press, 1972.

Kephart, N. C. *The Slow Learner in the Classroom.* Columbus, OH: Charles E. Merrill, 1960.

Kirk, S. A. & Kirk, W. D. *Psycholinguistic Learning Disabilities: Diagnosis and Remediation.* Urbana, IL: University of Illinois Press, 1971.

Kirk, S. A., McCarthy, J. J., & Kirk, W. D. *Examiner's Manual for the Illinois Test of Psycholinguistic Abilities,* Revised. Urbana, IL: University of Illinois Press, 1968.

Landis, D. Review of the Purdue Perceptual Motor Survey. In O. K. Buros (Ed.), *The Seventh Mental Measurement Yearbook.* Highland Park, N.J.: Gryphon Press, 1972.

McCarthy, D. *McCarthy Scales of Children's Abilities.* New York: The Psychological Corporation, 1970, 1972.

McCarthy, J. J. & Kirk, S. A. *The Construction, Standardization, and Statistical Characteristics of the Illinois Test of Psycholinguistic Abilities.* Urbana, IL: University of Illinois Press, 1963.

Osgood, C. E. A behavioristic analysis. In: J. Bruner (Ed.), *Contemporary Approaches to Cognition.* Cambridge, MA: Harvard University Press, 1957a.

Osgood, C. E. Motivational dynamics of language behavior. In: M. R. Jones (Ed.), *Nebraska Symposium on Motivation.* Lincoln, NE: University of Nebraska Press, 1957b.

Roach, E. G. & Kephart, N. C. *The Purdue Perceptual-Motor Survey.* Columbus, OH: Charles E. Merrill, 1966.

Sattler, J. M. Review of the McCarthy Scales of Children's Abilities. In: O. K. Buros (Ed.), *The Eighth Mental Measurement Yearbook.* Highland Park, N.J.: Gryphon Press, 1978.

# CHAPTER 9

# Projective Assessment Instruments

The projective instruments differ in their purpose from the intellectual, achievement, and developmental procedures described in the last three chapters. Each class of instruments previously discussed assesses some aspect of cognitive functioning. By contrast the projectives are designed to describe and assess the domain of personality. Cognitive function and style only partly determine the individual's performance on a projective task.

All projective devices rest upon the assumption that the manner in which the person is organized psychologically will determine the content and style of that person's perceptions. The nature of personal symbolism is assumed to be determined by the characteristics of that person and not to be random in nature. This assumption of the deterministic nature of symbolism and perception is called the projective hypothesis. Specifically, symbolism and perception are assumed to be shaped by the needs, fears, defenses, and coping mechanisms of the person and to be revealed in projective data whether the product is stories a person tells, perceptions of inkblots, or responses to incomplete sentences or other ambiguous stimuli. Likewise, drawings are assumed to be visual-motor projections.

Underlying the development of specific projective techniques are assumptions about personality theory and the originator's preference for an approach which uses a particular form of expression. Thus, Murray spent an enormous amount of time delineating a personality theory and using projective stories as a data base for the descriptions of individuals using his personality theory as the framework for the interpretation of the stories they told. Rorschach used visual stimuli in the form of ink-blots and elicited associations to them. It is usual for the developer of a projective technique to describe some standard format for administration, to develop a scoring system that is explicit, and to provide guidelines for interpretation. If the originator's personality theory is not explicitly stated elsewhere, it will be implicit in the guidelines for interpretation of the projective data. Henry Murray's (1943) interest in drive or need and in the way the individual responded to the environment eventually expressed itself in the formal scoring system and interpretation of stories told in response to the Thematic Apperception Test (TAT) cards. Since the publication of the TAT in 1943, there has been a vast amount of research on this test, in normative, anthropological, theoretical, and methodological studies, and all manner of validation studies. Henry (1956) provides a good discussion and examination of the TAT. Readers who wish to trace the development of the ideas behind the instrument may find it fascinating to read Murray's earlier work and to follow for themselves the manner in which the instrument developed as a function of Murray's interests in personality. For many of the other projective devices there is not as much in the way of continuity between written material relating the originators' theoretical ideas to the methods and interpretations of the techniques.

Projective techniques have been the subject of controversy because criterion measures which are agreed upon by professionals are less well defined than in the area of cognitive function and cognitive tests. As a result the literature which deals with standardization, and particularly with validity issues, has been hotly debated for the past four decades. Many psychologists do not believe that projective testing is valuable because it makes assumptions regarding motivations that are not directly accessible to awareness of the individual. Others reject projective assessment because the methods are more clinical than psychometric in terms of the types of data available concerning their construction and usefulness. Since the literature on projectives is not directly comparable to that concerning cognitively based tests, but has been criticized on the basis of the same criteria that are used for cognitively based tests, users of projective tests have often assumed a defensive stance regarding them. Recent discussion by Exner (1974) has addressed the nature of some of these criticisms and pointed out some of the improprieties embodied in many of them.

Proponents of projective techniques usually hold that they can develop an impression or description of a person based on the manner in which the person approaches the material and the style with which the material is processed. Information about needs, perceptions, goals, and defenses are deduced both from the stylistic features of the material and from the content. Comparisons of intratest material and intertest material across the battery of tests are used to develop some estimate of the reliability of the findings for that person. This approach has been labeled idiographic by some writers since it is the intensive study of a given person.

Some assessment techniques which are used as projectives have also been used to study and compare individuals and, therefore, share some of the nomothetic characteristics with the cognitive tests. Examples of these tests would be the MMPI and various forms of the Sentence Completion Test which have associated scoring systems (such as the one developed by Loevinger & Wessler, 1970). The MMPI items are standard presentations and the subject merely endorses them as true or false but the patterns of profiles have the capability of being interpreted either as a function of cookbook comparisons to those of known clinical populations, or a function of the interrelationships among the clinical scales. In order to perform the latter type of analysis the clinician must be familiar with the content of the scales and the degree of item overlap among them. Either method of analysis should result in comparable descriptions, but the cookbook method relies more heavily upon the research already done on clinical populations, while the pattern analysis just described depends upon an intimate knowledge of the properties of the test and how the characteristics of the test must be taken into account in the final clinical formulation. Most clinicians probably actually use some information from both sources in arriving at a diagnostic impression. Likewise, while the Loevinger approach permits one to gain a rating of ego development level, the content of the completed sentences contributes data which may bear on important themes and coping mechanisms used by the patient.

In the pages which follow we will introduce the reader to each projective instrument, its administration and scoring. We will also discuss the interpretations and clinical uses of the instruments. Because of the volume of research literature that abounds on these instruments, we refer the reader to Buros Mental Measurement Yearbooks and to extensive reviews found in journal and annual review publications.

## TASKS OF EMOTIONAL DEVELOPMENT (TED)

*Manual*

Manual to Accompany the Tasks of Emotional Development Test. Cohen, H. & Weil, G. R. Brookline, MA: T.E.D. Associates, 1971.

*Purpose*

The Tasks of Emotional Development is a projective test which was devised so that professionals working with children and adolescents could evaluate emotional health problems which might be interfering with a patient's functioning. Both the description of personality in terms of overall adjustment and the areas of conflict and symptoms were considered important. Like the TAT (see p. 239), this test is assumed to reveal information about the subject and his or her interaction with the environment. Because of some of the difficulties with TAT stimulus materials, the authors based the pictures used for the TED upon a range of tasks which are related to social and emotional development of children. These are assumed to be ego tasks in that mastery is involved in optimal adjustment of internal needs and environmental demands, and that both coping and defensive mechanisms might be used by the subject. Age is taken to be a rough measure of development and children are assumed to have a developmental sequence through which they accomplish these tasks of emotional maturation, an approach which draws upon the theoretical background of Erikson (1950) and others.

*Format*

Tasks chosen were considered for age-appropriateness and importance, as well as their ability to be portrayed in a photograph. Thirteen tasks were included:

1) Socialization within the peer group
2) Establishment of trust in people

3) Acceptance and control of aggressive feelings toward peers
4) Establishment of positive attitudes toward academic learning
5) Establishment of respect for the property of others
6) Separation from mother
7) Identification with same-sexed parent
8) Acceptance of siblings
9) Acceptance of limits set by adults
10) Resolution of oedipal conflict (affection between parents)
11) Establishment of positive attitudes toward orderliness and cleanliness
12) Establishment of positive self-concept
13) Establishment of positive heterosexual socialization

Using the literature on the TAT as their guideline, the authors chose to use photographs with the idea that they might provoke responses with clear behavioral relationships to reality. Photographs were chosen to include characters of the same sex as the subjects and a series was constructed for younger children and for adolescents for each sex. The photographs were clear and focused upon the tasks chosen for inclusion. Two psychiatrists selected photographs to match the tasks and rated them for goodness of fit. The photographs included were those which provoked total agreement as most representative of each task of emotional development. The total number of photographs was 49 (one card for heterosexual socialization and four for each of the other twelve tasks to include both sex and age level combinations). Thus each child receives only those cards appropriate for age and sex level.

*Administration*

Instructions given to the subject include asking for what is happening in the picture and what the characters might be feeling and thinking as well as how the story ends. The instructions also include a definition of feelings and ask the subject to indicate when the story is finished. No specific instructions for the order of questioning are given but the manual appears to depart from the TAT type inquiry in suggesting an inquiry after each original story and in suggesting specific types of probes for specific stimulus cards in the series. No special instructions are given as to how to record the subject's stories, but presumably verbatim recording is implied.

*Scoring*

Rating scales for Perception (subject's description of what is seen), Outcome, Affect, Motivation, and Spontaneity are described. Each of the 13 developmental tasks represented by the photographs is scored for each of these variables. Data are summarized in three different ways: obtained scores, which are the original categories of the rating scales; normal order scores, which assign a numerical value to the obtained scores; and rank order scores, which convert the obtained scores to rankings in terms of degree of maturity. Tables containing data from two normal and three clinical samples are included.

*Standardization*

Together the two normal samples consisted of approximately 1,100 boys and girls from six through 11 years of age from two public school systems of different socioeconomic levels: lower-middle to middle and middle to upper-middle. Age, grade, IQ, and fathers' occupations were noted and reported. The sample appears to have been drawn from a somewhat higher-middle class than lower-middle class population and there is some variability between the two groups, as expected. The clinic samples included 600 children referred for suspected emotional problems. The clinic sample falls between the two normal samples on age, grade, and socioeconomic level.

*Reliability*

Inter-scorer reliabilities are reported and are generally high. Neither test-retest nor split-half reliabilities are appropriate because of the nature of the test.

*Validity*

Stories for the first six tasks were collected on latency boys and girls. Comparisons were made between these stories given by clinic children and the reasons for their referral. These children were then compared with those in the normal sample. Both authors made the comparisons and when they agreed that a child had a given problem on a given task the child was assigned to the Relevant Clinic Sample (a subset of the entire clinic sample). Many children could not be placed in the Relevant

Clinic Sample. The authors performed analyses of tasks and between clinic and normal samples, which are described in Cohen and Weil (1971), concluding that the TED elicits stories with lower scores for clinic children than for normal children.

*Critique*

No reviews have yet appeared in the Mental Measurement Yearbook and only one brief notation in Personality Test Reviews. The status of the TED as a test seems dubious. There are no data which really establish it as a test, either in terms of validation work of a substantial nature or reliability data. The authors' contention that test-retest reliabilities are unnecessary is questionable in that under some conditions in which no change is expected such data might prove valuable.

The TED does probably offer the examiner an opportunity to present children and adolescents with standard stimulus material whereby clinical data may be elicited. The scoring procedure suggested seems cumbersome and unnecessarily detailed considering the lack of validity and reliability data. However, a systematic method of interpretation seems called for, and the authors do suggest one. The method suggested by Murray for the TAT would be an alternative, or some other systematic approach, such as that suggested by Bellak (1975) or Schneidman (1952) for other projective instruments, might be useful. In any case, the data from the TED should be considered as hypotheses and used in conjunction with a full assessment rather than as a single diagnostic method.

## MAKE A PICTURE STORY METHOD (MAPS)

*Manual*

Manual for the Make A Picture Story Method. Schneidman, E. S. New York: Projective Techniques Monograph No. 2, 1952. The Society for Projective Techniques and Rorschach Institute.

*Purpose*

The Make A Picture Story was developed to provide a thematic projective method which gave the subject greater latitude than that used in some other tests for choice of situations and characters which serve as the stimulus material for the stories which are produced. The MAPS was designed to be used in both psychodynamic interpretation of personality and in psychiatric classification with subjects from age six to ages beyond 60, and with both normal and clinical subjects.

*Format*

The MAPS consists of 22 situations or backgrounds which are on printed cards, of which one is blank, some are very ambiguous, some are partly structured, and some are clearly recognizable scenes. The kit, which can serve as a stage for the stories, also contains 67 figures, both males and females of varying age in various stances. Minority group figures are included as well as some mythical figures, animals, and ambiguous figures. Some of the characters are partly dressed or nude. The examiner is provided with a figure location chart for aid in recording the choice and placement of figures and also with a figure identification card to aid the examiner in recording.

*Administration*

Instructions are provided in the manual. The examiner places the background LIVINGROOM before the subject and explains that he will show the subject similar pictures one at a time. The figures are then produced and the examiner explains that the subject is to take one or more figures and put them on the background as they might be in real life, after first looking at each figure. After the subject looks at all the figures, the examiner asks the subject to choose some figures and to tell a story about them, including what they are feeling and thinking and how the story ends.

The examiner records the story verbatim, as well as the choice and placement of the figures. The subject is instructed to tell a story to each background as the examiner presents it. Ordinarily, 10 pictures are given. The subject is usually permitted to choose two of the backgrounds. Inquiry is suggested to follow the method used by the examiner for the TAT administration. (The subject may use the same or different figures on the backgrounds. The blank background is given last.) The form of the inquiry is recommended to be minimal as in "Can you tell me more?" or "Go on" and "What might you call this story?" or "If you were going to give this story a title, what would it be?" A method of forcing the limits is recommended when the examiner wants to investigate a particular hypothesis and consists of presenting a specific background and figures and asking the subject to make up a story about them.

## Scoring

The author recommends a story-by-story analysis, using one of five frameworks: normative, hero-oriented or need-press oriented (Murray, 1943), an intuitive method using the examiner's empathetic insight, an interpersonal (social) approach, or a form approach which examines perceptual, logical, and linguistic distortions. Nineteen areas are suggested for inclusion in the report which is based on the stories. Schneidman suggests the thematic pull of the backgrounds and offers sample interpretations, although no data are presented in this regard.

## Reliability

A scant amount of reliability data (inter-rater reliability) is reported by Jensen (1965) in the Sixth Mental Measurement Yearbook.

## Validity

Practically no data exist on the MAPS validity. The original work was done on a sample of 50 hospitalized psychotics (mostly paranoid schizophrenics) and a sample of 50 hospitalized nonpsychotics. The data were analyzed for 800 signs which might discriminate the groups.

## Critique

Jensen (1965) concludes that very little research has been inspired by the MAPS and finds little practical basis for its use. Earlier reviews in the Fourth Mental Measurement Yearbook had been more optimistic about the use of the MAPS. While it should not be considered a psychometric instrument, it is a standard method of inquiry in that the examiner asks the same general task from the subject. Since the stimulus materials may vary, it is far from a standardized task in this regard. However, the task is interesting to children, who often respond to it when they will not respond to pictures or photographs alone. The task must be modified and very carefully structured with children who are hyperactive (the materials may end up all over the room) or who are below normal intelligence (they will need more structure). Even when the stories are rather sparse, the characters introduced and the methods of interacting reveal something of the child's phenomenological world with somewhat more confidence than when the child has no choice in the characters presented.

## CHILDREN'S PERSONALITY QUESTIONNAIRE (CPQ)

*Manual*

Handbook for the Children's Personality Questionnaire. Porter, R. B. & Cattell, R. B. Champaign, IL: Institute for Personality and Ability Testing, 1972. 1602 Coronado Dr., Champaign, IL 61820.

*Purpose*

The Children's Personality Questionnaire was designed to provide a personality test for use with children which might be of value in academic, recreational and clinical settings. The authors wanted to develop a test which was convenient, dealt with personality characteristics with functional unity, and could be related to psychological theory. The test is designed for children from eight through 12 years of age and overlaps two other tests of Cattell and his associates (the High School Personality Questionnaire and the Elementary School Personality Questionnaire).

*Format*

The CPQ requires a normal reading vocabulary of an average eight-year-old child. There are equivalent forms available so that retesting for intervals shorter than two weeks is possible. The test may be administered either individually or in groups and there are both long and short forms. All forms include test booklets and answer sheets, but the test may be administered orally if the subject cannot read the material. Forms are scorable by hand or by computer. The test forms are composed of forced choice statements such as, "Are you usually sure of yourself?" or "Do you often not feel very sure of yourself?"

*Administration*

Instructions printed on the test form are self-explanatory. Scoring stencils are provided for hand-scoring. The CPQ yields 14 independent factor scores which are labeled A through $Q_4$ to maintain the same designations as previously used on the 16PF test of Cattell. The factors have also been given names and interpretations for high and low scores on each factor. For example, factor A low scores are described as reserved, detached, critical, and cool, whereas higher scores are described as warm, outgoing, easygoing, and participating. Factor B is a general intellectual factor, Factor C a measure of ego strength, Factor G a measure of superego strength, etc. The test is designed to take no more than 45 minutes and is composed of 140 items per form (10 items per factor). However, each form may be broken into two parts (short forms).

*Reliability*

Reliability figures are presented in the manual and in the handbook. Test-retest figures for a one-week interval range from .28 to .82 for Forms A, B, C, and D. The sample is simply described as 93 boys and girls for Forms A and B and 106 boys and girls for Forms C and D. Kuder-Richardson Formula 21 values computed for A+B and C+D range from .26 to .83 for the various personality factors. Parallel form correlations for the 14 personality factors are too low to permit use of factor scores for comparative purposes. The sample is described as 1,407 boys and girls.

*Validity*

The manual presents data on construct validity based on 836 boys and girls. Coefficients range from .20 to .90 (A+B+C+D on Factor B, General Intelligence). Data presented in the handbook pertain only to Forms A and B and are based on 124 boys and girls. The construct validity values for these computations are somewhat higher, ranging from .33 to .95. No other validity data are presented in the manual, i.e., no data external to the test itself. Data in the handbook are arranged by age and sex and presented as age trends (although these appear to be cross-sectional rather than longitudinal samples).

Second order factors (extraversion, anxiety, tough poise, and independence) may be computed by means of a weighting method described in the handbook. Additional data are presented with regard to school achievement, clinical populations, and cultural patterns.

*Critique*

While the CPQ has undergone further study since the 1959 edition, not a great deal has changed with regard to the general characteristics of the instrument. Reviews have appeared in both the Sixth and Eighth Mental Measurement Yearbooks. As Anastasi (1965) noted in the Sixth Mental Measurement Yearbook, the data presented with regard to sources external to the test are sparse and in many cases not easily accessible to the user (unpublished studies and reports). Again, the instrument is difficult to evaluate because of the scanty and indefinite nature of the reporting about the validity data and the lack of information about the normative samples. Layton (1965) concluded that because of the small samples and lack of cross-validation, the CPQ should be considered a research instrument rather than an applied instrument. Gough (1978) expressed concern that the CPQ lacks adequate operational or pragmatic validity work. In addition, he felt that the intrascale reliabilities were too low to permit the use of the factor scales as a foundation for a science of personality, one of Cattell's aims. Moreover, the interform scale consistency was lower than desirable for many of the factors between the A and B forms. Finally, Gough observed that the statements in the manual and handbook may be partisan, and felt that the claims for the instrument may have been overstated.

The CPQ probably does have value as a research tool, but based on the material presented, its value as a clinical instrument remains to be demonstrated if further work is done to standardize it and make it readily interpretable with respect to appropriate clinical issues.

SENTENCE COMPLETION TESTS

Sentence completion tests are considered a semi-structured form of projective technique. In this procedure the patient is asked to read sentence stems consisting of one to a few words and to supply the remainder of the sentence. The idea is that the free associations of the subjects will provide relevant material. While no particular training is necessary for the administration of the form, the interpretation of material will vary greatly with the training and professional experience of the examiner. Because the material presented in the sentence stems is pretty obvious, a patient or subject may avoid material more easily than in some of the less structured forms of projective devices. Likewise the subjects must be able to read if the test is to be administered in written form. Illiteracy, retardation, and any interference with ability to concentrate may impair the subject's ability to perform. Forms of the sentence completion test which do have standardization data were almost always presented in written form. Therefore, the effect of oral examination of the subject is unknown and obviously open to the influence of interpersonal variables to a greater extent than is true in the written form.

There are a number of forms of sentence completion tests which have been used with children. Some of them, such as that devised by Sanford et al. (1943) use an approach analyzing needs and presses (similar to Murray's system of analysis for the TAT). Others use sentence completion tests as screening devices (Rotter et al., 1954), divide content into specific areas for examination (Forer, 1957), or examine the structure of the responses (Loevinger, 1976). Consequently there are many approaches to interpretation which reflect the framework characteristic of the analytical approach. Rabin and Haworth (1960) present a brief description of some of the standardization efforts that originators of different forms of sentence completion tests have made, as well as a reproduction of the Forer Structured Sentence Completion Test. Researchers have been successful in obtaining good inter-rater reliability for scoring various forms (correlations in the .90s) with somewhat lower reliabilities for test-retest (Rohde, 1957). Very few validity data are cited for any of these forms.

Most forms of sentence completion used with children range in length from about 25 stems to around 60 stems. The language used may be quite simple, as in the Rotter Incomplete Sentences Blank — High School Form (Rotter et al., 1954) with stems such as "I like . . . ," "The happiest time . . . ," or "I want to know. . . . " Others have considerably more complexity, e.g., the Rabin Adaptation of Sacks and Levy Sentence Completion Test (Rabin & Haworth, 1960), which has stems such as "To me the future looks . . . ," or "I would do anything to forget the time I . . . ," and require more reading ability.

Some forms of sentence completion tests are very specific in focus, attempting to assess some variable of particular interest to the examiner. The Self-Focus Sentence Completion (Exner, 1973) is designed to assess egocentricity. The Sentence Completion Form (Felhusen et al.,

1966) focuses on classroom behavior in elementary and high school students. At the opposite extreme is the strategy employed by Loevinger (1976) of evaluating ego development as a global estimate of the person's functioning.

The age level suggested for use of various forms of sentence completion tests ranges from elementary school age to high school age. However, most of the forms have high school levels and almost all of them include about a third grade level (probably because of the reading level required).

An examiner should take into account the age of the subject, the type of measure desired (global versus focused), the type of analysis desired, the length of the instrument and the reading level required. No single source appears to present a comprehensive list of sentence completion tests; nor do good data on standardization or various forms of reliability and validity appear to be easily available. For most clinical purposes a form should probably be of intermediate length with enough family-oriented, school-oriented, peer- and self-referent stems to survey a range of problem-related content. There should be enough repetition to gain some notion of whether a single answer is capricious or relevant to an important issue. The scoring should probably attempt to include both structural and content aspects, e.g., complexity versus subject matter. Sometimes children or adolescents will be more revealing on this semi-structured form of projective than with other types of projective devices. For the amount of time and energy involved in the sampling of the child's responses, the sentence completion is probably a highly cost-effective clinical assessment procedure.

## PROJECTIVE DRAWINGS

Hammer (1975) has enunciated principal assumptions made by users of drawings as a projective device, which include the belief that the figure drawings (whether of humans or not) are determined by central psychodynamic factors which reflect "body image" concepts. In addition, drawings are believed to be determined by a variety of external factors that can be differentiated from the body image concept. Analysis of the drawings should properly be sensitive to both external and internal concerns.

A variety of techniques has been employed to elicit projective drawings. Early in the history of projective drawings the basic task was defined so that the subject was given a standard-sized sheet of paper and a medium soft pencil and asked to draw a person (Draw-A-Person technique). Since that time various modifications of this approach have been developed. Among them are: the House-Tree-Person Test (H-T-P), Draw-A-Family, Kinetic Family Drawings, Human Figure Drawings, Most Unpleasant Concept, drawings of animals, and any number of other variations.

Generally interpreters of drawings focus on both the content of the drawings and some formal aspects of the drawings. For example, the size, placement, pencil pressure, amount of detail, organization, and sequence of drawings have all been the source of hypotheses about the personality characteristics of the subject. Discussions of these formal aspects of drawings can be found in Hammer (1975) and in other writers (Buck, 1948; Burns & Kaufman, 1972; Di Leo, 1973; Machover, 1949). In some of these techniques the order of the drawing is prescribed (e.g., the H-T-P) while in others there is more latitude for the choice of the first figure to be drawn and the order in which the others are produced.

Even when the artistic ability of the subject is poor, drawings can be quite revealing. For example, the formal aspects of the drawings have been used to estimate intelligence, reality contact, and a variety of psychodynamic considerations, including the conflictual areas of concern, defenses, and coping mechanisms. Hypotheses based on the content and the formal aspects of drawings should be tentative. Data from other sources are necessary to strengthen impressions gained and caution should be observed in making predictive statements which are not thus confirmed. Projective drawings should be considered as a part of a battery of tests and clinical procedures rather than an independent diagnostic method.

The behavior of the subject during the course of the drawings is the third source of information of clinical interest to the examiner. Subjects frequently comment upon themselves, the task, the reason for the referral, and other matters of interest. The attitude of the subject toward the task as well as the content and formal dimensions of the drawings all provide a data base for interpretation. This richness of material and the multidimensional determination of the product invite speculation and hypothesis generation. At the same time, without confirmation from other sources which have some external validation, this very richness of material can become the occasion for the examiner to indulge in his own projections about the patient, rather than for analysis of the patient. The clinician is open to the "Barnum Effect." In other words, a few statements which are accurate may lead to a sense of acute clinical intuition which may obscure the fact that most of the hypotheses generated about the person were inaccurate, or that acuteness of perception on the clinician's part may reflect an overly general set of statements.

Despite these cautions about the tentative nature of inferences based on drawings, their use does offer a nonverbal method of performance that allows the subject to be distinctly self-expressive. As such, personal concerns may be expressed. The complexity, intensity, and organization of drawings often draw the attention of the clinician to areas which are not spoken about or which are obscured by the verbal adequacy of subjects in conversation. Although there are more comprehensive and reliable indices of intelligence, brain function, and personality assessment, drawings are economical in terms of time, and may serve a useful function as part of an overall assessment.

## ADOLESCENT MMPI PROFILES

Marks, Seeman, and Haller (1974) present tables based on data for 1,800 normal Minnesota adolescents mainly between the ages of 14 and 15 but with some subjects ranging from 13 through 18 years of age. Of these 1,800 subjects, 100 boys and 100 girls ages 14, 15, and 16 and a smaller sample of 17-year-olds, together with 1,046 subjects from six states distributed around the U.S., were chosen for study. The subjects from the more general population were sampled so as to include urban-rural distribution and private versus public school distribution. All subjects were white, living at home, and not currently being treated for emotional disturbance.

The profiles of these adolescents were plotted without K correction (due to its lack of suitability, including some empirical evidence contraindicating the propriety of using K with adolescent profiles). The normal profiles for adolescents indicate greater elevations than for normal adults of scales 4 through 0, indicating the need for profiles of adolescents to be adjusted for adolescent norms.

A sample of 3,000 emotional disturbed adolescents, 834 of whom were in treatment, comprised an abnormal sample. Raw scores were converted to T scores for age and sex and plotted. Each profile was given a two-point code and the high points with ties were awarded the scale designation with the lowest numerical value. In order to establish a two-point code, a minimum of 10 cases was required as a criterion. Twenty-nine two-point codes were established, but in 15 cases in which the minimum of 10 cases was not available, the third highest code point was used as the basis of classification. There were 14 code types which could be compared for high and low profiles (minimum N=20). When all classifications were made, 22 code types remained. Each of these 22 code types was averaged for a sum of male and female profiles, except for Scale 5 which was a defining scale. For Scale 5, T scores of 50+ indicate the direction of the opposite sex for both males and females.

Marks, Seeman, and Haller caution that their norms cannot be applied with confidence to groups not conforming to the characteristics of their sample. Thus profiles of normal minority adolescents and of adolescents not living at home bear an unknown relationship to the profiles of normal adolescents in the Marks, Seeman, and Haller group, rendering interpretation of elevations for these adolescent patients more uncertain. Likewise, mothers of adolescent patients in the abnormal sample saw themselves as homemakers, now unlikely to be the case with so many working mothers (a change since the 1940s, 1950s, and 1960s when these cases were collected). What effects these changes in family circumstances might be related to is also unknown.

The distinction between early and late adolescence must be considered in the interpretation of MMPI profiles. Marks, Seeman, and Haller suggest that the use of adult norms may be more appropriate with 17- and 18-year-old subjects if their circumstances are more like those of adults. Recently new profile forms have been devised which take account of the differences between adult and adolescent norms (MMPI Profile Form Adolescent Norms, 1980). These profiles are available for both sexes and for four age groups, 14 to 18.

## THEMATIC APPERCEPTION TEST (TAT)

*Manual*

Thematic Apperception Test Manual. Murray, H. A. Cambridge, MA: Harvard University Press, 1943. 79 Garden Street, Cambridge, MA 01451.

*Purpose*

The Thematic Apperception Test was designed to permit a trained interpreter to study the personality of a subject. By personality Murray meant that the interpreter would be able to describe the drives, conflicts, and emotions of a subject, even when these psychological characteristics were not obvious to the subject. Although the TAT was used for studies of nonpathological personalities, Murray saw it as particularly useful for use with patients above four years of age.

*Format*

There are 20 cards, 19 of which have been printed with pictures and one of which is blank. The pictorial material is divided into two sets of 10 cards each. The first set is more clearly related to everyday life experiences, while the second set is more bizarre and ambiguous as to form. Some cards are especially designed for males and some for females and are marked as such for the examiner.

*Administration*

Good rapport should be established so that the subject feels the interest and receptivity of the examiner. The subject should be made comfortable and given the instructions. Murray provides verbatim instructions for the subject which involve giving a beginning, what is happening at the time of the picture, and an end to the story. The subject is instructed to make the story as dramatic as possible and to describe the feelings and thoughts of the characters. There are also instructions for children and less educated or intelligent adult subjects. Murray advises against using instructions indicating that this is a test of imagination, since this may be threatening to the subject. The exact wording of the instructions is seen as less important than fitting the instructions to the understanding of the subject.

After the subject has given the first story, the examiner may probe to ask for any omitted material (e.g., the outcome, how a figure was feeling or thinking). Otherwise the examiner should only encourage the subject where necessary or cut off a story that gets too long by asking for its ending, but should not get into a discussion of the stories with the subject.

Many examiners prefer to tape-record the stories and transcribe them later, but they may be written down in some shorthand fashion. Since the average story given by an adult is about 300 words long and it is important to get a verbatim record, the examiner should use whichever method guarantees the greatest exactness. Originally Murray intended two days for administration, with the second set of more unusual cards given on the second day. The blank card has special instructions in which the subject is asked to imagine a picture and then tell a story about it.

An inquiry is then conducted during which the examiner reminds the subject of the story given and asks about points of interest. These should also be recorded.

## Scoring

Murray's scoring system included identification of the hero, description of forces arising from the hero, and forces which *pressed* upon the hero from the environment. The interpreter was free to use any framework for interpretation, given these restrictions. Murray used a list of some 28 needs and classified them for valence and strength (based on the intensity, duration, frequency, and importance in the plot). Likewise the environmental forces are scored for some 30 presses (which may be personal or impersonal) as to their significance and strength. Outcomes are described for active versus passive nature, content of emotions such as guilt, and happy versus unhappy conclusions. Themas (the interaction of a press and the needs or drives of a hero) are described. In this way dynamic aspects of the subject can be described and interpreted.

Interpretation should take account of behavioral and conceptual functioning. Attributes of the heroes are construed as important to the subject's own personality, while those attributed to the environment are taken to reflect the subject's view of his or her world.The analysis of the stories should be taken as working hypotheses, not as definite conclusions.

Since the time of Murray's original work, various other systems have been devised for the scoring and interpretation of the TAT. Bellak (1975), for instance, suggests an ego psychology theoretical framework. He also reviews some relevant literature concerning aspects of interpretation.

## Critique

Many critics of the TAT condemn it as not being predictive of overt behavior, although, as Dana (1972) points out, fantasy may be a substitute for overt behavior. Issues of importance include the effects of instructions and examiner characteristics on the fantasy productions. Studies have shown women to produce richer stories than men, while men and women respond differently in terms of hostile-aggressive response to arousal. Cultural differences occur with respect to types of relationships portrayed and interpretation must take these differences into account. In general the TAT does not fulfill the requirements of test and measurement theory to qualify as a psychometric instrument. Rather, it is seen and used as a method of describing personality. While it may result in working hypotheses, these must be used in conjunction with other methods when attempting to predict or serve other purposes of tests. Eron (1972) comments on the usefulness of the TAT as part of a diagnostic process because of its differential findings with contrasted groups of subjects, despite the lack of cross-validation studies.

## CHILD AND ADOLESCENT RORSCHACH PERFORMANCE

### Purpose

The Rorschach (see Ames et al., 1971, 1974; Exner, 1974, 1978) has been used as a method of studying the personality and personality disturbance. It is one of the most unstructured projective techniques available.

### Format

The Rorschach consists of 10 cards, of which five are achromatic and five have color. The inkblots presented on these cards vary in complexity and organization.

### Administration

The subject is usually given instructions similar to those of Ames et al. (1974): "I have some things to show you. What do you see?" or "People see all sorts of things and I want to know what they look like to you." Instructions of this nature are given prior to the Free Association period in which subjects report their responses. Instructions for the Inquiry period which follows the Free Association period are usually phrased in such a manner as to make it clear to the subject that the examiner is reviewing the subject's responses in order to "see it like you do." No leading questions are permitted and the examiner focuses on aspects of the percept originally voiced by the subject. Questions are phrased in terms of "What about the blot helps you to see _____?" Some examiners advocate an inquiry after each card (Ames et al., 1974), while most others suggest an inquiry which follows the entire free association period so as to avoid any influence on the subject's responses. Some examiners also use a third period (Testing the Limits) to clarify any unclear responses which remain after the subject has produced the responses and explained them.

## Scoring

Records are scored for area or location, determinants, content, and popularity of response. Formal scoring is too involved to discuss here, but Exner (1974, 1978) and previous systems by Klopfer, Beck, and others are well known. The administration and scoring of the Rorschach require individual training and considerable practice. The use of the technique by untrained examiners is likely to result in the examiner's projections about the subject, rather than information about the subject, being studied. It is ill-advised to attempt to use the Rorschach without formal training and practice.

## Standardization

The Rorschach Inkblot Technique was first developed and used with adults. When the procedure was imported to this country, it was applied by a number of researchers who developed scoring systems which partially overlapped but were idiosyncratic in many details. Exner (1974) has an excellent discussion of the history of these applications and methods of scoring. The use of the Rorschach with children and adolescents has had an even more problematic history than with adults.

Ames et al. (1974) published data on child Rorschach responses based on records of 650 children of above average intelligence and above average socioeconomic levels. These children were aged two through 10 years and all lived in the New Haven and Waterbury areas, with the exception of a few clinical cases also from the northeastern part of the United States. The records were scored and typical profiles were constructed at each of the age levels sampled. It was found that the total number of responses, the F+%, H, and P increased with age across the entire period sampled. Other trends which appear reliable were that boys gave more responses than girls, while girls gave more F+% up to age four and a half, after which boys gave more F+%. Other findings were not consistent across age and sex.

Ames et al. (1971) conducted a study of adolescents aged 10 through 16 with 50 boys and 50 girls at each age level. The socioeconomic status of the subjects was higher than average (over half in the professional category) and the mean IQ was 116, with no IQ level falling below 113 and standard deviations ranging from approximately 10 to 14.6. Of the 700 records, 398 were from different children, the remainder being retesting. (Retested children provided 429 records from 27 subjects.) Subjects were given similar instructions to those for children. The Inquiry for location and nonleading questions for determinants was conducted immediately after the Free Association period. Other questions necessary to make scoring decisions were made after the entire set of cards had been presented. Subjects were also asked for their best-liked and least-liked cards. Scoring included location, determinants, content, and popularity, with many features of scoring based on the Hertz tables.

Boys were found to give a higher number of W responses, while girls gave higher numbers of D and Dd. All subjects gave more W responses than would be expected for an adult record with fewer D responses and fewer Dd responses. F+% was slightly higher for girls for most ages. Slightly more responses and fewer refusals occurred than for children's records. Generally age changes during the period of adolescence were small and variable from one age to another.

Exner (1978) reports data on 2,545 records of subjects aged five years through 16 years. His goal was to collect 100 subjects per cell yearly at each age for nonpatients, children with behavior problems, and withdrawn children. The sample most closely approaches a N=100 for the nonpatients and deviates the most for the withdrawn sample. Exner reports no socioeconomic data but comments that comparison of various socioeconomic groups resulted in no significant differences for structural data. No other descriptors of the samples are reported for sex, geographical location, minority status, or other usual demographic data. Exner's data for number of responses are more variable over younger childhood than Ames', and reach a higher level, but in view of the standard deviations the differences do not appear to be significant for the two samples. The same pattern applies to F+% and popular responses.

*Critique*

In view of the ambiguities resulting from samples which lack sufficient description to serve as normative data for much of the population, the use of the Rorschach remains in the realm of a clinical rather than a psychometric instrument. The most reliable data across studies suggest that younger children give fewer responses than adults, while adolescents approach the lower limit of adults in terms of number of responses. The same is true for the use of populars, while other variables are more inconsistent in the patterns which occur in their use across the age range from two through 16. Low F+ and low perception of humans also seem to be unusual for children and adolescents. However, the best use of the Rorschach is probably in terms of how the subject brings determinants and locations into play in response to the differential stimulus properties of the blots. This type of sequence analysis takes into account both formal scoring properties and content. Analyses of this type are usually taught in clinical practice as students work with case study material.

In assessment batteries, the Rorschach may provide information about the reality contact, richness of resources, productivity, organizational ability, defenses, affect, and areas of conflict. Comparison of performance on more structured instruments with the Rorschach may produce useful information about how ambiguity affects the subject. It should be noted that most of the data on children have been derived from normal subjects and that many of these were above average in terms of socioeconomic level and intelligence. Rorschach records of children who are retarded tend to be brief and unelaborated. Records of disturbed children are sometimes helpful in defining problems of thought and affect, as well as specific content which is problematical for these children.

## Comparison of Projective Techniques

Lindzey's (1959) review of methods of classifying projective techniques includes use of the degree of structure inherent in the test, its theoretical versus empirical basis, the type of analysis (formal versus content), its purpose, method of administration, and the nature of the response elicited. As Rabin and Haworth (1960) point out, the potential number of multidimensional categories that could be generated from Lindzey's classification would be too large to be useful. They suggest a classification based on the type of response elicited, e.g., completion (as in Incomplete Sentences tasks) versus construction (story-telling as to a TAT card).

Of the instruments reviewed in this chapter we have chosen a range of techniques which represent varying amounts of structure inherent in the materials. Thus the Rorschach is an unstructured technique, while the sentence completion is a semi-structured technique, and the MMPI and CPQ are quite structured. The structure is defined by the restriction of the subject's answers to a particular type of content. Rorschach cards may be defined entirely according to a subject's perceptions. Incomplete sentences have a defined subject matter but little specification as to how that subject matter should be handled. The MMPI and CPQ are quite specific and restrict the subject's replies to a narrow range of answers. Each of these procedures can be useful and many times a comparison of clinical material derived from a combination of materials is informative about the nature and extent of a child's defenses. For example, a child may be more responsive and productive to the Rorschach than to a more structured technique in which social demands are implied. This may be helpful information if compliance or defiance is an issue. On the other hand, very anxious children may "freeze" on less structured material but feel more comfortable and be more revealing with techniques which involve more familiar stimulus material, such as is the case with TAT or TED cards.

The material reviewed contains some procedures based on theoretical grounds (TED), while others are more empirically determined (MMPI). Yet it is safe to say that regardless of the origin of the technique none of them possess the breadth of representation in the standardization samples or the psychometric data typical of some of the intelligence and achievement tests. The analyses are based more on the clinical (ideographic) method in which a person is studied intensively. Comparisons made with others are based more on configurations (MMPI code types or Rorschach ratios) of clinical findings than on summary scores (such as IQs). In some cases quantitative methods of comparison are lacking altogether and more global and qualitative methods of analysis are employed (e.g., drawings).

We have included several techniques administered by an examiner (Rorschach, TAT, TED, MAPS) and self-administered tasks (Incomplete Sentences and MMPI). We have chosen individually administered measures, although the MMPI and Incomplete Sentences can be used in group administration. The nature of the responses elicited from these different instruments varies from orally produced responses (stories, precepts) to written material (sentences) to drawings to multiple choice answers. Few tasks could be categorized clearly as constructional as opposed to expressive or completion.

We have not included free or structured play, free story-telling techniques, wishes, and other less structured projective techniques which may be very effective, but which lack some minimal standard methods of administration and analysis. We have commented on techniques which are useful with young children (MAPS), preadolescents (TED), and adolescents (MMPI). We have also included techniques which may apply across these age ranges (Rorschach, TAT, drawings, Incomplete Sentences), thus permitting comparisons across testing occasions if a child is seen more than once.

All of the projective techniques reviewed were developed with children of normal or above normal intelligence. It is the experience of clinicians that more restricted responses characterize retarded children as a group. There are, of course, some exceptions. As a result many clinicians avoid extensive use of projective techniques with moderately to severely retarded children. The amount of information gained may be more economically obtained in less time and energy with other methods. For borderline or mildly retarded children, however, some of the strengths and problems which are important in the children's adjustment may be clarified by use of projective testing.

Other clinical groups may have more complex patterns of responses than retarded children but may still differ from responses of normals. For example, the MMPI profiles of adolescents which are coded 4-9 are conduct problems. The 4-9s are also likely to be runaways and to use acting-out as their major defense.

Decisions which are based on psychological assessment of children often rely upon information derived from projective testing. Because of the more clinical than psychometric nature of the data produced by the use of projective techniques, caution is urged in the interpretation of projective material. The interpretations are more tentative. The clinician will feel on firmer ground when several projective devices of varying structure or utilizing different methods of analysis produce results which are congruent across tests. Likewise, if the content produced within a single projective device is internally consistent, there will be greater confidence in the findings. This internal consistency may be observed in the repetition of themes within an instrument, or it may be observed that relationships which are delineated in one story or other type of production are consistent in their structure with other examples referring to that type of relationship. Because of the plaguing problems of reliability and validity that characterize projective devices, these methods of comparison across and within instruments assume great importance in estimating the confidence with which the clinician can make interpretations.

It may be that the clinician will find great internal consistency in the content of projective data, but have no life history data or other input which suggest the validity of the perceptions of the child. In such cases it is clear that the child's perceptions will color his experience of relationships and situations. Decisions which have to be made about children often need to take account of these perceptions, even when they are unrealistic. In custody cases, for instance, the alacrity with which a child may be expected to adjust to a specific situation may be as much a function of the child's perceptions as it is of the realistic situation into which the child will be placed.

Projective testing is often desired to assess the reality contact of the child, and whether there are emotional components to behavioral problems. Reality contact is evaluated by whether the child can achieve some consensual perceptions with others. This question is evaluated by the child's ability to use good form on the Rorschach, correctly appraise situations (tell appropriate stories to TED cards pulling for certain developmental themes), and demonstrate the use of appropriate thought processes and affective reactions. Gross disturbances in the child's ability to function appropriately signal the probability of serious problems. Disturbances which are found on projective testing can be observed in thought processes, in affective processes, or in the integration of the two processes.

On the other hand, one must not be too quick to interpret fantasy productions as a sign of serious disturbance of reality contact. The examiner of a child once was given an involved story to the blank TAT card. The story concerned this child's white horse and how much she loved it. The child referred at several points in the testing to the horse, and the examiner was told the details of the boarding arrangement for the horse and other facts about when the child rode the horse and with whom. It was not until the examiner was giving feedback to the parents that she discovered that the child, who had a wry sense of humor and did not particularly want to be tested, had no horse. Because the child's reality contact did not have any impairment, the only conclusion that the examiner could come to was that she had been the victim of an elaborate hoax by a superficially compliant child who was resisting in a socially acceptable manner, but one which challenged the examiner and her use of projective devices. It should be noted that the child did ride and love horses, and used active methods of expression. She was imaginative and oppositional, and had a sense of humor, all of which were expressed in her bogus "facts." This style and method of approach were consistent with other data. A defensive examiner might over-interpret the child's fantasy productions.

Rabin and Haworth (1960) provide an excellent source of material, much of it written by the originators of projective techniques for children. Many of the techniques included in that volume are rarely used in clinical settings, and others have declined in popularity since the time they were reviewed. We have included some techniques not reviewed in Rabin and Haworth, including the MMPI, which is often classified as an inventory but does deal with the same type of content as projective devices. Psychologists who are interested in specific projective devices, which were not included in their training, will find it helpful to practice administration and scoring and be trained in the use of a particular technique before using it clinically. Fortunately, continuing education programs and workshops make such training reasonably easy to obtain.

## REFERENCES

Ames, L. B., Learned, J., Métraux, R. W., & Walker, R. N. *Child Rorschach Responses: Developmental Trends from Two to Ten Years. Revised Edition.* New York: Brunner/Mazel, 1974.

Ames, L. B., Métraux, R. W., & Walker, R. N. *Adolescent Rorschach Responses: Developmental Trends from Ten to Sixteen Years.* New York: Brunner/Mazel, 1971.

Anastasi, A. Review of the CPQ. In: O. K. Buros (Ed.), *The Sixth Mental Measurement Yearbook.* Highland Park, N.J.: Gryphon Press, 1965.

Bellak, L. *The TAT, CAT, and SAT in Clinical Use.* New York: Grune & Stratton, 1975.

Buck, J. N. The H-T-P technique: A qualitative and quantitative scoring manual. *Journal of Clinical Psychology,* 1948, *4,* 317–396.

Burns, R. C. & Kaufman, S. H. *Actions, Styles, and Symbols in Kinetic Family Drawings (K-F-D): An Interpretive Manual.* New York: Brunner/Mazel, 1972.

Cohen, H. & Weil, G. R. *Manual to Accompany the Tasks of Emotional Development Test.* Brookline, MA: T.E.D. Associates, 1971.

Dana, R. H. Review of the TAT. In: O. K. Buros (Ed.), *The Seventh Mental Measurement Yearbook.* Highland Park, N.J.: Gryphon Press, 1972.

Di Leo, J. H. *Children's Drawings as Diagnostic Aids.* New York: Brunner/Mazel, 1973.

Erikson, E. H. *Childhood and Society.* New York: W. W. Norton, 1950.

Eron, L. D. Review of the TAT. In: O.K. Buros (Ed.), *The Seventh Mental Measurement Yearbook.* Highland Park, N.J.: Gryphon Press, 1972.

Exner, J. E., Jr. The self-focus sentence completion: A study of egocentricity. *Journal of Personality Assessment,* 1973, *37,* 437–455.

Exner, J. E., Jr. *The Rorschach: A Comprehensive System.* New York: Wiley-Interscience, 1974.

Exner, J. E., Jr. *The Rorschach: A Comprehensive System. Volume 2: Current Research and Advanced Interpretation.* New York: Wiley-Interscience, 1978.

Felhusen, H. F., Thurston, J. R., & Benning, J. J. Sentence completion responses and classroom social behavior. *Personnel and Guidance Journal,* 1966, *45,* 165–170.

Forer, B. R. *The Forer Structured Sentence Completion Tests.* Santa Monica, CA: Western Psychological Services, 1957.

Gough, H. G. Review of the CPQ. In: O. K. Buros (Ed.), *The Eighth Mental Measurement Yearbook.* Highland Park, N.J.: Gryphon Press, 1978.

Hammer, E. F. *The Clinical Application of Projective Drawings.* Springfield, IL: Charles C Thomas, 1975 (fourth printing).

Henry, W. E. *The Analysis of Fantasy.* New York: John Wiley, 1956.

Jensen, A. R. Review of the MAPS. In: O. K. Buros (Ed.), *The Sixth Mental Measurement Yearbook.* Highland Park, N.J.: Gryphon Press, 1965.

Layton, W. L. Review of the CPQ. In: O. K. Buros (Ed.), *The Sixth Mental Measurement Yearbook.* Highland Park, N.J.: Gryphon Press, 1965.

Lindzey, G. On the classification of projective techniques. *Psychological Bulletin,* 1959, *56,* 158–165.

Loevinger, J. *Ego Development: Conceptions and Theories.* San Francisco: Jossey-Bass, 1976.

Loevinger, J. & Wessler, R. *Measuring Ego Development. I: Construction and Use of a Sentence Completion Test.* San Francisco: Jossey-Bass, 1970.

Marks, P. A., Seeman, W., & Haller, D. L. *The Actuarial Use of the MMPI With Adolescents and Adults.* Baltimore: Williams & Wilkins, 1974.

Machover, K. *Personality Projection in the Drawing of the Human Figure.* Springfield, IL: Charles C Thomas, 1949.

*MMPI Profile Form.* Adolescent norms: Male and female. Odessa, FL: Psychological Assessment Resources, 1980.

Murray, H. A. *Thematic Apperception Test Manual.* Cambridge, MA: Harvard University Press, 1943.

Porter, R. B. & Cattell, R. B. *Handbook for the Children's Personality Questionnaire (CPQ).* Champaign, IL: Institute for Personality and Ability Testing, 1972.

Rabin, A. I. Comparison of American and Israeli children by means of a sentence completion technique. *Journal of Social Psychology,* 1959, *59,* 3–12.

Rabin, A. I. & Haworth, M. R. *Projective Techniques with Children.* New York: Grune & Stratton, 1960.

Rohde, A. R. *The Sentence Completion Method.* New York: Ronald Press, 1957.

Rotter, J. B., Rafferty, J. E., & Lotsof, A. B. The validity of the Rotter Incomplete Sentences Blank, High School Form. *Journal of Consulting Psychology,* 1954, *18,* 105–111.

Sanford, R. N., Adkins, M. M., Miller, R. B., & Cobb, E. A. Physique, personality, and scholarship. *Monograph of the Society for Research in Child Development,* 1943, *8*(1), Whole No. 34.

Schneidman, E. S. *Manual for the Make A Picture Story Method.* New York: Projective Techniques Monograph No. 2, 1952.

# CHAPTER 10

# *Behaviorally-based*

# *Measures*

With the rise of behavioral views of personality, there has been an emphasis on the development of assessment methods which may be helpful in designing effective treatments (Mash & Terdal, 1981). In line with this point of view, measures have been developed which are less concerned with global personality factors and more concerned with situational or temporal consistency of behavior. These measures usually assess ongoing behavior rather than report past behavior. In addition, they are usually based upon observable behavior rather than upon inferred states of mind, and the nature of the variables which control the behavior are the focus rather than some other type of content. The goals of behavioral assessment techniques are essentially the accumulation of information about the problems in question, and the types of assessment tools used are remarkably diverse.

Mash and Terdal (1981) point out that general behavioral patterns may be stable over time. They note the need to acknowledge the controversy over the use of diagnosis and classification based on nonverbal bases, particularly because of the unreliability of these classifications and the lack of demonstrated validity. The measures we have chosen to include in this chapter have been developed because adults concerned with the care of children believe that a particular behavior is maladaptive or producing negative consequences and they are concerned with the dysfunction.

There is a myriad of techniques and assessment procedures subsumed under the rubric of behaviorally-based measures. These procedures include direct observational procedures, structured and unstructured interviews, self-reports, behavior checklists, and rating scales which can be completed by parents, teachers, and others. We do not advocate that the psychologist use only these methods, rather that they be used in conjunction with clinical interviews, and other psychometric and clinical methods which are appropriate to the individual child.

The assessment methods reviewed in this chapter have been grouped according to the source of the obtained information. We review assessment procedures which are broadly based, in the sense that they are not problem-specific. The range of behaviors assessed by these methods varies considerably with the instrument. The clinician is usually desirous of surveying the child's behavior in order to determine the nature and type of problems which should be explored further.

Parent report measures have been among the most widely used behavioral assessment methods. The respondent is asked to rate the child on recent observations of the child's behavior. These checklist and rating scales can provide data that would be difficult to obtain from other sources or people less familiar with the child and his behavior.

Teachers are an additional source of relevant material concerning the child's behavior in situations not easily observed by the clinician or parent. Data concerning direct observation of peer interactions, development of appropriate social skills, conformity to group expectations, and other more academically related variables may be easily obtained from the child's teacher. The large range of behaviors that teachers can observe across a variety of situations (e.g., classroom, playground, cafeteria) can provide an excellent basis for rating behavior.

Individual interview assessment procedures, conducted by trained clinicians, provide an opportunity for direct observations of the child's behavior and also permit the child to report on his or her perception of the problems. Behaviorally-based interview schedules may be highly structured in format with predetermined questions and very little flexibility with regard to the questions or answers. On the other end of the continuum, an interview schedule may consist of open-ended questions and answers which allow the option of exploration of problematic content areas. Within this format, great flexibility is permitted to both examiner and respondent.

Finally, self-report measures are widely used as measures of indirect samples of behavior which have occurred in the child's past. Morris and Kratochwill (1983) have suggested that self-report measures can vary upon several dimensions: "specific vs. global measures, publically observable vs. private events, relatively permanent characteristics vs. more transient aspects of performance, direct vs. indirect" (p. 98).

Depending upon the structure of the assessment situation, it is sometimes the case that prior to the clinician's actually meeting with the child or parents, some pencil and paper material is obtained. In those cases the material may direct the clinician's attention to specific problem areas. In other cases, checklist and questionnaire material which deals with a broad range of behavior may serve as a method of ascertaining which content can be ruled out as unimportant in a given case, even if the topic has not been introduced in the interview or was not obvious in situations involving direct observation. Aside from these screening functions, Wilson and Prentice-Dunn (1981) advocate the use of behavioral assessment techniques for the purpose of problem definition, pinpointing target behaviors, progress-monitoring, and follow-up. This orientation reflects the approach in which assessment and treatment follow a behavioral model rather than that of broadband personality constructs or traits. In such an approach the screening stage of assessment is a survey of a great many behaviors, while successive stages of assessment "funnel" attention directly to specific behaviors of concern. Wilson and Prentice-Dunn also examine the use of rating techniques, whereas much of the previous literature has focused on self-report schedules and inventories (Tasto, 1977). Because we assume that the screening function is likely to be common to psychologists operating from a number of different assessment orientations, we will restrict our review to those instruments which deal with the screening function; hence the instruments are more global than some of those which might apply to the four later stages described by Wilson and Prentice-Dunn.

We have chosen some of the questionnaires and checklists which have received attention because of the research which has employed them (Behavior Problem Checklist [Quay & Peterson, 1975]; Child Behavior Checklist and Child Behavior Profile [Achenbach, 1978]) and others because they have been used with various clinical populations.

We will describe the purpose, age, format, administration, and scoring of these instruments. When available, we will also provide material on standardization and psychometric properties of the instruments.

## ADAPTIVE BEHAVIOR SCALE (ABS)

*Manual*

*American Association on Mental Deficiency Adaptive Behavior Scale: 1975 Revision.* Fogelman, C. J. (Ed.) Washington, D.C.: AAMD, 1975.

### Purpose

The AAMD Adaptive Behavior Scale is a behavior rating instrument first published in 1969 and designed to provide a general description of the "adaptive functioning" of impaired people, particularly those who are mentally retarded. The logic for the development of the scale is that standard tests of intelligence produce only partial and limited information relevant to a person's overall capacity to function adequately in his or her environment. Also, treatment decisions based only on an IQ may be misleading, usually through an underestimation of a person's ability to function adequately. The ABS was designed to yield a comprehensive measure of an individual's personal, social, and vocational adaptation within his or her environment.

### Format

The ABS is composed of two major parts, each of which yields a profile of the person's level of functioning in a number of behavioral domains or groups of related activities. Part I produces scores on 10 domains, including Independent Functioning, Physical Development, Economic Activity, Language Development, Numbers and Time, Domestic Activity, Vocational Activity, Self-Direction, Responsibility, and Socialization. Within each domain, various test items pertinent to behavioral functioning are ordered developmentally, so that the higher a person scores on a given domain, the more developmentally advanced he or she will be considered to be.

Part II is concerned with "maladaptive" behavior or behavior that would be considered deviant within the person's usual environment. The domains included in Part II are Violent and Destructive Behavior, Antisocial Behavior, Rebellious Behavior, Unacceptable or Eccentric Habits, Self-Abusive Behavior, Hyperactive Tendencies, Sexually Aberrant Behavior, Psychological Disturbances, and Use of Medications. Scores for domains on Part II are not considered to have developmental significance but are helpful in identifying areas of maladaptive functioning. The higher a person's domain score on Part II, the greater his or her maladaptive functioning in that domain.

*Administration and Scoring*

The ABS manual delineates three methods of administration: 1) first person assessment – the person who completes the ABS knows firsthand the subject's behavior; 2) third party assessment – the person who completes the ABS booklet solicits information from other people who are directly familiar with the subject's behavior in various ways; and 3) interview assessment – the person who completes the ABS interviews someone who is directly familiar with all aspects of the subject's behavior and uses a semi-structured format to elicit the information. This third method is often used clinically with parents of impaired children.

The information derived from any of these methods is used to complete an ABS booklet for the subject. The booklet describes the scoring methods used to derive the domain scores for both Part I and Part II. The scoring is primarily additive. Then, the subject's domain scores are used to construct a profile based on age-related norms provided in the manual. This profile indicates the subject's functional level relative to peers who are *institutionalized* due to the mild to profound mental retardation. Norms are based on individuals from age three to age 69.

Interpretation is straightforward. Low percentile scores on Part I are taken to indicate developmental deficits, often secondary to mental retardation. Low Part I scores may or may not be related to high scores on Part II, which are taken to indicate specific maladaptive behaviors. If an individual scores high on Part II but does not produce low scores on Part I, this usually indicates disabilities due to emotional problems rather than mental retardation. For treatment purposes, moderate deficits (rather than severe deficits) on Part I probably stand a better chance of producing change.

*Standardization*

Data are presented on subjects by age level for both Part I and Part II. These data were derived from samples varying from 97 subjects at age three to 528 at ages 10 to 12. The samples are all composed of people in residential institutions and are provided yearly through age five, for two-year spans through age 18, and by decades thereafter. For each age level, raw scores are plotted by deciles for each domain and maximum scores for each domain are noted. The total sample employed was approximately 4,000 residents of 68 facilities in the United States for previous versions of the scale. The revised scales contain new sections on profiling, interpretation and application, rather than any major content changes. More complete descriptive data about the standardization samples can be obtained from the AAMD Central Office.

*Reliability*

The ABS manual reports mean test-retest reliabilities of .86 for Part I (range .93 for Physical Development to .71 for Self-Direction) and .57 for Part II (range=.77 for Use of Medications to .37 for Unacceptable Vocal Habits).

*Validity*

Factor-analytic study showed that the 24 ABS domain scores load on three factors: Personal Independence or the ability to function independently on personal care; Social Maladaptation or the presence of inappropriate social behavior; and Personal Maladaptation or the presence of psychological disturbance. Brief review of studies which are criterion-related is provided in the manual. These studies involved placement in various types of administrative units and also subjects who had been classified clinically at various levels of adaptive behavior.

*Critique*

The ABS has a limited but useful application for institutionalized patients, primarily in the mild to profound levels of mental retardation. However, the referral question to psychologists is often how well a retarded person may be likely to function *outside* of an institutional setting. The ABS can only answer this type of question in a negative direction, when the scores are even lower than those expected in an institutional setting. The ABS should not be the sole source of determination of an individual's level of adaptive function. The scale deserves continued study.

## BEHAVIOR PROBLEM CHECKLIST (BPC)

*Manual*

*Manual for the Behavior Problem Checklist.* Quay, H. C. & Peterson, D. R. Obtain from Dr. H. C. Quay, Director, Program in Applied Social Sciences, University of Miami, Miami, Florida.

*Format*

The Behavior Problem Checklist presents 55 items describing problem behavior traits occurring in childhood or adolescence. In addition a face sheet contains seven items of demographic information and information about the respondent. Each of the problem behaviors is rated on a three-point scale (no problem, mild problem, severe problem).

*Administration and Scoring*

The parent or respondent rates each behavior item. The scale usually requires about 10 minutes to complete and can be scored in about five minutes. Because weighted scores were highly correlated with unweighted scores, the weighted scores have been discontinued and the score for each subscale is simply the number of items checked either mild or severe.

*Standardization*

Factor analytic studies of deviant and normal subjects are reported in the manual. Three primary scales have been identified: Conduct Problem, Personality Problem, and Inadequacy-Immaturity. There is also a Socialized Delinquency Scale derived from case history records and a four-item group which serve as flag items specifically for psychotic behavior.

The original 58 behavior items were selected from over 400 representatively selected cases from a child guidance center (Peterson, 1961). Next, teachers rated 831 children from kindergarten through the sixth grade. Factor analysis revealed two independent clusters: Conduct Problems and Personality Problems. Later studies on older children revealed an additional Inadequacy-Immaturity factor.

*Reliability*

The manual presents internal consistency estimates which have been reported to be approximately .90 for Conduct Problems, the low .80s for Personality Problems. Interrater reliabilities are moderate (mid .70s) for young children and lower for older children, based on teacher ratings. The ratings for older children are based on less contact time with the children who may only spend an hour a day with the teacher making the rating. Parent agreement reliability estimates were also moderate and parent-teacher agreement was low. Test-retest reliability estimates for two-week intervals range from .74 for boys on Personality Problems to .93 for girls on Inadequacy-Immaturity.

*Validity*

Several studies are cited in the manual demonstrating that concurrent validity has been established through differentiation of clinical and nonclinical samples. Other studies (also cited in the manual) indicate that expected patterns on specific scales appear for specific clinical samples which score higher than normals or other clinical groups.

*Critique*

The BPC is a convenient and efficient method of surveying problem behaviors. The factors compare well with Achenbach's CBCL factors in terms of both the Internalizing-Externalizing broadband factors and the appearance of the Inadequacy-Immaturity factor for older children.

There is no "national" norm group and no framework within which the data are interpreted. However, the BPC does permit descriptive analysis of the child's behavior problems as seen by adult caretakers. Of course, the BPC is subject to respondent bias, whether that occurs from inaccurate reporting, emotionally laden perceptions, or other factors which may detract from objective behavioral description.

## CHILD BEHAVIOR CHECKLIST (CBCL)
## AND CHILD BEHAVIOR PROFILE (CBP)

*Manual*

There is no manual as such. The following references contain information on the construction and use of the CBCL and CBP:

*Instructions for Hand Scoring the CBP.* Achenbach, T. M. Burlington, VT: Child, Adolescent, Family, and Community Psychiatry, 1980. University of Vermont, 1 South Prospect Street, Burlington, VT 05401.
The Child Behavior Profile: I. Boys Aged 6-11. Achenbach, T. M. *Journal of Consulting and Clinical Psychology,* 1978, *46,* 478-488.
The Child Behavior Profile: II. Boys Aged 12-16 and Girls Aged 6-11 and 12-16. Achenbach, T. M. & Edelbrock, C. S. *Journal of Consulting and Clinical Psychology,* 1979, *47,* 223-233.
The Classification of Child Psychopathology: A Review and Analysis of Empirical Efforts. Achenbach, T. M. & Edelbrock, C. S. *Psychological Bulletin,* 1978, *85,* 1275-1301.
Behavioral problems and competencies reported by parents of normal and disturbed children aged 4 through 16. Achenbach, T. M. & Edelbrock, C. S. *Society for Research in Child Development Monographs,* 1981, *46*(1), 82.

*Purpose*

The Child Behavior Checklist and Child Behavior Profile were developed to provide a standardized format of descriptions of behavior that would be useful to both clinicians and researchers. The CBCL and CBP were devised to include special narrow-band syndromes, competencies, and adaptive behaviors. They also permitted grouping children on etiology and other bases, and allowed quantitative assessment of behavior change. Separate patterns for age and sex were derived.

*Format*

The CBCL can be filled out by parents or other caretakers. The checklist takes about 20 minutes to complete and consists of 118 behavior problem items. A three-point scale is used in considering each type of behavior. Current instructions ask respondents to consider the child's behavior during the last six months.

*Administration*

Parents rate behaviors. Some items require further elaboration. For example, Social Competence items (e.g., sports, activities, jobs, etc.) are presented in a different format which elicits parent estimates of amount of time spent in the activity and how well the child performs relative to his or her age group. Other items (Social Scale) evaluate individual and group relationships. The School Scale is also completed for children of school age. Scoring may be done by hand as all items use three- or four-point scales. Raw scores are converted to percentiles and to T-scores. Profiles may be plotted as a function of the converted scores.

*Standardization*

Data obtained from parents of 450 boys seen in 20 East Coast mental health settings were the basis of the Behavior Problems Scales derived by factor analysis. Approximately 80% of the sample was white and 19% black. The children were mainly from middle-class homes. Approximately equal numbers of boys at each year of age were represented for the sample 6–11 years of age. For other age and sex groups, comparable samples were collected. In addition, 50 normal children served as the basis for data collected from parents at each age level and each sex. The same sample characteristics applied except that the normal children were from the Washington, D.C., area and had had no mental health services for the previous year.

Table 10.1 indicates the narrow-band or first order factors found for each age group and sex studied. As can be seen, the somatic scale for the Internalizing factor (broadband or second order factor) and the aggressive and delinquent scales for the Externalizing factor hold up across ages and both sexes. Scales which might indicate developmental patterns (uncommunicative for boys), atypical developmental patterns (cruel for girls), or neurotic patterns show less comprehensive distribution. Older boys tended to obtain more Externalizing scores, while in the clinical sample older girls increased in Internalizing scores.

*Social Competence Scales* were derived from data on normal subjects. Normalized T-scores were obtained. Clinical samples scored lower than normals on Social Competence Scales. Social competence increased with socioeconomic status but showed no age effects. Socioeconomic status effects for boys stemmed from the Activities and School Scales, but for girls were due to changes on the Social Scale.

# Table 10.1

## Child Behavior Problems Checklist: Factors by Age and Sex

| Broadband Factors | Internalizing | | | | | | | Mixed | Externalizing | | | | |
|---|---|---|---|---|---|---|---|---|---|---|---|---|---|
| Narrow Band or First Order Factors by Age and Sex | Schizoid | Depressed | Uncommunicative | Obsessive-Compulsive | Somatic | Immature | Schizoid-Obsessive | | Hyperactive | Aggressive | Delinquent | Sex | Cruel |
| Boys 6-11 | X | X | X | X | X | | | Social With-drawal | X | X | X | | |
| Girls 6-11 | | X | | | X | | | Social With-drawal | X | X | X | X | X |
| Boys 12-16 | X | | X | X | X | X | | Hostile With-drawal | X | X | X | | |
| Girls 12-16 | X | Depressed Withdrawal | | Anxious-obsessive | X | | | Immature Hyper-active | | X | X | | X |

261

*Reliability*

For younger boys, the test-retest reliabilities ranged from .72 on the Activity Scale to .97 on total score (N=12 normals with an intertest interval from seven to 12 days). Test-retest reliability estimates for small samples of subjects in other age and sex cells were comparable. There was a general decrease in reported behavior problems from occasion 1 to occasion 2.

Interparent agreement on 37 younger clinic boys ranged from .58 for Activity to .87 for the School Scale. Mean correlations between parents were comparable for older boys, but mothers reported more problems for the 6–11 year old girls.

*Validity*

Highly significant and large differences were found between the clinical group and the normal group on the Behavior Problems Scales. Clinical samples also earned lower scores than normals on the Social Competence Scales. The Immature syndrome occurred only for the adolescents. Some patterns reflect cultural bias. For example, although more cruel behavior was reported for boys, it was more discriminating for girls (for whom it is probably less culturally acceptable).

*Critique*

The studies were conducted on outpatients and therefore the CBCL and CBP may underestimate behavior characteristics for inpatients. The authors point out that the lack of evidence for a depression factor for adolescent boys may not reflect the impropriety of such a diagnosis. For boys this age, many items on the Schizoid, Uncommunicative, and Hostile Withdrawal factors were the same as those which entered the Depression factor for younger boys. Whether these behaviors should be interpreted as "depressive equivalents" is subject to controversy.

The CBCL and CBP are convenient and easily scored. The instrument holds promise as further data become available. However, relatively small samples with lack of geographical representation and unknown distribution on other dimensions make interpretation tentative. The instrument promises to be useful in settings in which clinical research is combined with clinical practice. The broadband factors of overcontrol, undercontrol, detachment, and learning problems, which were found across a number of studies and researchers and which Achenbach and Edelbrock (1978) discuss, correspond reasonably well with the DSM-III categories. Narrow-band factors (first order factors) usually were derived from scales with fewer items (and were probably less reliable). Therefore, studies of both etiology and treatment, as well as reports of disturbed behavior, may be improved by the more precise definitions possible through use of the CBCL and CBP. The CBCL is subject to problems relating to responder bias such as unreliability of informants due to either inaccurate or distorted reporting.

## CONNERS SYMPTOM CHECKLIST

*Manual*

The Conners Symptom Checklist is referenced in: Symptom patterns in hyperkinetic, neurotic, and normal children. Conners, C. K. *Child Development*, 1970, *41*, 667–682.

*Purpose*

The Conners Symptom Checklist was devised to permit discrimination among groups of normal, hyperkinetic, and neurotic children based on a report of their symptoms.

*Format*

A checklist containing 73 items describing symptoms is presented to be rated on a four-point scale from "not at all" to "very much present" by the respondents. The symptoms are grouped into 24 categories to reduce the effect of any particular item. (Thus sleep disturbances might include restless, nightmares, awakens at night, and cannot fall asleep.) These groups form the basis of five factors: 1) Aggressive-Conduct Disorder; 2) Anxious Inhibited; 3) Antisocial Reaction; 4) Enuresis; and 5) Psychosomatic Problems.

*Standardization*

The children included 316 outpatients at a psychiatric clinic, with an IQ of 80 or higher. There were 258 males, 58 females. Forty-three of the children were black, the rest white. There were 166 hyperactive and 137 neurotic children; 13 children were of unknown diagnosis. Normal children were obtained from Baltimore public schools representing middle-class and lower-class backgrounds. The children were without psychiatric history or adjustment problems. Parents provided data consisting of 365 usable questionnaires. The age of the clinical sample ranged from five to 15 years and of the normal sample from five to 16 years. The distribution of the normal sample was comparable to the clinical sample in racial distribution.

*Reliability*

No reliability data are presented.

*Validity*

Discriminant function analyses were performed which provided evidence that the checklist could identify normals from clinical samples on 21 of the 24 categories, with 70% of the patients correctly classified and 83% of the normals correctly classified (p > .005). The second analysis correctly classified 77% of the neurotics and 74% of the hyperkinetics within the clinical sample (p > .001). The hyperkinetics scored significantly higher than the neurotics on aggressive-conduct and enuresis factors. The neurotics scored more highly on the anxious-inhibited factor. Lower-class children also had significantly more reported symptoms than middle-class children, primarily on the antisocial and psychosomatic factors. Racial differences consist mainly in the lower social class for a broad range of categories. Only school problems were higher for black children in the middle-class sample, but more problems were reported by parents of black children for nine of the 10 categories on which differences were found in the lower-class sample.

*Critique*

There are no general population norms and no reliability data. The data are consistent with other instruments which have identified conduct problems and personality problems. The usefulness of the checklist as a research instrument seems reasonable. However, the scale is used primarily in psychopharmacology studies (Quay & Werry, 1979).

A 39-item Teacher Rating Form has also been developed (Conners, 1973) which produces five factors (not identical to the parent form reviewed above); these appear to be reliable on test-retest (r ranged from .72 to .91 over a one-month interval). Probably other scales of a more general nature would be useful for most clinical screening purposes since the parent questionnaire does not identify some relevant clinical groups and the teacher questionnaire does not identify other clinical groups.

## DEVEREUX CHILD BEHAVIOR RATING SCALE (DCB)

*Manual*

The Devereux Child Behavior Rating Scale Manual. Spivack, G. & Spotts, J. Devon PA: The Devereux Foundation Press, 1966.

*Purpose*

The Devereux Child Behavior Rating Scale was designed to describe and measure behavioral symptoms that characterize an atypical child from the ages of eight to 12. Emotionally disturbed or mentally retarded children are rated by clinicians, childcare workers, parents, or others who have had intimate contact with the child over an extended period of time. The scale takes approximately 15 minutes to administer.

*Format*

The DCB consists of 97 items comprising 17 factors. Fifty-three of the items are of the form, "Compared to normal children, how often does this child . . . ," with a 5-point Likert-type scale response blank. The remaining 44 items are rated on Likert scales with scores ranging from 5 to 8 points. The 17 factor scores are distractibility, poor self-care, pathological use of senses, emotional detachment, social isolation, poor coordination and body tonus, incontinence, messiness-sloppiness, inadequate need for independence, unresponsiveness to stimulation, proneness to emotional upset, need for adult contact, anxious-fearful ideation, impulse ideation, inability to delay, social aggression, and unethical behavior.

*Standardization*

The original scale was given to a subject pool of 140 children (107 male and 33 female) between five and 12 years of age. All of the subjects were enrolled in the Devereux Schools and had a variety of psychiatric diagnoses ranging from schizophrenia (N=22) to chronic brain syndrome (N=35). The 68 items chosen reflected easily observable behaviors in terms of frequency or the degree to which they were typical of the child. The raters were house parents or supervisors of the residential units of eight Devereux Schools. The authors concluded that the DCB factor scores related to clinical diagnosis. A later study was conducted by Spivack and Spotts (1965) with 252 children (179 males and 73 females between the ages of 6 and 12) enrolled at the Devereux Schools. These institutionalized children had a variety of clinical diagnoses with an average IQ of 71 and a standard deviation of 27 points. Raters were houseparents and childcare workers. In this study, an expanded item pool of 121 behavioral symptoms was used. These ratings were factor-analyzed with 20 interpretable first-order and six second-order factors emerging. The authors concluded that the DCB correlated with the clinical diagnosis of the children.

*Reliability*

The authors report inter-rater reliability coefficients ranging between .77 and .93 for the factor scores with a median correlation of .83. A median one-week test-retest reliability was reported to be .83.

*Validity*

No validity data were reported by the authors with the exception that the factor scores agreed with the clinical diagnosis of the children.

*Critique*

The DCB is a widely used clinical scale despite the lack of studies reporting empirical data on the test. The DCB was standardized on a group of institutionalized children having a variety of diagnoses of significant emotional problems and chronic brain dysfunction. Its generalizability to other children is limited despite its widespread use in a variety of settings. Thus far, there have been no demonstrated external criteria validity of the factor scores, nor are there separate norms available for different age and diagnostic populations.

The apparent strengths of the DCB lie in the high face validity of the items and factors. Factor scores and item responses are likely to be of considerable practical interest to individuals concerned with classification of behavioral symptoms and evaluation of behavioral problems in children. Administration and scoring are quite easy and a completed DCB may provide useful guidelines for topics to be followed up in a clinical interview.

### EYBERG CHILD BEHAVIOR INVENTORY (ECBI)

*Manual*

Copies of the Eyberg Child Behavior Inventory may be obtained from Sheila Eyberg, Ph.D., Department of Medical Psychology, University of Oregon Health Science Center, Portland, Oregon 97201.

*Purpose*

The Eyberg Child Behavior Inventory is a behaviorally specific rating scale designed to assess parental perception of behavior problems in their children. The ECBI is applicable to children between the ages of two and 16 and is completed by the child's parent.

*Format*

Thirty-six behaviors comprising the scale were selected from case record data on an unreported number of cases over a two-year period. The authors selected items that reflected parents' specific descriptions of commonly occurring behavior problems. Behaviors which were clearly age-limited (e.g., thumb sucking) or unobservable by the parent (e.g., disruptive in school) were eliminated. Based upon the selected behaviors, two ECBI scales were constructed. The Problem Scale is used to identify relevant or applicable behaviors and requires the parent to circle "yes" or "no" to each question. The total Problem Score is calculated by adding the total number of problem behaviors circled (scores range from

0 to 36). The Intensity Score is calculated from the summation of frequency for each behavior on a scale ranging from (1) never to (7) always occurs. The Intensity Score has a range of 217 points (36 to 262).

*Standardization*

The normative sample included 512 children between the ages of two and 12 who were evaluated at a pediatric clinic. The majority (65.8%) of the children were brought to the clinic for a physical examination because of minor illness, 25% were chronically ill, and 9% of the children were suspected of having developmental delays or were conduct problems. All were white and came primarily from lower and lower-middle-class families. Eighty-five percent of the inventories were completed by the child's mother and the others were completed by relatives (10.6%) or others (2.8%). Eyberg and Ross (1978) collected data from the parents of 44 children ranging in ages from two to nine and a half from "normal families" who were paid to participate in the study. This sample was compared to additional groups of children referred for psychological evaluations (N=43), a control group of 20 children who were referred for intellectual or developmental assessment, and 10 children who had been in treatment. The ECBI scores significantly differentiated the problem versus non-problem groups with almost no overlap.

*Reliability*

Test-retest reliability of .86 and the Intensity and Problem Score split-half reliability of .95 and .98 have been reported by the authors (Robinson & Eyberg, 1978). Item and scale analyses data from the normative sample (n=512) indicate that all 36 items were checked as a problem significantly more often than from the normal group. The authors found both the Intensity and Problem Scales to be stable and internally consistent.

*Validity*

Validation data (Eyberg & Ross, 1978) indicate that the ECBI significantly differentiated between groups of problem and non-problem children between the ages of two and seven (p < .001). In an adolescent population (ages 13 to 17), the inventory was found to differentiate between conduct problem and normal adolescents. Robinson, Eyberg and Ross (1980) reliably demonstrated in a study of 512 children ages two to 12 that each individual item, in addition to the total Intensity and Problem Scores, differentiated conduct problem from non-conduct problem children. After reporting data from several validation studies, the authors concluded that the ECBI is an "internally valid scale which measures a unitary construct, 'conduct problems'."

*Critique*

The ECBI is an easily administered test which is normally completed by the child's parents; however, anyone familiar with the child can be the rater. Any rating scale completed by a parent or other caretaker is subject to a halo effect which should be taken into account when interpreting the data. The standardization sample included only children from lower to lower-middle-class families; therefore, caution should be exercised when comparing data from other populations to these norms. In addition, within the standardization data, a significant difference was found in the data when fathers completed the inventory. Fathers tended to endorse fewer items and rated the items less frequently on 21 of the 36 items when compared to the mothers in the sample.

The ECBI has good initial reliability and validity data and shows promise as a screening device to pinpoint specific problems in children. It is easily administered and scored, yielding quantifiable data which could be helpful in planning specific treatment approaches.

## LOUISVILLE BEHAVIOR CHECKLIST (LBC)

*Manual*

Louisville Behavior Checklist Manual. Miller, L. C. Los Angeles: Western Psychological Services, 1977. 12031 Wilshire Blvd., Los Angeles, CA 90025.

*Purpose*

The Louisville Behavior Checklist was designed to aid mental health professionals in screening for deviant behavior and to help parents communicate concerns they have about their children. There are two forms: E1 for ages four through six and E2 for ages seven through 13.

*Content*

The original items were selected from clinical literature, inventories, and intake material given at a child guidance clinic. There are 164 items which represent behaviors. Factor analysis provided 11 scales: Infantile Aggression, Hyperactivity, Antisocial Behavior, Social Withdrawal, Sensitivity, Fear, Academic Disability, Immaturity, Aggression, Inhibition, and Learning Disability. Normal Irritability (behaviors which appear at least 25% of the time in normals) and Rare Deviance (items which appear less than 1% of the time in normals) were added, as were seven scales based on clinical judgment: Psychotic Behavior, Neurotic Behavior, Sex, Somatic, School Disturbance Predictor, Severity Level, and Prosocial Deficit. All of these scales are found on E2. On E1 the academic disability scale is replaced by an intellectual deficit scale, composed of items mainly from the Minnesota Child Development Inventory. Also, the Learning Disability scale was changed to Cognitive Disability scale. E1 was constructed after the content changes for E2 but no reanalyses of data were performed on E1.

*Administration and Scoring*

The parent is given the checklist and answer sheet with the directions to mark each item either true or false. A sixth grade reading level is required in order to complete the checklist.

Scoring templates for each scale are provided. The raw scores are converted to scaled scores and percentile scores (tables are in the manual). Profile sheets may be plotted with either scaled scores or percentile scores. There are profile sheets for each sex. Standard scores above 65 are suspect. Scores above the 85th percentile on Neurotic Behavior and two or more items on Rare Deviance, Psychotic, Somatic or Sex scales should be considered significant.

*Standardization*

A random sample of 133 male and 154 female children was used for Form E1. These children were balanced for family income and race to represent the general population of Jefferson County, Kentucky. For

Form E2, 114 male and 122 female children were used, balanced for the same factors. In addition, data on socioeconomic status, religion, parents' marital status and educational level are included in the manual.

*Reliability*

Split-half reliabilities were computed for each scale of Form E1 for the sample of 287 children. These estimates ranged from .85 to .97, except for Sex which was .60. Test-retest estimates for a three-month period ranged from .45 to .89 for Form E2. Split-half reliability estimates for E2 (N=236) ranged from .44 to .90. Because most of the items represent either very severe or very mild behaviors on some of the scales (especially Somatic and Sex scales), the split-half reliability estimates may be lower than would be the case with more adequate scaling.

*Validity*

Content validity appears to have been established through the method of item selection. In addition, there are two studies reported which differentiated clinic and non-clinic samples, but the test forms are not the same as the 1977 edition (Miller, 1967, 1977). Other studies reported in the manual involved a phobic group (N=64), an autistic group (N= 18), a learning disabled group (N=50), and a general population group (N=64). The author concluded that discrimination of all groups could be made, normal from pathological and within pathological groups. Data are presented in the manual for this criterion-related validity. Construct validity was studied through parent and teacher ratings of children's behavior. While aggressive behavior and learning disability appeared to have cross-situational congruence, other behaviors showed little cross-situational relationship.

*Critique*

A wide variety of problems is sampled, making the LBC a good screening device. Some parents will, however, check items indicating severe behavior simply because they have little experience with very deviant behavior and have observed benign behavior which appears to be described similarly. The manual gives an example in which a compulsive ritual is described and notes that parents may check this item when the child merely repeats a particular game. Likewise parental anxiety may result in over-endorsement of certain items. The Normal Irritability scale provides good information on the parent's set. The reliability and validity data are weak and based on a small sample of Jefferson County, Kentucky, children with a high proportion of lower socioeconomic level families. Most of the prior research was done on Form D which was developed during the late 1960s. Form D later evolved into Form E2 and then E2 later served as the basis for E1. Further reliability and validity studies need to be done. However, the Louisville Behavior Checklist appears to have promise as a screening device.

## LOUISVILLE FEAR SURVEY SCALE FOR CHILDREN (LFSC)

*Manual*

Louisville Fear Survey Scale for Children. Miller, L. C., Barrett C., Hampe, F., & Noble, H. Unpublished manuscript. Child Psychology Research Center Bulletin No. 1. Louisville, Kentucky, 1974. Survey copies available from: L. C. Miller, Child Psychiatry Research Center, 608 South Jackson Street, Louisville, KY 40202.

*Purpose*

The Louisville Fear Survey for Children was designed to assess the number of fears and intensity of fears of children as rated by their parents. The authors consider the scale applicable for children ages four through 18.

*Format*

The LFSC contains 104 items, to which the subject responds on a Likert-type format, checking one on a five-point scale from "not at all" to "very much." The parent rates his child for each item in terms of his perception of his child's intensity of fear. Sample items include the ocean, being touched by others, going to sleep at night, getting a shot, etc. Factor analysis (Miller et al., 1972) extracted three factors purported to describe major dimensions of children's fears. The factors are: 1) natural and supernatural dangers (e.g., storms, the dark); 2) physical injury (e.g., having a shot, getting a serious illness); 3) social stress (e.g., being touched by others, being criticized).

The items included on the LFSC were extracted from clinical literature, child anxiety inventories, and adult anxiety inventories.

*Administration*

The original score was developed to use either parent or child as the rater. Form B is recommended only for parental ratings. On each item, the parent rates the child on a five-point scale ranging from "not at all" to "very much." The scores are summed for the three factor scores.

*Standardization*

The standardization sample included children from the ages of six through 16 rated by their parents. Seventy-eight children in the sample had been diagnosed phobic by a team of clinicians and 101 children were drawn from the general population. Less than 5% of the children from the general population sample were found to be excessively fearful. While boys and girls were found to be alike in terms of general areas of fearfulness, girls were typically rated as having more intense fears than boys. General population norms are available from the authors.

*Reliability*

For the general population sample, a split-half reliability of .96 has been reported. For each scale Johnson (1976) reports reliabilities ranging about .80, although the type of reliability was not reported.

*Validity*

Johnson (1976) reports that the major difference between the clinically diagnosed phobic group and the general population sample was on the social stress scale.

*Critique*

Thus far, available reliability and validity data are minimal and the standardization sample was extremely small. The generalizability of available norms is questionable as these are based on small samples.

The LFSC is a relatively simple, economic screening device for fearful or phobic children; however, caution should be used in interpreting the results, as they present the parental impressions of children's fears.

## MINNESOTA CHILD DEVELOPMENT INVENTORY (MCDI)

*Manual*

Minnesota Child Development Inventory Manual. Ireton, H. & Thwing, E. Behavior Science Systems, 1974. Box 1108, Minneapolis, MN 55440.

*Purpose*

The Minnesota Child Development Inventory is designed to be completed by the child's mother and to yield information about the developmental level of the child from one to six years of age. The MCDI is meant to be considered a supplementary measure and is not intended to serve as a substitute for a parental interview.

*Format*

The MCDI contains 320 items about observable child behaviors. The statements are grouped into eight scales: General Development, Gross Motor, Fine Motor, Expressive Language, Comprehension-Conceptual, Situation Comprehension, Self-help and Personal-Social. The scales were not selected by a factor analytic method but by the authors, as those which would be most meaningful to clinicians, teachers, and parents, and which would generally be included in the child developmental literature.

*Administration and Scoring*

The MCDI booklet and answer sheet are given to the child's mother to be completed. Instructions are printed on the booklet, but the examiner should be aware that the MCDI requires an eighth grade reading comprehension level. Raw scores are calculated for each scale by the use of scoring templates and are recorded on a profile form and transformed into developmental age levels for each scale. Scores below the mean score for children 30% younger than the child being evaluated are considered to provide an indication of developmental retardation. Scores below the mean score of children 20%–30% younger are considered to be in the borderline range of development.

*Standardization*

The 320 items of the MCDI were derived from an original item pool of about 2,000 statements collected from child development literature and psychological tests for preschool-age children. The items were selected as representative of developmental skills, observable in everyday situations, readily described, and possessing age-discriminating power. The age level of an item is that age at which at least 67% of mothers first answered yes to the statement and is thus considered characteristic of that age.

An item validation study was conducted to determine the age discrimination power of 673 items from the original item pool. From this study the final 320 statements of the questionnaire were established. The normative study was then conducted in Bloomington, Minnesota, a suburb of Minneapolis. The sample consisted of 796 white children (395 male and 401 females) from six months to six and a half years of age. Most of the parents had 12 or more years of schooling (94% of fathers and 95% of mothers), most of the mothers were full-time housewives (86%), and most of the fathers' occupations (92%) were above the level of unskilled labor, with 43% being classified as professional-managerial. The families in the sample were small and intact. The authors state that other normative studies of urban, urban poor, and minority children will be conducted and caution against using the current norms for children from lower socioeconomic levels or for other races.

*Reliability and Validity*

Internal consistency for each scale was computed using the split-half method. The data are presented in the discussion section of the manual for each scale. The General Developmental Scale, which consists of 131 of the most age-discriminating items from other scales, has the most uniformly high reliability coefficients (.83 to .93) for ages nine months to five years eleven months. Scale validity is demonstrated in the manual with graphs for each scale showing a systematic increase in the number of items passed with increasing age. Several of the scales have a limited age range, reflecting the pattern of development for certain skills. For example, gross motor skills beyond age three generally consist of refinement of established skills rather than the acquisition of new ones; therefore, this scale tops out at age three. The profile forms indicates the age range for which each scale can be interpreted with confidence.

## Critique

The MCDI samples a wide range of behaviors over the ages included. It is quick and convenient to administer and to score and has an excellent manual with adequate explanations, charts, and appendices. Its limitations include the requirement that the informant have an eighth grade reading level and its highly selective normative sample. While the inventory is not a substitute for an interview with parents of white, middle-class, suburban children, it is useful in that specific observable behaviors are reported by the informant and these behaviors can be used in the context of a comprehensive assessment to supplement other data. The first entry in the Eighth Mental Measurement Yearbook contains a review by Goodwin (1978), who cites in detail shortcomings in the nature of the standardization sample and who points out that validity has not yet been convincingly established. Despite these obvious inadequacies in the psychometric foundation of the instrument, the items do appear to be well chosen and it can be hoped that future work will place the MCDI on a more substantial measurement basis.

## MISSOURI CHILDREN'S BEHAVIOR CHECKLIST

### Manual

No manual as such. The Missouri Children's Behavior Checklist is found in: Identification of clinically relevant dimensions of children's behavior. Sines, J. O., Pauker, J. D., Sines, L. K., & Owen, D. R. *Journal of Consulting and Clinical Psychology*, 1969, *33*, 728–734.

### Purpose

The major reason for the development of the checklist was to provide a method of identifying children who were clinically deviant on one of several dimensions of behavior. Criterion groups so identified were to be used in the development of an objective, nonverbal, personality test for children.

*Format*

The Missouri Children's Behavior Checklist consists of 70 items which were derived from a longer original list chosen from the literature and other checklists. Six dimensions were represented: aggression, inhibition, activity level, sleep disturbance, somatization, and sociability. There are no overlapping items. Items are based on direct observation of the child or refer to statements the child has made about him- or herself.

*Administration and Scoring*

The parent is given a copy of the checklist and asked to circle "Yes" or "No" according to whether the child has shown that behavior in the previous six months. Scoring is indicated in a table in the article.

*Standardization*

Data were collected in the U.S. and Canada from 15 child psychiatric, pediatric, and mental health clinics. The children, seen for psychological evaluation, comprised 404 boys and 250 girls, ages five through 16. Data are based on analyses of the boys only.

Items were retained if they correlated highly enough with the total score and if they could be assigned to a dimension because the item was associated with that dimension more than any other. Statistical requirements are discussed in the article.

*Reliability*

Internal consistency was studied by odd-even correlations, which ranged from .67 to .86 for the six dimensions. Aggression was the most reliable, followed by activity level, sleep disturbance, and inhibition. Somatization and sociability were moderate in level. Agreement between parents ranged from about 53% to 93% on individual items, while for scales it ranged from about 69% to 93%.

*Validity*

Checklist scores for 24 boys seen in a child psychiatric clinic were compared with checklist scores for 24 normal non-referred boys. Both groups ranged from six to 14 years of age and were comparable in terms of IQ (range 80 to 134 in nonclinic group and 80 to 137 in the clinic group). Significant differences were found on aggression, inhibition, activity level, and sociability dimensions.

*Critique*

The Missouri Children's Behavior Checklist is easy to administer and score. As yet the checklist appears to be in its developmental phase with little in the way of psychometric data for boys and none for girls. The standardization remains to be done. However, this brief instrument appears to have value in that it has dimensions which may be independent and able to discriminate clinic versus nonclinic children on relevant behavioral dimensions.

## PERSONALITY INVENTORY FOR CHILDREN (PIC)

*Manual*

*Multidimensional Description of Child Personality: A Manual for the Personality Inventory for Children.* Wirt, R. D., Lachar, D., Klinedinst, J. K., & Seat, P. D. Los Angeles: Western Psychological Services, 1977.
*Actuarial Assessment of Child and Adolescent Personality: An Interpretive Guide for the Personality Inventory for Children Profile.* Lachar, D. & Gdowsk, C. Los Angeles, CA: Western Psychological Services, 1979. 12031 Wilshire Blvd., Los Angeles, CA 90025.

*Purpose*

The Personality Inventory for Children was developed to facilitate the personality descriptions of children and adolescents, primarily within the age range six to 16 years, although profiles may be obtained for children from three to five years. The questionnaire contains 600 items, usually answered by the mother or someone who has known and cared for the child since early childhood. The PIC was intended as a preliminary procedure to provide screening information prior to the intake interview and which might serve to help focus attention on appropriate areas for concern and possible treatment. The PIC was also seen as a possible screening device for locating children who may suffer psychological problems.

*Format*

The PIC consists of 600 true or false items which are statements about the child (e.g., "My child has many friends") or about family relationships. The administration booklet provides written instructions and the answers are marked on an answer sheet supplied to the respondent. The PIC may be handscored with templates supplied for that purpose. The raw scores are tabulated on the profile form for the PIC and are then graphed on the form. The profile forms are constructed so that the female version is printed on one side of the sheet and the male form on the opposite side. Three validity scales and an Adjustment Scale as well as 12 clinical scales are displayed. T-scores are printed to the side of the graph. A separate form for the less stable profiles of three to five year olds is available.

*Standardization*

A total of 2,390 boys and girls served as the standardization sample for the PIC. The distribution was approximately equal for sex with children sampled at years six through 16. The lowest number of children sampled was 167 at year six and the highest was 298 at year seven. Because preliminary analyses yielded many sex and age effects, the data were examined further. Only the Intellectual Screening Scale produced large enough age differences to merit age norms.

A preschool sample of 102 boys and 90 girls who were between three and five years of age served for the development of preschool norms. Lie Scale norms were added to the inventory after the standardization had been completed for both the school and preschool samples. Thirty-eight protocols provided a test-retest reliability for normal children and indicated no differences for age or sex. The Lie (L) Scale correlates with other scales indicating a defensive method of responding and appears to be elevated when the respondent desires to avoid close attention to the problems of the child or the family.

The F Scale probably reflects severity of symptoms and was constructed to avoid age or sex effects. It has moderate correlations with many of the clinical scales. Defensiveness (DEF) measures a response set on the informant's part to deny problems or place blame for them elsewhere. Low negative correlations were obtained for DEF with most other scales.

The Adjustment Scale (ADJ) was based on 600 normal and 200 maladjusted boys. This scale correlates moderately with clinical scales and with the F Scale.

Achievement (ACH) reflects academic difficulties, impulsivity, and problems in concentration and motivation. It is most closely related to the cognitively oriented scales and second with the psychological adjustment scales. Poor readers (PIAT) are most closely related to high ACH scores. Intellectual Screening (IS) contrasted protocols of retarded and normal children (N=65 retarded and 325 normal) matched for age and sex. IS correlates best with ACH and other cognitively oriented scales, and is negatively related to antisocial behavior reflected in other scales. The Development Scale (DVL) is a broad spectrum developmental screening scale and overlaps somewhat with other cognitive scales and scales reflecting reality contact and social skills. The correlations are based on a clinical sample of 764 subjects. The Somatic Concern Scale (SOM) reflects a variety of physical symptoms, severity, and frequency of illness. This scale relates to other scales indicating anxiety, withdrawal, and depression, all of which taken together reflect a mode of internalization (INT). Depression (D), using a definition which includes moodiness, social isolation, pessimism, loss of interest, lethargy, and crying, produces correlations with scales reflecting withdrawal, poor social skills, anxiety and disturbed thought processes. Few children (only nine) with a primary diagnosis of depression were found in the heterogeneous clinical sample of 764 children. Family cohesion and effectiveness (FAM) through items which tap family stability, atmosphere, communication, and other aspects of family life overlap very little with other scales. Even so, FAM correlates significantly with scales which measure acting-out behavior and somewhat with those measuring psychological discomfort. The Delinquency Scale (DLQ) was based on 107 delinquents matched for age and sex with 321 normal children. The scale reflects a broad range of antisocial tendencies and a disregard for limits. The Withdrawal Scale (WDL) reflects social and physical isolation and emotional distance. WDL overlaps with D and is correlated with most of the internalization scales as well as those reflecting somatic, social skill deficits and psychotic concerns. The Anxiety Scale (ANX) contains items reflecting worry, irrational fear, various correlates of anxiety, poor self-concept, and pessimism, and correlates highly with D. The Psychosis Scale (PSY) was based on 60 psychotic hospitalized children who had diagnoses of various forms of psychosis and 300 normative protocols matched for age and sex. There is little item overlap with other scales. Most of the children diagnosed as psychotic obtained scores over 100T. The Hyperactivity Scale (HPR) includes emotional lability, interpersonal relationship items, impulsivity, restlessness, and lack of compliance. T scores in the low 60s appear to identify most hyperactive children. The Social Skills Scale (SSK) reflects lack of friends, and the reasons for this failure. The scale correlates with D, WDL, and ANX, as well as PSY, DVL, and ACH.

Seventeen supplementary scales may be derived including scales for adolescent maladjustment, aggression, asocial behavior, cerebral dysfunction, delinquency, ego strength, externalization-internalization, learning disabilities, and others.

*Reliability*

Three different samples provided test-retest reliabilities for the 16 scales of the PIC. The estimates were .86, .71, and .89, for intervals ranging from four to 102 days. The normal standardization sample provided internal consistency estimates from .72 to .84 and from .72 to .89 in a general male clinical sample (Ns respectively 2,390 and 198).

*Validity*

Several studies cited in the manual indicate that the PIC could predict clinically meaningful external criteria. Additional studies (by Lachar et al., 1978) indicate that adolescent PIC and MMPI data are congruent and that response to medication can be predicted for hyperactive children (Voelker, 1979). Further studies are reported in Wirt and Lachar (1981).

*Critique*

The PIC is easy to administer and seems to have some good psychometric properties. There was, for example, an effort to obtain a sample representative of census data for each age level for the normal sample and a sizeable sample was collected. Clinical samples were also collected and compared with the normal samples in the derivation of many (but not all) of the scales. Validity studies have been published on samples collected since the time of the construction of the inventory. The PIC gives descriptions of relevant childhood personality dimensions. At the present time many of the clinical criterion groups have been males, which limits the applicability of the PIC for girls. Some of the scales appear to have stronger psychometric foundation than others. There may be some bias because of the large number of cases obtained from one geographical region.

Several limitations are mentioned by the authors and should be observed carefully in making interpretations based on the PIC. First, the informant should be someone who has known the child well from early childhood. The data will only be as reliable as the informant. Second, even though standard scores are obtained which convert raw scores into T-values, these T-values can only be interpreted appropriately with regard to the values obtained by the criterion groups which have been studied. Thus a T-score on the Psychosis Scale cannot be equated with the same T-score on the Hyperactivity scale. T-values for Psychosis must approach the value of 100 before the authors feel sure of the interpretation, whereas T-values for Hyperactivity which reach 62 may be interpreted with confidence. The variability in interpretation of T-scores on the PIC appears even greater than with the MMPI, to which the authors compare this method.

A more basic criticism is lodged by Achenbach (1981) who points out that the instrument is not standardized on samples independently diagnosed, as was the MMPI, for example. This lack of reliably diagnosable criterion groups "makes it difficult to identify a basic test structure underlying essentially ad hoc scales that may have limited generalizability (p. 333)."

Given all the limitations of the PIC and questions about the assumptions upon which it is based, the advantage of the instrument is that it may serve as a preliminary screening device so that the clinician's attention may be directed to areas which might be overlooked otherwise, or to the confirmation of impressions from the intake interview. In cases in which ambiguity exists about a diagnosis, the instrument may prove helpful. Because the parent defensiveness measure is incorporated into the questionnaire, a clinician may be able to detect bias in this form of parent report which may be unavailable in some of the other paper and pencil methods.

## WASHINGTON SYMPTOM CHECKLIST (WSCL)

*Manual*

There is no manual as such. The WSCL is found in: A behavioral checklist for use in child psychiatry clinics. Wimberger, H. C. & Gregory, R. J. *Journal of the American Academy of Child Psychiatry*, 1968, 7, 677–688.

*Purpose*

The Washington Symptom Checklist grew out of a need for a screening device for use with child psychiatry patients which might be used both as a clinical tool and in research dealing with emotionally disturbed patients. The checklist is intended to survey symptoms of children who are referred by their parents.

*Format and Content*

The WSCL is divided into three sections. The first section consists of 66 symptoms which are rated on a four-point scale from "never" to "very often." The second section contains five questions which are intended to assess motivation. The third section has four open-ended questions which probe for additional information concerning motivation and psychopathology. Examples of the items are: Part I. Forgets things, disobeys father, cries easily. Part II. Do you think that your child has an emotional problem? Do you feel in part responsible for your child's problems? Part III. Who originated the idea of coming to the clinic?

*Administration and Scoring*

The WSCL usually takes 15 to 20 minutes to complete. Parents or others who know the child may fill out the checklist, usually just prior to the intake interview. Items are scored 0 through 3 with a higher total score taken to indicate a greater degree and extent of disturbance. Instructions are included on the form. The language is direct, but some parents with poor reading levels may find some of the vocabulary difficult. No reading level is specified in the article.

*Standardization*

Parents of 40 clinic children and 40 nonclinic children were used to establish psychometric characteristics of the checklist. No general standardization sample was mentioned in the article; however, the sample served by the clinic was described as lower-middle and upper-middle class in terms of socioeconomic status. The two groups were described as similar in terms of education and socioeconomic levels, but no other description was mentioned.

*Reliability*

Test-retest reliability estimates were performed with 66 parents of clinic children and 74 parents of nonclinic children after a 30-day interval. The reliability estimate for the clinic group was .84 and for the nonclinic group it was .87.

Item reliability was studied by noting which items yielded high enough frequencies to be considered. Mothers and fathers were given the checklist over the 30-day interval. Item reliability from one rating period to the next was studied for the 53 items in which sufficient frequency existed to permit reexamination. The 53 items were reported to hold up well.

*Validity*

Parent report on the checklist was compared with therapist report for 22 cases. Agreement beyond the .001 level of confidence led the authors to assume a high degree of validity exists for the WSCL.

*Critique*

The Washington Symptom Checklist is an unstandardized instrument which surveys some problem behaviors often thought to be characteristic of child psychiatry patients. Despite its ease of administration, no data of any major import are cited to support its usefulness with a general child psychiatric population, or to other socioeconomic levels. Results are cited only in terms of children older or younger than 12 years of age, but with such a small sample any attempt to characterize the usefulness of the instrument seems untenable. One positive characteristic of the checklist is the open-ended part which may permit the clinician to determine something of the parental attitudes and reliability as an informant. Other checklists appear to be better studied with broader samples and better psychometric characteristics.

### ADAPTIVE BEHAVIOR SCALE (ABS)—PUBLIC SCHOOL VERSION

*Manual*

*AAMD Adaptive Behavior Scale: Public School Version, 1974 Revision.* Lambert, N., Windmiller M., Cole, L., & Figueroa, R. Washington, D.C.: AAMD, 1975.

*Purpose*

The public school version of the AAMD Adaptive Behavior Scale is a revision of an earlier AAMD scale for institutionalized people, mainly because of mental retardation. Domains sampled in the institutional version which are not pertinent to school and which cannot be observed in school settings have been eliminated, e.g., Domestic Activity. Both the institutional and public school versions are based on the need for broader and more comprehensive information about a person's ability to function adequately than can be obtained from intelligence tests alone. In the school setting, the ABS may be of service when decisions must be made regarding the educational placement of children who have intellectual deficits, learning disabilities, or behavior disorders.

*Format*

The public school version of the ABS is identical to the institutional version (see previous review in this chapter), except that items relevant to behaviors which cannot be observed at school have been omitted. In Part I of the public school version of the ABS, the entire Domestic Activity domain has been omitted, along with items included in other functional domains that are not readily observed at school (e.g., self-care at toilet, dressing behavior). In Part II, the domains of Self-abusive Behavior and Sexually Aberrant Behavior have been omitted.

*Administration and Scoring*

The public school ABS is administered and scored in an identical fashion to the institutional ABS. After the raw scores are obtained for each functional domain, the appropriate set of norms given in the public school version of the ABS manual is used to determine a person's functional "profile."

*Standardization*

The norms for the public school ABS were derived from a different population than that used for the institutional version. The public school ABS was standardized on several subpopulations: 1) normal children in regular classrooms; 2) children in special classes for the "educable mentally retarded" (EMR; IQ range=50 to 75 ± 5); 3) children in special classes for the "trainable mentally retarded" (TMR; IQ range=35 to

50 ± 5); 4) children in special classes for the "educationally handicapped" (EH₁), meaning that they were of normal intelligence but had chronic learning and/or behavior problems and were below grade level in achievement; and 5) children similar to those in category #4 except that they had less severe learning disabilities and did not require special classes most of the school day (EH₂). The standardization sample included 2,600 children in California schools who were aged between seven and 13 years. Separate norms are given for each of the five subpopulations at each age level (age units=1 year). These data were analyzed by sex and race. No significant differences were found on these variables for Part I domain scores, but some differences existed in Part II. This has resulted in three sets of norms for Part II domain scores (i.e., by sex, age, and ethnic group) for each of the five subpopulations.

The public school version of the ABS is interpreted like the institutional version in that high domain scores indicate adaptive functioning on Part I and maladaptive functioning on Part II. The norms used for percentile comparisons are determined by the person's level of intellectual functioning, but the profile may be compared to more than one set of norms. Thus, a child's adaptive functioning could be described as being above the 80th percentile for an EMR population, but below the 30th percentile for a normal population.

The manual for the public school version of the ABS specifies how interpretations may be based on clusters of functionally similar domain scores. Part I produces five clusters that permit broad inferences about relative strengths and weaknesses: 1) Physical Development; 2) Cognitive Development (includes Language Development and Numbers and Time domains); 3) Functional Skills (includes Independent Functioning, Economic Activity, Vocational Activity domains); and 4) Socialization. Part II produces two broad clusters: 1) Social Maladaptation (includes Violent and Destructive Behavior, Rebellious Behavior, Untrustworthy Behavior, and Psychological Disturbances domains); and 2) Personal Maladaptation (includes Stereotyped and Odd Mannerisms, Unacceptable Vocal Habits, Unacceptable Eccentric Habits, Self-abusive Behavior, and Hyperactive Tendencies domains). The ABS manual emphasizes that high domain scores on Part II may simply reflect frustration secondary to inappropriate school placement and that this frustration may subside with proper placement.

*Reliability*

No reliability studies were conducted with the public school version, since fairly extensive studies were done on the institutional version.

*Validity*

The public school ABS manual reports data which generally show that children's domain scores discriminated among their actual school placements except at the highest age levels (12–13 years).

*Critique*

The public school ABS appears to be a useful procedure for evaluation of the adaptive and maladaptive behavior of schoolchildren. While the ABS should not be the sole source of information about a child, the specificity of items and domains do provide useful information which may be helpful in decisions affecting school placement. The ABS and its institutional version both rest upon the reliability of report provided by the respondent. In the case of bias or inaccuracy, the instrument is subject to unreliable impressions.

## DEVEREUX ELEMENTARY SCHOOL BEHAVIOR RATING SCALE (DESB)

*Manual*

*Devereux Elementary School Behavior Rating Scale Manual.* Spivack, G. & Swift, M. Devon, PA: The Devereux Foundation Press, 1967.

*Purpose*

The Devereux Elementary School Behavior Rating Scale was specifically developed to assist the teacher in evaluating the adjustment of schoolchildren by measuring classroom behaviors.

*Format*

The DESB is comprised of 47 behavioral items which are considered to be relevant to the teacher's assessment of a child's classroom behavior and/or emotional adjustment. The 47 items are assigned to 11 factors containing three to five items each and three items not belonging to any factor. The 11 factors are Classroom Disturbance, Impatience, Disrespect-Defiance, External Blame, Achievement, Anxiety, External Reliance, Comprehension, Inattentive-Withdrawn, Irrelevant Responsiveness, Creative Initiative, Need for Closeness to Teacher. Three items — e.g., Unable to Change, Quits, and Slow Work — are scored singularly. The DESB is completed by a teacher or teacher's aide who is familiar with a child's classroom performance. Scores are added together according to factor membership. Factor scores may be compared to norms contained in the manual. The DESB is designed for use from kindergarten through sixth grade.

*Standardization*

The authors began with a pool of 111 items derived from meetings with 72 teachers of regular public elementary school classes, public school special education classes, and from the Devereux Schools. The 111 items chosen were representative of adaptive and maladaptive classroom behaviors which were easily observable to the teachers. Teacher ratings were provided for 225 boys and 102 girls either in public school special education classes for emotionally disturbed children or in residential treatment centers. Additional ratings of 126 boys and 126 girls in a regular elementary school were obtained. Of the normal sample, which was selected by sex, grade, and IQ, 75 children from first grade through sixth grade were included, with the remainder of 30 boys and girls from kindergarten. The mean age for the public school group was 9.2 years and the mean IQ was 108. The children selected on the basis of emotional problems requiring placement in either public school special education classes or in the Devereux Schools were in ungraded classes with instructional levels ranging from readiness to fifth grade. The average age of this sample was 11.9 years and the IQ level for the entire sample ranged from 50 to 133 with a mean of 87. The raters used in the standardization of the DESB were 20 regular classroom teachers and 29 teachers working with children having emotional and/or behavioral problems.

*Reliability*

The authors provided a test-retest reliability coefficient of .87 for the 11 factors for a sample of 128 children rated after a one-week interval. The reliability coefficients for these individual items were lower, ranging from .71 to .80. Other reported test-retest reliability coefficients of a sample of 67 children over a one-year interval range from .49 to .86 with median values of .73 (Schaefer, Baker, & Zawel, 1975; Wallbrown,

Wallbrown, & Blake, 1976). Schaefer et al. (1975) also report teacher/ teacher-aide inter-rater reliability estimates ranging from .61 to .87 with a median of .80.

## Validity

Spivack and Swift (1967b) report concurrent validity data which included low but significant correlations between the 11 factors and achievement measures. Within this study, 80% of the children who were A and B students had none or one deviant factor scores in comparison with the 85% of the D and E students who had two or more deviant scores, and 65% students had four or more. In a sample of 174 males and 147 females in grades one through six randomly selected from public schools and 284 males and 128 females in grades two through six referred for social and/or emotional problems by their teacher, the item level validity of the DESB was assessed (Willis, Smithy, & Holliday, 1979). The results of that study suggest that the DESB responses are skewed for "normal" children as the item means fall near the positive end of the behavioral continuum and have small standard deviations. In contrast, item means of the sample of children referred for social/ emotional problems were more consistently closer to the middle of the distribution and had much higher standard deviations. Willis et al. (1979) suggested that the DESB is unlikely to be useful in attempting to identify normal children with normal problems. The DESB appears to be more effective in the identification of problems among children with more significant emotional problems.

## Critique

The DESB is a relatively brief, easily administered and scored rating scale, which is completed by teachers who have had daily contact with the child. Therefore, the DESB should provide an accurate assessment of the child's current behavior. However, test-retest reliabilities have been reported ranging from .49 to .86 for a one-year interval, which suggests that the DESB may not be a stable measure for an individual child over time.

One should keep in mind that the standardization sample was quite small and several authors have questioned the fact that the DESB derives 11 proportedly different factors from only 45 items on the scale.

## DEVEREUX ADOLESCENT BEHAVIOR RATING SCALE (DAB)

*Manual*

*The Devereux Adolescent Rating Scale Manual.* Spivack, G., Spotts, J., & Haines, P. E. Devon, PA: The Devereux Foundation Press, 1967.

*Purpose*

The Devereux Adolescent Behavior Rating Scale was designed to evaluate and describe readily observable behavior problems in adolescents between the ages of 13 and 18. The DAB is not designed to measure personality characteristics. The DAB is appropriate for use by professional mental health workers as well as nonprofessionals. The DAB takes approximately 15 minutes to administer.

*Format*

The DAB is a checklist comprised of 84 items which break down into 12 factor scores, three cluster scores, and 11 item scores. The factor scores are: unethical behavior, defiant-resistive, domineering-sadistic, heterosexual interest, hyperactive expansive, poor emotional control, need approval and dependency, emotional distance, physical inferiority-timidity, schizoid withdrawal, bizarre speech and cognition, bizarre action. The three cluster scores are: inability to delay, paranoid thought, and anxious self-blame. The 11 item scores are: persecution, plotting, bodily concern, external influences, compulsive acts, avoids competition, withdrawn, socialization, peer dominance, physical coordination, and distraction.

The items were selected from a review of clinical and research literature of adolescent behavior problems, available child and adult behavior rating scales, interviews with the Devereux clinical staff, and a review of clinical material from the case records of adolescents enrolled at the Devereux Schools. The items selected cover a wide range of adolescent behavior problems and supposedly avoid the use of technical words and phrases, as well as being explicitly defined and unambiguous. The raters are not supposed to make inferential judgments about the behavior, only to rate it. The final items were selected according to clarity of meaning and generality, as well as the results of several factor analyses. The ratings for an individual adolescent are plotted on a profile that shows his scores on 12 factors, three clusters, and 11 individual item scores.

The score may be compared to two normative samples: institutionalized and normal adolescents.

## Standardization

The standardization sample was composed of 548 institutionalized adolescents from the Devereux Schools, Norristown State Hospital, and the Bethany Children's Home (a foster care facility). The large majority of these adolescents had a variety of clinical diagnoses including psychosis, chronic brain syndromes, personality disorders, and other severe nonpsychotic disturbances. An additional sample of 305 normal children was included to allow comparison of ratings of each factor, cluster score, and item score with the institutionalized adolescents.

## Reliability

The authors report a mean inter-rater reliability of .42 and a median intra-rater reliability at a seven-to-10-day interval of .82. In his review of the DAB, Jessness (1972) indicated that the reliability was adequate, despite the heterogeneity of the sample. However, the inclusion of redundant items may have spuriously inflated the reported reliability coefficients.

## Validity

Construct validity is supported by the reported significant differences between the various diagnostic groups and between the clinical and nonclinical sample.

## Critique

The DAB is one of the few behavior rating scales specifically designed for an adolescent population. As such, it includes items particularly relevant to this age group without including more childlike or adult behavior problems. The quantifiable data obtained from the DAB can be used to examine the presence or absence of behavioral problems at a single time or to monitor progress and change in an individual. Because of the brief administration time required, the DAB is an efficient instrument to screen for severe behavior problems.

Although the DAB was designed to avoid inferences about behavior, not all of the items are explicitly defined, thus requiring the rater to make value judgments about the behavior, e.g., "sneaky." The DAB is designed for nonprofessional use; however, the inclusion of such terms as "echolalia" may make the scale difficult to administer by one who is not trained in psychiatric nomenclature.

Considering the standardization of the DAB on a severely disturbed inpatient adolescent population, the DAB may be limited in its application to other adolescents and may be more appropriate for use with very disturbed adolescents. Some of the test items refer to infrequent, grossly abnormal behaviors, e.g., "speaks in a way that is disconnected, incoherent," or "echolalia"; therefore, the scale may not be appropriate for looking at behavioral differences in normal adolescents. Most noninstitutionalized adolescents score in a narrow range so that the scores often do not differentiate between normal, neurotic, and delinquent adolescents. The DAB does appear to be able to identify psychotic adolescents; however, these subjects might easily be identified without employing the DAB because their behavioral deficits are so obvious. However, Jessness (1972) gives an example of an extremely anxious adolescent who would not be identified by the DAB. This adolescent would not receive a high score on the anxious self-blame factor scale since three of the four items (e.g., obsessions, delusions, and self-condemnation) are extreme symptoms. Therefore, other than the use of the DAB as a screening device to pinpoint overt behavior problems, caution should be exercised with outpatient adolescent populations.

## CHILDREN'S DEPRESSION INVENTORY (CDI)

*Manual*

Rating scales to assess depression in school-aged children. Kovacs, M. *Acta Paedopsychiatrica,* 1981, *46*(5–6), 305–315.

*Purpose*

The Children's Depression Inventory is a self-report scale designed to assess and define depression in children aged seven through 17.

*Format*

The CDI is a self-report measure consisting of 27 items with each consisting of statements graded from 0 (absent) to 3 (severe). The scale purports to reflect the child's feelings during the past week based upon commonly accepted symptoms of depression, e.g., insomnia, withdrawal, sadness, shame, pessimism. The items chosen for the CDI are a modification of the Beck Depression Inventory for adults and are considered more appropriate for children, e.g., work becomes homework, guilty becomes ashamed. Several revisions have followed resulting in the elimination of items considered to be irrelevant to childhood problems and the inclusion of six items which assess difficulties in appropriate areas of childhood problems, e.g., schoolwork. Cutoff levels for varying degrees of depression have been established (Carlson & Cantwell, 1980; Kovacs et al., 1976).

*Administration and Scoring*

The CDI is an easily administered, easily scored self-report measure consisting of 27 items, with each item consisting of statements which are rated by the child. The three alternatives from which the child selects the items most applicable to him are graded from 0 to 2 in the direction of increasing severity (i.e., 0 = symptom is absent; 2 = symptom is severe and is present all the time). The total CDI scores for an individual child may range from 0 to 54 depending on presence and severity of symptomatology. Cutoff levels for degrees of severity of depression have been identified for children based upon studies by Carlson and Cantwell (1980) and Kovacs et al. (1976).

*Standardization*

The initial version of the CDI was administered to 39 consecutively admitted hospitalized patients and 20 "normal" children aged eight to 13 years. The controls had no history of psychiatric treatment and no evidence of mental retardation and were matched with the psychiatric sample only on age. The clinicians utilized the Interview Schedule for Children, as a structured clinical interview, to obtain a global severity rating of depression. A highly significant correlation occurred between the independent ratings of depression and the scores from 20 items of the CDI. This study also provided preliminary support of discriminant validity based upon the higher mean and modal scores for the psychiatric sample versus the "normal" groups.

Additional field testing with 127 fifth and sixth grade students (age 10 to 13 years) resulted in a more psychometrically acceptable instrument, having 27 items and employing a three-choice format.

*Reliability*

Friedman and Butter (1979) report acceptable internal consistency (coefficient alpha=.86) and statistically significant item total score correlations ranging from .31 to .54. Within this study, no discernible age or sex effects were noted. The CDI scores for this sample of 875 Canadian children aged 10 to 17 years, attending fourth through eighth grades in public school, ranged from 0 to 51 (mean=9.27; S.D.=7.29; mode=7). Kazdin (1981) reports that additional data on internal consistency for both clinic and nonpsychiatric samples and inter-item and item-total score correlations have yielded correlations which are moderate but statistically significant. Test-retest reliability, assessed by Friedman and Butter (1979) over a one-month interval, indicated that the CDI is a reasonably stable measure of depressive symptoms in children (r=.72, N=28).

*Validity*

Carlson and Cantwell (1980) administered the CDI to 102 randomly selected children between the ages of seven and 17 years. Of the 102 children who were evaluated on an outpatient basis, 93 were given Axis I DSM-III clinical diagnoses. Of the remaining nine children, five were undiagnosed and four were not found to have indications of emotional problems. Twenty-eight children diagnosed as having affective disorders had significantly higher scores on the CDI when compared to children with behavior disorders or anorexia nervosa. Global ratings of depression given by clinicians at the end of an interview revealed a similar trend. Poor self-esteem, which is considered an indication of depression in children, was found to be correlated with high CDI scores (Piers-Harris correlation=.66) by Friedman and Butter (1979). Kovacs and Beck (1977) found a highly significant correlation (r=.55) between the Interview Schedule for Children (a structured interview yielding global depression ratings) and scores from 20 items of the CDI in a sample of 39 hospitalized children. Interestingly, the CDI has a low correlation (r=0.23) with peer ratings obtained by the Peer Nomination Inventory for Depression (Lefkowitz & Tesiny, 1980). Hodges et al. (1982b) also found significant correlations between the depression symptom complex of the Child Assessment Survey and the CDI (r[77]=0.53, p<0.0001).

*Critique*

The CDI relies exclusively upon the child's ability to accurately report the number and degree of severity of depressive symptoms. Some authors have questioned the ability of the child to report his symptoms, as some children avoid the expression of depressed affect (Cytryn & McKnew, 1974). In addition, differing levels of cognitive and language functioning in children may quite possibly influence the interpretation of the questions and the answers the children provide to a self-report inventory.

The multiple choice format and necessity of ranking symptoms by degree of severity may be too complicated for young children or children having intellectual limitations. Multiple items per page may contribute to the possibility of a response set, and reactivity or social desirability will color results.

The advantages of this instrument are that the scoring is simple and the CDI has extensive field testing which has resulted in careful item selection and development. The CDI has good preliminary discriminant and convergent validation with normal and psychiatric populations.

The CDI appears to be a promising instrument; however, additional validation work focused upon the intercorrelations between self-report inventories and other measures of childhood depression remains to be completed.

## CHILDREN'S MANIFEST ANXIETY SCALE (CMAS)

*Manual*

There is no manual as such. The scale may be found in: The children's form of the Manifest Anxiety Scale. Castenada, A., McCandless, B., & Palermo, D. *Child Development,* 1956, *27,* 317–326.

*Purpose*

The CMAS was developed as a paper and pencil children's self-report measure of the tendency to experience general or chronic anxiety across a variety of situations. It has been used in numerous studies to investigate the relationship between anxiety in children and other cognitive, affective, and achievement variables.

*Format*

The CMAS consists of 53 items, 42 of which are Anxiety items, and 11 additional items that constitute a Lie Scale which provides an index of the subject's tendency to falsify his answers. A revised edition of the CMAS is available (Reynolds & Richmond, 1978) which utilizes 37 items (28 Anxiety items and 9 Lie items). The scale consists of statements to which the child responds by circling "yes" or "no." The score for the Anxiety items and Lie items is calculated by summing the number of items circled "yes." The CMAS has been used with children in grades one through 12 and may be read aloud to children in lower grades.

*Administration and Scoring*

The CMAS may be administered on an individual basis with oral instructions or explanation of word meaning if necessary. It is also applicable for group administration. The child is asked to circle "yes" or "no" as each item applies to him. A scoring sheet is provided which breaks the items into the Anxiety and Lie Scales. All items endorsed "yes" by the child are summed for each scale which yields total scores. These scores can be compared to the normative tables.

*Standardization*

The authors initially adapted the Taylor's Manifest Anxiety Scale for use with children. The resulting scale (CMAS) was standardized on a sample of 386 Caucasion boys and girls from four schools. Additional normative samples included 136 black elementary schoolchildren in grades four, five, and six; 37 adolescent, educable, mentally handicapped adolescents ages 13 to 18 years with IQ ranging from 57 to 60; 27 non-institutionalized, educable, mentally handicapped children ($\bar{x}$ age=12 years 11 months). A bibliography of research utilizing the CMAS is available from Reynolds (1977). In response to criticism of the CMAS, a revised edition of the CMAS is provided by Reynolds and Richmond (1978). Criticism of the original CMAS involves teachers' complaints that it does not measure enough areas of anxiety and that some words in the scale are too difficult for younger children, slow learners, and the mentally retarded. In addition, data have been provided indicating that only 12 of 42 items of the original CMAS Anxiety Scale meet the criteria of a good test item (Reynolds & Richmond, 1978). These authors revised the CMAS and standardized the measure on a group of 329 school children from grades one to 12. The 37 items were cross-validated on a sample of 167 children from grades two, five, nine, 10 and 11. The revision of this CMAS represents a 33% reduction in the length of the scale and offers good reliability.

*Reliability*

Reliability coefficients for both scales have included the following results: test-retest reliability of .90 for the Anxiety Scale and .70 for the Lie scale over a one-week interval with white children grades four, five, and six; .59 to .91 for black children in the same grades for the Anxiety Scale and .77 to .80 for the Lie scale over a one month interval. Test-retest reliability for emotionally disturbed children was .77. The intercorrelations between the Anxiety and Lie Scales have been found to be low, ranging between −.11 to .22. When the 37-item revised version of the CMAS was used, the Anxiety Scale recorrelated significantly with the Lie Scale. A three-way ANOVA indicated that black children scored significantly higher than whites on the Lie Scale.

*Validity*

Concurrent validity measures have been obtained by correlating the CMAS with the State-Trait Anxiety Inventory for Children (STAIC). The results indicate low but significant correlations between the Anxiety portion of the CMAS and the A-State (.47) and the A-Trait (.38) Scales of the STAIC. The Anxiety Scale of the CMAS was not significantly correlated with the Lie Scale (−.19). Girls commonly report more anxiety on the CMAS than boys. A correlation of .49 was obtained between the CMAS scores and the Fear Survey Schedules for Children when administered to 59 boys (aged 10) and 40 girls (aged 10) from two parochial schools.

Validity studies have shown that children in residential treatment centers for emotional and behavior disorders do receive significantly higher scores than normal children of the same sex and age (Finch, Kendall, & Montgomery, 1974). In general, girls report more anxiety on the CMAS than boys (Castenada et al., 1956; Reynolds & Richmond, 1978).

A factor-analytic study of 245 children by Finch et al. (1974) reported that the CMAS measures three types of anxiety in children. The three identified factors or types of anxiety are: Factor I Anxiety: Worry and Oversensitivity, a thought or cognitive dimension; Factor II, Anxiety: Physiological, a body-oriented, psychosomatic dimension; Factor III, Anxiety: Concentration, behavioral interference. Additional factors have been reported by Scherer and Nakamura (1968): Anxiety-Worry, similar to the first factor of Finch et al. (1974); and Anxiety-Neurosis, whch seems to include items from the second and third factors of Finch et al. (1974).

*Critique*

The CMAS is an easily administered and scored test with good reliability. The validity coefficients obtained by comparing the CMAS with other instruments purporting to measure anxiety or fear in children have been low but significant. The CMAS has been used with a variety of populations and to investigate the effect of anxiety upon performance and behavior in numerous studies. It is difficult to know exactly what type of anxiety is being measured as it has been argued that anxiety is a multidimensional concept. It has been assumed that the CMAS is a measure of trait anxiety (Finch et al., 1974); however, additional work needs to be done to clarify this issue as studies have reported low correlations between the CMAS and the A-Trait Scale of the STAIC (Finch & Nelson, 1974). Higher correlations between the CMAS and the A-State Scale of the STAIC suggest the possibility that scores on the CMAS may be more reflective of transitory anxiety states than is commonly assumed.

Research on the Lie Scale of the CMAS suggests that this scale may be indicative of defensiveness or social desirability factors rather than a lack of validity of the child's score (Reynolds & Richmond, 1978). Accordingly, a high Lie score would invalidate the Anxiety score; however, it could provide useful information about the child's personality.

Additional study is needed to determine the validity of the CMAS and what type of anxiety the scale is measuring. Many clinicians have found this scale to be a useful screening device, although the relatively high Lie Scale scores found in first and second grade children suggest that caution be exercised when using this instrument with young children.

## STATE-TRAIT ANXIETY INVENTORY FOR CHILDREN (STAIC)

*Manual*

*Preliminary Manual for the State-Trait Anxiety Inventory for Children* ("How I Feel Questionnaire"). Spielberger, C. D. Palo Alto, CA: Consulting Psychologists Press, 1973.

*Purpose*

The STAIC was developed as a research tool to study anxiety in elementary school-age children. It contains separate self-reports for measuring State Anxiety (A-State) and Trait Anxiety (A-Trait). The STAIC is very similar to the STAI which may be used with adolescents (grades 9 through 12) and adults.

*Format*

The STAIC is a self-report inventory which may be administered individually or in groups. Instructions are printed on the Test Form for both the A-State and A-Trait Scales. It is designed for elementary age children and typically requires approximately 20 minutes to complete.

The A-State scale is comprised of 20 "I feel" sentence stems designed to assess the child's feelings at a particular moment in time. For each of the 20 different adjectives, the child responds by circling one of the three alternatives that describes him best, e.g., very happy, happy, not happy. The key items in half of the sentence stems are indicative of anxiety (troubled, frightened), while the remaining 10 sentence stems reflect the absence of anxiety (cheerful, good). For items which are indicative of anxiety, "very" and "not" are assigned weights of 3 and 1 respectively, a value of 2 is given when the child circles only the adjective. The order of weighting the values is reversed for items which indicate the absence of anxiety.

The A-Trait Scale is composed of 20 statements to which the child responds by marking an "X" in the appropriate box indicating the frequency of occurrence of the behavior. The scoring weights assigned to "hardly ever," "sometimes," and "often" are 1, 2, and 3 respectively for all items. This scale is designed to measure relatively stable individual differences in anxiety or in the tendency to experience anxiety in children. Children's scores on both the A-State scales may range from a minimum of 20 to a maximum of 60. For large groups, the STAIC may be administered with a machine-scorable answer sheet. A scoring key is provided in the manual for individually administered tests.

*Standardization*

The initial item pool of 33 A-State and 40 A-Trait items was derived after examining other anxiety inventories for children and adults. The format of these preliminary items was similar to the STAI but simplified to facilitate their use with elementary school-age children. The number of response categories was decreased from four to three in the children's version.

The preliminary items were field-tested on a large number of fourth, fifth and sixth grade children and were revised based upon their responses to the test. The final selection of items for the A-Trait Scale was based on a combined criterion defined in terms of internal consistency and concurrent validity. The selection of items for the A-State Scale was based upon internal consistency and construct validity.

The STAIC was standardized on a sample of 60% white and 40% black children from a wide range of socioeconomic backgrounds. Two large samples of fourth, fifth, and sixth grade students from three schools in Tallahassee and Leon County, Florida (456 males and 457 females), and 281 males and 357 females in Brandenton and Manatee County, Florida, comprised the standardization sample. The norms are based on the combined data for both samples. Norms for the STAIC Scale have been extended to third grade based upon a sample of randomly selected third and fourth grade black disadvantaged children (407 males and 425 females in fourth grade and 342 males and 348 females in third grade [Papay & Hedl, 1978]).

*Reliability*

Test-retest reliability coefficients for the STAIC were calculated for 246 children in the normative sample after a one-week interval (Spielberger, 1973). Coefficients of .65 for 132 males and .71 for 114 females were reported for the A-Trait Scale. The reliability coefficients for the A-State Scale were somewhat lower, as expected, since a valid measure of state anxiety would be expected to reflect the influence of transitory situational variables existing at the time of each test administration.

The reliability coefficients for the 132 males and 114 females on the A-State Scale were .31 and .47 respectively. Spielberger (1973) also reported, as a measure of internal consistency, median item-remainder correlations of .38 and .48 (for females) on the A-State Scale and .35 for males and .40 for females on the A-Trait Scale.

Papay and Hedl (1978) report similar internal consistency measures for their sample of 1,522 third and fourth grade black disadvantaged children. Median A-State item-remainder correlations of .49 and .40 for third and fourth grade males and .46 and .35 for third and fourth grade females respectively were reported. In comparison, third and fourth grade males obtained lower item-remainder coefficients on the A-Trait Scale (.36 and .40), while the coefficients obtained by the third and fourth grade females (.35 and .35) were more similar to their scores on the A-State Scale.

*Validity*

Evidence of concurrent validity of the STAIC was obtained by Finch and Nelson (1974) in their study of 50 emotionally disturbed children. The subjects were given the STAIC and the Children's Manifest Anxiety Scale (CMAS). Low but statistically significant correlations were found between the A-State Scale (.27) and the A-Trait Scale (.54) and the Children's Manifest Anxiety Scale. In 1974, Montgomery and Finch conducted a study with 60 children (49 males and 11 females) having an average age of 11.2 years who were in a residential treatment center and 60 normal children having an average age of 10.4 years. The two groups were given the STAIC and the CMAS. On both the A-State and the A-Trait Scales of the STAIC and the anxiety portion of the CMAS, the children diagnosed as having emotional problems scored significantly higher than the normal control group. Point-biserial correlations were also obtained between the scores of both groups and the scores on the STAIC and the CMAS. The data indicated that the A-State scores had a significant correlation with the Anxiety score of the CMAS (.47) and the A-Trait scores were also significantly correlated with the Anxiety Scale of the CMAS (.52).

*Critique*

The STAIC was standardized on a sample for fourth, fifth and sixth grade students and, therefore, may have limited generalizability to other populations. For example, disadvantaged fourth grade black males have been found to score considerably lower than the normative sample on the A-Trait Scale. Further research is needed to extend the norms for the remainder of the elementary school-age children and for varying populations. While statistically significant correlations have been found between the STAIC and other measures of anxiety in either children, these correlations have been low and are not as good as the STAI after which this scale was modeled. Additional data from convergent and discriminant validity studies need to be obtained, as anxiety is frequently reported to be associated with or masked by other symptoms of childhood disorders.

The A-State and A-Trait distinction on the STAIC may be blurred between special groups of children at specific times. For example, young children who have recently experienced an emotional trauma, e.g., loss of a parent or life-threatening illness, may score higher on both scales than other children. Evidence that the STAIC distinguishes children within these special populations from other groups of children would add support to the A-State/A-Trait distinction and to the validity of the STAIC. Further support would be evident if the children who experienced recent emotional trauma evidenced less anxiety on the A-State Scale over time.

Although additional research is needed in several areas, the STAIC does supply minimally acceptable reliability and validity and warrants further study as a clinical instrument.

## BELLEVUE INDEX OF DEPRESSION (BID)

*Manual*

None. The Bellevue Index of Depression is based upon the Weinberg et al. (1973) criteria for childhood depression, which may be found in: Depression in children referred to an educational diagnostic center: Diagnoses and treatment. Weinberg, W. A., Rutman, J., Sullivan, L., Penick, E. C., & Dietz, S. G. *Journal of Pediatrics*, 1973, *83* (6), 1065–1072.

*Purpose*

The BID is a semi-structured interview for depressed children from the ages of six to 12½ years. The BID can be administered separately to the child, parents or others who know the child.

*Format*

The BID consists of a semi-structured interview format consisting of 40 items to which the child or other raters respond. The items are subsumed under 10 general content areas which are purported to be indicative of childhood depression. The 10 content areas are: dysphoric mood; self-deprecatory ideation; aggressive behaviors; sleep disturbance; change in school performance; diminished socialization; change in attitude toward school; somatic complaints; loss of usual energy; and unusual changes in appetite and/or weight. Each of the 40 items is rated on two separate 4-point scales. The severity scale scores range from 1 to 4 based upon whether the symptom is rated from "not at all" to "very much." The severity criterion was that the item endorsed was a change from the child's "usual self." The duration scale criteria included the stipulation that identified symptoms had to be present for one month. For a symptom of depression to be scored positive, the criteria for both scales must be met. The severity criteria are summed and if the child's score exceeds 20, the child is considered clinically depressed. In addition, for a child to be considered depressed he must have at least one item from the first two categories. The first category is dysphoric mood and includes appearance of sadness; moodiness; irritability; cries easily, etc. The second category, self-deprecatory ideation, includes such sample items as feelings of being worthless, death wishes, suicidal ideation and attempts. Furthermore, the child has to have at least one item from any other two of the remaining eight categories.

*Standardization*

The BID was developed at the Bellevue Psychiatric Hospital on the basis of the Weinberg et al. (1973) Index of Depressive Symptomatology (WIDS). The WIDS is a refinement and extension of the Ling et al. (1970) criteria of childhood depression. Petti (1978) administered the BID and the WIDS to 73 children aged six to 12½ years old who were admitted to the Bellevue Psychiatric Hospital Unit for acutely ill and emotionally disturbed children. The BID and the WIDS were scored using self-report data from the child, data from parents or guardians who were able to provide a reliable history, and additional information from the child's school. Thirty-nine children and their parents were interviewed by the author and completed the WIDS and the BID. Information was obtained from their school records, and their primary psychiatrist and/or ward attendant submitted information concerning the diagnosis of depression. This sample of 39 children was referred to as the "independent" sample. The other 34 children comprised the "dependent" sample in which their primary psychiatrists were not asked for their diagnosis of depression. Petti (1978) found statistically significant agreement between the clinician's judgment of depression and the WIDS and the BID scores for the independent, dependent samples and for the total sample.

## Reliability and Validity

Petti (1978), using the WIDS and the BID and an independent clinician's judgment, evaluated a total of 73 children admitted to Bellevue Psychiatric Hospital from May 1974 to June 1975. Each of these children was judged to have or not have depression based upon each of these measures. An 89% agreement between the WIDS and the BID scales for the 73 children was obtained with 23 children rated as not depressed and 42 children rated as depressed by the scores on both scales (p<.001). The clinician's judgment and BID scores for the 34 children in the dependent sample reached 82% agreement and 84% agreement was found between the two measures for the independent group (N=39). The majority of children who were not found to be depressed by the results of their scores on the WIDS and the BID, but were diagnosed as depressed by the clinician, were considered as having an acute depressive reaction. It was found that for this group of children symptoms of depression failed to meet the one-month criterion of duration. A total of 61% of the sample of 73 children was diagnosed as depressed by the judgment of the clinician as compared to 59% of the children diagnosed depressed by their scores on the BID.

## Critique

The BID provides quantifiable data for severity and duration of depression in children from the ages of six to 12½ years. The semi-structured interview format requires the examiner to be familiar with the categories of the BID so that a stilted interview will not result and endanger rapport with a depressed child. The BID has acceptable agreement with previously established criteria for childhood depression.

The sparse standardization, reliability, and validity data and lack of use with a diversity of both clinical and nonclinical populations require that considerable research be conducted before the clinical ability of the BID can be assessed.

## CHILD ASSESSMENT SCHEDULE (CAS)

*Manual*

The Child Assessment Schedule: A diagnostic interview for research and clinical use. Hodges, K., Kline, S., Fitch, P., McKnew, D., & Cytryn, L. Washington, D.C.: American Psychological Association, 1981. Order Manuscript No. 2313 and remit $7.00 to Catalog of Selected Documents in Psychology, Order Department, American Psychological Association, 1200 17th Street N.W., Washington, D.C. 20036.

*Purpose*

The Child Assessment Schedule was developed to provide a standardized diagnostic interview appropriate for use with children. The CAS is designed to obtain information useful in clinical evaluations, for research and training purposes, and to determine a diagnosis and develop a treatment plan. The authors report the CAS is appropriate for use with children between the ages of seven and 14.

*Format*

The CAS requires an experienced clinician to administer it properly and it takes between 45 minutes and one hour. The CAS is divided into two parts. The first part consists of 75 questions considered to be relevant to the child's functioning in several areas including: family; fears; school; friends; self-image; mood; expression of anger; somatic concerns; activities and hobbies; and thought disorder symptoms. The examiner codes each response as either true, indicating the presence of a symptom, or false, suggesting the child does not have the symptom. The items may also be scored as ambiguous, indicating the symptom occurs infrequently, or as not being applicable to the child, or no response from the child can also be scored. Affirmative answers indicate the child has a particular symptom or behavior. The second part of the CAS contains 53 items which are focused upon the following areas: estimation of cognitive ability; grooming; motor coordination; activity level; quality of verbal communications; insight; quality of emotional expression; and clinical impressions of interpersonal interactions.

Quantified scores can be derived for comparison on total symptom scores, content areas (e.g., number of items indicative of problems on the topic of school) and symptom complex scores, which are comparable to childhood diagnoses found in the DSM-III. In addition to these formal scoring procedures, the CAS also provides information about the specific area of dysfunction (e.g., school, family, peer relationships) which is obtained by the sum of items affirmatively endorsed by the child for each area. As another set of scores can be generated, which are analogous to the DSM-III diagnostic criteria, the clinician can formulate a diagnostic impression of the child.

*Standardization*

Standardization data were not provided by the authors.

*Reliability*

Fifty children referred to a children's mental health center, including 32 behaviorally disordered outpatients and 18 behaviorally disordered inpatients, comprised the original sample studied. These 27 girls and 23 boys were all Caucasian, having a mean age of 10 with a range from seven to 14 years. The control group, which also had a mean age of 10, was recruited from two Girl Scout and two Boy Scout troops, with children having a history of psychiatric illness or recent significant life stress being excluded. Adequate inter-rater reliability of .90 was found for the total CAS score. Content area inter-rater reliabilities ranged from .59 to .84 with the lowest content area being worries. Inter-rater reliabilities for symptom complexes ranged from .44 to .82, the three symptom complexes having the lowest inter-rater reliabilities (Attention Deficit Without Hyperactivity, Socialized Conduct, and Separation Anxiety) contained fewer items and were felt to require fine discriminations by the raters.

A revised edition of the CAS containing modifications of the scales in the original CAS which failed to meet acceptable criteria for inter-rater reliability was used in the 1982 NIMH study. Ten latency-age children of mothers having affective disorders and mothers without emotional problems were rated independently by two raters. An item-by-item comparison for all categories was computed yielding a mean scoring agreement of .91 with a range of .87 to .96. High inter-rater reliabilities were reported for content areas (average .93) and for symptom complexes (mean agreement=.93).

*Validity*

Hodges et al. (1982a) collected three types of validity data on their original sample of 32 psychiatric outpatients, 18 psychiatric inpatients, and 37 normal controls. The subjects were given the Children's Depression Inventory (CDI) (Kovacs et al., 1978) and the State Trait Anxiety Inventory for Children (STAIC) (Spielberger, 1973). A parental rating of their children's behavior was also obtained via the Child Behavior Checklist (CBC) (Achenbach, 1978). On nine out of 11 content areas and on eight out of nine symptom complexes, the psychiatric inpatients scored significantly higher than the outpatients, who obtained significantly higher scores than the controls.

In addition, the same trend was reported for the CAS total score. The only two score subscales which failed to differentiate between groups were Fears and Worries and Attention Deficit Without Hyperactivity. The results of a discriminant analysis indicate that the CAS correctly classified 72.2% of the inpatients, 83.8% of the controls, and 40.6% of the outpatients in the original sample.

Concurrent validation was assessed by comparing the CAS total scores with maternal reports of child pathology (CBC). The number and severity of problems were found to be significantly correlated ($r = .53$, $p < .001$ and $r = .57$, $p < .001$, respectively). Significant correlations were also found between the CAS and the STAIC ($r = .53$, $p < .001$) and the CDI and one symptom complex (Depression) on the CAS ($r = .53$, $p < .001$).

*Critique*

The CAS is a new instrument demonstrating excellent inter-rater reliability obtained for both experienced clinicians and less experienced technicians for symptom complexes and content areas. Good concurrent validity data have been reported in two studies as the CAS has differentiated between groups of children in terms of levels of psychopathology. The CAS total scores correspond with maternal reports of symptoms and other self-reports by the children.

A particular advantage of the CAS is that it has been designed to elicit information which explicitly corresponds to the DSM-III diagnostic categories. Further research is needed to determine whether the CAS can differentiate among children with various disorders, including thought disorders.

The CAS appears to be a promising clinical instrument; however, in view of the limited reliability and validity data, much research is required before a final determination of its utility in clinical assessment and research can be made.

## COMPARISON OF BEHAVIORALLY-BASED MEASURES

Several authors have noted that the availability of behaviorally-based assessment measures should not imply that the assessment technology is well developed (Humphreys & Ciminero, 1979; Kazdin, 1981, Morris & Kratochwill, 1983). The criticism of these techniques involved the overall paucity of data on standardization, reliability, and validity and concluded that very few of the instruments which have been developed come close to satisfying the psychometric standards which are desirable in evaluation of these assessment procedures. Of particular concern is the fact that very often the issue of validity has been addressed by indicating that one assessment instrument correlates with another instrument designed to measure the same construct. The resulting correlation between two measures, neither of which has been carefully validated, may be difficult to interpret. The measures may correlate significantly because they reflect response styles (e.g., social desirability) or simply because of the degree of underlying psychopathology of the child. Convergent and discrimination validity data are particularly important in the assessment of childhood disorders, as some clinical symptoms (e.g., depression and anxiety in children) may be masked or associated with symptoms of other disorders.

The advantages of these behaviorally-based assessment procedures are that they are convenient in terms of their administration and scoring and provide easily quantifiable data. They are usually economical in terms of therapist time and cost involved. The scales can often provide the clinician with information from people well acquainted with the child (e.g., teachers), who are not available at the time of the evaluation. Such data would be difficult to obtain from sources other than rating scales or checklists.

However, all of the instruments reviewed are subject to respondent bias which may arise from a variety of sources. Test items that reflect very strong opinions held by the respondent may often be answered in a way which is consistent with ingrained biases of the respondent and may be irrelevant to the content of the items. Retrospective data obtained from parents may be highly subject to respondent bias, including inaccurate observation and defensiveness on the part of the parent, whether out of desire to gain social approval or because of parental psychopathology or out of ignorance of the importance of behavior patterns in children. In particular, when using any self-report measures, it is necessary to recognize the possibility that the respondents are reporting what they assume the examiner wants to hear. The use of self-report inventories for children has been questioned by several authors, as the ability of children to accurately portray their feelings is doubtful. For example, some children may avoid the expression of depressed affect (Cytryn & McKnew, 1974). Kazdin (1981) noted that differing levels of language ability and cognitive development in children at different age levels may significantly influence the way they perceive questions or test items, as well as the answers given. In addition, severity of symptomatology or intellectual limitations may also influence the type of information obtained from self-report data from children.

The interview assessment format is a widely used method of evaluating children and most of the interviews available for children are currently undergoing development and refinement. However, the reliability and validity of interviewer assessments have been criticized (Hay et al., 1979). Sources of low reliability data may arise as different clinicians are likely to obtain different information from the same child. Some checklists, such as the Washington Symptom Checklist, include open-ended questions which permit the clinician to gain an estimate of the respondent's attitude and motivation, but most do not. Some of the scales provide only measures of presence or absence of a particular problem (Devereux Elementary Behavior Rating Scale), while others give frequency of occurrence or severity of measures (Eyberg Child Behavior Inventory).

Due to the fact that we are only beginning to approach anything like a typology of child behavior patterns for deviance (Edelbrock & Achenbach, 1980), the instruments which have been developed are quite variable in their focus and scope. Some of them (e.g., the Conners Symptom Checklist) are concerned with specific types of behavior (hyperactivity in this case), while others are more concerned with both adaptive and maladaptive behaviors (the AAMD Adaptive Behavior Scales). Deviance is described in terms of lack of normal development on some instruments, such as the Minnesota Child Development Inventory, while both developmental and psychopathological patterns are surveyed in other cases (the Personality Inventory for Children).

In cases in which developmental problems are suspected, the AAMD Scales, the Minnesota Child Development Inventory, and the Personality Inventory for Children seem best suited to survey parent observations of their children's behavior. In cases in which psychopathology is a major focus, the broad screening seems best accomplished by the Behavior Problem Checklist, the Child Behavior Checklist and the Child Behavior Profile, and the Personality Inventory for Children. While all of the parent report measures covered are available, not all of them are easily accessible at the present time.

The choice of appropriate parent or child report measures would appear to depend upon the purpose for which they are intended. We have chosen instruments which might serve a general screening function for behavior problems and adaptive behavior. The scales chosen may be grouped according to respondent.

Parent scales are:

1) Adaptive Behavior Scale
2) Behavior Problem Checklist
3) Child Behavior Checklist and Child Behavior Profile
4) Conners Symptom Checklist
5) Devereux Child Behavior Rating Scale
6) Eyberg Child Behavior Inventory
7) Louisville Behavior Checklist
8) Louisville Fear Survey Scale for Children
9) Minnesota Child Development Inventory
10) Missouri Children's Behavior Checklist
11) Personality Inventory for Children

Teacher scales are:

1) Adaptive Behavior Scale (Public School Version)
2) Devereux Elementary School Behavior Rating Scale

Self-Report scales are:

1) Children's Depression Inventory
2) Children's Manifest Anxiety Scale
3) State-Trait Anxiety Inventory for Children

Clinician scales are:

1) Bellevue Index of Depression
2) Child Assessment Schedule

These instruments serve as corroboration for interview contacts and to elicit material from others who may be unable to attend interviews, e.g., teachers and other caretakers. Few of the instruments are marketed in the same fashion as other clinical instruments. Because most of these checklists and scales were derived as part of research efforts, they also have some limitations in terms of basic standardization work, often representing somewhat esoteric populations.

Psychologists will find parent report measures helpful in checking themselves as to the thoroughness of the inquiry conducted concerning the complaints which originated referral. Likewise the congruence of the child's behavior across different situations may be easier to determine (if indeed it is congruent) by multiple reports from the adults who have opportunity to observe the behavior. The third function of these measures is in providing some estimate of the reliability of the informant. This latter information can be detected on some instruments through the use of scales which measure parental defensiveness (e.g., the PIC) or on the open-ended questions from the Washington Symptom Checklist or because parents and others may endorse such an extravagant number of items that almost no child could earn such dismal descriptions.

In many cases, if the clinician arranges appointments in advance and sends out preliminary packets of information, the inclusion of a parent report measure will prove helpful in formulating some ideas about the nature of the problems and the direction of the assessment approach. If the clinician needs to obtain specific types of assessment materials, some lead time can be gained before the face-to-face contact. In short, parent report measures are good supplementary sources of clinical data. They are not intended and should not be used as substitutes for interview and other assessment procedures.

## REFERENCES

Achenbach, T. M. The child behavior profile: I. Boys aged 6–11. *Journal of Consulting and Clinical Psychology,* 1978, *46,* 478–488.

Achenbach, T. M. *Instructions for Hand Scoring the CBP.* Burlington, VT: Child, Adolescent, Family & Community Psychiatry, 1980.

Achenbach, T. M. A junior MMPI? *Journal of Personality Assessment,* 1981, *45,* 332–333.

Achenbach, T. M. & Edelbrock, C. S. The classification of child psychopathology: A review and analysis of empirical efforts. *Psychological Bulletin,* 1978, *85,* 1275–1301.

Achenbach, T. M. & Edelbrock, C. S. The Child Behavior Profile II. Boys aged 12–16 and girls aged 6–11 and 12–16. *Journal of Consulting and Clinical Psychology,* 1979, *47,* 223–233.

Achenbach, T. M. & Edelbrock, C. S. Behavioral problems and competencies reported by parents of normal and disturbed children aged 4 through 16. *Society for Research in Child Development Monographs,* 1981, *46*(1), 82.

Carlson, G. A. & Cantwell, D. P. A survey of depressive symptoms, syndromes and disorders in a child psychiatric population. *Journal of the American Academy of Child Psychiatry,* 1980, *18,* 587–599.

Castenada, A., McCandless, B., & Palermo, D. The children's form of the Manifest Anxiety Scale. *Child Development,* 1956, *27,* 317–326.

Conners, C. K. Symptom patterns in hyperkinetic, neurotic, and normal children. *Child Development,* 1970, *41,* 667–682.

Conners, C. K. Rating scales for use in drug studies with children. *Psychopharmacology Bulletin,* Special Issue, Pharmacology of children, 1973, 24–84.

Cytryn, L. & McKnew, D. H. Factors influencing the changing clinical expression of the depressive process in children. *American Journal of Psychiatry,* 1974, *131,* 879–881.

Edelbrock, C. S. & Achenbach, T. M. A typology of child behavior profile patterns: distribution and correlates for disturbed children aged 6–16. *Journal of Abnormal Child Psychology,* 1980, *8,* 441–470.

Eyberg, S. M. & Ross, A. W. Assessment of child behavior problems: The validation of a new inventory. *Journal of Clinical Child Psychology,* 1978, *7,* 113–116.

Finch, A., Kendall, P., & Montgomery, L. Multidimensionality of anxiety in children: Factor structure of the Children's Manifest Anxiety Scale. *Journal of Abnormal Child Psychology,* 1974, *2,* 331–335.

Finch, A., Jr. & Nelson, W. Anxiety and locus of conflict in emotionally disturbed children. *Psychological Reports,* 1974, *35*(1), 469–470.

Fogelman, C. J. (Ed.) *AAMD Adaptive Behavior Scale: 1975 Revision.* Washington, D.C.: American Association of Mental Deficiency, 1975.

Friedman, R. J. & Butter, L. F. Development and evaluation of a test battery to assess childhood depression. Ontario Institute for Studies in Education. Unpublished manuscript, 1979.

Goodwin, W. L. Review of the Minnesota Child Development Inventory. In: O. K. Buros (Ed.), *The Eighth Mental Measurement Yearbook.* Highland Park, N.J.: Gryphon Press, 1978.

Hay, W. H., Hay, L. K., Angle, H. V., & Nelson, R. D. The reliability of problem identification in the behavioral interview. *Behavioral Assessment,* 1979, *1,* 107–118.

Hodges, K., Kline, S., Fitch, P., McKnew, D., & Cytryn, L. The Child Assessment Schedule: A diagnostic interview for research and clinical use. *Catalog of Selected Documents in Psychology,* 1981, *11,* 56. Washington, D.C.: American Psychological Association.

Hodges, K., Kline, S., Stern, L., Cytryn, L., & McKnew, D. The development of a child assessment interview for research and clinical use. *Journal of Abnormal Child Psychology,* 1982a, *10*(2), 173–189.

Hodges, K., McKnew, D., Cytryn, L., Stern, L., & Kline, S. The Child Assessment Schedule (CAS) diagnostic interview: A report on reliability and validity. *Journal of the American Academy of Child Psychiatry,* 1982b, *21,* 468–473.

Humphreys, L. E. & Ciminero, A. R. Parent report measures of child behavior: A review. *Journal of Clinical Child Psychology,* 1979, *8,* 56–63.

Ireton, H. & Thwing, E. *Minnesota Child Development Inventory Manual.* Minneapolis, MN: Behavior Science Systems, 1974.

Jessness, C. F. Review: Devereaux Adolescent Behavior Rating Scale. In: O. K. Buros (Ed.), *The Seventh Mental Measurement Yearbook,* Volume 1. Highland Park, N.J.: Gryphon Press, 1972, 134–135.

Johnson, O. G. *Test and Measurements in Child Development: Handbook II.* San Francisco: Jossey-Bass, 1976.

Kazdin, A. E. Assessment techniques for childhood depression. *Journal of the American Academy of Child Psychiatry,* 1981, *20,* 358–375.

Kovacs, M. Rating scales to assess depression in school-aged children. *Acta Paedopsychiatrica*, 1981, *46*(5-6), 305–315.

Kovacs, M. & Beck, A. T. An empirical clinical approach towards a definition of childhood depression. In: S. G. Schulterbrandt and A. Raskin (Eds.), *Depression in Children*. New York: Raven Press, 1977.

Kovacs, M., Betoff, N. G., Celebre, S. G., Mansheim, P. A., Petty, L. K., & Reynek, S. T. (1976) Childhood depression. Philadelphia, PA (unpublished data). In: E. A. Petti, Depression in hospitalized child psychiatry patients. *Journal of the American Academy of Child Psychiatry*, 1978, *17*, 49–59.

Lachar, D., Butkus,M., & Hryhorczuk, L. Objective personality assessment of children: An exploratory study of the Personality Inventory for Children (PIC) in a child psychiatry setting. *Journal of Personality Assessment*, 1978, *42*, 529–537.

Lachar, D. & Gdowsk, C. *Actuarial Assessment of Child and Adolescent Personality: An Interpretive Guide for the Personality Inventory for Children Profile*. Los Angeles, CA: Western Psychological Services, 1979.

Lambert, N., Windmiller, M., Cole, L., & Figueroa, R. *AAMD Adaptive Behavior Scale: Public School Version, 1974 Revision*. Washington, D.C.: AAMD, 1975.

Lefkowitz, M. M. & Tesiny, E. P. Assessment of childhood depression. *Journal of Consulting and Clinical Psychology*, 1980, *48*, 43–50.

Ling, W., Oftedal, G., & Weinberg, W. Depressive illness in childhood presented as severe headache. *American Journal of Diseases of Children*, 1970, *120*, 122–124.

Mash, E. J. & Terdal, L. G. *Behavioral Assessment of Childhood Disorders*. New York: The Guilford Press, 1981.

Miller, L. C. Louisville Behavior Checklist for males, 6–12 years of age. *Psychological Reports*, 1967, *21*, 885–896.

Miller, L. C. *Louisville Behavior Checklist Manual*. Los Angeles: Western Psychological Services, 1977.

Miller, L. C., Barett, C., Hampe, E., & Noble, H. Factor structure of childhood fears. *Journal of Consulting and Clinical Psychology*, 1972, *39*, 264–268.

Montgomery, L. & Finch, A., Jr. Validity of two measures of anxiety in children. *Journal of Abnormal Psychology*, 1974, *2*, 293–296.

Morris, R. J. & Kratochwill, T. R. *Treating Children's Fears and Phobias: A Behavioral Approach*. New York: Pergamon Press, 1983.

Papay, J. P. & Hedl, J. J. Psychometric characteristics and norms for disadvantaged third and fourth grade children on the State-Trait Inventory for Children. *Journal of Abnormal Child Psychology*, 1978, *6*(1), 115–120.

Peterson, D. R. Behavior problems of middle childhood. *Journal of Consulting Psychology*, 1961, *25*, 105–109.

Petti, E. A. Depression in hospitalized child psychiatry patients. *Journal of the American Academy of Child Psychiatry*, 1978, *17*, 49–59.

Quay, H. C. & Peterson, D. R. *Manual for the Behavior Problem Checklist*. Miami, FL: Program in Applied Social Sciences, University of Miami, 1975.

Quay, H. C. & Werry, J. S. *Psychopathological Disorders of Childhood*. New York: John Wiley, 1979.

Reynolds, C. R. A bibliography of research employing the Children's Manifest Anxiety Scale: 1956–1977. Unpublished manuscript, 1977.

Reynolds, C. R. & Richmond, B. O. What I think and feel: A revised measure of children's manifest anxiety. *Journal of Abnormal Child Psychology*, 1978, *6*, 271–280.

Robinson, E. A. & Eyberg, S. M. Behavior problems present in an adolescent population. Paper presented at the meeting of the Oregon Psychological Association, Eugene, Oregon, 1978.

Robinson, E. A., Eyberg, S. M., & Ross, A. W. The standardization of an inventory of child conduct problem behaviors. *Journal of Clinical Child Psychology*, 1980, *13*, 22–29.

Schaefer, C., Baker, E., & Zawel, D. A factor analytic and reliability study of the Devereaux Elementary School Behavior Rating Scale. *Psychology in the Schools*, 1975, *12*, 299–300.

Scherer, M. & Nakamura, C. A fear survey schedule for children (FSS-FC): A factor analytic comparison with manifest anxiety (CMAS). *Behavior Research and Therapy*, 1968, *6*, 173–182.

Sines, J. O., Pauker, J. D., Sines, L. K., & Owen, D. R. Identification of clinically relevant dimensions of children's behavior. *Journal of Consulting and Clinical Psychology*, 1969, *33*, 728–734.

Spielberger, C. D. *Preliminary Manual for the State-Trait Anxiety Inventory for Children*. Palo Alto, CA: Consulting Psychologists Press, 1973.

Spivack, G. & Spotts, J. The Devereux Child Behavior Scale: Symptom behaviors in latency age children. *American Journal of Mental Deficiency*, 1965, *69*, 839–853.

Spivack, G. & Spotts, J. *The Devereux Child Behavior Rating Scale Manual*. Devon, PA: The Devereux Foundation Press, 1966.

Spivack, G., Spotts,J., & Haines, P. E. *The Devereux Adolescent Rating Scale Manual*. Devon, PA: The Devereux Foundation Press, 1967.

Spivack, G. & Swift, M. S. The Devereux Elementary School Behavior Rating Scale Manual. Devon, PA: The Devereux Foundation Press, 1967a.

Spivack, G. & Swift, M. S. The Devereux Elementary School Behavior Rating Scales: A study of the nature and organization of achievement-related disturbed classroom behavior. *Journal of Special Education*, 1967b, *1*, 71–90.

Tasto, D. L. Self-report schedules and inventories. In: A. R. Ciminero, K. S. Calhoun & H. E. Adams (Eds.), *Handbook of Behavioral Assessment*. New York: Wiley-Interscience, 1977.

Voelker, S. L. Methylphenidate in the treatment of hyperactivity in children: Prediction of short-term response and multi-source assessment of long-term effects on behavior and academic achievement. Unpublished doctoral dissertation, Wayne State University, 1979.

Wallbrown, J. D., Wallbrown, F. H., & Blake, S. Stability of teacher ratings on the Devereux Child Behavior Rating Scale. *Journal of Experimental Education*, 1976, *44*, 20–22.

Weinberg, W. A., Rutman, J., Sullivan, L., Penick, E. C., & Dietz, S. G. Depression in children referred to an educational diagnostic center: Diagnoses and treatment. *Journal of Pediatrics*, 1973, *83*(6), 1065–1072.

Willis, S., Smithy, D., & Holliday, S. Item level validity of the Devereux Elementary School Behavior Rating Scale. *Journal of Abnormal Child Psychology*, 1979, *7*, 327–335.

Wilson, D. R. & Prentice-Dunn, S. Rating scales in the assessment of child behavior. *Journal of Child Clinical Psychology*, 1981, *10*, 121–125.

Wimberger, H. C. & Gregory, R. J. A behavioral checklist for use in child psychiatry clinics. *Journal of the American Academy of Child Psychiatry*, 1968, *7*, 677–688.

Wirt, R. D. & Lachar, D. The Personality Inventory for Children. In: P. McReynolds (Ed.), *Advances in Psychological Assessment*, Volume 5. San Francisco: Jossey-Bass, 1981.

Wirt, R. D., Lachar, D., Klinedinst, J. K., & Seat, P. D. *Multidimensional Description of Child Personality: A Manual for the Personality Inventory for Children*. Los Angeles: Western Psychological Services, 1977.

# CHAPTER 11

# *Neuropsychological Assessment Techniques*

Neuropsychological assessment of adults has become recognized as a special branch of clinical assessment. New techniques and data have shown that the psychological sequelae of neurological dysfunction can be described, and that these descriptions of behavioral change contribute to better understanding and care of many adults who suffer neurological impairment. Inevitably, as these techniques have developed, there has been an increasing demand for similar neuropsychological assessment of children who suffer neurological impairment.

## NEUROPSYCHOLOGICAL ASSESSMENT OF CHILDREN

There are major differences in the neurological statuses of normal children and normal adults (Boll & Barth, 1981). The neurological structures, connections, and functions of the adult present a much more stable condition against which the effects of trauma or disease may be measured. For the period from birth to about 12 years of age, the neurological structures, connections, and functions are in a state of rapid development, about which current knowledge has provided only partial descriptions. Efforts to conduct neuropsychological assessment of children must take place within the context of the neurological development of the child, the behaviors associated with the neurological development,

315

and through the use of procedures which permit one to ascertain whether the expected behaviors can be demonstrated. Sources of error in neuropsychological assessment may be due to ignorance of structure or behavior, or due to problems with the assessment procedures themselves.

Boll and Barth (1981) point out that neuropsychological problems in children vary with age and with type, severity, and location of lesion. No single test is comprehensive enough to ascertain presence of all possible neuropsychological deficits. Despite the need for use of comprehensive assessment batteries, there is still widespread use of single, often unidimensional tests in clinical practice, e.g., the use of the Bender-Gestalt test as a measure of brain damage. The Bender-Gestalt, which is primarily visual-spatial and perceptual in nature, is not an adequate method for detecting neuropsychological problems which do not depend upon those functions.

Neuropsychological assessment procedures have their origins in extensions of behavioral aspects of neurological examination and in the intellectual assessment used to establish IQs and other standards for cognitive behavior. The knowledge of these procedures and the data which have been derived through their use with both normal and neurologically-impaired children are one major component of adequate neuropsychological assessment of children.

In this chapter we will assume that most readers are not knowledgeable about neurological structures. (A basic reference for this information is Walsh, 1978.) However, as the course of neurological development is even less familiar to most psychologists, we will sketch that course. We limit ourselves to the period between four or five years of age and about 12 years of age. Little neuropsychological assessment is conducted prior to this period, and after this period most neuropsychological assessment procedures and behavior are the same as for adults. We will also describe behavior associated with neurological maturation and mention appropriate associated techniques of neuropsychological assessment. Following this information we will describe some individual neuropsychological assessment procedures.

While some neuropsychological assessment procedures have been studied and have data based on a sizable number of children (Reitan & Davison, 1974), other procedures have little child data available. As is so often the case with neurologically-based problems, the association between structure and behavior and between lesion and behavioral deficit often requires only a small number of cases to be established. However, because cases obtained clinically are the basis of the data, there are seldom cases with identical amounts and types of damage. Because of the complexity of the functioning brain, such differences, even though they may be slight, render ambiguous many decisions about the relationships between structure, function, and behavior.

Walsh (1978) has written of the neuropsychological examination as a descriptive (rather than a predictive) enterprise. He contends that the description of behavior associated with known damage is a primary function of the neuropsychologist. Clinically, however, the psychologist is often asked whether there is evidence for brain dysfunction, and this question may be asked in a predictive vein. Both neurological and psychological techniques for the study of the relationship between brain and behavior are becoming increasingly sophisticated. Walsh's position appears well taken, as criteria for damage are improved by better neurological examination and as techniques for detecting and analyzing behavior are improved by psychologists.

Many children who are referred for neuropsychological examination come to the attention of professionals because they are hyperactive or because they have learning problems. Others are referred because they have suffered brain trauma or disease which causes concern about the possible sequelae of these events. In almost all these cases the neurologist, the psychologist, the educational curriculum designer, and often the speech pathologist collaborate as a team for the most effective care to occur. No single discipline encompasses all the skills and issues which permit adequate translation of assessment information into effective treatment. If such a team is not available, the psychologist should make sure that enough consultation and communication occur and that the results of the neuropsychological examination are clear and speak directly to the relevant issues of diagnosis and treatment. It is, for example, of no direct value to label a child brain-damaged, because such a global descriptor does not describe the child's adaptive behavior, or his strategies for approaching information, or the types of errors that he makes – all of which are critical information for the design of a suitable curriculum or treatment program.

The psychologist focuses upon behavioral functions which develop during the period of childhood. These behavioral functions depend on the development of a language system, a motor system, a sensory system, attentional processes, learning, and memory. Each system and its functions can be related to brain development. We turn now to a brief description of the course of brain and behavior change and the methods which are used to detect these changes psychologically.

## BRAIN-BEHAVIOR RELATIONSHIPS

Brain development may be detected through the establishment of myelinated fibers. Not all brain areas myelinate at the same time. In fact, the cycles of myelination may be used as a gauge of when some behavioral functions may be expected to appear. The time span within which these brain and behavior changes occur will also determine the period during which neuropsychological evaluation may be expected to provide useful information. Figure 11.1 illustrates the cycle of myelination (reprinted from Yakovlev & Lecours, 1967). As can be seen, major sensory tracts are established in the early months of life. Later on, and by about four years of age, most of the other tracts are well on their way to myelination. After about age four what remain to be established are the cortico-subcortical connections, the development of the reticular formation, cross-hemisphere connections, the supra-association area, and some frontal structures.

Neuropsychological examination can establish whether behavior is attained within the expected age span and, if not, what types of errors are made. The procedures used for examination must be age-appropriate, which means that not all procedures are used in the examination of a given child. In addition, the election to use particular procedures will be shaped by the intake information and by the child's performance on an individually administered intelligence test such as the WISC-R or WPPSI. The individually administered intelligence test not only is a method for the establishment of the general level of intelligence, but it also serves as a screening test for the detection of a number of cognitive deficits which may direct some specific neuropsychological assessment. The Wechsler tests are preferred to other tests, such as the Stanford-Binet, because the performance on the various subtests of the Wechsler may make it easier for the clinician to detect certain problems and deficits.

Before we discuss the neuropsychological assessment procedures (and these are clinical procedures, for the most part, rather than tests which fit the psychometric requirements fulfilled by intelligence tests), we will chart the brain, behavior, and test relationships which may be expected during the period starting at about four and extending to about 12 years of age.

Since most of the sensory and many of the motor tracts are established by four years of age, cross-modal integration of sensory information begins to appear at this time. This integration is a necessary precursor

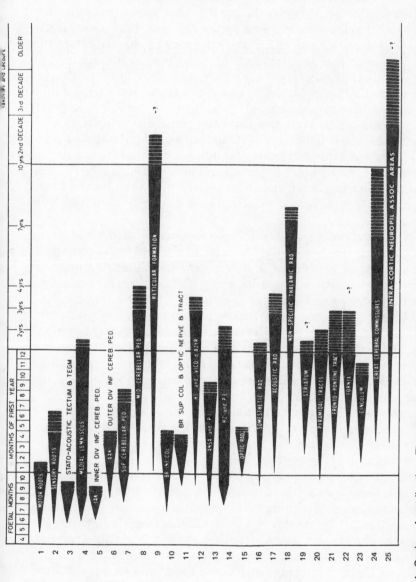

FIGURE 11.1. Cycles of myelination. The width and length of graphs indicate progression in the intensity of staining and density of myelinated fibres; the vertical stripes at the end of graphs indicate approximate age-range of termination of myelination estimated from comparison of foetal and postnatal material with the material from adults in the third and later decades of life. (Reprinted with permission from Yakovlev and Lecours, 1967.)

319

to the ability to read, a skill in which graphemic and phonemic codes must be coordinated. It is also during the same period that imitation of a motor behavior demonstrated by the examiner may occur. If the examiner executes a hand action, the child may be able to imitate the action. However, it is likely that at this age the child will imitate the action with both hands rather than only with the appropriate hand. Before the inhibition of the second hand can occur, some frontal lobe functions will have to be developed. This inhibitory and motor programming landmark is thus a criterion for a later period of development, after which its absence is indicative of immaturity or of pathological processes. Also during this early part of childhood, children are learning to develop categories, by both the methods of inclusion and exclusion. The categories must be simple and must depend on a very limited memory span. For this purpose the Categories Test may be used (Reitan & Davison, 1974).

Likewise hand preference is established for some children, while others do not mature in this fashion until later on, at least not with a consistent preference. Hand preference is determined by asking the child to perform a number of actions and observing whether there is a consistent preference for one hand. Another method is to use the Tapping Test (called Finger Oscillation in the Reitan Battery) to observe preference and facility of use. Motor behaviors related to handedness may be tapped by the McCarthy Motor Scale. At this age a number of other motor skills are not yet developed. These skills which depend on additional cerebellar development include the ability to hop or to walk in heel-toe fashion along a straight line.

Memory functions may be tested by parts of the McCarthy or the Ostreicher Sentences, which provide increasing amounts of vocabulary (Lezak, 1976). Haptic memory may be assessed by the child version of the Form Board.

Usually by age five, a clear hand preference is demonstrated. Likewise the body schema is established in space (for one's own body but not for extrapersonal space). The brain at this period is continuing to myelinate with some frontal lobe development, establishing tracts both within the cortex and subcortically. Tracts are also becoming established between various other cortical areas. There is greater hemispheric dominance established for both language and motor functions. As a result, foot preference is established and certain language behaviors become possible, e.g., automatic naming, which is the ability to name objects within categories. At this age automatic naming occurs within concrete categories; thus, the child may be able to name objects found in the kitchen whereas he may not be able to name objects in more abstract categories (such as means of communication).

During this period planning and coordination of motor behavior undergo improvement so that now the child can connect two objects with a line and can demonstrate organized search by scanning space effectively. There are also fewer problems with fine motor behavior which crosses the midline. With the establishment of the body schema the child is able to perform on Finger Localization and to match directions relative to his body, e.g., front versus back, up versus down. At this age the mirror movements discussed in the previous period should be disappearing when the child is asked to imitate a movement expressed by the examiner. Likewise the child is able to make ordinal arrays, although the middle parts of the array may not be accurate. Fine visual-spatial discrimination is improving, so that now the child may be able to discriminate between letters even if he does not yet know their names.

By age five and a half, most children can recognize 15 to 18 letters of the alphabet. They still make errors of commission (which are due to impulsivity or lack of inhibition) rather than errors of omission (which are due to attentional problems). These errors can be tested by means of a continuous performance task in which the child is asked to circle each of a given stimulus, e.g., the letter A. Similarly children continue to respond to the most salient features of stimuli even when these are not the aspects of the stimulus to which they are asked to respond. For instance, they will name the colors on tests such as the Stroop rather than report the content. During this period the child is able to identify common objects by feel (the haptic system is becoming better developed). Children are also able to perform on the Children's Form Board, even if they cannot name the objects. Because of major cerebellar development, children are now able to perform complex motor behavior such as touching finger to nose or standing on one foot. At this point neurological soft signs may be significant. Thus if the child continues to execute imitated actions poorly, there may be concern that problems exist. On the other hand the child may execute the actions well but more slowly, which would not be particularly significant.

Language development during this period of time permits the comprehension of the conditional. Language is still at an elementary level in terms of the use of action rather than reflexive verbs.

Because the frontal lobes are now more operational, there is improved use of sets. This is reflected in the child's ability to perform Part A of the Trail Making Test (Reitan & Davison, 1974). However, because the child cannot yet change sets well, Part B is beyond the level of many children at this age. Frontal development also accounts for the child's ability to inhibit overflow movements, so that imitation of examiner movements is more smoothly performed. However, because powers of abstraction and the ability to perform changes in sets are relatively undeveloped, the child may make errors when asked to perform mirror commands with the child facing the examiner. If the examiner can provide enough structure ("act as the child's frontal lobes"), many times the child will be able to respond to commands to inhibit behavior when unable to do so spontaneously.

During this period the types of errors that are often made reflect this concrete approach to instruction, so that the child may be stimulus-bound and lose sight of directions. Within the visual-spatial area this might be exhibited in simplification on the Bender-Gestalt, loss of set in imitation of movements, and poor performance on Part B of the Trail Making. Such errors are not indicative of pathology at this period but are within normal limits. More primitive errors would be cause for concern.

Around age seven, the supra-association area is developing, as a result of which there is better definition of the haptic system. Testing for finger localization should be improved. Single finger identification should be good, while there may be some evidence of suppression with simultaneous stimulation of two fingers. This suppression effect is probably attentional rather than sensory in nature.

At the same time the cross hemispheric connections are being rapidly developed, permitting language-directed discrimination of visual objects. Thus, on command the child is able to identify given objects. Errors will lead the child to pick out similar objects, e.g., pointed objects for "stars" because of the child's response to the salient features of the stimulus.

As the frontal system continues to develop, the attentional processes improve and the child is less subject to distraction. Testing for this development may be accomplished by the use of a continuous performance task.

Reading skills, which depend upon attentional processes, integration of transmodal stimulation, and the other functions just described, will vary to some extent with the individual differences in maturation of these systems. Testing for problems in reading will require determination of whether attentional processes are at fault or whether the child does not perform cross-modal integration of stimuli, or does not have letter or phonemic recognition.

The next period of development spans the years up to about age 11. During this time there is continued frontal development, along with cortico-cortical and cortico-subcortical development. The commissure also continues to mature. As these changes occur, attentional processes and ability to inhibit continue to improve. As a result, programming of motor events becomes established. In order for this motor programming to occur the child must attend, must compare behaviors, and must be able to inhibit behavior. Some of the procedures which test for the establishment of motor programming are relatively easy to administer. The examiner may instruct the child to write lines composed of alternations of the letters m and n, e.g., mnmnmnmn. Another relatively simple test is to instruct the child to observe the examiner and when the examiner holds up one finger, the child should hold up the left hand; when the examiner holds up two fingers, the child should hold up the right hand. Other tests which evaluate planning are Mazes and Trail Making.

The continued development of the supra-association area facilitates the cross-modal association of stimuli of increasing complexity. As a result, extrapersonal space is now constructed so that the child can correctly identify the verbally designated parts of the examiner's body – "my left hand."

Neurologically the right hemisphere is developing, which permits the identification of common objects that are felt but not seen. Without the cross-hemisphere connections and the development of the right hemisphere, this would not be possible. As a result, both ipsilateral and contralateral identification of objects is possible. Performance on the Form Board shows a large transfer of learning during this period.

Cerebellar development now permits the achievement of complex motor acts. The child has achieved a sense of the body in space. The motor part of the McCarthy will demonstrate a finer ability to throw a bean bag, to walk on a tape in a heel-toe fashion, to throw with one hand, etc.

After about 11 years of age, the major changes occur in the increased complexity of behavior and the more efficient management of it within shorter time limits. Children also acquire cognitive skills which are possible in part because of a longer span of memory, ability to reason by analogy, and reversible operations of a logical nature. As a result, mathematical operations, word problems, and memory problems are now attainable by the child.

Table 11.1 summarizes the developments during this period between about four years and 12 years of age. Comparison of the data contained

TABLE 11.1

## Chronological Development of Neural Tracts and Behavior with Associated Behavioral Tests

| | 4-5 Years | 5-5½ Years | 7 Years | 8-11 Years | 11+ Years |
|---|---|---|---|---|---|
| BRAIN | Sensory tracts established; Motor tracts established; Pyramidal tracts developing; Mid-cerebellar tracts; Fronto-pontine tracts developing | Frontal lobes develop: cortico-cortical tracts; Motor dominance beginning; Language dominance beginning | Supra-association; Cross-hemisphere connections; Frontal | Frontal development: cortico-cortical tracts cortico-subcortical tracts; Right hemisphere development; Cross-hemisphere development; Further supra-association area; Cerebellar development | Frontal development; Intercortical association areas |
| BEHAVIOR | Cross-modal integration; Imitate hand movements; Beginning hand preference; Develop categories | Hand preference established; Foot preference established; Body schema | Haptic development; Language-directed discrimination of objects; Attention matures; Cross-modal integration of graphemes and phonemes | Programming of motor events; Haptic functions develop; Extrapersonal space established; Complex motor acts | Cognitive skills; Logical and reasoning skills |
| TESTS | Hand preference; Tapping Test; Children's Form Board; Associate letters and sounds; McCarthy Memory; Ostreicher Sentences; Categories Test | Automatic naming (concrete); Can identify own body in space (finger localization); Organized search of space; Makes ordinal arrays; Identify common objects by feel (astereognosis); More complex language; Trail Making (A) | Finger identification (single stimuli good; double weaker); Identify objects by description or by name; Continuous Performance Tasks; Reading tests | Can alternate responses to a sequence of stimuli; Identify objects by feel (Form Board); transfer of training between hands; Identify body parts, extrapersonal space (e.g., examiner's left hand); Toss bean bag accurately, walk heel–toe on straight line | Achievement tests; Memory; Math |

in Table 11.1 with Figure 11.1 indicates that although most of the neurological development discussed has been accomplished, there are still other tracts which have not yet matured. These include the reticular formation and some of the intracortical association areas, which do not reach maturity until the third decade of life or perhaps later.

## ISSUES IN NEUROPSYCHOLOGICAL ASSESSMENT

Lezak (1976) stresses the importance of the individualized approach to neuropsychological assessment, taking into account an appreciation of the specifics which prompted the referral as well as the examiner's repertoire of assessment techniques. The later chapters of her book review a wide variety of neuropsychological measures, a few of which have data pertinent to children's performance.

One individualized approach to neuropsychological assessment is that of Christensen (1975), who followed Luria's approach to the form of the examination. This method is essentially developmental in nature and therefore can be used with children as well as adults. The method is a clinical examination of behavior in which the various behavioral functions associated with brain function are systematically surveyed. While statistical analyses are not performed as part of this type of examination, there are direct relationships between structure and behavior which provide the examiner with confidence in the results. Moreover, some of the examination procedures provide converging estimates of the same types of function or dysfunction, a method of evaluation which is essentially criterion-related in nature rather than purely statistical in approach.

Many of Luria's ideas have been incorporated into the Luria-Nebraska Battery (Golden, Hammeke, & Purisch, 1978). The Luria-Nebraska Battery is appealing to those trained in the psychometric tradition of American psychology. It appears to offer a straightforward method of scoring and evaluating the behavior of neuropsychologically-impaired patients. However, for those who have little or no background in neurology and neuropsychology but who might encounter referrals requesting neuropsychological evaluation, the Luria-Nebraska approach may be deceptively simple. Spiers (1981) points out that Golden has essentially reified the groupings employed by Christensen, and that the scoring of the Luria-Nebraska bears little relevance to Luria's concepts of brain-to-behavior relationships. There is serious question that the Luria-Nebraska

Battery can provide a standardized measure for assessment of neuropsychological function. The key to the issue is whether procedures employed by Luria are useful without the conceptualization of the results in a manner that takes into account legitimate brain-to-behavior relationships.

It should be obvious that cookbook application of neuropsychological examination procedures is professionally irresponsible. Interpretation of findings requires knowledge not only of brain functions but also of a repertoire of assessment procedures. It also requires an individualized approach to the examination of each patient. Although many neuropsychologists may use approximately the same examination procedures with different patients, the information from these procedures is combined and evaluated specifically with regard to the referral questions which must be confronted. The professional competence required in the test administration is miniscule compared to the professional competence required in the understanding and interpretation of the obtained data. Perhaps nowhere else, other than in the assessment of personality functions, must the examiner have such depth of psychological background to back up the technical skills of the assessment procedures.

## METHODS OF NEUROPSYCHOLOGICAL ASSESSMENT

The usual neuropsychological assessment performed in the United States reflects both behavioral, neurological examination and psychological examination. Generally examiners begin the asessment with an interview, which in addition to providing some basic information about the patient's past history also gives indications as to his present condition, including orientation, attitudes toward his problems, and the specific nature of his problems. Of particular interest are changes in basic physiological functions as well as presence of headaches, seizures, aberrations of sensation or motor behavior, speech, or memory.

An intellectual assessment is performed (individual administration of a standardized IQ test, usually a Wechsler for the appropriate age level), as well as an individually administered achievement test, where appropriate. Specific neuropsychological procedures which follow this initial interview and intellectual and achievement evaluation vary with the age of the patient as well as some preferences of the examiner. We have previously mentioned standardized neuropsychological batteries used by Boll (1981), Christensen (1975), Golden et al. (1978) and Reitan and Davison (1974). Other neuropsychologists use a variety of methods, in addition to or instead of parts of these procedures, the differences usually being attributable to the type of patient population and research, which often occurs concomitantly with the clinical service being performed. Thus in settings such as the Aphasia Research Center at the Boston VA Hospital, the focus on the development of techniques for assessment of aphasia becomes a major thrust. The Adult Neuropsychology Battery (Boll, 1981) consists of the Halstead Category Test, Tactual Performance Test (Form Board), Rhythm Test (Seashore Test of Musical Talent subtest), Speech Sounds Perception Test and Finger Oscillation Test (Tapping Test). A number of additional procedures routinely included are the Trail Making Test, Strength of Grip (hand Dynamometer), and unilateral and bilateral assessment of tactile, visual, and auditory perception. Aphasia screening is also performed.

The Reitan extension of the Adult Neuropsychology Battery was accomplished in two separate versions, one for older children (nine through 15) and one for younger children (five through eight), taking into account developmental differences in ability to perform on some tasks. The Battery for older children includes a modified Category Test, Tactual Performance Test and Trail Making Test, and also a Speech Sounds Perception Test. No other modifications were made. For younger children more extensive modifications had to be made. For example, the Category Test had to be redesigned, the orientation of the Form Board was placed in a horizontal position so that younger children could reach all of the blocks, a smaller apparatus was used for Finger Tapping, and some new tests were added. The Marching Test surveys gross motor functions; the Color Form Test and the Progressive Figures Test were added to evaluate cognitive processes including organizational ability, flexibility in thinking, abstraction, and concept formation. Younger children were also presented with a Matching Pictures Test, which requires appreciation of relevant categories. Other visual spatial tests include a Target Test in which the subject must remember and reproduce a figure tapped out by the examiner, and an Individual Performance Test in which the subject has to copy figures which range from simple to complex. This approach produces scores on each test and in this manner normals and neuropsychologically-impaired subjects can be compared. The appendices in Reitan and Davison (1974) provide tables for children which are useful for this purpose.

By comparison, Christensen (1975) outlines a neuropsychological examination which first evaluates motor functions of the hands (including optic-spatial organization) and complex forms of praxis (tie shoes, unbutton coat), and continues with oral motor behavior including speech regulation. Next, acoustic-motor organizaton is assessed, then cutaneous and kinesthetic functions, complex visual functions, receptive and expressive speech, and reading, writing, and arithmetic skills. Learning and memory functions are also assessed. No statistics are involved in this clinical approach, which was developed out of Luria's neurological examination of patients. The individual items of testing were selected because behaviors elicited by those items were subserved by particular brain structures. Thus the individual item functioned diagnostically rather than in a probabilistic nature, unlike items on achievement tests, for example, where the items are only partially related to some criterion.

Most neuropsychological examinations also take into account the personality, particularly the affective aspects of it. Questions relating to motivation are important in evaluating specific performance, as well as the patient's orientation to being evaluated. In addition, some neuropsychological disorders are characterized by affective changes. At the minimum, personality inventories are usually included as part of the neuropsychological examination. However, in other cases far more extensive personality assessment, including projective procedures, may be employed.

## SPECIFIC EXAMINATION PROCEDURES AND
## THE NEUROPSYCHOLOGICAL REPORT

Lezak (1976) is an excellent source of descriptions of specific examination procedures. Several chapters of her book provide brief introductory material relating to these procedures. We will present here only a few descriptions of materials as a vehicle for discussing the neuropsychological report. We will include both clinical procedures and a few of the usual items from the more psychometrically-based examination procedures. Since reports are typically based upon some of each of these types of assessment procedures, the reader will be able to consider reports in the light of the methods by which conclusions have been reached. For fuller understanding of these and other specific examination practices, the reader should consult Christensen (1975) and Lezak (1976).

The first group of tests we review concern the assessment of sensory and motor functions tested through the use of the hands. However, these procedures also provide information pertinent to other issues.

*Tapping Test (Finger Oscillation)*

The subject is seated comfortably at a table with the apparatus consisting of a board to which is attached a key that may be depressed. Each depression of the key activates a counter which records the number of depressions. The examiner demonstrates the use of the apparatus and the position in which the arm should rest on the table with the hand upon the key. The subject is instructed to take a few practice trials, depressing the key fully and as rapidly as possible, using only the index finger. The examiner observes whether the subject is in the correct position and whether the key is being depressed enough to activate the counter. Following the practice trials, the subject is instructed to tap as rapidly as possible and to stop upon request. Each hand is tested for 10-second intervals, alternating hands to prevent fatigue effects, until five trials have been administered to each hand.

The Tapping Test is thought to reflect the function of the motor strip of the postcentral gyrus. However, the test is probably best utilized as a general indicator of lateralized brain damage, because disturbances due to such damage may be associated with generalized motor slowing. One problem in the interpretation of the Tapping Test is that an individual's motivation for tapping rapidly may not be high and a potentially normal score may not be attained for this reason. Clinical attention to motivational factors is, thus, extremely important. Norms for the Tapping Test have been established (Reitan & Davison, 1974). In general, the indications for dysfunction take into account the hand preference of the subject, as well as a differential performance between the two hands.

*Finger Localization and Agnosia Screening Test*

In this procedure the examiner assesses the subject's ability to name or otherwise indicate which finger or fingers have been stimulated tactilely. The subject is seated at a table opposite the examiner. A screen shields the subject's vision of his or her own hands from direct observation. The subject is instructed to place the left hand, palm up, on the screen. The examiner numbers the fingers aloud for the subject, beginning with the thumb as number one, and checking with the patient to determine if there was any difficulty in detecting the touch of the pencil point. After this the subject is told that the examiner will touch a finger and should then report the number of the finger touched. The examiner records the subject's answers, touching each finger separately in a prescribed order. Next, the right hand is examined. Finally both hands are examined with the instruction to the subject to report which hand and which finger is being touched.

This clinical procedure is used to detect lesions in the dominant hemisphere in the parietooccipital area (Benton, 1959). In association with other deficits (agraphia, acalculia, right/left disorientation), dysfunction on the finger localization task contributes to the Gerstman syndrome, which indicates high probability of a dominant parietal lesion (Walsh, 1978).

Additional procedures employed in Finger Localization use essentially the same format, but include the use of diagrams of the hand to which the subject points with the non-tested hand to indicate which finger has been touched. Another procedure is to write a block letter on the subject's finger tip and have the subject report which letter has been written. These variations permit one to infer additional hypotheses based on the brain functions which require the use of vision or of symbolic processes. The procedure yields findings which may be informative by virtue of the pattern of errors produced in the performance of the various tasks. In order for the examiner to feel confident in the results, there should be no evidence indicating a receptive language disorder. Norms for children between six and nine years of age are found in Benton (1959).

*Consonant Trigrams*

This memory task is usually affected by left temporal dysfunction which interferes with the verbal learning functions mediated by it. The examiner introduces the task with the explanation that after he (the examiner) has said three letters the subject is to repeat them. Several items are given so that the subject's performance indicates understanding of the task and ability to remember and repeat the trigrams. Next the examiner informs the subject that more three-letter groups will be given, but this time the subject will delay until signaled to repeat the letters, offering an opportunity to observe variable delays of say three, nine, and 18 seconds (in order to see if short-term memory and storage occur beyond that point). Following the delayed condition, the subject is told that three letters and a number will be presented. The subject's task is to count backwards from the number given by ones. For example, given QLX 10, the subject counts 10, 9, 8 . . . until the point where the examiner asks the subject to repeat the trigram presented.

This task would be expected to be difficult for younger children.

There are no norms on the task for children and the data on adults have been drawn from both college students and neurological cases (Lezak, 1976).

*Rey-Osterrieth Complex Figure Test*

Some tasks are much more complex than others, thereby requiring very careful attention on the part of an examiner in order to analyze the import of the subject's performance with regard to a number of hypotheses, some of which may be interrelated. The Rey Figure was standardized by Osterrieth on 230 children ranging from four to 15 years of age (Osterrieth, 1944; Rey, 1941). Smaller numbers of children with learning difficulties and adjustment problems were also investigated. The task is first presented with instructions to the subject to copy the design. The examiner gives the subject a different colored pencil as each part of the design is finished, noting the order of the colors. Three minutes later the subject is asked to draw the design from memory. Often a second delayed drawing is elicited after 20 or 30 minutes.

The examiner is interested in the manner of the subject's performance as well as the final product. Frontal functions affect the planning and programming of the approach. The types of errors or rotations which may occur may indicate lateralization effects, and the subject's retention of material is also an important consideration. Accuracy of copying approaches an adult level by about age eight. Visual problems can complicate the performance on the Rey-Osterrieth Figure Test. However, assuming the eyes are intact and functional, neglect of one side or the other of the figure may signal posterior cortical dysfunction, usually indicating parietal lobe involvement as well as occipital lobe damage.

*Visual Memory Tests*

There is a variety of other visual memory tests, some of which are recognition tests, and some of which require the subject to try to reproduce the stimuli presented to him. While tasks which require reproduction invoke the function of different cortical functions than those which depend purely on recognition, the examiner who selects the visual memory task must be aware of the differences in these tasks in order to interpret findings appropriately. Where questions relate to complex behavior such as reading, the clinician may have questions as to whether visual discrimination, visual recognition, visual memory, integration of visual and auditory stimulation, or more verbal problems are involved. In such cases the type and combination of assessment procedures will reflect the hypotheses which are being investigated. By now it should be clear that the hypotheses formulated in a case of dyslexia, for example, will be the guide for the selection of instruments that may be appropriate for a neuropsychological examination. If no visual problems appear to be contributing to the dyslexia, it may be that the integration of phonic material with graphic material is faulty. This situation which may be due to not having learned or not being able to learn phonics, or not being able to make the integration of material which the subject is capable of learning independently in each of these areas. Unless one is interested in the neurological issues it is highly unlikely that a dyslexic child would be administered all the material which might help the clinician narrow down the possibilities. Generally, some indication of a more global area would be sufficient to alert educational specialists that a curriculum needed to be designed which would compensate for the disability. Such a curriculum would incorporate compensatory strategies or provide practice in areas of weakness. One might never know, if such a curriculum were successful, what neurological bases permitted the success.

*Verbal Function Tests*

Because so many language functions are lateralized (almost always in the left hemisphere), dysfunctions can be powerful indicators of the types of problems that a patient is suffering. The area where the temporal, parietal, and occipital areas converge (supra-association area and the adjacent areas) is of particular importance. A review of the neuropsychology of this area and the associated functions is beyond the scope of this book, but Lezak (1976) and Walsh (1978) offer a basic survey level of material for the interested reader. Many procedures have been developed which help the neuropsychologist differentiate among the possible dysfunctions which may be observed.

If the patient is observed to have difficulty with language, one is interested in whether the difficulty is expressive or receptive. While simple information of this sort can be determined from the use of the vocabulary on an IQ test and a comparison with performance on the PPVT, there may be more complex issues at hand. Suppose, for example, that the subject understands the examiner's question but has motor problems which affect the production of speech. Written answers may indicate that the subject is able to handle the material at a conceptual level. It should not be assumed that because the subject does not respond he does not comprehend. The task of the clinician is to separate out the various types of production problems from those that relate directly to problems of comprehension. We will now briefly mention a few procedures that pertain to the assessment of verbal functions.

The left parieto-temporo-occipital region is vital to the communication functions which involve the understanding and use of symbolic stimuli. Starting at the posterior of the brain and working forward there is a range of difficulties which are encountered with cortical impairment. Occipital-parietal impairment may interfere with reading. Moving forward, temporal and/or parietal impairment may interfere with writing. Temporal lobe problems are implicated in the impairment of the ability to understand speech (Wernicke's aphasia). Impairment in Broca's area, where the organization and pattern of speech take place, may result in inability to speak normally even though language can be comprehended. Even farther forward, frontal lobe impairment can result in concreteness and inability to organize and regulate behavior—functions necessary to initiate and spontaneously produce creative behavior and to adapt to changing conditions.

There are a number of reading tests which can be used to detect level of comprehension, word recognition, and oral versus silent reading. The Diagnostic Reading Scale has been reviewed in Chapter 7. It requires the subject to read silently and answer questions (usually in an oral response), to read aloud and answer questions in an oral response, and to listen to the examiner read and answer questions in an oral response. If there are obvious problems with speech production, the examiner can test for comprehension by asking the subject to write the answers to the questions. The interaction with the patient on this test permits the separation of a number of difficulties mentioned above. Other tests which depend upon written forms only may not be so helpful in some respects. The choice of reading test should depend upon the type of information the examiner wishes to elicit and the nature of the responses demanded by the test.

Fluency tests may require either an oral or a written response from the subject. In the oral form, the examiner gives the subject an instruction, such as, "I'm going to give you a letter. I want you to give me as many words as you can that begin with that letter." The subject is instructed to avoid proper names and variations of the same word. Usually the patient is given three letters, one at a time, and allowed 60 seconds in which to respond. Performance will be affected by age and by education. There are norms for adults (Lezak, 1976). For children between the ages of two and a half and eight and a half the verbal fluency subtest of the McCarthy Scales of Children's Abilities may be used (McCarthy, 1972). Norms are provided for a measure which consists of four trials in which the subject is asked to name as many 1) things to eat, 2) animals, 3) things to wear, and 4) things to ride, as possible, This more concrete version is more suitable for young children.

A written form of the verbal fluency test appears in the Primary Mental Abilities Test which has norms for adults (Thurstone & Thurstone, 1962). Comparison of oral and written fluency may be of value in understanding the nature of the deficits suffered by the patient. A systematic examination of speech functions is found on the Christensen neuropsychological examination (1975). The subject first repeats words after the examiner, singly and then in series and sentences. The subject is asked to name objects, name from descriptions, and provide categories for objects. The fluency – the ability to generate spontaneous descriptions, give a narrative, and identify and manipulate verbal material – is surveyed. The same type of analysis is possible with written language through a similar survey.

The usefulness of the neuropsychological examination is enhanced by the collaboration of the neurologist and the educational specialist and/or speech pathologist. Neuropsychological evaluation may be helpful in medical settings in which the purpose of the examination is to aid in the diagnostic determination of the type of impairment, corroborating the evidence from neurological examination. The neuropsychological examination data may be helpful in the selection of treatment approaches for patients who have suffered neurological impairment. Sometimes the help comes in the form of finding alternative or compensatory mechanisms which enhance the patient's ability to communicate. Sometimes, understanding the specific nature of the deficits which have been suffered are of enormous help to the patient and family who can better understand what to expect as sequelae to the impairment.

In addition to the procedures which have been reviewed here and those reviewed in Lezak (1976), there are many other assessment procedures which have been devised or used as neuropsychological procedures. For example, the Harris Tests of Lateral Dominance (Harris, 1974) were designed to be given in cases where children exhibit reading, spelling, or writing disorders, speech difficulties, or neurological problems. The Harris Tests are composed of items, some of which deal with body schema and some of which permit observation of motor behaviors of various types. There is no good evidence for validity, other than face validity, of the procedure. The Harris Tests may be a more complicated form of assessing hand, eye, and foot preference than those methods usually included in neuropsychological examinations. The tests are not a test of lateral dominance at the level of discourse in which one is concerned about lateralization of speech and symbolic functions. Many tests, of which the Harris is only an example, were developed because of the interest that psychologists and educators have had in the relationship between brain functions and reading or other academic performance. Because theories waxed and waned concerning the importance of hand preference and cortical dominance, a number of tests have been developed which have focused upon hand preference and reading, with the belief that data relating these measures might advance knowledge about the relationship between neurological function and reading. This does not appear to have been particularly fruitful.

Other tests, e.g., the Southern California Sensory Integration Tests, were constructed because of interest in children with learning disabilities (Ayres, 1972). These tests are lengthy in terms of administration time and contain surveys of various sensory and perceptual functions as well as motor responses. The difficulty with the use of such instruments is not that they do not permit one to obtain information which may be relevant to neuropsychological evaluation, but that they have been divorced from the conceptual framework within which their data would be useful. Tests such as the Harris and the Southern California Sensory Integration Tests are attractive to educators and others who might be interested in learning-disabled children. To the examiner who may learn how to administer these examinations, there may be a false sense of confidence that one can interpret the neurological import of the subject's performance. This is not necessarily the case. As has been pointed out, there are many factors which can interfere with performance – some motivational factors and some due to disabilities that may keep the subject from making an appropriate response because of the limitations of the test. Without a good understanding of neuropsychological theory and the assessment procedures, the examiner is left with only a rote application of cookbook administration and interpretation. Such use of tests is not only incompetent but also dangerous, in that patients may incur costs in time, money, and consequences which are inappropriate for their conditions.

It is safe to say that neuropsychological evaluation should always be linked to neurology, and to consultation with neurologists. Research utilizing and developing new assessment techniques is perfectly legitimate within such a context. Separated from this context, however, esoteric theories bearing little relationship to the neurology of the subject may develop and spawn "assessment procedures" of doubtful use.

## REFERENCES

Ayres, J. A. *Sourthern California Sensory Integration Tests*. Los Angeles: Western Psychological Services, 1972.

Benton, A. L. *Right-Left Discrimination and Finger Localization*. New York: Harper, 1959.

Boll, T. J. The Halstead-Reitan Neuropsychology Battery. In: S. B. Filskov & T. J. Boll (Eds.), *Handbook of Clinical Neuropsychology*. New York: John Wiley, 1981.

Boll, T. J. & Barth, J. T. Neuropsychology of brain damage in children. In: S. B. Filskov & T. J. Boll (Eds.), *Handbook of Clinical Neuropsychology*. New York: John Wiley, 1981.

Christensen, A. L. *Luria's Neuropsychological Investigation Manual*. New York: Spectrum Publications, 1975.

Golden, C. J., Hammeke, T., & Purisch, A. Diagnostic validity of a standardized battery derived from Luria's neuropsychological tests. *Journal of Consulting and Clinical Psychology*, 1978, *46*, 1258–1265.

Harris, A. J. *Harris Tests of Lateral Dominance, Third Edition. Manual of Directions for Administration and Interpretation*. New York: The Psychological Corporation, 1974.

Lezak, M. D. *Neuropsychological Assessment*. New York: Oxford University Press, 1976.

McCarthy, D. *McCarthy Scales of Children's Abilities*. New York: The Psychological Corporation, 1972.

Osterrieth, P. A. Le test de copie d'une figure complexe. *Archives de Psychologie*, 1944, *30*, 206–356.

Reitan, R. M. & Davison, L. A. *Clinical Neuropsychology: Current Status and Applications*. Washington, D.C.: V. H. Winston, 1974.

Rey, A. L'examen psychologique dans les cas d'encephalopathie traumatique. *Archives de Psychologie*, 1941, *28*, (112), 286–340.

Spiers, P. A. Have they come to praise Luria or to bury him?: The Luria-Nebraska battery controversy. *Journal of Consulting and Clinical Psychology*, 1981, *49*, 331–341.

Thurstone, L. L. & Thurstone, T. G. *Primary Mental Abilities* (Revised). Chicago: Science Research Associates, 1962.

Walsh, K. W. *Neuropsychology: A Clinical Approach*. Edinburgh: Churchill Livingstone, 1978.

Yakovlev, P. I. & Lecours, A. R. The myelogenetic cycles of regional maturation of the brain. In: A. Minkowski (Ed.), *Regional Development of the Brain in Early Life*. Philadelphia: F. A. Davis, 1967.

PART III

# Applications
# of Principles
# and Methods

# CHAPTER 12

# *Illustrative Case Material*

In previous chapters we have examined some of the normal developmental processes which are relevant to distinguishing between age-appropriate behavior and behavior that is indicative of psychopathological problems. We have also discussed the deviant varieties of children's behavior, reviewing the major problems which usually bring children to the psychologist's office or clinic. We have considered the assessment process in terms of the issues which are raised by referral questions and other information, and we have synopsized information relevant to the standard psychometric and clinical assessment procedures used with children. What remains is to put the meat on the bones of these domains of interest.

In this chapter illustrative case material will be presented.* In each case the assessment process will be traced from the point of referral through various decision steps, reporting the findings of assessment procedures, and conclusions based upon these findings. The cases have been selected to represent a range of presenting problems typical of a practice with a number of types of sources which result in child assessment referrals. These cases will be discussed in terms of the logic of the assessment process as well as the specific material which is presented.

---

*The cases presented are composite and fictionalized, chosen for their representation of clinical problems rather than serving as actual reports on living people.

The logic of the assessment process, as discussed in Chapter 5, depends upon the active and inquiring involvement of the clinician. The hypotheses which are generated depend upon having an open mind and trying to explain the data available at each step in as many plausible ways as possible. Only when the clinician has discarded some of the possibilities based on the assessment information elicited is it appropriate to focus the formulation sharply. While it is true that good clinicians have hunches and impressions which are labeled as intuitive, it is probable that these feelings are based upon observation and interpretation of historical and behavioral material. While some people are better observers than others, the process is not mystical. Attempts to articulate the basis for impressions will lead to more explicit identification of the data important to the assessment procedure.

We will being our case illustrations with a chronically ill child. While such referrals may occur more often in medical settings and child guidance centers, their frequency is likely to rise. As new medical techniques have prolonged life for many of these children, they are brought to the attention of mental health professionals. Often these children have to cope with problems other than those of the illness itself, because the resulting social difficulties are usually quite complex.

### LATANYA: A CHRONICALLY ILL CHILD

Latanya, an eighth grade black female who has suffered from sickle cell anemia since birth, was referred by her pediatrician. Latanya has a history of strokes, pneumonia, and numerous other ailments. Her medical records at 14½ years of age already fill several large charts which detail numerous emergency room consultations as well as hospitalizations. Currently, Latanya's pediatrician wants to know whether there is an emotional component to some reported fainting spells and to her learning and behavioral problems at school.

The interview material from Latanya and her mother indicates that there are eight children in the family. The mother also has a history of sickle cell anemia with many medical problems. The mother supports the family through public assistance and some work when she is able. The parents are divorced and the father has remarried. He refuses to contribute to the care of the family because he has a new family. He does not visit the children. The mother reports that Latanya is moody and has a bad temper, leading to many fights at home and school. Both

Latanya and her brother have been in trouble at school due to their behavior. Although the mother sees Latanya as the cause of most of these problems, the girl insists that her brother Darrell is responsible for most of the fights. Latanya's mother also feels that the school has been remiss in providing for her daughter's education. The school history reveals many absences due to illness and Latanya's performance has been so poor that she is failing. In the interview Latanya did not volunteer any information about school, but when asked she seemed to feel little concern about her reported failure and behavior problems.

When Latanya and her mother came to the clinic for the evaluation, the girl was attractively dressed as if she were going to a party. She was a pretty, somewhat reserved girl who glanced at herself frequently in the mirror in the room. While she was cooperative, her answers were minimal, unless she was urged to give fuller replies.

Following the intake interview and review of the medical records, the psychologist entertained several possibilities as to the problems that Latanya faced. First, the medical problems were severe and chronic and could have contributed both to the behavioral and learning problems. Second, the family was large and poor, without a father. Although Latanya had received good medical care through public assistance, conditions which might have reinforced the importance of school were largely missing. Third, there was some doubt about the mother's ability to deal with the implications of the illness, on the one hand, and her ability to control the behavior of her children, on the other. The mother's frustration may have led to an unrealistic blaming of the school and others for Latanya's problems, especially since she had many of the same problems with her daughter at home. Fourth, neither the girl or her mother showed much insight or motivation to become personally involved in making changes in Latanya's behavior. Rather, the attitude was passively dependent, indicating that others should take the responsibility for making things better and then being critical of the results.

Based on the possibilities noted, there appeared to be a need for both intellectual and personality evaluation. The models presented in Chapter 5 may be reviewed at this point. The clinician's first question, with regard to the school problems, is, "How bright is the child?" Latanya was administered a WISC-R to determine the answer to this question. Her scores were found to be in the low 80s, Full Scale IQ of 81, with very little scatter on the subtests. The comprehension score and the picture arrangement score were higher than the others and this was seen as consistent with Latanya's social orientation and visual alertness. The performance also was characterized by a lack of strategies to approach problems.

Because of the poor attendance record, the failing grades, and the mother's feeling that the school was not doing the best by her daughter, an achievement test was administered to determine how much basic information Latanya had acquired. Latanya was given a Woodcock-Johnson Test and it was found that her achievement was markedly deficient in all areas. Her scores were as follows:

|  | Grade Score | Age Score |
|---|---|---|
| Reading | 2.8 | 7-10 |
| Math | 4.5 | 9-9 |
| Written Language | 3.9 | 8-11 |
| Knowledge | 2.8 | 8-2 |

Given that Latanya is 14½ years old and in the eighth grade, it is obvious that she is very much behind both her age group and grade level. The fact that she has a WISC-R score in the low 80s would lead one to expect a better level of achievement under normal conditions. However, Latanya lives in a broken home with a large number of children and suffers from a chronic and severe physical condition, all of which could interfere with her ability to perform, or her motivation for doing so. The intelligence test material suggests that Latanya had few cognitive strategies at her disposal so that she adopted a passive attitude toward problem-solving and performance. This lack of cognitive strategies could be responsible for some of her learning problems, as could the passivity noticed in her response to task demands. However, additional personality problems might also be involved. Both the pediatrician and the mother have expressed concern about Latanya's behavior. In the interview Latanya did not volunteer information about her feelings about herself.

The clinician decided to administer the TED to Latanya and also to give her the Sentence Completion Test and other open-ended procedures to elicit material relevant to her emotional life. The stories told to the TED indicated that the girl saw mother figures as punitive. She understood social demands of different situations and tried to present a façade of happiness and a close-knit family. However, at variance with this were many indications of low self-esteem, some self-destructive thoughts, and a strong use of denial. For instance, she told stories about a girl who was very dedicated to her schoolwork and who would not break rules. The Sentence Completion Test indicated considerable concern with her own illness and that of her mother, problems in school, and difficulties getting along with peers. Despite the long period since the parents' divorce, Latanya still expressed a strong desire to have her parents reunited.

Latanya was given an opportunity to express several wishes and again her desire for the parents' reconciliation was foremost. After that she wished not to be sick any more. Projective drawings indicated a desire for a happy home life where all the family members were present.

The psychologist felt that Latanya's projective productions did add to the picture considerably. It was not surprising to find a focus on illness, but it was somewhat unexpected to find that she focused on the needs of others (particularly her mother) before herself. Although she sees her mother as punitive, it is clear that she has a strong dependence on her and is concerned about any possible threat to the mother's welfare.

It can be seen from the way the clinician approached this case that many ideas were raised early in the assessment process due to the nature of the referral. After the interview, the psychologist had some impressions which came from the information provided by the girl and her mother and some impressions which grew out of the nature of the interpersonal interactions which took place during the interview. These impressions raised still more questions. The intellectual and personality assessment which was conducted through the use of standardized and clinical procedures did not result in a complete ruling-out of the questions raised in the referral. It did result in an integrated picture of the girl's emotional and academic adjustment and some of the bases for the specific problems that the girl was experiencing.

With regard to the question of prognosis, the clinician would have to be very cautious. Unless the social and emotional support for this girl improve, little more will be accomplished by the efforts of the school and health authorities who have tried to intervene for her benefit. The home conditions and the length and severity of the health and emotional problems may be too severe to show much improvement. Even so, the possibility exists that Latanya may be helped by personal and genetic counseling, so that she may make some decisions about how she lives which will be in her own best interests.

Now that we have traced the case of this chronically ill child, Latanya, through the evaluation processes and demonstrated the type of thinking that went into the evaluation, we turn to the reporting of the results. The report follows the general form outlined in Chapter 2. It may be helpful to read the report and then reread the case so that the reader can follow how and why the clinician chose to word material in certain forms and also the intricate links between observation and interpretation.

---

## PSYCHOLOGICAL EVALUATION

Latanya, an eighth grade black female, was referred by her pediatrician. Latanya has been reported to faint at school and also to experience both learning and behavior problems at school. The pediatrician asked whether there might be an emotional component to the fainting spells and for more information and recommendations pertinent to the learning problems and other behavior problems at school.

### Pertinent History

Latanya suffers from sickle cell anemia. She has had many severe illnesses associated with this congenital disease, including episodes of pneumonia, strokes, and infections. Her medical records fill several charts and report numerous emergency room consultations and hospitalizations.

Latanya's mother also suffers from sickle cell anemia and also has had many severe medical problems. When the mother is able she does work, but most of the time the family is supported through public assistance. The parents are divorced and the father has remarried. There are eight children in the home and there is discord based on their problems among themselves. There is little family agreement about why there are so many fights. The mother sees Latanya as moody and having a bad temper and as the cause of most of the problems. The mother also feels that the school has been at fault in not educating her children better.

Reports from the school indicate that Latanya has many absences and that she does not pay attention and do her work when she is in school. In addition, she has been in fights at school. Teacher reports indicate that Latanya's mother is hostile and defensive, ready to blame the school for her daughter's problems and providing little guidance for the girl at home.

### Behavioral Observations

Latanya accompanied her mother to the clinic. She was attractive and neat but inappropriately dressed, as if going to a party. Although Latanya was reserved, she did look at herself frequently in the mirror which was in the room. She initiated no comments and when asked a question directly she was minimally compliant, giving brief, unelaborated answers unless pressed for further details. There was no evidence of tension between the girl and her mother, although the mother frequently made comments which were critical of Latanya. In general, Latanya adopted a passive, dependent attitude, while her mother took an active, critical, and dissatisfied posture.

*Procedures:*

WISC-R, Woodcock-Johnson Achievement Test, Tasks of Emotional Development, Sentence Completion Test, Three Wishes

### WISC-R

Latanya scored a Full Scale IQ of 81, with very little scatter on the subtests. The comprehension score and picture arrangement score were higher than the others and this was consistent with Latanya's social orientation and visual alertness. There was a marked lack of strategies on matters that required problem-solving, a finding consistent with Latanya's passive attitude and her general disinterest in abstract material.

### Woodcock-Johnson

Latanya's achievement scores were deficit in all areas indicating that she has not acquired much basic information relative to other children her age (14½ years). The distribution of scores was:

|  | Grade Score | Age Score |
|---|---|---|
| Reading | 2.8 | 7-10 |
| Math | 4.5 | 9-9 |
| Written Language | 3.9 | 8-11 |
| Knowledge | 2.8 | 8-2 |

Thus Latanya is behind both in terms of age and grade levels. Her IQ score would lead to an expectation of a better level of achievement under normal conditions. However, because of her disinterest in abstract content, her lack of cognitive strategies, her passive orientation, and her numerous school absences, she has not acquired information at an expected level. Other personality factors may be involved and projective testing explored these.

*Tasks of Emotional Development*

Latanya was able to interpret the social demand of the portrayed situations, a finding consistent with her social orientation found on the WISC-R. She gave superficial stories with a façade of happiness and family closeness. However there were indications of low self-esteem, self-destructive thoughts, a strong use of denial, and a perception of mother as punitive.

*Sentence Completion Test*

The content of the answers indicated preoccupation with her mother's illness, school problems, peer problems, and a desire to have her parents reunited. The ego level of the answers was immature, self-protective, and conformist.

*Three wishes*

Latanya's first wish was for her parents to be reunited; her second wish was not to be sick anymore; and finally, she wished for a happy home.

*Summary and Recommendations*

Latanya, a 14½-year-old eighth grade student, was seen for psychological evaluation. Latanya, who suffers from sickle cell anemia, was referred by her pediatrician in connection with fainting, other school behavior problems, and learning problems. Latanya comes from a large family and a broken home, in which there are few material resources. The home is characterized by fighting among the children and Latanya is seen as the cause of many family problems, according to the mother.

Latanya is an attractive eighth grader who functions at the lower end of the low average IQ range. She seems able to understand and learn from social situations, although her performance socially does not match her comprehension. She is well below grade and age levels with regard to more abstract information. In addition, Latanya lacks cognitive strategies and adopts a passive attitude when confronted with a problem-solving situation.

Projective evaluation indicates that Latanya is very worried about her mother's illness as well as her own. Very little information about sickle cell anemia appears to be understood either by the girl or her mother, even though they both assert that they do understand the illness. The discrepancy between the information level and the assertion appears related to the use of denial, which is Latanya's psychological approach to many problems by which she might otherwise be overwhelmed. Latanya expresses concern about social rejection, school problems, and self-destructive thoughts, while wishing for a happy home and successful school situation.

The material obtained indicates a strong need for school placement which can provide help with Latanya's academic deficiencies. She may need tutoring as well, both because she needs help with developing cognitive strategies and because of her passive, dependent personality. The problems with low self-esteem and passive dependence on others, as well as Latanya's overuse of denial, indicate a strong need for psychological help, probably in the form of a therapeutic relationship. On the basis of the present evaluation the fainting episodes are consistent with escaping from stressful and unpleasant situations, and therefore an emotional component cannot be ruled out. Also, it is noteworthy that Latanya has never injured herself in falling during these attacks. However, it would appear that the fainting episodes should not be a major focus of attention since they result in reinforcing Latanya's avoidance of responsibility in the school situation. Rather, the school should be advised as to how to handle these episodes so as to reduce the social attention that they have involved. In addition, both Latanya and her mother would benefit from genetic counseling concerning sickle cell anemia and they should have an opportunity to discuss the care, problems, and consequences of the disease in lay terms.

---

Our second case illustrates the extreme behavior problems which arouse the concern of both family and school personnel. Extreme behavior problems of a destructive nature usually attract the attention of law enforcement authorities when they occur in adolescence. In younger children, if no crime has been committed or if the destructive behavior takes place within the confines of the home, the child is more likely to be referred to mental health professionals. Often the question which prompts the referral is whether some emotional problem is at the root of the behavior problems. Sometimes the behavior problems are tolerated at home until the child gets into trouble at school, at which point the parents may be forced to focus upon them despite reluctance to do so.

## TONY: A SEVERE BEHAVIOR PROBLEM

Tony, a nine-year-old boy, was referred by his parents after he got into trouble at school. Tony was reported to have attacked and severely beaten a classmate. Because of his behavior he was suspended from school and his parents were told that they would have to seek help for Tony or he would not be allowed to reenter school. Tony was accompanied by his parents and a family friend to the clinic where he was scheduled for a psychological evaluation, with the understanding that he might also be a candidate for individual treatment if the evaluation indicated that this might be appropriate.

When the referral was first received the psychologist wondered whether the behavior which got Tony into trouble was typical of his school deportment or whether it was also apparent at home. The evaluation was scheduled for the parents and Tony. The friend who accompanied the family was first seen sitting in the waiting room and it was not clear whether she was a family member. She was introduced by her first name only and when the family and the psychologist departed for the interview room she accompanied them saying that she could probably be of some help.

The interview began with the psychologist still unsure of the friend's identity, but interested in a pattern of interaction that left this person so undefined. It was reported that Tony was a fourth grade student who lived with his parents and an 11-year-old brother. The father, a construction worker, spends much time away, sometimes coming home to spend a few days between jobs. The mother, previously a waitress and a construction worker, is now a housewife. Two other members of the household include the female friend who visited the clinic with them and a male teenager whom the family took in to help with his own drug and adjustment problems. Emotional problems were reported in the extended family, with several members of the family having served time in prison for impulsive behavior. Tony's father reported that he himself also had a bad temper.

Tony's early history contained no reports of illness or accidents or developmental problems. However, school problems had been evident from the beginning: He had repeated the second grade and been placed in a special class in the third grade. His parents felt that Tony was bright but only performed if he was interested. Although this was not the reason for the referral, Tony had recently drowned the family cat and beaten a dog to death. He was also responsible for a number of fires set in the family home, one of which had occurred while his parents were sleeping. It was only the coughing due to heavy smoke which had aroused them in time to save the house and themselves from destruction. Recently Tony's grades had dropped at school and his disruptive behavior in the classroom preceded the incident in which he beat and kicked a classmate to the point of unconsciousness.

Tony's behavior in the interview was reticent. He refused to comment on any of the material reported by the parents but was not particularly hostile or tense. He had adequate eye contact but simply did not respond verbally. The psychologist wondered if Tony had a story of his own that he wanted to tell when the parents were not present, but neither in the joint interview nor after did Tony volunteer any information or perception that was not directly elicited. He was noncommittal when his parents reported that he was oppositional and very jealous. The family friend was finally identified when the interviewer asked how she fit into all this and what her perceptions were. It developed that she was a "friend" of the father, having met him on a construction job and come to live with them. Her relationship with the mother and her plans for the future were never defined. She corroborated the parents' story about Tony's behavior. The psychologist observed many signs of indirect communication within the family and had a strong impression that the family focused upon problems and activities of people outside the family, ignoring stresses and problems within the nuclear family group. The mother was found to be ineffective in controlling Tony's behavior and, in fact, he responded to no one but the father during the latter's infrequent visits home, and then only out of fear. Tony and his brother were described as frequent liars about their behavior, even when such deception was unnecessary. Tony was described as having almost no friends and those that he had were episodic due to many disagreements and feuds.

The clinician had the impression that Tony comprehended well and was very adept at social manipulation but, because there was relatively little overt behavior and there was evidence of poor school performance, felt that a good measure of intelligence would be called for. Accordingly, a WISC-R was given and found to provide scores in the average range (VIQ=106, PIQ=102, and FS IQ=104). There was wide scatter among the subtests which was obviously due to the level of cooperation that Tony gave at any given time. Because he was easily frustrated and gave up prematurely on many tasks, his scale scores ranged from 1 to 18. At times he wanted to leave the room and he threatened the examiner with aggressive behavior. At other times he threatened to break the mirrors in the room. However, the examiner was very firm with Tony and told him he would have to remain until the procedures were completed. The examiner informed Tony that he could control the amount of time he spent in the assessment situation by cooperating and completing the tasks or he could make himself take longer by being un-cooperative. Under these instructions Tony complied, although at every opportunity he complained or resisted to the limit that he could.

Tony was administered a Rorschach. He was productive (24 responses) with good reality-testing (good form) and no signs of psychosis. He produced responses primarily on the basis of form and showed other signs of affective constriction. There were also indications that Tony was prone to act out impulses with little cognitive mediation and that his affective constriction could result in being emotionally distant from people. The content of his responses was mostly immature (animals or pairs of animals, usually not in movement) and he was very stimulated by the color cards, although his responses were almost entirely determined by form. Over two-thirds of his responses were to the color cards but without the use of color.

Projective drawings were done impulsively and carelessly, complying only in a minimal way with instructions. The kinetic family drawing showed a powerful father looming over the tiny figures of the rest of the family. Incomplete sentences admitted a bad temper and close involvement with the family but denied closeness with others or other problems. Tony also ridiculed the examiner. Projective stories told to the TED were generally sparse and reported little affect. Stories about peers were structured in terms of competitiveness and isolation. Stories with both parental figures were somewhat distorted by telling about one parent and some other more distant figure. A strong emphasis on sources of dependency gratification (food, money, gifts) and power (winning, overcoming others) were the main features of the stories.

The examiner frequently had to structure, limit, and push Tony to get his cooperation. Problems with impulse control, low tolerance for frustration, and anger and dependency were clear in his interactions as well as in the test material content.

The psychologist felt that Tony was much brighter than his scores on the WISC-R indicated, probably in the range of 125. Both his pattern of responding and the content of material he produced were congruent with reported behavior. Tony's anger was extreme during evaluation and he once took a swing at the examiner who stopped him and set limits upon such behavior immediately. While Tony responded to this within the evaluation setting, his behavior at home appeared to be out of control at times, and vindictive at other times (such as the killing of the family pets and the fire-setting). There was no evidence of psychosis but rather a very severe oppositional orientation and one which was devoted to getting his own way at all costs. This, combined with Tony's anger and needs for attention and affection, were very prominent features of the likelihood of his destructive acting-out.

The psychologist felt that the family problems were severe, with little communication between members, denial of the severity of the problems and consequences of Tony's misbehavior, and displacement of concern onto those outside the nuclear family. The presence of the two non-family members made the situation worse since Tony felt he had to compete with them for attention and affection. The family also was active in helping others outside the home. In view of the amount of denial and the severity of the problems, the psychologist was not sanguine about the hope that either individual or family outpatient therapy was likely to prove helpful for Tony. It was probable that he would not really become engaged in the process. Tony was seen as very likely to continue his destructive behavior pattern until someone was either seriously injured or killed as a consequence of it. In view of the fact that the parents only came to the evaluation under pressure from the school and the threat that the juvenile court would intervene, prognosis seemed very poor indeed. Given all this information the psychologist recommended inpatient residential treatment. While not hopeful that Tony would make major changes, this treatment alternative seemed to present the most favorable conditions under which some change might be possible.

---

## PSYCHOLOGICAL EVALUATION

Tony, a nine-year-old Caucasian boy, was referred by his parents for evaluation after he was reported to have attacked and severely beaten a classmate at school. The school insisted on the evaluation and is to be sent a copy of the report.

### Clinical Interview

Tony lives with his parents and his 11-year-old brother. The father, a construction worker, spends much time in other cities due to his work, often coming home only a few days between jobs. The mother, previously a waitress and a construction worker, is now a housewife. Two other members of the household include a female friend, who accompanied the family to the clinic, and a male teenager, whom the family took in to help with his own drug and adjustment problems. Emotional problems were reported in the extended family, with several members of the family having served time in prison for impulsive, aggressive behavior. Tony's father also reported that he had a bad temper.

No reports of illness, accident, or developmental problems marked Tony's early years. When Tony started school he had problems from the beginning and repeated the second grade. He was placed in a special class in the third grade, although his parents believed he was bright and could have performed better if he had been interested. The parents reported that Tony had recently drowned the family cat and beaten a dog to death. He was responsible for setting a number of fires in the family home, one of which occurred while his parents were sleeping. Only because of coughing due to heavy smoke were they aroused in time to save themselves and the home from destruction. Recently Tony's grades had dropped at school and his disruptive behavior in the classroom preceded the incident in which he beat and kicked a classmate to the point of unconsciousness.

*Behavioral Observations*

When the interview began, Tony, his parents, and the woman who accompanied them all entered the interview room. The adults reported the content described above, but did not express feelings about the events. Neither did they clarify the role of the woman who accompanied them. Tony's behavior was reticent. He refused to comment on any material reported by the parents, but was neither hostile nor tense. He had adequate eye contact but simply did not respond verbally. When asked about his parents' report that he was oppositional and jealous, he did not reply. When the family was asked directly, they identified the woman who accompanied them as a "friend" of the father who had met him on a construction job and come to live with them. After the woman was introduced she corroborated the parents' report and stated that Tony obeyed no one but the father and him only out of fear. All adults agreed that Tony was a frequent liar, even when there was no reason, that his mother couldn't manage him, that he had almost no friends and that those he had were only episodic due to his temper.

*Procedures:*

WISC-R, Rorschach, Projective Drawings, Incomplete Sentences Test, Tasks of Emotional Development

### WISC-R

Tony was found to perform in the average range of intelligence (VIQ = 106, PIQ = 102, FSIQ = 104). The wide scatter (scale scores ranged from 1 to 18) was due to the level of cooperation that Tony gave at any given time. He was easily frustrated and gave up prematurely on many tasks. At times he wanted to leave the room and threatened the examiner with aggressive behavior. At other times he threatened to break the mirrors in his room. However, when given firm instructions that he had to stay and that he could control the situation by being cooperative, he did comply. Nevertheless, at every opportunity he complained or resisted to the limit.

### Rorschach

Tony was productive (24 responses) with good reality-testing (good form) and showed no signs of psychosis. He produced responses mainly on the basis of form and showed other signs of affective constriction. There were indications that Tony was prone to act out his impulses with little cognitive mediation and that his affective constriction could result in being emotionally distant from people. The content was mostly immature (animals or pairs of animals) and he was very stimulated by the color cards, although his responses were almost entirely determined by form.

### Projective drawings

The drawings were done impulsively and carelessly, complying only minimally with instructions. The kinetic family drawing showed a powerful father looming over tiny figures (the rest of the family). There was no elaboration and no common activity.

### Incomplete Sentences Test

The content of the test was concerned with bad temper, close family ties, no ties to anyone else, and ridicule of the examiner.

### Tasks of Emotional Development

Tony's stories were superficial and reported little affect. Peers were seen as competitive and isolated. The parents were not seen as close. The main emphasis was on material sources of dependency gratification (food, money, gifts) and on power (winning, overcoming or dominating others).

### Summary and Recommendations

Tony, a nine-year-old boy referred by his parents, was minimally cooperative during the evaluation and showed clear evidence of problems with impulse control, low tolerance for frustration, anger, and oppositonal behavior.

Tony's performance on the WISC-R was in the average range, but marked by inconsistent performance due to his negativism. He probably could perform in the range around 125 if he were cooperative and interested. During the testing Tony took a swing at the examiner who stopped him and set limits on his behavior immediately. While he responded to this limit-setting in the evaluation, his behavior at home appears to be out of control at times, and vindictive at other times (killing the family pets and fire-setting). While there was no evidence of psychosis, there was evidence for a severe oppositional orientation, an immature determination to dominate others in order to get what he wanted.

There appear to be severe family problems with little communication between members, denial of the severity of the consequences of Tony's misbehavior, and displacement of concern onto those outside the nuclear family. The presence of two non-family members adds to the number of people with whom Tony feels he has to compete. It is unlikely that either individual or family outpatient therapy will work, since neither Tony nor his family would have come without pressure from the school and the threat that the juvenile court would be involved if they did not. Given all of this, inpatient residential care is recommended. However, even so, the prognosis seems guarded and Tony should be considered to be an unsocialized aggressive child who is likely to hurt someone badly unless he improves.

---

In contrast to the previous two cases in which a substantial amount of family history and contact with family members was available to the psychologist, referrals of foster children are often characterized by very sparse information about the child prior to the time of evaluation. Several different case workers may have been involved with separate placements for these children with little or no continuity over time. Frequently the only information available is that the child is a candidate for placement and has a history of previous unsuccessful foster home care. It is likely that a caseworker will bring the child to the clinic or office, having had little previous direct contact with the child. This being the case, the child may be confused about the purpose of the visit and what will happen during the evaluation. Even if attempts have been made to prepare the child for meeting the psychologist, the child may not have grasped the explanation adequately. Children who find themselves in this situation will usually have a vague appreciation that the visit will weigh heavily in what will happen to them. However, the process may remain mysterious and threatening. The result is that the psychologist is faced with a child accompanied by a stranger to a strange situation in which another stranger decides his or her fate.

## TRACEY: A FOSTER CHILD

Tracey was referred by a social service agency for a psychological evaluation as part of pre-adoption procedures. Tracey, aged six, and her younger sister were removed from their parents' custody three years ago as a result of physical abuse by their mother. They were placed in a foster home in which Tracey once again experienced abuse and neglect. The children were removed after a year when the situation was discovered by a protective services worker. In the next foster care placement the younger sister was highly favored over Tracey and, as a result, Tracey became very withdrawn, shy, and timid. Although she had improved socially over the immediate past six months, she has remained introverted and has been repeating kindergarten. The teacher has raised the question of possible learning disabilities which preclude her achieving successfully at the first grade level. The teacher recommended that Tracey be evaluated. Recently the possibility of adoption for Tracey and/or her sister has also been raised by people (not the foster parents) in the community.

In view of Tracey's history, the psychologist formulated several questions. First, there was the question of how the repeated physical abuse and neglect had affected Tracey. Second, there was the question of the effects of the unsuccessful foster placements. Third, there was the question of how Tracey's cognitive strategies and development might have been retarded. Fourth, there was the question of the significance of the relationship between Tracey and her sister. One of the concerns about the relationship with her younger sister was whether Tracey and her sister should be placed together or in separate homes, if adoption seemed a suitable choice. Finally, there was the question of whether Tracey should be adopted at the present time.

In the absence of family input or direct contact with previous foster parents, the psychologist was faced with the need to generate sufficient and specific information which would bear on each of these questions. A fairly comprehensive evaluation describing Tracey's present adjustment seemed appropriate to address several of the questions formulated by the psychologist.

Because Tracey was six years old, doing poorly in school, with a known history of abuse and neglect, it was the psychologist's decision to use the Stanford-Binet rather than one of the Wechsler Scales to evaluate this young child. The Binet would avoid the problem of obtaining too little information about cognitive strategies which might be the case if the WISC-R had been used (she would be expected to ceiling quickly). Since she would be expected to perform near the top of the WPPSI, that test might require much longer administration time than the Binet. Also, in the event that her poor school performance was the result of retardation, the WISC-R scores might not reflect her true level of the performance (the lowest WISC-R score which could be obtained for a child aged six would be an FS IQ of 44). Therefore, the Binet would permit a better reflection of Tracey's abilities if they were very low.

The psychologist also wondered whether Tracey might have more ability to comprehend verbal material than to produce it, particularly in view of the history of abuse. Therefore, the decision to give the Peabody Picture Vocabulary Test was made to effect the comparison between comprehension and production.

As Tracey was repeating kindergarten and the question of learning disabilities had been raised, it was felt that a test of visual-motor integration would be appropriate as well as some readiness tests which focus on the type of material usually found in kindergarten and first grade curricula. Finally, the psychologist felt that projective testing would be helpful in assessing Tracey's feelings toward herself and other significant people in her life. Since the content of Tracey's conversation was restricted to the present and the future, it was difficult to tell from the interview just how hurt she was and the specific nature of possible problems which might have been associated with parental relationships. In view of Tracey's age, the examiner elected to use a variety of tests: House-Tree-Person, Kinetic Family Drawing, Children's Apperception Test (Human Form) and Sentence Completion for Young Children.

In the clinical interview the psychologist found Tracey to be a neat, attractive girl who was quiet and shy at first but who warmed up rapidly. She was confused about her living arrangements and was not sure where she belonged. She spoke openly of wanting a new family and appeared to be very close to and dependent upon her younger sister. She had a great need to please the examiner and worked very hard.

Tracey's performance on the Stanford-Binet Intelligence Scale, Form L-M, placed her within Borderline Defective range of intellectual ability (IQ=76). She passed all items at the IV=6 level and failed all items at the VII year level. She showed serious developmental delay in visual-motor coordination as she was unable to pass tasks in these areas at the V year level. Her vocabulary was at the VI level and was the only test passed at an age-appropriate level. She showed deficits in abstract thinking, awareness of details in her environment, and visual motor skills. On the PPVT, Tracey also exhibited a significant delay in receptive language as indicated by a mental age score of three years, 11 months (fourth percentile). Thus, both the Stanford-Binet and the PPVT provided congruent results suggesting significant cognitive deficits, although her vocabulary score on the Binet was higher than that on the PPVT, raising the question of fluctuation of attention during the testing. The Beery Developmental Test of Visual Motor Integration provided an age equivalent of four years four months, suggesting serious difficulties in eye-hand coordination and perceptual organization. This age equivalent is approximately one-and-a-half years below Tracey's chronological age. As would be expected, these cognitive deficits are reflected in academically related behavior. Tracey cannot recite the alphabet and cannot write the letters. While she is able to count from one to 10, she is not able to write her first name. She scored at the tenth percentile when compared to other children of her chronological age on the Metropolitan Readiness Tests (Form A).

The results of the personality assessment suggest that Tracey is a depressed, anxious girl who cannot understand the reasons for her mistreatment by adults. She wants to please adults and their caring and approval are deeply important to her. Physical abuse and emotional neglect were frequent themes in all of the projective material and obviously have had a highly traumatic effect on Tracey's psychological functioning and emotional well-being. The projective stories told in response to pictured situations clearly describe Tracey's depth of loneliness and insecurity and her lack of trust in adults as safe for her. For example, "Children waiting to eat – Dad standing in the back. He is watching, they know he is watching. They are sad because their Dad ain't feeding them. Crying. Daddy never comes, no one comes, they are going to get a whipping from Ma. Still no feeding. They just sit and wait, nobody comes."

Given all of these data, the psychologist's intepretation was that Tracey's basic psychological needs for love, nurturance, and acceptance simply have not been met in the past. Instead she has experienced the world as a dangerous place in which children are at the mercy of physically abusive, noncaring adults who are incapable of being pleased. Tracey's quiet, conforming, introverted personality makes it difficult for one to comprehend the intense feelngs of helplessness, worthlessness, insecurity, and unhappiness which she is currently experiencing. The psychologist concluded that Tracey was functioning across a variety of cognitive, visual-motor, and language tests within the mild mentally retarded range. Her academic prereadiness skills likewise were inhibited and it was felt that special education classes were warranted. She was seen as a depressed, insecure, anxious, and eager-to-please little girl whose basic psychological needs for warmth, love, approval, and attention had not been met. Consequently, major problems of depression and feelings of worthlessness need to be addressed, probably in play therapy. With regard to adoption, some cautions were advised. Her adoptive parents would need to be aware of this little girl's sensitivity and reluctance to express her feelings directly. She would need considerable support and indications of warmth and acceptance before she could feel safe with any family wishing to adopt her. Most likely, Tracey would be a slow-to-warm-up child who should be allowed to become acquainted at her own pace and not be rushed when adapting to new situations. Pre-adoptive counseling with prospective parents was strongly recommended. In view of the previous problems, an adoptive home in which there were no other children would seem preferable, all other things being equal. If Tracey were placed in the home with her younger sister, the adoptive parents would need to insure that Tracey had her own special attention, but not at the expense of slighting her sister.

## PSYCHOLOGICAL EVALUATION

Tracey, age six, was referred by social agency for a psychological evaluation as part of pre-adoption procedures. There is question of possible learning problems.

### Pertinent History

Tracey and her younger sister were removed from their parents' custody three years ago because of their mother's physical abuse of them. They were placed in a foster home and Tracey experienced both abuse and neglect. The children were placed in a second foster home after a year. The younger sister was favored and Tracey became increasingly withdrawn, shy, and timid. At the present time she is repeating kindergarten and remains introverted, although she has shown signs of some improvement over the past six months.

No information was available from the natural parents or previous foster parents. The child was unable to remember or report information about either situation.

### Behavioral Observations

Tracey was a neat and attractive girl who appeared to be well-nourished. She was quiet and shy at first but warmed up rapidly. She was very oriented toward pleasing the examiner and wanted a lot of social approval. She worked very hard at the tasks presented, even when she experienced difficulty.

### Procedures:

Clinical Interview, Stanford-Binet Intelligence Scale (Form L-M), Peabody Picture Vocabulary Test, Beery Developmental Test of Visual- Motor Integration, Metropolitan Readiness Test, Tasks of Emotional Development, House-Tree-Person, Kinetic Family Drawing, Children's Apperception Test (Human Form), Sentence Completion for Young Children.

#### Clinical interview

This indicated that Tracey felt very worried about whether she might be separated from her sister. She was confused about her current placement and what might happen to her. She spoke openly about wanting a new family, and appeared to feel very close to and dependent upon her younger sister.

### Stanford-Binet Intelligence Scale (Form L-M)

Tracey's performance on the Stanford-Binet placed her within the Borderline Defective range of intellectual ability (IQ = 76). She passed all items at level IV-6 and failed all items at the VII level. Tracey showed serious developmental delay in visual-motor coordination as she was unable to pass tasks in these levels at the V year level. Her vocabulary was the only test passed at an age-appropriate level. She showed deficits in abstract thinking, awareness of details in her environment and visual-motor skills.

### Peabody Picture Vocabulary Test

Tracey's receptive language performance also indicated a significant deficit as she received a score equivalent to a mental age score of three years 11 months. Thus, both the Stanford-Binet and the PPVT provided congruent results suggesting significant cognitive deficits, although her vocabulary on the Binet was higher than that on the PPVT, raising the question of fluctuation of attention during the testing.

### Beery Developmental Test of Visual-Motor Integration

Serious difficulties in eye-hand coordination and perceptual organization were suggested by Tracey's age equivalent of four years four months. This finding is congruent with the finding that Tracey cannot write the letters of the alphabet and cannot write her own first name.

### Metropolitan Readiness Test

Deficits previously noted are consistent with Tracey's poor performance on the readiness test. She scored at the tenth percentile with respect to children of her chronological age.

### Tasks of Emotional Development

Tracey's major themes dealt with physical abuse and emotional neglect. The stories reflect abandonment, abuse, sadness, and deprivation. Tracey appears to be depressed, anxious, and confused about her mistreatment by adults. She wants their approval and wants to please them, but is able to achieve neither acceptance nor basic security.

*Summary and Recommendations*

Tracey, a six-year-old foster child, was seen for evaluation for adoption. Tracey has been abused and suffers the consequences of neglect. Her quiet and conforming personality makes it difficult to detect the intense feelings of insecurity, unhappiness, helplessness, and worthlessness that this girl experiences. Tracey functions within the mildly retarded range of intellectual performance and is academically behind as well.

Recommendations for Tracey's care should include consultation with adoptive parents. They will need to understand that Tracey will need a long period of acceptance before feeling safe. While she might be superficially compliant and approval-seeking, she will be slow to warm up emotionally and will need time to establish a trusting relationship. Because of indications of feelings of rejection and depression, Tracey would benefit from some relationship in psychotherapy, probably play therapy. Tracey will also need special education classes. While Tracey wants a home very much, she probably needs to go to one in which no other children are currently placed. If placed with her sister, the adoptive parents will need to make sure that Tracey has her own special attention, but not at the expense of slighting her sister.

---

A sizeable number of referrals arise from cases in which children exhibit personality problems which frustrate, puzzle, and sometimes terrify their parents. It is difficult for parents who observe strange behavior to decide whether the child who exhibits unusual practices and verbalizations is seriously disturbed or whether they themselves are overinterpreting the significance of the behavior. By the time that parents refer their children, they usually believe that something is very wrong, and they have considerable anxiety about the consequences which they and their children may have to face. Particularly when conduct problems are absent and no major school problems exist, parents become more concerned about possible serious emotional disorder.

### HUGH: A SEVERE PERSONALITY PROBLEM

Hugh, aged 11 years three months, was referred by his mother who reported a complex family history. Hugh's mother reported a normal early developmental history. However, shortly after Hugh's birth she separated from her husband (subsequently divorcing him) and she suffered a period of depression. She was unsure of the effects of the separation and of her depression on young Hugh. Furthermore, according to the mother there was a strong "genetic" history of psychiatric problems on both sides of the family. This history included incidences of schizophrenia, bipolar depression, and alcoholism in various members of the family. While Hugh's parents were separated when he was three months old, they were divorced when he was four. His mother remarried a year later. Family relationships were and continue to be very poor, with episodes of physical and emotional abuse by the stepfather.

Currently Hugh is described by his mother as being well-behaved at school and in other situations outside the home. However, he is a serious behavior problem at home. His problematic behaviors include refusing to study, low frustration tolerance, moodiness, and manipulative behaviors. He had an "imaginary companion" until recently and reports auditory, visual, and tactile hallucinations.

One of the questions raised by the referral and interview material is whether Hugh is psychotically disturbed. Both intellectual and personality testing would be helpful in establishing the degree and nature of the cognitive and affective problems. The psychologist arranged an intake interview with Hugh, who was a very neat and attractive boy. He was distraught, anxious, and cried frequently during the interview. He spoke of being identified as the "bad" child in the family and clearly felt unloved and unwanted by his parents. Hugh saw his mother as rejecting and his stepfather as a demanding, frightening, and punitive man. He spoke of having nightmares from which he wakes up crying, disoriented, and unable to get back to sleep. He described hallucinatory experiences involving auditory, visual, and tactile features. Hugh was at a loss to explain the reasons for his misbehavior at home except that he could not control himself. There was a compulsive aspect to his manipulatory behavior and Hugh felt driven by it. One of Hugh's major concerns involves the possibility that he would be unable to continue therapy in the future. Hugh's mother described him as bright and creative, loving art, music, and poetry. She felt that he actively and deliberately tried to disrupt the family and cause problems with her husband. She was angry with him and felt he needed strict discipline and limits.

Hugh's performance on the WISC-R placed him at the top of the Superior range of intellectual ability (VIQ=128, PIQ=123, FSIQ=128). Due to the depressing effect of anxiety upon his ability to perform, these results may be considered as reflecting minimal levels, and it is possible that his intellectual ability is higher than these current results would suggest. On the WISC-R, Hugh demonstrated excellence in logical, abstract thinking and verbal reasoning. He also showed a superior level of social acculturation and comprehension, as well as a good ability to use this knowledge to plan how he will deal with everyday situations. He has a good vocabulary and a good fund of general information. He has good organizational ability, manipulates spatial relations well, and shows strengths in visual-motor coordination. Three subtests were relatively depressed (Arithmetic, Digit Span, and Coding) and probably reflect inability which may be due to anxiety and depression. However, on the basis of the intelligence test, any major thought problems can be ruled out.

The results of the personality assessment suggest the presence of depression, anxiety, insecurity, and a possible psychotic potential. His level of stress far exceeds his ability to cope with his feelings and has resulted in an inability to empathize or identify with others. Specific findings are described in the Psychological Evaluation.

Hugh's projective drawings reflect a compulsive tendency as well as generalized anxiety which at times is overwhelming. For example, the male figure is running blindly through a rainstorm and is described as "a boy feeling angry because his parents yell at him. He is running from his parents and he needs someone to be nice to him." The family drawing is highly suggestive of a pathological family situation and this family is described as "falling apart from mental problems . . . this family won't stay and solve their problems." The parents are described as "mean, cruel, acting as if they don't care, and only wishing to punish the children."

Recurring themes of rejection, unjust punishments, loneliness, and depression are found within the Sentence Completion and Thematic Apperception Tests. On the projective story task, each major character was described as lonely, frightened, rejected, and having deep-seated feelings of anger and hostility directed toward parental figures who are viewed as threatening, punishing, and rejecting. Hugh feels guilty about the angry and hostile feelings he has toward his parents and is unable to cope with his anger in acceptable ways. Consequently he wishes to leave the family. He views the situation as hopeless and feels helpless about changing things for the better. For example, here is one story Hugh related: "This is a story about a mother of a boy, thinking what a disgrace my child is, so angry at the boy she wants to kill him. Doesn't. The mother just sits and mopes. The son runs away and the mother is relieved."

The Rorschach protocol suggests the potential for disturbances in thought processes and judgment. Under stress, Hugh becomes disorganized and tends to interpret reality in terms of his own needs rather than realistically. He is anxious, insecure, and has strong ambivalent feelings toward paternal figures. There are indications of possible destructive impulses which are not acted out directly because of fear of retaliation and considerable guilt and anxiety over repressed hostility. Strong suggestions of apprehension and feelings of inadequacy relative to paternal figures are present as well as concomitant anticipation of maternal rejection.

The Personality Inventory for Children was administered, using Hugh's mother as the rater. The PIC assesses the respondent's opinion of a child's behavior, attitudes, and family relationship. The profile analysis suggests that Hugh's mother is defensive, tending to "disown" the relationship-based aspects of the problem. The Adjustment Scale is clearly elevated (ADJ-113T) indicating the presence of a pattern of highly dysfunctional behavior. Hugh is viewed as an overly active, anxious boy who is not depressed or withdrawn. Instead, he is seen as having well-developed social skills, although serious family disorganization is indicated. Primarily Hugh is described as an emotionally disturbed, anxious boy with clear-cut delinquent tendencies, including suggestions of inconsideration of the rights and feelings of others and total disregard for limits.

The psychologist concluded that Hugh was of superior intellectual ability, that he was a vulnerable child who was at risk for future psychological problems. He was seen as depressed, anxious, confused, and experiencing a high level of stress far above his ability to cope well. In addition, he was seen as an angry, guilt-ridden boy who could not express his hostility directly toward his parents, whom he sees as punitive, critical, demanding, and rejecting. As a consequence his manipulative behavior became an indirect expression of angry feelings and was experienced by Hugh as driven rather than self-directed. Finally, Hugh was suffering some distortion of reality which was characterized by hallucinatory experiences. Without therapeutic intervention, the potential for future psychotic disturbance could not be ruled out. While his present level of adjustment could be considered borderline, without therapy and without changes in the family Hugh could be expected to have further and worse episodes of dysfunction.

## PSYCHOLOGICAL EVALUATION

Hugh, age 11 years three months, was referred by his mother who has been worried by her son's deteriorating behavior. She wanted to know whether Hugh was very disturbed and what could be done to help him.

*Pertinent History*

Hugh's mother reported no problems with pregnancy, birth, and delivery. Hugh's early developmental history was normal as far as achieving milestones. However, when Hugh was three months old his parents separated, his mother suffered a depression, and after four years the parents were divorced. Hugh's family history includes numerous incidences of mental disorders including schizophrenia, bipolar depression, and alcoholism. The mother has been worried about a "genetic" basis for Hugh's behavior.

When Hugh was five his mother remarried, but family relationships continue to be problematic with Hugh's stepfather sometimes abusing him physically and emotionally. At home, Hugh exhibits poor frustration tolerance, moodiness, and manipulative behavior. His mother reports auditory, visual, and tactile hallucinations on his part.

Both the mother and teacher report that Hugh is well-behaved at school. The mother described her son as bright and creative, loving art, music, and poetry. On the other hand she was angry and frustrated by him and felt that he deliberately tried to disrupt the family and cause problems with her husband. He was defiant and needed strict discipline and limits, according to her point of view.

*Behavioral Observations and Interview*

Hugh was a neat and handsome boy. He was anxious, distraught, and frequently became tearful during the interview. Hugh saw his mother as rejecting and saw his stepfather as a demanding, punitive, and frightening man. Hugh reported having terrible nightmares from which he awoke disoriented, crying, and unable to get back to sleep. He described hallucinatory experiences congruent with those described by his mother. He also confirmed his misbehavior at home and stated that he felt he had no control over it. In fact, there was a driven and compulsive aspect to his manipulative behavior. He felt that he needed treatment and was afraid of what would happen if he did not get it, although he had not discussed this with his mother.

*Procedures:*

WISC-R, Projective Drawings, Thematic Apperception Test, Rorschach, Sentence Completion Test, Personality Inventory for Children.

### WISC-R

Hugh's performance on the WISC-R yielded a VIQ of 128, PIQ of 123, and FIQ of 128. However, because of the anxiety obvious during testing, it is likely that this estimate is lower than would be the case if Hugh were under less stress. Hugh demonstrated excellent logical and abstract reasoning. Three subtests were relatively depressed (Arithmetic, Digit Span, and Coding) and probably reflect the effects of anxiety and depression. Otherwise, Hugh organized material well and showed strengths in visual-motor coordination, social acculturation, and social comprehension.

### Projective drawings

Projective drawings were characterized by overwhelming anxiety and were very compulsively drawn. The male figure running blindly through the rainstorm was described as "a boy feeling angry because his parents yell at him. He is running away and needs someone to be nice to him." Great attention was paid to drawing the raindrops and the details of clothing, etc. Family was described as disintegrating and parents as mean and cruel.

### Thematic Apperception Test

On the Thematic Apperception Test each major character was described in lonely, angry, and rejected terms. Punitive parents were the targets for children's anger and fear. The stories indicated hopelessness and depression. For example, "This is the story of a mother of a boy, thinking what a disgrace my child is, so angry at the boy she wants to kill him. Doesn't. The mother just sits and mopes. The son runs away and the mother is relieved."

### Rorschach

The Rorschach is marked by breakdown in form and arbitrary percepts. When the content is frightening, e.g., a monster, Hugh becomes disorganized and uses both space and determinants very idiosyncratically and in poor form. His performance indicates anxiety, strongly ambivalent feelings about parental figures, and possible depressive and destructive feelings which have to be hidden to avoid retaliation by others. Father figures are more feared for punitive reasons and mothers are seen as the source of rejection.

### Sentence Completion Test

The Sentence Completion Test confirms the material found in the TAT and the Rorschach. The form of the answers reflects Hugh's level of intellectual functioning, but the level of ego development is below that which would be expected for a boy his age.

### Personality Inventory for Children

The PIC suggests that Hugh's mother, who completed the instrument, is defensive, tending to "disown" the relationship-based aspects of the problems. The Adjustment Scale is clearly elevated, indicating highly dysfunctional behavior. Hugh is viewed as an overly active, anxious boy who is not withdrawn or depressed. Rather, the mother describes him as more delinquent in his tendencies to be inconsiderate of other people and to disregard limits on his behavior.

### Summary and Recommendations

Hugh, an 11-year-three-month-old boy, is of superior intellectual ability. However, he is a vulnerable child who is at high risk for future psychological problems and he already is experiencing severe psychological problems. He is depressed, which is not obvious to his mother, and he is confused and experiencing a high level of stress. He is angry, guilt-ridden about it, and feels rejected and punished by his parents. His manipulative behavior appears to be driven by his angry feelings. Hugh's basic reality-testing is compromised and he suffers hallucinatory experiences at times. In addition, his judgment becomes arbitrary when he feels emotional stress and he is not able to use his high intelligence appropriately under those conditions. Hugh's present level of adjustment should be considered borderline. He needs immediate intervention in the form of psychotherapy. In addition, parental counseling seems critical if the home situation is to become more supportive. Both the mother and stepfather should be involved in this treatment. Without intervention Hugh can be expected to have further and worse episodes of dysfunction.

---

There is greater parental awareness of learning disabilities now than at any previous time. Likewise school personnel are sensitive to learning problems. When children do poorly in school, therefore, one of the first possibilities considered be either parents or teachers is that learning disabilities may have contributed to the child's failure. The psychologist receiving referrals related to school failure is often asked to determine whether the child is indeed suffering from a learning disability. Such was the case with our next clinical example.

### CORBIN: A LEARNING PROBLEM

Corbin, who is an 11-year-one-month-old white male, was born seven weeks prematurely. During his early development, Corbin was slow in attaining some developmental milestones, but by the age of three he was within normal limits. At this time he started wearing glasses. At age five he had his tonsils removed and after that he had several bouts with childhood diseases.

The history provided relevant information about Corbin's school performance. When Corbin was entered in kindergarten at age five, he was tested and placed in a special class for Specific Learning Disabilities (SLD). In the first grade Corbin attended special classes for a half day and was placed in a regular classroom for the remainder of the day. When Corbin was in the third grade, his family moved to another state where he was placed in a regular classroom. Corbin did not achieve at grade level in reading although he was able to do so in mathematics and in other subjects. For this reason Corbin was again placed in an SLD class. Sessions lasted about 45 minutes per day. Upon promotion to the fourth grade Corbin was also placed in an SLD class for 90 minutes per day. Just before the move in the third grade Corbin's parents were divorced and his mother remarried about six months after the move.

Both Corbin and his mother report reading difficulties and frustration which is secondary to them. Corbin also told the examiner that children have been teasing him for his reading problems and the fact that he wears glasses. Corbin feels close to both of his natural parents, despite their divorce, and feels that he can confide in them and in his stepfather. The court has decreed that Corbin may elect which parent he would prefer to live with when he gets a little older. However, the boy feels this may be a problem as he does not want to hurt either parent's feelings. Currently, Corbin is active in team sports, music, and plans to join Boy Scouts. His parents let him take piano lessons last summer.

Everyone, including Corbin, agrees that he has trouble reading. There were no reported emotional problems at home or at school. The psychologist noted in the interview that Corbin related easily and showed no signs of emotional disturbance. He was able to discuss matters frankly and was appropriate for his age and difficulties. The psychologist had screened for problems with the Behavior Problems Checklist, and again, there were no reported difficulties other than the reading problem. Therefore, the psychologist ruled out further assessment of emotional problems, unless something unexpected should appear during the course of the procedures which would be used to investigate Corbin's reading difficulty.

During the examination Corbin revealed himself to be a cooperative and attentive child who became involved in the tasks and who related easily with the examiner. Although he did not become upset when he had difficulty, it was clear that the tasks which involved visual perception or oral answers were easier for him than those which involved reading. Corbin was careful in his work and could break down a problem and analyze various courses of action before responding. Occasionally he experienced word-finding difficulty, but sometimes could think of the correct answers when this happened.

Several times Corbin mentioned that he wished he could talk to someone outside of the family about his problems. He wondered whether he could talk to someone at church or in scouting or even with his mother. Corbin was controlled in his expression of emotions even when he was discussing his problems. Basically he seemed motivated to get help for his academic and peer-related problems.

Corbin was administered a WISC-R on which he received a FSIQ of 107 with a VIQ of 96 and a PIQ of 120. His approach indicated a very careful style and possible mild attentional problems. His scaled scores for individual subtests were as follows:

| Verbal | | Performance | |
|---|---|---|---|
| Information | 8 | Picture Completion | 13 |
| Similarities | 9 | Picture Arrange- | |
| Arithmetic | 7 | ment | 12 |
| Vocabulary | 11 | Block Design | 15 |
| Comprehension | 12 | Object Assembly | 16 |
| Digit Span | 5 | Coding | 8 |
| | | Mazes | 8 |

Corbin's performance was remarkable in that despite some apparent difficulty with immediate attention (lowered Digit Span) he was capable of good performance on subtests in which all the parts were immediately available (several of the performance subtests). Arithmetic, Digit Span, and Coding were all lower than other tests, further suggesting the attentional problem.

Corbin was administered a PIAT on which he achieved as follows:

| Subtest | Grade Equivalent | Age Equivalent |
|---|---|---|
| Mathematics | 5.3 | 10-7 |
| Reading Recognition | 1.8 | 7-2 |
| Reading Comprehension | 2.4 | 7-6 |
| Spelling | 2.7 | 7-11 |
| General Information | 4.2 | 9-5 |

Although Corbin scored above his grade level in mathematics, those subtests which involved reading or recognition of words were well below grade level. In addition his age equivalents were all below his chronological age.

The psychologist had the impression from all of the observation and data gathered that Corbin was a child who had significant reading problems. The reading problems included difficulties with word recognition, spelling, and comprehension. In addition, the presence of attentional difficulties was indicated and these attentional problems might be expected to further compromise Corbin's reading performance despite his high motivation. The material derived from the testing indicates that difficulty with language-related performance was poorer with visual than with auditory presentation. Contrary to this was the finding that on nonverbal tasks Corbin was able to achieve at an above-average level on visuospatial tasks. Consequently, the difficulties with visually presented stimuli may be specific to reading. Taken together these findings suggest that Corbin might benefit from a reading program which emphasizes the use of phonics. This would allow him to use his relative strengths in developing better reading strategies.

The psychologist also felt that Corbin was experiencing moderate frustration occasioned by the difficulties he had with reading. Despite this frustration Corbin's motivation remained high for achievement and he continued to be involved in trying to improve his performance. The psychologist did not feel he should be retained in his current grade at the end of the year as that might damage his motivation to achieve. Instead, it was felt that he should be enrolled in a reading program which emphasized phonics. If the reading program failed to improve Corbin's reading, the psychologist feared that the boy's frustration might become a hindrance to his general academic performance. Rather than permit this to happen, it was felt that the school should monitor Corbin's progress and refer him to a counselor before the problem became too debilitating. If the reading program did not succeed, Corbin might be helped by the counselor to work out some other strategies for learning information necessary to other coursework. Because of Corbin's good attitude and his adequate intelligence, as well as his analytical mind, it was felt that he had a good opportunity to maximize his chances of adequate school performance.

---

## PSYCHOLOGICAL EVALUATION

Corbin, an 11-year-one-month-old white male, was referred for psychological evaluation by his mother who was concerned about his school performance.

### Pertinent History

Corbin was born seven weeks prematurely and was slow in attaining some developmental milestones. At three years of age, however, he was within normal limits. When Corbin was five he was entered in kindergarten in a special class for children with specific learning disabilities, because he was clearly not able to function in the normal kindergarten. Throughout his school history he has required some special class placement because of reading problems.

Corbin's parents were divorced when he was in the third grade and his mother remarried six months later. Relationships remain good with both parents, and Corbin also feels close to his stepfather. A court decision will permit Corbin to choose where he wants to live when he is older. The boy experiences this as a problem, according to his mother.

*Behavioral Observations*

Corbin was cooperative and attentive. He related easily to the examiner and became involved in the tasks, although material which required reading was clearly frustrating to him. Corbin was careful in his work, analytical in approaching problems, and reflected before responding. He did experience some word-finding problems, but could succeed at times.

*Procedures:*

Clinical Interview, Behavior Problems Checklist, WISC-R, PIAT

*Clinical Interview and Behavior Problems Checklist*

Interviews with Corbin and his mother, and Corbin alone, confirmed that everyone agrees that Corbin has trouble reading. There were no emotional problems at home or at school. Both the mother's and a teacher report on the Behavior Problems Checklist indicated no signs of emotional disturbance. Corbin seems to be an active and well-socialized child. He is learning to play the piano with a teacher who is aware of his reading problems and who permits him to compensate for these difficulties in her method of teaching. Corbin did express some need to discuss problems outside of his family. He was concerned about being teased at school for reading problems and he was also concerned about not hurting his parents feelings when he had to decide where to live, an event which would come up in a year or two.

*WISC-R*

The WISC-R indicated that Corbin had an FSIQ of 107, a VIQ of 96, and a PIQ of 120. His approach indicated a very careful style and some mild attentional problems. His individual subtest scores were:

| Verbal | | Performance | |
|---|---|---|---|
| Information | 8 | Picture Completion | 13 |
| Similarities | 9 | Picture | |
| Arithmetic | 7 | Arrangement | 12 |

| Verbal | | Performance | |
|---|---|---|---|
| Vocabulary | 11 | Block Design | 15 |
| Comprehension | 12 | Object Assembly | 16 |
| Digit Span | 5 | Coding | 8 |
| | | Mazes | 8 |

Arithmetic, Digit Span, and Coding were all lower than other tests, indicating some possible attentional problems which might be due to sequencing. On tests where all parts were immediately available Corbin did very well.

### PIAT

The PIAT indicated that Corbin scored above grade level in mathematics, whereas his reading scores were well below both grade and age levels, indicating problems with word recognition, spelling, and comprehension.

### Summary and Recommendations

Corbin, an 11-year-one-month-old boy, is experiencing reading difficulties. Corbin's history suggests his problems to be long-standing. Because he has obvious problems with word recognition, spelling, and comprehension, and some attentional difficulties, Corbin is experiencing frustration in his attempts to read. The boy is highly motivated and can perform well on nonverbal tasks which require visuospatial abilities. The findings suggest that Corbin might benefit from a reading program which maximizes his ability to learn auditorily. A reading program which stresses the use of phonics should be considered. If this program does not work, Corbin should receive some one-to-one counseling or tutoring to develop alternative strategies for learning, e.g., use of auditory tapes.

Also, because Corbin is facing some real life stresses, such as deciding where he will live and how to handle teasing at school, a brief consulting relationship with him would be beneficial. Corbin seems a very well adjusted boy who needs brief support in handling current stress and some special tutoring or counseling in the academic area.

In contrast to the relatively clear example of learning problems provided by Corbin, psychologists are often referred children who present difficult diagnostic problems for the referral source. Sometimes these children and adolescents have such complex histories that many possible formulations could be derived from the historical material. In such cases, the clinician may be consulted to rule out possible formulations and to provide the referral source necessary to help decide upon the best type of intervention.

## EVE: A PROBLEM OF DIFFERENTIAL DIAGNOSIS

Eve was referred by a psychiatrist who was treating her on an inpatient unit. Eve was a 15-year-old girl with a history of drug abuse and running away from home. She was apparently well-adjusted as far as anyone knew, until two years before her hospitalization. At that time she had been stabbed by a jealous ex-boyfriend. This led to the loss of her then current boyfriend and a lengthy hospitalization for medical problems. Eve felt that the boyfriend had been mentally deranged. Since the time of the stabbing, Eve's parents reported that she had been a heavy user of marijuana and other drugs.

Eve was an early developer and a flamboyant dresser. These facts apparently led to her acquiring a very questionable reputation in the private school she attended. As she lived in a city, Eve took advantage of her looks and dated a great deal, almost always with older boys who were involved with drugs or alcohol.

According to Eve, her parents did nothing to discourage this way of life and the girl often visited the apartments of young adults from the time she was about 12 years of age. Things continued in this manner until Eve's parents moved to a very small community where her father had taken a job. Eve was bored with the lack of excitement and began running away shortly after the family moved. She was usually picked up by the police in the city where she grew up (she was usually visiting some friends there). While Eve had generally justified her absences by saying she was invited, or needed, she had not consulted her parents. On at least one occasion when she ran away, she was raped. She has been reported to be sexually active by her parents, who describe her as impulsive, experiencing nightmares, and difficult to control.

Upon meeting Eve, the examiner was struck by her pleasant, cooperative, and superficially social behavior. She was inquisitive about the procedures and responded well to the structure offered her. There were no signs of nervousness or tenseness. The psychiatrist who had referred Eve was unsure how disturbed Eve might be. He mentioned some concrete thinking on her part and wondered if schizophrenic problems might be underlying her sociopathic behavior. Consequently, the examiner was interested in both the content and process of Eve's thinking and method of relating. Eve talked easily about the problems which led up to her hospitalization and also about her hopes for the future. She wanted to get into work doing television commericals. She felt that this might be a step toward a film career in the future. She talked about friends who had contacts in the business, the possibility of acting school, all at an appropriate but superficial level. The psychologist was impressed by Eve's social skills but noted that there was very little in the way of solid information which she produced during the course of the interview.

An intellectual evaluation produced scores in the dull/normal range of intelligence. Eve's WISC-R scores were a VIQ of 84, PIQ of 84, and FSIQ of 82. Although Eve seemed able to acquire and store information, her ability to process and organize the information was much lower. The psychologist found no evidence of bizarre thinking or illogical processes. Rather the picture was one of a young girl whose intellectual abilities were limited and concrete in nature.

In order to verify the impression of Eve's cognitive style, the psychologist administered an Object Sorting Test (to determine the level of concepts attained and patterns of thinking used in justifying the final products). Her answers were excessively concrete, sometimes personalized into a little story, and often overly general. At times she would focus on some interesting but irrelevant detail. There were no signs of bizarre thinking. With more structure Eve was able to give successful functional or abstract answers much more frequently and her errors were those of oversight with regard to what was the most important basis of grouping objects rather than any other reason. This pattern of errors was consistent with her intellectual level. Given structure Eve was able to be appropriate most of the time; however, without structure she became lost in details and personalized associations.

The examiner wanted to be able to describe Eve's affective responses in more detail. The projective testing revealed a concrete and arbitrary approach which was congruent with good reality-testing when structure was present and was much less realistic with greater ambiguity. Eve's Rorschach, for example, was impulsive, not very productive, dependency-oriented, and with considerable poor form. The immaturity, depression, dependency, and lack of an adequate intellectual approach to the cards were obvious. Eve's confusion and feeling of threat were such that despite the excitement she experiences, her world seems full of danger. The psychologist found that Eve feels inadequate and confused, resorting to arbitrary but ineffectual attempts to make things understandable. A Sentence Completion Test indicated a problematic relationship with her mother, needs for approval and acceptance from others. Her running away seemed related to feelings of rejection over which she felt she had little control. Her figure drawing was described as a 10-year-old child who was uncoordinated. The figure was that of an eroticized woman's head on a childlike body. An MMPI revealed a strong tendency to deny problems and to act out.

As a result of the examination, the psychologist felt that the concreteness described by the psychiatrist was probably due to Eve's level of intellectual functioning, which results in a concrete approach to life. She seemed better able to function with considerable structure which kept her oriented and appropriate. Without structure she was found to become impulsive, approval seeking, and determined by her need for dependency gratification. There was nothing to indicate schizophrenic problems. Eve seemed primarily immature and inadequate, with too few intellectual and personality resources to be independent. The move to the small town away from her friends and amusements was difficult for Eve to accept, particularly as it made her more dependent upon her mother, with whom she had a highly ambivalent relationship. While Eve is well developed physically and has good superficial social skills, her excessive need to be liked and accepted and her limited intelligence have made her vulnerable to feelings of rejection. Little internalized control appeared to be present, leaving Eve at the mercy of her impulses and the wishes of others. Her parents' permissiveness may have, thus, inadvertently contributed to her running away. Eve's need for structure, limit-setting, and guidance was clear, even though she might be expected to feel frustrated by attempts from adults to provide those limits. The stronger the impulses, the more frustration Eve would experience. However, even though she protested against limits, she was both appropriate and adjusted well when given clear and consistent guidelines as to acceptable behavior.

The psychologist felt that Eve would continue to need help in negotiating the teenage years. Without guidance she was likely to be manipulated by others, particularly in view of her attractiveness and sexual needs. With guidance Eve might adjust well if she felt accepted and knew what was expected.

---

### PSYCHOLOGICAL EVALUATION

Eve, a 15-year-old psychiatric inpatient, was referred by her psychiatrist for aid in the formulation of her problems and for consideration of treatment alternatives.

## Pertinent History

Eve has a history of drug abuse and running away from home. She was permitted to roam at will in the large city in which she lived from the time she was about 12 years of age. She spent time with boys who used drugs and alcohol and was often in their apartments. When Eve was 13 she was stabbed by an ex-boyfriend and had a long convalescence. Her parents report that Eve developed early and dated a lot. She began running away from home and was a problem when she was home.

## Behavioral Observations

Eve was well groomed and attractively, if somewhat seductively, dressed. She was pleasant, cooperative, and superficially skillful socially. Eve was curious about the procedures and responded well to the instructions. There was no indication that Eve was tense. She talked easily but did not give much information unless asked directly.

## Procedures:

Clinical Interview, WISC-R, Object Sorting Test, Rorschach, Sentence Completion Test, Figure Drawing, MMPI

### Clinical Interview

The Clinical Interview indicated that Eve thought her problems began when her parents moved to a very small town. She was bored and ran away when friends called her from the city in which she had previously lived. She was usually picked up by police. Eve felt this was unfair and that she was responding to friends who needed her. She reported being raped on at least one occasion. She felt that she could capitalize on her looks and wanted to try to do television commericals as a step toward a film career. She talked vaguely about some friends who had contacts in the business, and going to acting school. Eve's relationships with her parents were described as distant, although a high degree of emotional ambivalence was focused on her mother. She felt that she was misunderstood and her parents were unreasonable in expecting her to like the very small town to which they had moved.

### WISC-R

The intellectual evaluation indicated that Eve was performing with an FSIQ of 82, a VIQ of 84, and a PIQ of 84. Eve was able to acquire and store information reasonably well; however, her ability to process, organize, and apply information seemed much lower. There was no evidence of bizarre thinking or illogical processes. Rather, Eve appeared limited and concrete in her functioning. There was little scatter among the subtests and no problems were indicated with her ability to attend to the material.

### Object Sorting Test

The Object Sorting Test was administered both to examine the level of concepts and to determine patterns of thinking. Again there was no evidence of bizarre thinking, but Eve's productions were concrete, often personalized, and irrelevant when she had to sort the objects as well as produce the concept. When presented with structured sorts, Eve was able to give some functional level or abstract level concepts. Her errors on this part of the test reflected oversight or carelessness.

### Rorschach

Eve's Rorschach was not very productive (fewer than average responses) and was also indicative of few internal resources. Her performance indicated good reality-testing when structure was perceived accurately, but Eve's percepts to ambiguous parts of the blots were characterized by arbitrary and concrete approaches to the stimuli. The use of determinants indicated impulsivity and dependency, while the content not only confirmed these areas of conflict but also suggested that depressive feelings were present. Eve perceived the world as dangerous and confusing and her arbitrary perceptions were ineffectual attempts to make things orderly for herself.

### Sentence Completion Test

The Sentence Completion Test revealed a problematic relationship with her mother. The content related to feelings of rejection, which were also related to her behavior in running away. The form of the SCT was congruent with her level of intellectual functioning as described on both the WISC-R and the Object Sorting Test.

### Figure Drawing

Figure drawing was very immature and uncoordinated. The description of the figure as a 10-year-old child was inconsistent with the eroticized woman's head on the childlike body.

*MMPI*

The MMPI revealed a strong tendency to deny problems. The only other remarkable feature was a high elevation on the scale which describes tendencies to act out in behavior.

*Symmary and Recommendations*

Eve, a 15-year-old white runaway, was seen for psychological evaluation to aid in describing her psychological organization and pathology. Eve's behavior is probably attributable to her intellectual limitations and her immature and impulsive tendencies to act out her problems in behavior. There is no indication of psychosis or bizarre thinking. Her concreteness reflects her level of intellectual functioning. Her ambivalent relationship with her mother and her early sexual experience have made it difficult for her to gratify her dependency needs at home. Given her physical attractiveness and her need to be liked and accepted, she is likely to respond to demands from young adult males. In addition, Eve has little internalized control and her parents have been permissive with her so that her tendencies to act out have not been kept in check. Given structure, she does respond appropriately although she may protest against the limits.

Eve should receive counseling to help her during the teenage years. Her parents will also need counseling to help them learn to set appropriate limits on Eve, provide her with support, and consider her normal needs for social outlets. Under these conditions Eve could be expected to make a reasonable adjustment and her runaway behavior would probably be unnecessary.

---

## DISCUSSION OF ILLUSTRATIVE CASES

The purpose of psychological assessment of children is to describe them in a way that can lead to helpful recommendations which should have a beneficial effect on their lives. The evaluation should provide aid in setting priorities with regard to the needs of a given child. This setting of priorities should be based upon knowledge of the child, of basic psychological data, and of situations.

The psychological assessment is, therefore, more than a description of a child. To be a useful assessment, the psychologist needs to evaluate the child's life situations: for example, home, social, school, and peer relationships. Since the child's psychological state is expressed in these different situations, ignorance of environmental demands and conditions is apt to lead to either sterile or erroneous impressions of the meaning of the child's behavior at any given time. Before formal testing begins, the clinician's understanding of the environmental limits, which are gathered through the history, the clinical interview, or in consultation with others, stimulates questions about future recommendations which will be formulated. For example, in the case of Tracey, the young abused child in foster care, a recommendation that she be placed in a warm, accepting home is meaningless within the context of her present problems. Although a warm, accepting home is what Tracey ultimately needs, the first priority is to set the conditions which will make such a placement likely to be successful.

During the assessment of the child through interview and clinical evaluation, the psychologist is able to sift through a range of possible recommendations. The object is to choose a recommendation which will maximize use of environmental change that will best fit the child's individual needs. The range of this change may include adjustments in the family or school, or it may include the recommendation for psychotherapy which gives the child a private outlet. The clinician's recommendation will be based upon the most realistic choice of the match between the child's needs and the possible solutions.

The cases chosen for inclusion in this chapter were selected because they represent a wide range of typical problems presented to psychologists for evaluation. Seldom does a history leave fewer questions than it raises. We saw, for example, that Latanya had both medical and social histories that were complex and left the way open for many possible explanations for the complaints that originally raised the referral question. Likewise in the case of Eve a complex history, including problematical relationships with parents interacting with an inadequate level of intelligence, produced behavior which could be interpreted in many different ways.

The reader is reminded of the temperamental dispositions which were described earlier in this book. Consider Tony, whose manner was oppositional and unrestricted in early life. His antisocial behavior stands in sharp contrast to that of Eve, whose early life was agreeable and fairly easy. Eve's problems appear to stem from needs for acceptance and approval and to occur within the framework of a personality that was basically socially oriented. As may be seen, we are suggesting that the clinician interested in the psychological assessment of children should begin to make some comparative observations across patients.

Among the sample cases presented in this chapter we have rated the patients in terms of the temperamental dispositions of these children at the time of assessment.

| 0 | Tracey | Eve | Corbin | EASY |
|---|---|---|---|---|
| 0 | | Latanya | | SLOW TO WARM UP |
| 0 | Hugh | | Tony | DIFFICULT |

The amount of cognitive control and cognitive ability of these children has been assessed in each case. If we rank the children in terms of cognitive assets we find them arrayed as follows:

| IQ Level | Tracey Latanya Eve Tony Corbin Hugh |
|---|---|

In each case we have tried to outline major environmental influences which helped to shape the behavior and personality of the child. We found that Tracey had a very poor background in terms of parental relations, both with respect to affection and the manner in which limit-setting may have occurred. Both Eve and Latanya received some affection but limit-setting functions were seriously impaired for each of them. Tony had fewer limits imposed than any of the other children, while Corbin's case indicated that he had perhaps had the most limit-setting. Hugh appeared to have inconsistent limit-setting and not much affection. If the children were rated on these dimensions, we would probably see the following arrays.

| 0 | Tracey | Hugh | Tony | Eve | Latanya | Corbin | AFFECTION |
|---|---|---|---|---|---|---|---|

| 0 | Tony | Eve | Latanya | Hugh | Tracey | Corbin | LIMIT-SETTING |
|---|---|---|---|---|---|---|---|

The behavior problems illustrated include school, health, emotional, and social problems. As we have examined and discussed each child, it has become clear that the interaction of basic endowment, intellectual development, socialization, and the availability of appropriate resources for nurturance has shaped the particular expression of personal adjustment. Each of the children and adolescents we have described faces major tasks if the presenting difficulties are to be overcome. In each case the assessment indicates that a combination of interventions may be necessary.

Tracey's disposition is relatively easy, but she has a long history of mistreatment. Her cognitive abilities are limited, whether this is a function of her endowment or her history or both. Without sufficient love, limit-setting, and stability she may be expected to have severe problems. Corbin, on the other hand, has a restricted problem which he has handled quite well. He may be expected to continue to have good social relations, and to the extent that he may be able to compensate for his learning disability he may be expected to achieve well also. Because of his easy temperament, relatively high intelligence, and good motivation, Corbin's future appears the brightest of the group.

All of the children, except Tony, are socially oriented. Even though Hugh gives evidence of a very serious personality disturbance, he is also more open to intervention than Tony, whose extreme antisocial position makes his prognosis very poor. We have discussed social influences here mainly in terms of early affection and limit-setting. However, it should be clear that social orientation is very much a function of peer relations as well.

At this point the clinician is implicitly ranking the current environmental conditions as to how they will affect outcome or prognosis. This ranking is based on conditions prior to recommended changes which may be made after the evaluation is completed. Given the cases we have reviewed, the ranking for the six children as to how their current environmental conditions affect future prognosis would look like this:

0     Tony   Tracey   Latanya   Eve   Hugh        Corbin           100

From the historical material available we find that Eve has the least social disruption of all in terms of peer relations. True she was stabbed by a deranged ex-boyfriend, but she maintained relationships with old (though disreputable) friends and appeared happy before her move. Her parents do not set limits and this has lowered her prognosis. Latanya has problems with many of the children at school but within her own family she does have some close peer relations. Corbin, who is teased at school, has no apparent problems with most of his other peers and has had a satisfactory history of peer relations up to the point that his learning problems singled him out for unpleasant distinction. Corbin is also able to relate well with adults and has a sensitive social awareness. Both Tracey and Hugh, for different reasons, are less socialized than the other children. Although their behavior is provocative at home, neither of them would necessarily attract attention outside the home as behavior problems. This is not because they do not have social problems, but rather because their responses to their social problems outside the home tend to be in the nature of withdrawal and lack of expression. Tony has a documented history of poor peer relationships and those that he has maintained include indications of sadistic and overprotective patterns.

All of the findings we have just discussed in terms of these comparisons have rested upon several necessary conditions. The psychologist has had available referral questions, historical material, and direct behavioral observations. In each case the psychologist has conducted an interview with the child and with the parents when they were available. In addition, the psychologist has brought to the evaluation some knowledge of child development, child psychopathology, measurement, information about specific assessment procedures, and experience.

It is no accident that clinicians respect experience. Experience provides the opportunity for establishing expectations or internal norms which are extremely helpful in weighing data relevant to a formulation. However, all clinicians begin with a very limited fund of clinical material and limited confidence in their ability to formulate the material available to them. What the clinician may confidently bring to assessment, regardless of the amount of experience, is that fund of knowledge about normality, deviance, and methods of assessment to which we have referred throughout this book.

In each case presented in this chapter, the psychologist's work included formulation of possible interpretations of data. These formulations in turn depended upon being able to entertain a range of possible hypotheses which might account for the observations reported. The work of formulation begins with the referral question itself and the accompanying material that brings it to the psychologist's attention. Then throughout the assessment process the psychologist must evaluate and reevaluate the information available. Decision points occur throughout the assessment process on the basis of further investigation of specific hypotheses or ruling out further investigation on the basis of sufficient data to make additional evaluation unnecessary. In this chapter we saw that the psychologist ruled out further study of emotional factors in the case of Corbin; enough information had been gathered to allow formulation of the material. We saw that in the case of Eve, *both* affective and cognitive assessment were necessary to determine the nature of her concrete thinking.

The decision of how much data is sufficient is a clinical judgment.

By and large this decision will be a function of how well the clinician has formulated the available material and the richness of the material, together with his or her experience. As a rule, the novice will require more data because of less experience. Although experience helps to make some discriminations which are based upon clinical familiarity, the logic of assessment does require some minimal adequate data base. Thus, no amount of experience will compensate for lack of appropriate data. To the knowledgeable clinician, the ability to formulate appropriately must be the single most important clinical skill available. It is the ability which sets the confidence limits for how much information must be gathered and how it is to be organized and assessed. This process is an active process, not a mechanical one. Assessment rests upon both imaginativeness at the level of hypothesis generation and thoroughness at the level of ruling out various possibilities which are under consideration. The synthesis of the data without either of these components remains a sterile exercise. With the clinician's involvement as an active diagnostician, the process of assessment is a creative enterprise which requires reflectiveness, skill, personal commitment, and a sense of intellectual adventure.

# *Index*